ABOUT ISLAND PRESS

Island Press, a nonprofit organization, publishes, markets, and distributes the most advanced thinking on the conservation of our natural resources—books about soil, land, water, forests, wildlife, and hazardous and toxic wastes. These books are practical tools used by public officials, business and industry leaders, natural resource managers, and concerned citizens working to solve both local and global resource problems.

Founded in 1978, Island Press reorganized in 1984 to meet the increasing demand for substantive books on all resource-related issues. Island Press publishes and distributes under its own imprint and offers these services to other nonprofit organizations.

Support for Island Press is provided by The Geraldine R. Dodge Foundation, The Energy Foundation, The Charles Engelhard Foundation, The Ford Foundation, Glen Eagles Foundation, The George Gund Foundation, William and Flora Hewlett Foundation, The James Irvine Foundation, The John D. and Catherine T. MacArthur Foundation, The Andrew W. Mellon Foundation, The Joyce Mertz-Gilmore Foundation, The New-Land Foundation, The Pew Charitable Trusts, The Rockefeller Brothers Fund, The Tides Foundation, and individual donors.

ABOUT THE PACIFIC RIVERS COUNCIL

The Pacific Rivers Council (PRC), formerly the Oregon Rivers Council, is one of the largest and most successful river conservation organizations in the nation. Its mission is to develop scientific tools, public policies, and community development procedures to restore the ecological integrity and sustainable use of America's river systems. PRC's first successful initiative was to lead the effort that created the landmark 1988 Oregon Omnibus National Wild and Scenic Rivers Act, which protected 40 Oregon rivers, totaling over 1,500 miles, as Wild and Scenic rivers. The Oregon Act remains the largest river protection act in the nation's history for the lower 48 states. The Pacific Rivers Council has received national acclaim for its innovative river restoration approaches that merge contemporary ecosystem science with sustainable community development.

ENTERING THE WATERSHED

ENTERING THE WATERSHED

✌ A NEW APPROACH TO SAVE AMERICA'S RIVER ECOSYSTEMS

BOB DOPPELT
MARY SCURLOCK
CHRIS FRISSELL
JAMES KARR

The Pacific Rivers Council

ISLAND PRESS

WASHINGTON, D.C. ❑ COVELO, CALIFORNIA

Illustration by Dan Gilmore

Entering the watershed : a new approach to save America's river
  ecosystems / Bob Doppelt . . . [et al.] (The Pacific Rivers Council).
    p.   cm.
  Includes bibliographical references and index.
  ISBN 1-55963-274-7 (alk. paper). — ISBN 1-55963-275-5 (pbk. :
alk. paper)
    1. Stream conservation — United States.   2. Stream ecology — United
  States.   3. Watershed management — United States.   I. Doppelt, Bob.
  II. Pacific Rivers Council.
  QH76.E57   1993
  333.91'6216'0973 — dc20   993-8895
                                                                  CIP

*QH
76
E57
1993*

CONTENTS

PREFACE

This book is the product of a two-year project to develop new federal river protection and restoration policy alternatives. The project has its roots in a growing frustration, felt nationwide, that river conservation is overwhelmingly losing the battle with river degradation. That degradation spans the range from declining water quality and extinction of riverine species to reduced recreational value and aesthetic appeal, declining productivity of sport and commercial fisheries, and threats to human health. Too few effective restoration tools and policies are available to reverse these trends, and time is running out. Failure to take action soon may result in irreversible degradation.

Our first awareness of the severity of the problem occurred, ironically, as a result of one of the successful initiatives of the Oregon Rivers Council (the Pacific Rivers Council's original name). In 1988, we successfully led an effort to push through Congress the landmark Oregon Omnibus National Wild and Scenic Rivers Act. This Act designated 40 Oregon river segments totaling almost 1500 miles and including almost 500,000 acres of land. Many organizations, including the National Sierra Club and American Rivers, were vital to the process. The Act remains the largest river protection act in the history of the lower 48 states. Implementing the Act, however, introduced us to the magnitude of the challenge we face in effectively protecting and restoring our nation's river systems.

In 1989 we crafted a strategy to help develop effective Wild and Scenic river management plans. The Act protected primarily mainstem river segments within federal lands. The headwaters of the streams, tributaries, and the contiguous private land sections downstream were not included. Private landowner opposition killed most of our efforts to include private land segments in the 1988 Act. To address the other river areas, we tried to identify appropriate federal and private land river conservation policies. This was especially important because we were determined to protect the habitat for dwindling runs of migrating Pacific

Northwest salmon, steelhead and trout that inhabit these rivers and streams. Our search for effective policies was fruitless.

The Forest Service and Bureau of Land Management had no effective policies to protect tributaries outside the designated corridors or in the headwater areas. Timber cutting, grazing and other activities continued almost unabated, degrading the upstream federal land river reaches even as we had, in theory, protected the mainstem sections. The only private lands-protection mechanisms we found were the Oregon State Scenic Waterway Act and the Clean Water Act. The State Waterways Act is very limited and would have required an entirely new legislative campaign. Further, the state act again addressed only special river segments and not entire rivers flowing through private lands. The Clean Water Act seemed effective only at preventing point-source pollution, and failed to address riparian areas, riverine habitat, biodiversity or water projects. The other state and federal policies that even mentioned rivers were a convoluted mishmash of conflicting laws pointing in all directions and completely disconnected from the fundamental science of how the rivers function.

As a result, we questioned the value of what we had actually accomplished with the Wild and Scenic Rivers Act. Although the 1988 Act may be a landmark step for national river conservation, we wondered whether we had done something truly meaningful for the rivers. Some of the best scenic and recreational river segments were protected, along with some important riparian areas. Nevertheless, we ultimately began to feel that we had bought more doughnut hole than doughnut.

We canvassed conservation groups nationwide to determine if others felt as we did about the need for new river protection policies, and found an overwhelmingly positive response. We then sought the advice of the nation's top stream ecologists and fishery biologists to identify what was needed to protect and begin to restore river systems. We also sought the ideas of those in the trenches of river conservation to help craft new private land river-restoration mechanisms: conservationists, public interest attorneys, and public agency personnel. These groups came together to form our "Scientific/Federal Lands Committee," and our "Private Lands Task Force."

Numerous meetings were held to assess the problems, identify potential solutions and hammer out the underpinnings of new policy proposals. Subsequently, we developed a separate task force of scientists to assist us in developing a scientifically sound watershed restoration strategy. Workshops were held in several river basins, and the Rapid Biotic and Ecosystem Response (RBER) strategy proposed in this book emerged. The extensive research by our staff, feedback from experts nationwide, and the efforts of our task forces resulted in the policy assessments and final proposals in this book.

It is important to note that although we have had considerable assistance from our task forces and many others, the assessments and recommendations presented in this book are the sole responsibility of the Pacific Rivers Council.

We hope this book will prove helpful in stimulating a new day for America's river systems and biodiversity. This is certainly needed. Existing policies clearly have not been effective. We do not pretend to have all the answers. Other approaches may prove helpful, and as the science of rivers and ecosystem restoration evolves, even better policy proposals may emerge. No matter what new approaches and policies are finally enacted, if this book helps to stimulate a new national debate over riverine management and helps to catalyze a new age of restoration for America's river systems and biodiversity, it will have served its purpose.

ACKNOWLEDGMENTS

Many people gave their time, energy and careful thought to the development of this project and book. Special thanks go to the committee of scientists who joined us at our first task force meeting at the H.J. Andrews Experimental Research station near Blue River, Oregon. At this meeting, and through many subsequent letters, phone calls, and meetings, this committee helped us identify the scientific underpinnings and many of the specific federal land management directives proposed in this book. The committee members are: Dr. Art Benke, Dr. Ken Cummins, Dr. Stan Gregory, Dr. Marjorie Holland, Dr. Ron Pulliam, Dr. James Karr, Dr. Wylie Kitchens, Dr. Richard Marzoff, Dr. Judy Meyer, Dr. Wayne Minshall, Dr. Manuel Molles, Dr. Jack Stanford, Dr. Fred Swanson, Dr. Jack Williams, Dr. Bob Wissmar, Dr. Jim Sedell and Dr. Gordon Reeves.

Equally special thanks go to the task force of conservationists, public agency personnel and scientists who came together to discuss the private land issues. Specifically, we thank David Pfeiffer, Phil Wallin, Dennis Canty, Drew Parkin, Peter Lavigne, Scootch Pankonin, Beth Norcross, Barry Beasley, Pope Barrow (whose organization, the American Whitewater Affiliation, first proposed the National Rivers Registry concept), David Conrad, Chuck Hoffman, Bern Collins, Dr. Ron Pulliam and many others for their time and energy in debating the key issues.

We are particularly appreciative of the assistance provided "over and above the cause" by Dr. Benke, Dr. Holland, Dr. Meyer, Dr. Stanford, Dr. Gregory, and Dr. Pulliam.

We extend our very special appreciation to Dr. Jim Karr for his assistance in writing and editing many of the scientific aspects of Part I, and in many other ways supporting and assisting in this project. We also appreciate Dr. Chris Frissell's invaluable assistance in writing the RBER watershed protection and restoration strategy proposed in Part II of the book.

We are indebted to T. Charles Dewberry, Pacific Rivers Council stream ecologist, Mary Scurlock, J.D., our staff policy analyst, David Bayles, our Public Lands Director, and Debbie Gilcrest, J.D. Charles pulled off the first real coup of the project by organizing the H.J. Andrews meeting and somehow getting all 15 of the top scientists together to everyone's surprise. Charles also helped develop and write the first drafts of the federal lands management prescriptions. We especially appreciate Mary's extensive work on the federal policy analysis found in the Appendixes. Debbie Gilcrest provided valuable research and written contributions to the private land sections.

David Bayles played a major role in developing the project and the recommended strategies and policies. William Bowman provided countless hours of rewriting and editing of the document and deserves great thanks. Dan Gilmore created the graphic found in Chapter Two. Steve Mallory provided copy editing and helpful advice. Louise Bilheimer, Administrative Director of our staff, helped keep the project organized and offered editorial advice. Bob Parker of MLP and Associates did much of the early private lands policy analysis and proposal development. Michael Blumm of the Lewis and Clark College Northwestern School of Law, and Mike Jennings and Catherine Jope of the National Park Service provided valuable comments and advice.

A very special tribute goes to Dr. Jim Sedell and Dr. Gordon Reeves. They taught us early on that rigorous, holistic thinking could indeed begin to change existing riverine management practices and policies. They educated, inspired and chided us, and have made a large contribution to the overall development of the project.

We are very appreciative of the financial and personal support provided by David Nee and the Ittelson Fouundation, Connie Harvey and the Maki Foundation, the C.S. Mott Foundation, the Murdock Charitable Trust, Jim Compton and the Compton Foundation, and the James Ford Bell Foundation. We thank them all.

Finally, I want to thank Peggy Bloom, my wife, for constantly encouraging both the organization and me, while putting up with my late-night, early-morning and weekend-long writing and editing.

Bob Doppelt
Executive Director
The Pacific Rivers Council

DEFINING THE TERMS

One of the primary reasons for the lack of effective riverine protection and restoration policies in the United States is the limited awareness of the complex dynamics of streams and rivers. Few people understand that a river extends beyond the water flowing in the channel. To help change our thinking about the complex nature of rivers, we use specific terms throughout this book, including *riverine system, watershed ecosystem, riverine-riparian ecosystem, riverine-riparian biodiversity, watershed or catchment basin, biotic refuges* or *refugia,* and *biological hot spot.*

The term *riverine system* is used to describe the entire river network, including tributaries, side channels, sloughs, intermittent streams, etc. We use this term to provide a constant reminder that rivers are complex, dynamic *ecological systems.* We also use the term *riverine* as opposed to *aquatic* to distinguish between flowing freshwater systems and other aquatic systems such as lakes and ponds, which this report does not specifically address.

The term *watershed* or *catchment basin* refers to the entire physical area or basin drained by a distinct stream or riverine system, physically separated from other watersheds by ridgetop boundaries (a more strict scientific definition of the term *watershed* would just define catchment basin *boundaries,* but we use it to identify the entire basin).

Watershed ecosystem refers to all of the elements and processes that interact within the catchment basin or watershed, including but not limited to the riverine-riparian ecosystem.

The *riverine-riparian ecosystem* is nested within the watershed ecosystem and includes the processes and elements that interact in the riparian and flowing water areas throughout the entire riverine system. This generally includes the 100-year floodplain.

The *riparian area* (or streamside vegetation buffer zone), when stated alone, is the transition zone between the flowing water and terrestrial ecosystems and hence is a very important part of the riverine-riparian ecosystem.

Riverine-riparian biodiversity refers to all of the native aquatic and riparian organisms dependent upon the riverine-riparian ecosystem for life, including but not limited to fisheries and aquatic insects. Biodiversity (or biological diversity), is defined as the variety of the world's native biological elements, representing and integrated over organizational levels from genes to landscapes.

The terms *biotic refuges* or *refugia* refer to areas with relatively undisturbed, healthier habitat and processes that serve as refuges for biodiversity. Larger refugia can be the size of whole watersheds.

Biological hot spots are smaller intact riverine habitat patches that provide critical functions for the stream or biodiversity. Hot spots can include deep pools for fish habitat, a cold-water tributary junction that provides a small "thermal refuge" for biodiversity, or a small of section of complex, healthy riverine habitat.

Finally, we use the term *riverine systems and biodiversity* to encompass all of the above.

One must realize that little consensus exists even among scientists when it comes to specifically and uniformly defining such terms. We have used the terms consistently throughout the book according to the definitions above so that all readers may begin to think of riverine systems as complex, dynamic ecological and biological systems on a landscape level.

EXECUTIVE SUMMARY

The degradation of America's riverine systems and the depletion of riverine-riparian biodiversity have reached alarming levels. Not one riverine system in America has been spared. Fisheries, surface and groundwater quality and quantity produced by watershed ecosystems, and entire aquatic food chains are at risk nationwide.

This book assesses the capability of the nation's riverine conservation approaches and policies to address the crisis (see appendix for detailed policy assessments). We conclude that the nation's existing riverine protection and restoration approaches and policies are inadequate and have failed. Entirely new approaches and policies must be established quickly to stave off the impending collapse of many riverine systems and to prevent wholesale biological extinctions. Such losses erode nature's ability to provide basic ecological functions, degrade social and cultural climates and erode economic conditions.

Based on extensive consultation with some of the nation's leading scientists and our own research, we recommend a comprehensive new approach to the crisis facing America's riverine systems and biodiversity: a strategic national community- and ecosystem-based watershed restoration initiative. Only a coordinated federal initiative directed by the highest level of government will be able to cut through the myriad fragmented and ineffective approaches, policies and agency inertia that contribute to the growing problems.

The Extent of the Crisis

Only a few examples are needed to understand the extent of the crisis. In the 20 years since the enactment of the Clean Water Act and the National Wild and Scenic Rivers Act, almost 50% of the nation's waters still fail to meet water quality standards when biological criteria are used. Less than 2% of the nation's river miles even qualify for Wild and Scenic designation, leaving more than 98% of the miles with no protection options.

From one-third to three-fourths of aquatic species nationwide are rare to extinct, and aquatic species are disappearing at a faster rate than terrestrial species. An estimated 70-90% of natural riparian vegetation, vital to maintaining the integrity of riverine-riparian ecosystems and biodiversity, has already been lost or is degraded due to human activities nationwide. Seventy percent of the nation's rivers and streams have been impaired by flow alteration.

The economic and social impacts of lost and degraded riverine systems and biodiversity are severe. However, these impacts have not been accurately examined or systematically documented. Again, only a few of the available examples are necessary to demonstrate the alarming degree of loss.

The jobs and food resources once provided by the commercial and recreational fisheries nationwide have been decimated in this century. For example, two-thirds of the fishes of the Illinois River (Illinois) have experienced major population declines or disappeared from that watershed since 1850, and the commercial catch of the river, second in commercial catch to the Columbia River early in this century, declined to near zero over a decade ago. The Missouri River commercial fishery has declined by 80% since 1945. Since 1910, annual native salmon and steelhead runs of the Columbia river system have declined by over 95%, causing loss of fishery jobs. High rates of fish extinction are likely to persist into the future.

How would our nation respond if our agricultural productivity were reduced by three-quarters or were eliminated altogether?

Despite expenditures of at least $473 billion to build, operate, and administer water pollution control facilities since 1970, the nation's water resources continue to decline in both quality and quantity. Soil in America is eroding at the rate of 4 billion tons per year, and soil erosion costs the nation an estimated $3.2 billion each year. About one-third of the soil eroded by water from agricultural land enters streams and other bodies of water, annually causing $2-$9 billion in off-site damage to water-related activities such as recreation, water storage, irrigation and navigation.

In short, almost every segment of our society has been affected by and pays heavy direct and indirect ecological, financial, and job-related costs for the degradation of America's riverine systems and biodiversity, whether they are aware of it or not.

These issues are discussed in greater depth in chapter one.

The Problems That Must Be Addressed

The ecological problems: The problems facing America's riverine systems and biodiversity are caused by human activities. The cumulative result of the many human impacts has been called *ecosystem simplification*: huge reductions in the life-supporting complexity and diversity of watershed ecosystems. As the complexity and diversity are reduced, the system's ability to self-repair is eroded, leaving the system with reduced ability to perform ecological functions and with biodiversity depleted. In other words, the biological integrity of the system is weakened or destroyed. The most damaging impacts usually result from changes in the basic structure and function of riverine-riparian ecosystems and habitats.

Riverine ecosystem simplification is caused by the following human-related impacts:

* changes in water quantity or flow due to irrigation and other withdrawals

* the modification of channel and riparian ecosystem morphology caused by damming, reservoirs, channelization, drainage and filling of wetlands and dredging for navigation

* excessive nonpoint-source pollution, including erosion and sedimentation caused by damaging land-use practices, including agriculture, forestry, and urbanization

* the deterioration of substrate quality or stability

* the degradation of chemical water quality through the addition of point-source contaminants

* the decline of native fish and other species from overharvest and intentional or accidental poisoning, and

* the introduction of exotic species

These activities may occur anywhere within the watershed, along the riparian or floodplain areas, or in river channels. These issues are discussed in chapter one.

The policy problems: All levels of government have failed to stem the degradation of America's riverine systems and the extinction of riverine-riparian biodiversity. This failure has many dimensions. The United States has no national goal to protect or restore riverine ecosystems or riverine-riparian biodiversity. Consequently, there are no national policies that mandate coordinated federal, state and private management and conservation of whole riverine systems. Traditional river assessments have been ineffective because they fail to assess the biological status of America's riverine systems. No policies provide self-sustaining levels of riverine-riparian biodiversity. No policies require the identification and protection of the remaining healthy riverine habitats. No effective riverine restoration policies exist at any level of government. Finally, no policies effectively integrate riverine protection and restoration with local economic benefits and community revitalization. In short, our entire traditional paradigm for riverine conservation and management has failed, and an entirely new way of approaching the problems is needed.

The few riverine protection policies that exist, such as the National Wild and Scenic Rivers Act, focus on discrete stream segments, not ecosystems. This approach fails to address the actual processes and elements of riverine systems. Likewise, the restoration policies that exist generally focus on single species (usually game fish), the most degraded stream segments, or on the chemical aspects of water quality, and, consequently, have generally failed.

Existing protection and restoration strategies and policies at all levels of government are fragmented, extremely narrow in scope and ineffective. More effective ecosystem-based tools and policies are needed in the national riverine protection and restoration tool box.

The Watershed Ecosystem: A Dynamic System

Most people think of rivers simply as water flowing through a channel. This narrow view fails to capture the actual complexity and diversity of riverine systems, and is one of the reasons for failed policies. In the past 15 years many scientific studies and reports have documented that riverine systems are intimately coupled with and created by the characteristics of their *catchment basins*, or *watersheds*. The concept of the watershed includes four-dimensional processes that connect the longitudinal (upstream-downstream), lateral (floodplains-upland), and vertical (hyporheic or groundwater zone-stream channel) dimensions, each differing temporally.

Watersheds are ecosystems composed of a mosaic of different land or terrestrial "patches" that are connected by (drained by) a network of streams. In turn, the flowing water environment is composed of a mosaic of habitats in which materials and energy are transferred and, therefore, connected through biologically diverse food webs. Human activities can result in the fragmentation and disconnection of the habitat patches if management is not planned and implemented from an ecosystem and watershed perspective.

In-stream conditions, then, are largely determined by processes occurring within the watershed and cannot be isolated from or manipulated independent of this context. Disturbances in a watershed propagate downstream from headwater sources. Management and conservation activities absent from the watershed context run the risk of being ineffective, at best, and can be counterproductive and destructive, at worst.

The Importance of Headwaters, Biotic Refuges, Benchmark Watersheds, Riparian Areas, Floodplains, and Biological "Hot Spots"

Ecologically healthy watersheds require the maintenance and protection of the lateral, longitudinal, and vertical connectedness of the mosaic of habitat patches and ecosystem components within the watershed over time. However, almost all watersheds nationwide are already highly degraded and fragmented. The remaining relatively healthy undisturbed headwaters, biotic refuges, benchmark watersheds, riparian areas, floodplains, and biological hot spots, therefore, play a vital role in supporting existing levels of health for the system and in anchoring potential recovery efforts.

The small streams at the *headwaters* of riverine systems are the most vulnerable to human disturbance (especially timber harvesting, road building, grazing and related activities) because they respond dramatically and rapidly to disturbance to their riparian areas. Even where inaccessible to fish, these small streams provide high levels of water quality and quantity, sediment control, nutrients and wood debris for downstream reaches of the watershed. Intermittent and ephemeral headwater streams are, therefore, often largely responsible for maintaining the quality of downstream riverine processes and habitat for considerable distances.

Biotic refuges or *refugia* are discrete riverine areas which maintain habitat conditions conducive to at-risk biodiversity. Refugia can include the remaining relatively undisturbed smaller headwater watersheds that also provide some degree of ecological "control" for the system. As such, these refugia are often the linchpins of the existing health of riverine systems for considerable distances downstream, and for biodiversity.

The remaining undisturbed headwater streams also constitute many of the remaining *benchmark* watersheds with which to compare and monitor stream ecosystems over time. In many riverine systems, preserving the integrity of both the biotic refuges and fully intact benchmark watersheds may be the only hope of maintaining ecosystem and species health. Restoration of many of America's riverine systems may prove impossible unless these areas are quickly protected and secured.

Riparian areas and *floodplains* play a critical role in maintaining ecosystem health throughout the system, not just in headwater areas. It is imperative to protect and restore riparian areas and floodplains on federal and private lands nationwide.

The term *biological hot spot* is used to describe smaller, intact riverine habitat patches that provide a critical function for the stream. Although surrounding areas may be seriously degraded, they generally retain a degree of health, because of fortuitous historical land ownership patterns or simple chance. Hot spots remain throughout most systems nationwide.

Refugia and hot spots cannot exist in isolation indefinitely; under existing federal laws and management, degradation caused by inappropriate development will eventually threaten these areas as well. Therefore, one of the initial objectives of restoration must be to quickly protect these areas from further development. Following this, the areas must be secured. Securing an area means reducing or eliminating threats caused by past human activities (such as sedimentation from road building) to prevent further degradation to the remaining healthy areas. Protecting and securing an area are two separate yet connected steps.

Despite the growing riverine crisis, our traditional conservation and management approaches fail to take this type of comprehensive ecological approach. Consequently, riverine systems and biodiversity continue to degrade. Clearly, new approaches and policies are needed to protect and restore the key aspects of watershed ecosystem structure and processes, including the headwaters, riparian areas and floodplains, biotic refuges, benchmark watersheds and biological hot spots.

These issues are discussed in greater depth in chapter two.

RECOMMENDATIONS

A New Restoration Approach

We recommend a new approach to protect and begin to restore America's riverine systems and biodiversity: the Rapid Biotic and Ecosystem Response (RBER) approach. The RBER approach is founded on principles of watershed dynamics, ecosystem function, and conservation biology -- a community and ecosystem-based strategy that maintains and restores riverine processes and biodiversity at the watershed level. The new approach integrates ecologically and economically sustainable restoration strategies in a scientifically defensible and conservative way, emphasizing principles of the physical and ecological functions of watersheds and key spatial and temporal aspects of aquatic ecology. Simple in concept and pragmatic in application, this new approach provides a means for prioritizing protection and restoration interventions and policies and for creating more rapid and cost-effective biotic recovery.

This approach involves three interconnected components:

* The approach begins with the comprehensive identification and protection of the remaining relatively healthy headwaters, biotic refuges, benchmark watersheds, riparian areas, floodplains, and the network of biological hot spots found in patches throughout an

entire river system. This approach differs significantly from the traditional piecemeal protection approaches that focus on discrete river segments with little sense of their importance to the problems or needs of the entire system. This approach also places the emphasis on *preventing* further degradation rather than on attempting to control or repair damage after it occurs. Prevention is more effective and cost-efficient than control or repair measures, which have failed in most cases.

* Following the protection of these areas, restoration can begin, focused initially on reducing or eliminating the threats to the remaining healthy areas stated above, thus securing them. After these areas have been secured, restoration would focus on providing better management between the protected areas and, eventually, expanding and then linking the healthy areas. This approach differs considerably from the traditional restoration strategies that apply almost all resources to restoring the most degraded or worst-looking river reaches, single (usually game) species, or to improving water quality with little awareness of the needs of the overall ecosystem or of the greatest opportunities for cost-effective rapid biotic recovery.

* Finally, the approach calls for the active participation of local communities and citizens in implementing the steps, through support for ecologically sustainable economic development. Without support from local communities and citizens, any policy will fail. To help generate support, local jobs must be created in restoration technologies. Riverine-focused community revitalization projects and economic conversions (such as changes to agricultural crops that are less water- and energy-intensive, yet provide a good economic return) must also be generated. These projects are needed to

restore riverine systems, and they offer the benefit of providing jobs and economic benefits. Open space preservation, such as the protection of undeveloped floodplains, must also be encouraged. New incentives and technical assistance must be provided to encourage and support local involvement in these steps and in designing and implementing watershed restoration action plans.

The new approach is discussed in greater depth in chapter three.

Necessary Federal Steps

To implement the new protection and restoration approach, a coordinated strategic federal initiative is required. The program must become a top-level national priority. The first step in this initiative must be to establish new federal watershed protection and restoration goals and approaches.

We recommend that the federal government establish the following:

* An expanded national goal that builds on the existing goal of the Clean Water Act. This goal establishes the importance of a new public resource -- riverine-riparian ecosystems and biodiversity. The new goal should be: "To restore and maintain the chemical, physical, and biological integrity of the nation's waters *and the natural biological integrity of riverine-riparian ecosystems and biodiversity.*"

* A single department with clear policy-making authority to coordinate and implement watershed protection and restoration programs. We recommend that the program be operated by the Environmental Protection Agency (provided EPA is given cabinet status and its performance and authority are greatly improved).

* Explicit definition of riverine-riparian ecosystems and biodiversity and a commitment to protect these resources in order to prevent, rather than try to control or repair, problems.

* Uniform, consistent protection and restoration standards for all federal land management agencies.

* Ecosystem and watershed-level planning by all federal agencies.

* A comprehensive ecosystem-based watershed protection program for all federal land-management agencies. This includes the creation of a nationwide system of "Watershed Biodiversity Management Areas" and "Benchmark Watersheds" and full protection for riparian areas and floodplains.

* A comprehensive ecosystem-based watershed restoration program that focuses initially on securing, expanding and, eventually, linking the remaining relatively healthy ecosystems and habitats, then on the more degraded areas within carefully crafted system-level recovery strategies.

* Coordinated, bottom-up, private-land watershed restoration programs that support and generate local jobs in restoration technologies, river-oriented community revitalization projects and appropriate economic conversions.

* A moratorium on new dam construction until a national "protected river" program is established, along with a process to prioritize, remove, and/or alter the most damaging dams and water projects within river systems.

* A periodic "State of the Nation's Rivers" report and a data bank for information on the conditions and trends. of America's riverine systems and biodiversity.

* Stable, long-term funding through better use of existing resources and an Aquatic Restoration Trust Fund, and effective new financial and tax incentives for watershed restoration.

* Improvements to the existing federal and state riverine protection and restoration approaches and policies so that they adopt and support the protection and restoration approaches, goals and policies proposed in this book.

These proposed new goals and approaches are discussed in chapter four.

Implementation Policies

To implement the proposed goals and approaches, we recommend two new policies that can be enacted rapidly: the *Federal Lands Watershed Management Act* and the *National Watershed Registry*. We also recommend a comprehensive federal policy that may require more time to enact: the *National Riverine and Riparian Conservation Act*. Our approach is based both on pragmatism (what may be quickly achievable in today's sociopolitical climate) and on principle (what ultimately needs to be done).

The Federal Lands Strategy

In the near term, we propose a new *Federal Lands Watershed Management Act*, a comprehensive, uniform policy that would be applied to all federal land management agencies that mandates watershed-level, ecosystem-based protection and restoration. This immediate first step can and must be accomplished. One uniform federal policy is needed to cut across the many conflicting and ineffective policy fragments that exist today concerning riverine systems and biodiversity on federal lands. Much of the remaining natural ecological capital that supports the tenuous health of many of the nation's riverine systems and much of the remaining biodiversity is found on federal lands, especially in the West. These systems must be protected quickly to *prevent* further degradation and to provide the fundamental building blocks for long-term restoration.

Protection: Our proposal includes the implementation of the new protection approach previously described. This includes clear and unequivocal new rules and regulations to protect headwaters, biotic refuges, benchmark watersheds, riparian areas and biological hot spots on all rivers and streams on all federal lands.

The biotic refuges that have already been disturbed by human encroachment should be protected under a new national system of Watershed Biodiversity Management Areas. These refuges will need active restoration treatments to secure them by reducing or eliminating threats from previous management activities to remain productive.

Watersheds existing essentially in an undisturbed or wild state should be protected through a national system of Benchmark Watersheds. Benchmark Watersheds are needed to provide baseline data through scientific research and long-term monitoring of change in watershed ecosystems and riverine biodiversity over time. They would receive the highest protection afforded to federal lands.

In addition, we propose a moratorium on new dam construction until a nationwide protected-area program is instituted. Finally, all federal agency policies and management actions that address the resources stated above would be uniformly aligned within each watershed.

Restoration: Once protections are in place, restoration efforts would focus initially on securing, expanding and then linking the relatively healthy headwaters, Benchmark Watersheds, Watershed Biodiversity Management Areas, and biological hot spots, as opposed to initially treating the most degraded areas. Focusing on linking and expanding the healthy areas will provide for potentially more rapid and cost-effective recovery. Only after the remaining healthy areas are secured and restoration begun should restoration resources be applied to the more degraded areas. A priority system would be developed to determine which of the more degraded segments will receive restoration treatments within the context of watershed-level recovery strategies.

We believe that the combined effect of these actions will be to help maintain and recover watershed ecosystems, riverine habitats and riverine-riparian biodiversity on federal lands nationwide. Securing these resources on federal lands may, in turn, help maintain the existing health and anchor restoration strategies for degraded systems flowing through private (non-federal) lands.

Local participation and economic enhancement: Securing and restoring watersheds on federal lands will require applying new restoration technologies to abate problems caused by roads, timber harvesting, mining, grazing, dams and other human activities. Physical treatments that restore hydrologic systems, reduce sedimentation, secure soils and provide site preparation for the reestablishment of native vegetation succession are generally the most cost-effective treatments to prevent and correct problems. Local workers should be employed in this work to ensure that the jobs and economic benefits remain local. For example, a draft estimate of the costs of protecting and restoring federal-land watersheds with at-risk salmon in the Pacific Northwest indicates that roughly 20,000 to 30,000 person-years of employment would be created over the 5-10 year period of implementation. Much of this would involve heavy bulldozer and excavator equipment work to remove, upgrade or otherwise alleviate sedimentation problems caused by forest roads.

Initial implementation of the Federal Lands Watershed Management Act: We propose that the policies be initially implemented on federal lands throughout the Pacific Northwest. Over 200 anadromous salmonids (trout, steelhead, char, and salmon) are at risk of extinction, and watershed ecosystems are highly degraded regionwide. At the same time, the region is soon certain to protect critical habitat for the Northern Spotted Owl and other species. Implementing the new federal-land riverine policies, in conjunction with the impending protection for these species, will provide a more structured and integrated land protection and management scheme. It would also allow the policies to be refined, if needed, before application to federal lands nationwide.

The Private Lands Strategy

We propose the concurrent establishment of a *National Watershed Registry*. The program would support existing programs and initiate new voluntary, bottom-up local efforts to recover riverine systems on private lands.

It is clear that the purely regulatory top-down approach to private land riverine management has failed. Despite efforts to promulgate and apply Best Management Practices (BMPs), Total Maximum Daily Loads (TMDLs) and other approaches, through federal and state policies, degradation continues. A new approach is needed.

Despite the failure of federal and state policies, many local bottom-up river restoration efforts are under way throughout the nation. However, because no federal umbrella policy exists to guide and support these efforts, most are piecemeal and limited in their effectiveness. In addition, most fail to generate local jobs in restoration or community revitalization projects or to support appropriate economic conversions. They are, therefore, often opposed by rural communities. Sometimes they even exacerbate or precipitate riverine problems. The National Watershed Registry is intended to provide a new enabling mechanism to support and help initiate local bottom-up restoration programs. The goal is to provide a flexible menu of local, state and federal incentives, funding and technical assistance that local citizens can utilize as they best see fit in developing locally tailored restoration programs. Such a mechanism is needed to help local programs become more effective and to proliferate nationwide.

Communities and citizen groups concerned about a riverine system with special values or problems would, after approval by the state, petition the Environmental Protection Agency (EPA) for the river's inclusion in the National Watershed Registry. Criteria would be established to prioritize petitions. To develop cooperation and coalitions among those most affected by riverine degradation or in need of economic stimulus, priority would be given to those petitions that include full involvement of economically and socially disadvantaged groups and communities. The EPA would place the system on the National Watershed Registry if its assessment confirmed that the system holds special values or problems and if the local communities demonstrate sufficient commitment to implementing a watershed restoration strategy. As with a listing on the National Register of Historic Places, no Act of Congress or state legislature would be required.

Protection and restoration: Inclusion in the National Watershed Registry would initiate a process by which local citizens and communities, working with state and federal incentives and technical assistance, would establish an independent, non-profit watershed council (or task force) that would bring together all the interests and affected groups to plan and implement a Watershed Restoration Action Plan (WRAP). The strategy would be based on a set of minimum federal criteria, yet would not impose complicated basinwide land-use planning procedures. Instead, each WRAP would be locally tailored to focus on protection and restoration of the more narrowly defined riparian areas, floodplains, and biological hot spots, along with retirement or modification of damaging dams, dikes, levees and channelizations, and other sedimentation and run-off reduction strategies. The restoration plan may also provide a means of protecting open spaces for biological purposes. The programs would be linked with programs for the restoration of contiguous watersheds on federal lands where such programs exist or may be started. A key component of the WRAP would be to develop a system-wide policy alignment and consistency mechanism.

The Watershed Restoration Action Plan would be used by a state to develop a comprehensive state hydroelectric plan for the river. The plan would be included as part of a state comprehensive hydroelectric plan, thus meeting Section 10(a) requirements of the Federal Power Act. The National Watershed Registry may, therefore, force the Federal Energy Regulatory Commission to deny hydroelectric license applications and allow the state to deny Section 401 Clean Water Act permit requests for hydroelectric projects on the river. A state and federal consistency clause would be one of the key incentives provided for each WRAP approved.

Local community enhancement: As with the federal lands program, a major by-product of the program would be to generate local jobs in restoration technologies, compatible river-oriented community revitalization projects and appropriate economic conversions. To encourage participation and support for the process, a menu of flexible financial, tax and administrative incentives would be provided.

The National Watershed Registry is aimed at supporting local, bottom-up efforts to address private-land riverine systems and is, therefore, not a comprehensive solution. As stated, it is needed to support the many ongoing local efforts that have sprouted across the country but, currently, are limited in effectiveness. It should also stimulate the growth of many new local efforts nationwide. As such, the National Watershed Registry would be a starting point from which to nurture more comprehensive efforts from the ground up.

Many states have become active in riverine restoration and have begun to support local efforts. However, states have limited ability to influence federally licensed or constructed dams or water projects, or federal lands where they play a major role in the watershed. Further, many states face increasingly limited financial and technical resources. Most state programs also fail to directly support the creation of jobs in restoration technologies, compatible community revitalization projects or economic conversions to restore rivers. Federal leadership, guidance and incentives are required to make local bottom-up programs more effective and abundant nationwide.

The Long-term Policy Solution: the National Riverine and Riparian Conservation Act

Ultimately, a comprehensive policy is needed that would combine regulatory and non-regulatory approaches to protect and restore every riverine system nationwide, regardless of land ownership. The *National Riverine and Riparian Conservation Act* would complement and build upon the Clean Water Act, which already applies to every body of water in the nation. A federal National Riverine and Riparian Conservation Act program would be established within the EPA to administer state programs, distribute grants and funding, and establish standards and criteria.

Protection and restoration: The National Riverine and Riparian Conservation Act would mandate the restoration of riverine systems based on a priority list of systems statewide. The priority list would not initially highlight the most degraded systems. Instead, the program would confer a high priority to two types of rivers: those systems where a sufficient degree of ecosystem and biodiversity health remains to maintain at-risk riverine-riparian biodiversity and to stimulate a rapid biotic and ecological recovery; and those rivers where sufficient local interest exists, as in the National Watershed Registry. If a high-priority riverine system lacks sufficient local support to be included in the National Watershed Registry, or the National Watershed Registry program has failed to lead to effective recovery steps, the National Riverine and Riparian Conservation Act would apply. The most degraded riverine systems would be addressed only after sufficient resources are applied to begin restoration efforts on those with the best chance of more rapid recovery.

The program would focus on three primary activities: riparian and floodplain protection and restoration, system-wide policy coordination and alignment, and dam and water-project removal and changes using the RBER restoration approach described earlier. Although disturbances to riverine systems and biodiversity have many causes, we believe it is possible to ameliorate a significant percentage (perhaps 60-80%) of the impacts by focusing on these three activities. Again, the initial emphasis would be placed on *preventing* further degradation rather than on controlling or repairing damage after it begins.

Every state would be required to implement a Watershed Restoration Action Plan (WRAP) to meet federal standards on each priority riverine system. The restoration action plans would be crafted through the auspices of an independent, non-profit umbrella watershed council composed of those with interests or concerns about the river in a process similar to the National Watershed Registry.

The statewide assessment would also identify systems or segments to be permanently set off-limits to future hydroelectric projects, thus initiating the state-protected rivers program. The system-wide hydroelectric plan for priority rivers would serve as a "comprehensive hydroelectric plan." Both the protected area program and the system-wide comprehensive hydroelectric plans for rivers would meet the Section 10(a) requirements of the Federal Power Act. Thus, states would have the right to deny Section 401 Clean Water Act permits for hydroelectric projects proposed on these riverine systems.

In addition, public agencies at all levels of government would be required to uniformly align their policies and management within the entire riverine system. However, no federal agency would be allowed to amend its policies to provide less protection than is required under the proposed Federal Lands Watershed Management Act.

Local community enhancement: Like the Federal Land Riverine Management Act and National Watershed Registry proposals, the NRRCA would place a major emphasis on involving the local communities in a bottom-up planning and implementation program, and in generating local jobs in restoration technologies, compatible river-oriented community revitalization projects and appropriate economic conversions. The focus would be on generating opportunities that will enhance both the river and local communities.

The National Riverine and Riparian Conservation Act is a concept whose time has come. What may seem like a distant ideal today may be within reach tomorrow. The nation must establish healthy riverine systems and biodiversity as vital national resources and move decisively to protect and restore these systems.

These three policy recommendations are discussed in greater depth in chapters five and six.

The Imperative of Change

Although we evaluated numerous federal and state riverine policies and programs in the appendixes of this report, we have not spent a great deal of time recommending improvements for each. We believe that improving existing policies, although important to do, will still not provide the effective approaches or policies needed to initiate an era of comprehensive watershed restoration nationwide. No existing restoration approaches or policies appear to be based on contemporary scientific knowledge, or effective implementation strategies and mechanisms. Until new approaches are adopted and new policies are enacted, most efforts in improving, properly applying or enforcing existing policies will remain primarily "rear guard" actions. That is, they may (but likely will not) maintain the existing levels of health for some riverine systems for a short time. However, they are certain to fail to maintain riverine health in the long run or lead to comprehensive recovery. New federal and state restoration goals, approaches and policies are needed.

It may appear contradictory that we have divided our near-term recommendations into those for federal and private lands while calling for watershed-level policies. We have done this for both practical and political reasons. The near-term steps are within reach and are needed to quickly stop the hemorrhaging of America's riverine systems by protecting and securing the remaining relatively healthy areas and initiating priority recovery actions. These steps should be viewed as building blocks to educate the public and to build a national consensus for enactment of the comprehensive National Riverine and Riparian Conservation Act.

To implement the new goals, approaches and policies proposed in this book, ten keystone issues must be addressed:

* First, we must fully acknowledge the severely degraded state of riverine systems and biodiversity nationwide, and make a national commitment to change this.

* Riverine systems must no longer be defined as "renewable" energy and water resources.

* Larger numbers of riverine systems must be addressed simultaneously and comprehensively.

* Current assumptions, approaches, and policies must be redesigned, from the stream-segment and single-species focus to the watershed (landscape), ecosystem and biodiversity perspective.

* Local investment in river conservation must be encouraged.

* Long-term, stable funding must be provided.

* Accounting procedures must be expanded to fully account for external costs of proposed riverine developments.

* The terms "sustainability" and "restoration" must be clearly defined.

* A commitment to prevention rather than repair or control is required.

* Finally, and most importantly, we must rapidly implement the comprehensive protective measures as described in this report, along with the separate but connected set of recovery actions.

These issues are discussed in chapter seven.

We hope this book will help guide the nation toward new approaches and policies that will protect and restore America's riverine systems and biodiversity.   Riverine systems are the life-support system of our nation.   These systems support the production of food, timber, fiber, water, and many other products that provide jobs, economic benefits and sustenance. From the remaining healthy riverine systems will come vital genetic resources to recolonize the environment for future generations. And it is the natural beauty and recreational opportunities of America's rivers that uplift the human spirit.

It is in our self-interest to protect and restore America's riverine systems and biodiversity.   It is also our moral responsibility.

PART I

FORGOTTEN WATERS

by

Bob Doppelt
Dr. James Karr
Mary Scurlock

CHAPTER ONE

THE HIDDEN CRISIS

The degradation of America's riverine systems, and the depletion of their biodiversity, have reached alarming levels. The problems affect the smallest streams to the largest rivers and all forms of riverine-riparian biodiversity. Not one river system in the United States has been spared. Even Idaho's Middle Fork of the Salmon -- one of the nation's most isolated rivers and an original Wild and Scenic River -- has been damaged by increased sedimentation caused by overgrazing and mining which started over 100 years ago.[1] Consequently, once plentiful colonies of freshwater mussels are now close to extinction. Fisheries, surface and ground water quality and quantity produced by watershed ecosystems, and entire aquatic food chains are at risk nationwide.

America has tamed almost all of its great rivers, and this development has provided obvious benefits to human beings. Riverine systems support many human uses and needs, such as industrial and municipal water supply, energy production (hydroelectric power, cooling of thermoelectric generating plants), irrigation, flood control, transportation, commercial fisheries and the assimilation of human waste. The recreational value of rivers and streams is also widely recognized, from "consumptive" recreation such as sport fishing, to "non-consumptive" recreation such as river-running, swimming, streamside hiking, camping and wildlife observation, and to the general appreciation of scenic values and aesthetics.

However, at what cost have these benefits accrued? What are the real ecological, economic, and social costs of such development?

The proportion of freshwater organisms that are threatened with extinction is far greater than that for terrestrial organisms; 10%-15% of terrestrial vertebrate organisms are classed as rare to extinct, but 33%-75% of aquatic organisms are rare to extinct.[2]

Among riverine organisms, the distributions and abundances of fishes are better known than those of any other

1

taxonomic group.[3] A recent survey by the Endangered Species
Committee of the American Fisheries Society (AFS) documented
the status of inland fishes in the United States, and the status of
native anadromous salmonids on the West Coast. These studies
found that more than 500 North American species, subspecies, and
stocks (populations) of fishes are considered to be at risk of
extinction. The studies further found that 40 more species and
subspecies of freshwater fishes have already become extinct, and
more than 106 stocks of anadromous salmonids have been
documented as extinct in the Pacific Northwest and California.[4]
The draft Northern Spotted Owl Recovery Plan found that more
than 750 of 1100 native fish populations (including resident and
estuarine) in 348 streams were at risk of extinction from the
Cascade Mountains west to the ocean in the Pacific Northwest.[5]

Overall, one third of all North American fish are
endangered, threatened, or of special concern, a significant increase
in levels of fish endangerment during the past decade.[6] High rates
of fish extinction are likely to persist into the future.

Not only fish are at risk. All forms of riverine and riparian
biodiversity are endangered. Among aquatic organisms, only a
few major species are sufficiently well known to provide data
necessary to count the proportion of species classed as rare or
extinct. Those proportions for fishes, crayfish and unionid mussels
are 34%, 65% and 73%, respectively.[7] The status of freshwater
mollusca may provide an indication of the seriousness of the
imperilment. About half the freshwater mussel species in the U.
S. are either federally listed (that is, endangered or threatened) or
are proposed for listing. Twenty percent of the mollusca (clams,
snails and their relatives) of the Tennessee River have been lost,
and 45% of the remaining species are endangered or seriously
depleted.[8] From the Cascade Mountains in the Pacific Northwest
to the Pacific ocean at least 132 riparian-associated species were
found to be at risk of extinction, including three birds, four
mammals, 12 amphibians, 45 mollusks and 43 arthropods.[9]

The ecological makeup of riverine systems has been
degraded nationwide. For example, overall an estimated 70%-90%

of natural riparian vegetation, vital to riverine health, has already been lost to human activities nationwide.[10] Clearing for urban and agricultural uses has reduced riparian forest area by 66%. In many areas of the arid West, the Midwest and the lower Mississippi Valley, riparian vegetation has been reduced by more than 80%.[11] Flow alteration has degraded 70% of this country's rivers and streams.[12] Once biological criteria are considered, almost 50% of the nation's waters fail to meet water quality standards, according to the Ohio EPA.[13]

How would our society respond if our agricultural productivity declined by over 75%? How can we continue to ignore declines of that magnitude in riverine resources that are essential to the economic and ecological health of human society?[14]

The status of riverine systems and biodiversity is indicative of the health of surrounding landscapes in the same way that blood samples provide important insight into the health of humans. The analogy is apt because rivers are in many ways the lifeblood of human society, and we cannot continue to tolerate their rapid degradation. The systematic reduction in the biological diversity of riverine systems is symptomatic of wider biotic impoverishment, the progressive decline in the earth's ability to support living systems and, thus, human society.

We are part of the natural richness provided by riverine systems. We depend on the systems for food, medicines, timber, water, fiber and many other products. They provide vital genetic resources. In this rapidly changing world, it is the remaining riverine-riparian species and genetically different biotic populations that can recolonize the systems in the future. And it is the natural beauty, aesthetic and recreational values of America's rivers that uplift the human spirit.

We are precariously close to a point where further losses may push the majority of riverine systems and species over the edge -- to a point where natural recovery may not be possible.

The Economic and Social Consequences of Riverine Degradation

The economic and social impacts of degraded riverine systems and lost biodiversity are severe. However, they have not been accurately examined or systematically documented. Only a few examples are necessary to demonstrate the alarming degree of loss.

Humans have suffered. Thirty-seven states reported fish consumption closures, restrictions or advisories in 1989,[15] reflecting threats to wildlife[16] and human health.[17] Recent demonstrations of intergenerational consequences from consuming contaminated fish raise new concerns: infants born to women with a history of consuming Lake Michigan fish (relative to infants of women who did not consume those fish over extended periods) experienced cognitive, motor and behavioral deficits in postnatal exams, and the patterns persisted to four years of age.[18]

The jobs and food resources once provided by the commercial and recreational fisheries nationwide have been decimated in this century. For example, two-thirds of the species of the Illinois River (Illinois) have experienced major population declines or disappeared from that watershed since 1850, and the commercial catch of the river, second in commercial catch to the Columbia River early in this century, declined to near zero over a decade ago. The Missouri River commercial fishery has declined by 80% since 1945. Since 1910, annual salmon and steelhead runs of the Columbia river system have declined from approximately 10-16 million to 2-2.5 million, a loss of 85% if hatchery fish runs are counted, and a loss of over 95% if, as is more appropriate, those runs are not included.[19]

The recreational value of flowing rivers and streams nationwide was estimated in 1985 by the Fish and Wildlife Service in its National Survey of Fishing, Hunting, and Wildlife-Associated Recreation. This survey reported that $17.8 billion was spent by 38.4 million people for non-Great Lakes freshwater fishing in 1985 and that 45% of these anglers fished in rivers and streams. Assuming that fishermen spend comparable amounts regardless of fishing location, the economic value of flowing-water fisheries is estimated at more that $8 billion annually. Additional economic value is derived from rivers and streams when non-consumptive recreation, such as kayaking, canoeing, and wildlife observation, as well as premiums for streamside properties, are added to the equation. What would the economic value be if riverine systems and fisheries nationwide were in healthier states?

Many rural communities are dependent on tourism, which, in large part, is derived from the availability of sport fishing and clean, free-flowing rivers. Moreover, it is now believed that the economic value of the tourist industry in many western states equals or exceeds the value of the forest products and other resource extraction industries. The availability of clean rivers and streams and their immediate environs is a primary draw for many of these tourists. Given the degree of riverine degradation, we must consider what has already been lost economically, and what is at stake if further degradation occurs.

Despite expenditures of at least $473 billion to build, operate and administer water pollution control facilities since 1970, the nation's water resources continue to decline in both quality and quantity.[20] These costs will continue to escalate as riverine degradation proceeds.

Soil loss caused by agricultural runoff, timber harvest, road building and grazing causes depleted growing capacity from farm and timber lands, increased water treatment costs and decreased water quality and habitat for riverine-riparian biodiversity and other riverine uses. The eventual buildups behind dams slowly eliminates the water storage capacity of reservoirs. Soil in America is eroding at the rate of 4 billion tons per year, and costs the nation an estimated $3.2 billion each year according to the Council on Environmental Quality.[21] About one-third of the soil eroded by water from agricultural land enters streams and other bodies of water, causing $2-$9 billion in off-site damage annually to water-related activities such as recreation, water storage, irrigation and navigation.

The lost potential of riverine food resources may become a much more important issue as the nation's traditional game fish decline and the population and need for new food resources grows. It may seem very unlikely that large numbers of people will develop a taste for non-game fish or other riverine species, but this notion is not that far-fetched. People today eat crayfish, bullhead and sunfish; pioneers ate caddisflies; and frogs and turtles are eaten in many cultures. France, a nation famous for the culinary arts, consumes many foods that Americans would not consider eating. The diversity of oriental cuisine is even broader. The Chinese, for example, eat scorpions complete with stingers and many kinds of snakes. With global population set to double in the next 40 years or so, the food potential from America's riverine systems must be fully considered. Who knows what potentially important medicinal resources have also been lost through riverine degradation?

The loss of fishery-related jobs, which should be long-term sustainable jobs, has significantly harmed many communities dependent on fishing and tourism to support their economies. The billions spent on water pollution control facilities are dollars that could have been kept within local communities, thus enhancing local economic vitality. The millions of tons of soil lost yearly and the billions of dollars lost in association with this must be viewed as ecologically and economically unacceptable to our nation.

In short, almost every segment of society has been adversely affected by the degradation of America's riverine systems and biodiversity, and we all pay heavy direct or indirect ecological, financial and job-related costs, whether we realize it or not. It is in our self-interest to protect and restore America's riverine systems and biodiversity.

CHAPTER TWO

RIVERINE SYSTEMS: THE STEPCHILD OF ENVIRONMENTAL EFFORTS

The Watershed Ecosystem

The degradation of America's riverine systems and biodiversity continues almost unabated, for a number of reasons. One of the most basic reasons is that most people typically think of rivers as simply water flowing through a channel. This view fails to appreciate the actual complexity and diversity of riverine systems and is reflected in failed policies. In the past 15 years many scientific studies and reports have documented that riverine systems are intimately coupled with and created by the characteristics of their catchment basins or *watersheds*. Watersheds involve four-dimensional processes that connect the longitudinal (upstream-downstream), lateral (floodplains-upland) and vertical (hyporheic or groundwater zone-stream channel) dimensions, each differing temporally.

Watersheds are ecosystems composed of a mosaic of different land or terrestrial "patches" that are connected by (drained by) a network of streams. In turn, the flowing water environment is composed of a mosaic of habitats in which organisms, materials and energy move in complex, yet highly integrated, systems. Physical and chemical processes and complex food webs depend on these movements. Given the dynamic connectedness of a watershed, management activities can fragment and disconnect the habitat patches if they are not planned and implemented from an ecosystem and watershed perspective.

In-stream conditions, therefore, are largely determined by processes that occur within the watershed, and they cannot be isolated from or manipulated independently of this context. A riverine system is an "open" ecosystem because a large proportion of the materials and energy in the system are derived from the surrounding terrestrial system, yet flow outward. Disturbances in a watershed propagate downstream from headwater sources. The protection of sensitive headwater areas in watersheds is therefore critical to maintaining and restoring riverine habitat and ecosystems for considerable distances downstream. Management of riverine systems absent from the watershed context run the risk of being ineffective at best, and counterproductive and destructive at worst.

Flowing freshwater systems are directly linked with the terrestrial environment -- the land base -- for shade and input of nutrients and organic materials. The riparian area is the area where that interface occurs. The riparian area is linked with the flowing water ecosystem to such an extent that the former is the essential part of the latter. Thus, the term *riverine-riparian ecosystem* more accurately describes the entire area.[22]

When described alone, the riparian area means an *ecotone* (transition region) between flowing water and terrestrial ecosystems, which serves as the area of continuous exchange of nutrients and woody debris between land and water.[23] Riparian vegetation is an especially critical component of the watershed because it provides an estimated 99% of the in-stream nutrients in the aquatic food web.[24] Although riparian areas constitute a relatively small proportion of the nation's land area (probably from 1% to 8% in the western United States, though a higher percentage in the Mississippi Delta, the Everglades and a few other areas), they are of vital importance to the ecological and biological health of watershed ecosystems.[25]

Riparian vegetation provides shade, helping to maintain water temperatures at the levels to which native riverine-riparian biodiversity are best adapted. Leaves and woody debris from the riparian area feed the water with nutrients for growth of aquatic plants and provide food and habitat for the insects upon which fish feed. This debris also contributes to the physical structure of the system by slowing water velocity and deflecting its course. As the water is slowed and deflected, it pushes against the banks and into the soils underlying the adjacent floodplain, thereby contributing to the local water table. Riparian areas are a vital source of important structural components of the entire riverine system.

Because riparian vegetation is vital to ecosystem health and yet so degraded nationwide, one of the primary goals of new national riverine conservation approaches and policies must be the protection and restoration of riparian corridors or buffers, especially on private agricultural and forest lands. This principle is fundamental to understanding how riverine-riparian ecosystems are degraded, and how they might be restored. As the National Research Council observes:

> The important concept from a management point of view is that streams are products of their catchment basins or watersheds and that the terrestrial environment closest to the stream (the riparian zone) has the greatest impact, with the influence diminishing with distance from the stream. Restoration and management of the riparian area are usually more cost-effective in improving water quality and fish habitat than practices applied farther from the watercourse.[26]

Healthy riverine systems are dynamic, changing systems that tend to meander. Their movement contributes to the health of the ecosystem because it slows water velocity in flood stages, burying and storing organic materials upon which certain species depend while releasing the degraded materials that are crucial to the survival of other species. It also creates a complete mosaic of seasonal habitats for riverine-riparian biodiversity. The dynamic nature of the systems is an important consideration in any restoration approach -- the system's ability to move and change must be protected.

For example, the fertilizing effect of floodwaters from rivers provides an important benefit to society. During floods, nutrients and soil are deposited on floodplains, renewing the fertility of agricultural lands. In modern America, as in most developed countries, however, the costs of floods are believed to outweigh the benefits, so dams and dikes are used to keep floodwaters out of fields, and chemical fertilizers are used to maintain soil productivity. Dams, dikes and channels have allowed economic developments that are not adapted to the flood cycle, a circumstance that disrupts the natural riverine-riparian ecosystem, beginning a process of soil and plant degradation, often lowering the water table and destroying floodplains, forests, and wetland vegetation.

Rivers transport and deposit sediment naturally. All too often, however, sediment delivery rates are disturbed by human actions that accelerate what may be a natural 500-year sedimentation rate into a 20-to-30-year period, thus overstressing the system.

Riverine-riparian ecosystems play an important role in producing habitats for both terrestrial and riverine biodiversity. Riverine habitats support the greatest biodiversity of any aquatic habitat types, including lakes and springs.[27] Riverine-riparian ecosystems provide life-supporting habitat for multitudes of non-fish vertebrate and invertebrate species -- key links in the aquatic food chain. They are also natural highways for migratory birds and other forms of biodiversity. Almost 80% of terrestrial species in the Western United States are dependent on riparian vegetation for food, habitat or migration corridors. Many birds nest in riparian areas, feed on aquatic insects and fish, deposit their wastes in the stream, and are, in turn, preyed upon by other species. The biological diversity supported by riverine-riparian ecosystems is a critical link in the entire natural food chain of which human beings are a part.

The Definition of an Ecologically Healthy Watershed

Ecologically healthy watersheds can be understood by evaluating the status of the elements and processes that affect biodiversity, productivity, nutrient and chemical cycles, and evolutionary processes that are adapted to the climatic and geologic conditions of the region. Collectively, these elements and processes provide a measure of system health. Some tangible measures of ecologically healthy watersheds include water yield and quality, species composition, diversity and abundance, wildlife use, and genetic diversity. A key indicator of these measures is the degree to which native riverine-riparian biodiversity survives in large landscapes throughout their historic range. This means that we must protect or restore riverine-riparian biodiversity at the ecosystem level (biodiversity fills a vital role in ecological processes), species level and genetic level (many subpopulations of species have uniquely adapted to different streams, and hanging on to these diverse genetic characteristics is vitally important).

Truly ecologically healthy watersheds may be said to have *biological integrity*: "the capability of supporting and maintaining a balanced, integrated, adaptive biological system having the full range of elements and processes expected in natural habitat of the region."[28]

The Importance of Headwaters, Riparian Areas, Biotic Refuges, Benchmark Streams and Biological "Hot Spots"

Because almost all riverine systems nationwide are already highly degraded and fragmented, it is important to understand the critical role that the remaining relatively healthy headwaters, riparian areas, floodplains, biotic refuges, benchmark watersheds and biological hot spots play in supporting existing levels of health for systems and species, and in anchoring potential recovery efforts.

The ecological significance of riparian areas is often accentuated in small *headwater stream* reaches. These small streams are the most vulnerable to human disturbance (especially timber harvesting, road building, grazing and related activities) because they respond dramatically and rapidly to disturbances to their riparian areas and are most sensitive to changes in riparian vegetation in the surrounding watershed. Even where inaccessible to fish, these small streams provide high levels of water quality and quantity, sediment control, nutrients and woody debris for downstream reaches of the watershed. Intermittent and ephemeral headwater streams are, therefore, important contributors to the entire riverine-riparian ecosystem. Thus, especially in the highly degraded systems, headwater streams serve as critical ecological anchors for riverine systems and important refuges for biodiversity.

Biotic refuges or *refugia* are discrete riverine areas, up to the size of entire tributary watersheds, that maintain habitat conditions conducive to at-risk biodiversity. The word refugia refers to the fact that the biodiversity supported by the area exists in isolation from other populations (as a refuge from degraded areas) and thus depends on the remaining relatively healthy area for survival. As such, refugia are often the "linchpins" of existing levels of ecosystem and biodiversity health. These areas must be identified and fully protected to maintain existing levels of health and to anchor recovery efforts.

The remaining undisturbed watersheds are *benchmark watersheds* with which to research, compare and monitor stream ecosystems over time. In many riverine systems, preserving the integrity of both the biotic refuges and fully intact benchmark watersheds may be the only hope of maintaining the health of ecosystems and species. Restoration of many of America's riverine systems may prove impossible unless these areas are quickly protected and secured to form the fundamental reconstructive building blocks.

It is not just in headwater areas that riparian areas play an important role. *Riparian areas and floodplains* play a critical role in maintaining ecosystem health throughout the system. It is imperative to protect and restore riparian areas and floodplains across the nation if we are to have any hope of maintaining or recovering riverine systems and biodiversity.

Biological hot spots are generally smaller riverine habitat patches that provide critical biological elements and processes essential to healthy riverine systems. Although surrounding areas may be seriously degraded, hot spots generally retain a degree of health for various reasons, such as fortuitous historical land ownership patterns or simply chance.

The *hyporheic zone*, for example, is the biologically active groundwater area most commonly found within alluvial floodplains. It is biologically and hydrologically connected to the surface water of the system. Though few management policies acknowledge these vital areas, the hyporheic zone is important for riverine organisms, especially invertebrates, during periods of disturbance to the system (floods, droughts, and so forth). The hyporheic zones have also been identified as intimately associated with fish spawning and rearing areas and are an important source of energy and nutrient transport. The zones can extend from a few centimeters on small streams to include large floodplain aquifers in gravel-bed rivers. The importance of the hyporheic zone and its role in providing refugia in streams is just now being recognized. A number of undeveloped floodplains still exist within most riverine systems. Their hyporheic zones are consequently important biological hot spots.[29]

Biotic refuges, benchmark watersheds and biological hot spots cannot exist in isolation indefinitely. Under existing laws and management, degradation caused by inappropriate development will eventually threaten these areas as well. One of the primary objectives of a new conservation approach must be to quickly protect and secure the areas from further development.

Many of the nation's riverine systems originate on or flow at least partially through federal lands. Although most of the federal-land riverine systems are seriously degraded, nearly all of the remaining relatively healthy headwaters, biotic refuges, benchmark streams, riparian areas, floodplains and biological hot spots are found on federal lands. This is especially true in the western United States and Alaska, where watersheds in the headwaters within federal roadless areas effectively constitute most of the remaining refugia for native riverine biodiversity whose populations are at-risk and declining.[30]

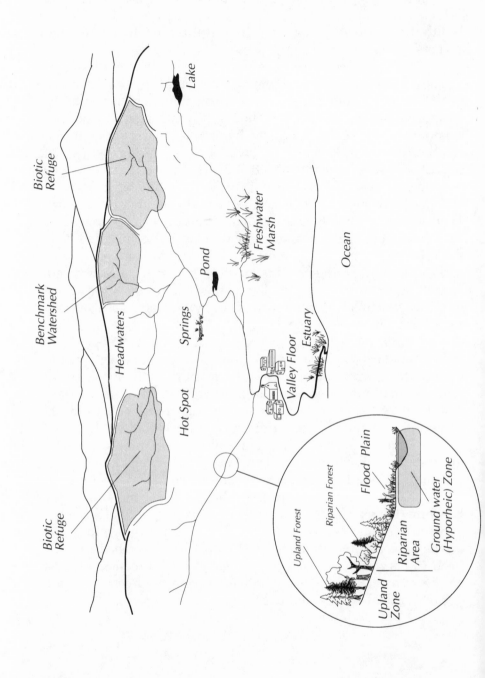

Biotic
Refuge

Benchmark
Watershed

Biotic
Refuge

Headwaters

Lake

Springs

Pond

Hot Spot

Freshwater
Marsh

Valley Floor

Estuary

Ocean

Upland Forest

Riparian Forest

Flood Plain

Riparian
Area

Ground water
(Hyporheic) Zone

Upland
Zone

Riverine Ecosystem Simplification: Slow Death By A Thousand Wounds

Human activities continue to degrade America's riverine systems and biodiversity in a variety of ways. The cumulative result of the many impacts has been called *ecosystem simplification*: huge reductions in the life-supporting complexity and diversity of riverine ecosystems. As complexity is reduced, the system's ability to repair itself after natural and human-caused disturbances erodes, leaving many systems and species seriously harmed or extinct, and with reduced ability to perform ecological functions. The most damaging impacts usually result from changes to the basic structure and function of riverine-riparian ecosystems and habitats.

Riverine ecosystem simplification is caused by a number of factors, including: 1) changes in water quantity or flow due to irrigation withdrawals; 2) modification of channel and riparian ecosystem morphology through dams, reservoirs, channelization, drainage and filling of wetlands and dredging for navigation; 3) damaging land use practices, including agriculture, forestry, and urbanization; 4) degrading water quality through addition of point- and nonpoint-source contaminants; 5) the decline of native fish and other species from overharvest and intentional or accidental poisoning; 6) and the introduction of exotic species.[31]

These activities may occur anywhere within the watershed, along the riparian or floodplain areas, or in river channels.[32] A brief discussion of each of these issues follows:

Changes in Water Quantity or Flow

One of the most extreme forms of disturbance to riverine-riparian ecosystems (most common in the arid West) is the almost complete appropriation of flowing surface water, either by direct withdrawal or by pumping from the riparian area -- "only slightly less extreme is the conversion of reaches of free-flowing rivers to a series of lake-like impoundments."[33] In either case, a free-flowing system no longer exists. Reduced in-stream flows leave insufficient water for fish and other riverine biodiversity, while altering the system's natural balance. By definition, a river is not a river without sufficient amounts of flowing water.

Modification of Stream Morphology

Dams have profound effects on rivers. Over 600,000 miles of America's rivers are already dammed,[34] and many more miles are affected by channelization and levying.[35] Estimates of the number of large dams on the nation's rivers varies from 68,000 (U.S. EPA) to 75,000 (National Park Service).[36] Untold millions of additional small dams exist nationwide.[37] Few riverine systems have escaped some form of alteration by damming or other flow alteration. In the contiguous 48 states, only 42 "free-flowing" rivers over 120 miles long remain, and only two large, free-flowing river systems remain -- the Yellowstone in Wyoming and Montana and the Salmon in Idaho.[38]

When a river is blocked, it is depleted of oxygen, and temperatures often change, depending upon the level of water release from upstream reservoirs. Rivers deepen and widen in the impoundments behind dams, often stratifying by temperature. Lower strata are oxygen poor, cool and often too dark to allow plant growth. Upper strata develop warmer temperatures that may be too warm for native aquatic species. Dams change the natural sedimentation transport process on which some fish species depend, trapping sediment (and food) that would naturally flow downstream or choking downstream reaches with sediment that would naturally have been dispersed by floods. In addition, unnatural pulses of water released from dams may erode streambanks, causing increased downstream sedimentation, which can block fish gills, smother food sources and cover spawning beds.[39] Dams also alter the natural cycles of inundation, abrasion and deposition, causing ecological and geological changes at the damsite and within the entire riverine landscape.

Dams also block passage for anadromous and other migratory fish that were naturally abundant, such as sturgeon, paddlefish, lampreys, salmonids (salmon, sea-run cutthroat trout and steelhead). Consequently, dams create huge changes in the entire food chain within a riverine system and in biomass, which, in turn, is reflected in declines in species such as eagles, fishers, martens and many other species that depend on riverine biomass for food. These changes eventually reach up to the highest echelons of the food chain.

Channelization means that a stream is straightened and usually lined with concrete or rock. The goal is usually to control flooding and divert water. These practices destroy the complex and dynamic function and structure of riverine systems.

The only time that the U.S. government attempted to quantify the mile of channelized streams in America was in 1972. At that time, the Council on Environmental Quality's report estimated that approximately 235,000 miles of streams and rivers had already been channelized, or were slated for channelization. Certainly, the total number of river miles affected today has increased dramatically from the 1972 estimates.

Drastic disturbance of riverine-riparian ecosystems also occurs where the river channel is prevented from interacting with the riparian and floodplain areas, generally creating incised, single-channel streams and substrate changes. Incised streams often cut the streambed down to bedrock, thus eliminating stream gravel that holds water during low flow periods. The process generally results in lowered water tables and decreased summer flows, which causes riparian vegetation to dry out and in many cases disrupts the hydrologic and regenerative cycles within the entire watershed. This loss of connectivity may occur directly, through channelization, levying, and the cleaning out of natural in-stream woody debris as well as indirectly, through the regulation of flood regimes via navigation dams.

The creation of reservoirs alters stream ecology in other ways. Impounded water drowns vegetation and even plants above the water level die when their root zones are flooded. Damage varies according to reservoir storage and release cycles. The more water stored, the more downstream flows are decreased. Mud flats are often exposed when water is released from reservoirs. Because of the large surface area of reservoirs, evaporation rates increase, concentrating salts in the stored water. Sediments gradually fill reservoirs, reducing their storage capacity.

Damaging Land Use Practices

One of the greatest causes of riverine-riparian ecosystem simplification derives from timber harvest and associated road building, grazing and mining. Timber harvest in the riparian area can reduce soil stability and bank structure. Extensive destruction of trees from timber harvest, grazing and road building harms rivers by increasing sedimentation, over-nutrifying the water and interfering with the reproduction of natural plant and wildlife communities.

Aside from logging in riparian and upland areas, timber that has fallen into rivers and streams is often removed as salvage or for navigational purposes. Without leaves and woody debris, stream velocity increases and the natural tendency of the stream channel to meander decreases. Roads, dikes, and construction along banks also tend to restrict a stream's lateral movement and keep it in a single channel. Undeflected, fast channelized currents erode the stream bottom, cutting deeply into the stream bed and lowering the elevation of the active channel. Stream water is no longer pushed into the soils under the floodplain, thus reducing water storage levels and capacity in the floodplain and lowering the local water table. Changes to the water table can greatly affect nearby vegetation, including agriculture. Increased water flow in the stream, plus the severance of the stream and floodplain by roads and other development, increases water inputs from upper stream reaches through precipitation and runoff. Although increased water velocity reduces the height of flooding in smaller upstream reaches, it increases the magnitude of downstream floods in the larger rivers.

Grazing simplifies riverine-riparian ecosystems because livestock favor riparian vegetation and tend to congregate in and along rivers, wetlands and streams. Animals grazing in these areas trample and consume riparian vegetation, inhibiting the regeneration of natural plant communities and increasing sedimentation rates, which covers stream beds and kills aquatic organisms. This depletes sources of large woody debris that are vital to channel stabilization and sinuosity. Shade is reduced, which increases water temperature and leaves biotic organisms such as aquatic insects and fish vulnerable to predation. Livestock also urinate and defecate in or near streams, increasing nutrient input beyond levels normal for natural aquatic communities.

Mining is another significant contributor to the simplification of riverine ecosystems. Current mining policies, although somewhat improved over the years, have led to a legacy of destruction for America's rivers. Approximately 50 billion tons of mining and processing waste have been left at mining sites. It is estimated that over 12,000 miles of rivers and streams are adversely affected by mining in the United States; at least one-third of this damage is caused by acid drainage associated with coal mining in the East and metals mining in the West.[40] Formed from the oxidation of iron pyrite, acid mine drainage (AMD) can coat stream bottoms with rust-tinted iron precipitate, adding sulfuric acid to the water and killing aquatic life.[41] Thousands of additional miles are indirectly affected.

Aside from acidification, mining and fossil fuel-related exploration activities have other negative impacts. Mineral exploration usually requires road building, which contributes to the sedimentation of rivers and streams. Development requires increased traffic, construction and accompanying surface disturbances.[42] The waste rock left after mining, called tailings, may contain heavy metals and processing chemicals that can leach into streams and groundwater. Even after mining activities cease, their impacts may continue.

Urbanization leads to development on floodplains, with subdividing of open space and destruction of riparian ecosystems, as homes, shopping malls, parks and industry are built along the edges of rivers. Urbanization and home development are often impossible to reverse. Urbanization generates point and non-point source pollution, and demands municipal and industrial water and often hydroelectric energy. The technology of transporting water in man-made channels over hundreds of miles and building huge dams have helped foster urban development even in the most seemingly inappropriate desert locations, such as Phoenix and Los Angeles. These factors have also led to extremely inefficient uses of water in many areas of the West. In fact, the United States is one of the most wasteful and inefficient water users in the world.

Point and Non-point Pollution

Over the past 25 years, progress has been made in controlling conventional point sources of pollution, such as sewage and other organic wastes, primarily through the implementation of point-source permit programs under the federal Clean Water Act. In some cases, however, water quality in critical river reaches is maintained only by diluting the systems with impounded water. Fish and other riverine species continue to be affected by the persistence of toxic substances in sediments. Furthermore, as will be discussed, national water quality assessments provide a very inadequate reflection of the true biological status of river systems because they are based on lake or channel sampling that does not include floodplain pools or backwaters, which are important nursery areas for fish and wildlife.[43] Water quality assessments also fail to address the structural, functional and biotic health of a riverine system, factors which are critical to support riverine-riparian biodiversity.

Excessive sedimentation and erosion creates nonpoint-source pollution. For all river miles in the United States, the Association of State and Interstate Water Pollution Control Administrators estimates that 11% were moderately to severely impaired by nonpoint-source pollution.[44] The estimated percentage contribution of the various types of nonpoint sources were: 64% from agriculture, 9% from mining, 6% from silviculture, 5% from urban runoff, 4% from hydromodification, 2% from construction and 1% from land disposal.[45] Regardless of the source, sediment accounted for a full 47% of the nonpoint-source pollution in affected rivers.[46]

On federal lands, the most prevalent causes of non-point pollution are deforestation and grazing. Both of these result in the loss of riparian vegetation and increased sedimentation. Logging carries with it the equally damaging practice of road building that can cause chronic and catastrophic sedimentation problems.

For example, recent surveys by scientists at the Pacific Northwest Research Station (PNWRS) of the USDA Forest Service documented the continuing decline of fish habitat in selected upper Columbia River basins since the 1930s. The PNWRS re-surveys provide direct evidence of the degradation of pool habitat (a critical element of riverine habitat) from the 1930s and 40s until the present. These habitat losses were associated with sedimentation and loss of large wood caused by timber harvesting, road building, grazing and related factors: ". . .relatively unharvested sub-basins in the Columbia basin in 1937 had frequencies of large pools exceeding 15 per mile. The present frequency of these streams averages less than 7 per mile. The exceptions are in the wilderness areas and low gradient willow-dominated streams. . . Streams on agricultural lands have also shown a steady loss in the frequency of large pools."[47]

On private (non-federal) lands, the most prevalent non-point pollution problems are caused by agriculture and urban development. According to a national fisheries habitat survey conducted by the U.S. Fish and Wildlife Service,[48] these factors are the most prominent in the deterioration of non-federal stream habitats. In 1985, several states reported that agriculture was the primary nonpoint-source pollutant in 64% of affected river miles.[49] Agricultural non-point pollution is degrading water quality on 29% of all streams, according to the USDA in its second Resource Conservation Act appraisal of conditions and trends on non-federal lands. "Existing soil conservation programs are designed to reduce soil erosion or cropland, but they do not necessarily improve or even maintain water quality or habitat in adjacent streams. Greenways along waterways in cities usually serve as recreational parks rather than as a means of restoring the natural functions of rivers, and most urban flood detention basins bear little resemblance in form or function to natural backwaters and floodplain pools."[50]

Agricultural runoff causes soil erosion as well as pollution problems. Selenium, a chemical toxic to humans and animals in large doses, is a major problem in areas near at least 15 major irrigation projects; 43 sites are under investigation. Soil erosion is the largest source of non-point pollution.

Overharvest

Overharvest of fisheries most often takes a back seat to habitat destruction and ecosystem dysfunction due to human activities in the depletion of biodiversity. However, overharvest in combination with other factors leads to biological extinctions. Although overharvesting alone is generally unlikely to drive many species to extinction, overfishing does deplete once abundant species to numbers too low to sustain natural reproduction. In addition, the functioning of the riverine biodiversity communities and ecosystems is greatly altered by the diminished presence of a fish species with particular feeding habits, body size, and life cycle.

Introduction of Exotic Species

More than 160 species of exotic (non-native) fishes from some 120 countries are listed on the international register kept by the United Nations, which reveals the problem of exotic species worldwide.[51] The exotic species occupy habitat and consume food otherwise used by native species and cause other ecological disruptions such as predation, hybridization, and the introduction of diseases and parasites. The establishment of exotic species in freshwater throughout the nation is rising sharply. In 1920, for example, only six species of exotics were established and by 1945 just three more were added. By 1980, at least 35 exotics had been established and at least 50 other exotic species had been recorded.[52] Hybridization and interbreeding with hatchery-reared counterparts of different genetic make-ups is an especially critical issue. Hybridization was found to be a factor in 38% of the recorded extinctions of North American fish species.[53]

One of the most catastrophic examples of the result of the introductions of exotic species is now occurring in Lake Victoria, Africa, which was noted for its high diversity of cichlid fishes (perhaps 400).[54] Nile perch was introduced in the late 1950s, which has resulted in a successful fishery that earns much-needed foreign currency, but the ecological and social costs have been high. Because hundreds of native species are becoming extinct, many local people have lost a source of protein and income.[55] Unfortunately, once established, exotic species are almost impossible to eradicate; hence, prevention is key.

Ecosystem simplification is the cumulative result of these impacts. It is the dramatic reduction of the complexity and diversity of structure, function and biological factors of America's riverine systems.[56] This leaves the ecosystems, habitats and species unable to withstand disturbances, both natural and human-induced, and ultimately unable to perform ecological functions or to repair themselves.

It seems clear that to abate the problems, an ecologically comprehensive program focused on key components of watershed ecosystem structure and function, including the headwaters, riparian areas, floodplains, biotic refuges, benchmark watersheds and biological hot spots will be needed. Yet, our traditional approaches to understanding and managing these systems fails to take an ecological approach.

The Failure of Traditional Assessments

Perhaps one of the most serious problems with riverine management approaches is the ineffectiveness of traditional riverine assessments. Although a number of studies tried to catalog the existing values of streams regionally and nationally, all have failed to assess the biological conditions of American riverine systems. This failure is attributable to two fundamental errors. First, previous studies did not assess rivers in their entirety because of the tendency to focus on river reaches as disjunct entities. Second, earlier studies provided only fragmentary information ". . . much like the information collected about an elephant by a group of humans with limited sensory abilities. Some can detect the odor, others hear the trumpeting, while others touch the trunk, leg or ear. None perceive the elephant in its entirety. Similarly, our society does not see rivers in their entirety."[57] To see rivers in their entirety means to see them at the catchment or watershed level.

From an ecological perspective, the health of a riverine system depends on the status of all components of the watershed. A river is not a collection of segments that can be managed as individual units. Therefore, understanding the ecological health or integrity of a river requires an understanding of the river as a complex ecosystem.

Previous riverine quality assessments neglected the biological components of water resource systems by concentrating on flow volumes and the chemical content of the water. Most regulatory approaches to protection of water quality concentrated on chemical criteria. For most of this century, agencies responsible for protecting water resources were constrained in their approach by a narrow view of pollution. Until recently, pollution was defined almost exclusively as chemical contamination of water resources. The Clean Water Act of 1987 provided a more comprehensive definition of pollution: "[Human] or [human-induced] alteration of the chemical, physical, biological or radiological integrity of water." This more comprehensive definition includes any human action (or result of human action) that degrades a water resource, even if the Act does not specifically address the action. As previously stated, humans may degrade or pollute water resources by chemical contamination, destruction of aquatic habitats, withdrawal of water for irrigation, overharvest of fish, or introduction of exotics.[58]

The only approach to the evaluation of water resources that is sensitive to all of these forms of pollution is biological monitoring, the assessment of biological end points.[59] This approach is in line with the recent Science Advisory Board recommendation to "attach as much importance to reducing ecological risk as . . . reducing human health risk."[60] As we begin to recognize the value of biological evaluations as the most direct and effective approach to assessment of their condition, we approach the threshold of a major transition in the way we manage riverine ecosystems. Failure to do so in the past resulted in continued degradation. The impediments to the use of biological monitoring have been complex: 1) the dominance of reductionist viewpoints; 2) a limited conceptual framework of legal and regulatory programs; 3) the poor definition of the biological integrity goal of PL 92-500; 4) the lack of an integrative, broadly applicable approach to the measurement of biological integrity; 5) the lack of a region-based quantitative definition of ecological health; 6) the lack of standardized field methods; 7) the inability to link field measurements and analyses to enforceable management options; and 8) the belief that biological monitoring is too expensive. Although advances in all these areas are still possible, widespread recognition of the value of biological monitoring has resulted in numerous state and federal actions to advance its use in a more holistic approach to river management.[61]

A comprehensive assessment and high-level national report on the ecological health of America's riverine systems and biodiversity are urgently needed. The report should be similar to the National Wetlands Report, which helped elevate public awareness of wetland function and loss. Such an assessment must use biological monitoring processes so that an accurate understanding of conditions nationwide can be established.

The River Conservation Movement Coming of Age

Not just assessment procedures require changing. The national environmental movement must begin to focus on riverine systems and biodiversity from an ecological perspective. Most national environmental organizations address riverine issues only when they overlap with their primary missions (wilderness, wildlife, water quality, and so forth). Only relatively recently have a few national river conservation organizations become more visible and effective.

The history of the river protection movement mirrors the evolution of America's environmental movement; in both, the emphasis originated with and in many cases remains focused on preserving sections of wild areas and/or pollution control. Only recently has the focus begun to shift to biodiversity or ecosystem concerns.

America's river protection movement began with a dominant focus on saving wild, primarily recreational river sections and on preventing inappropriate dams. The movement was spawned by environmental efforts to protect high-volume recreational boating rivers in the West, such as the battle to stop the Echo Park dams in Dinosaur National Monument.

Passage of the National Wild and Scenic Rivers Act in 1968 was in many ways the result of a capitulation to developers -- the belief was that if Congress would protect the best remaining scenic and recreational river segments, environmentalists would concede the rest. Unfortunately, at the time few people understood the need to manage riverine systems on an ecosystem and watershed basis, and the river protection movement, in its infancy, was incapable of organizing for larger battles. We now realize, however, that riverine systems cannot be effectively protected by focusing only on the best scenic and recreational segments. Nor can they be effectively protected only by preventing inappropriate dams or water projects, or by addressing water pollution. As the predominant riverine conservation strategies, these approaches are too narrow.

In addition to neglecting the biological integrity of riverine-riparian ecosystems, the historic emphases on protecting wild river segments has limited the existing protection policies largely to federal and state Wild and Scenic designations. This narrow approach requires separate legislative acts for each river or group of rivers to be protected. Further, this misplaced emphasis has failed to coalesce what should be the natural constituency for rivers. Often people addressing clean water, human health, instream flows, forestry and agriculture, soil productivity, fishery enhancement, or Wild and Scenic issues on the same riverine system fail to realize the commonality of issues or ecosystem processes they all focus on. The fragmentation of the constituency reflects the fragmentation of existing policies.

It is now time to expand beyond the more narrow, fragmented approach and add watershed-level, ecosystem-based protection and restoration approaches and policies to the river conservation tool box.

The Science-Policy Gap

Contemporary science and existing riverine restoration approaches and policies are separated by a 10-to-15-year gap, a problem that has helped render most policies ineffective. Existing riverine protection and restoration approaches and policies fail because they fail to address the way riverine systems actually function. Approaches to protect and restore riverine systems must address the watershed. Yet, as the assessments in the appendix of this book describe, no policies at any level of government effectively address these issues. This does not mean that complicated, basinwide land-use structure and planning processes are needed. It does mean that the areas most critical to riverine-riparian ecosystem and biodiversity processes and functions must be identified, protected, secured, and then strategically restored. Contemporary science now has the ability to move us much closer to these goals.

Jobs vs. Jobs

Finally, the traditional riverine conservation approaches have failed because of the difficulty in countering the jobs and economic benefit arguments. Efforts to stop dams, logging, urbanization, or other types of inappropriate development are typically framed as classic "jobs vs. the environment" issues. These arguments often seem persuasive to those who have established roots, traditions, and communities based on the jobs provided by the "trickle-down" effects from industries that may degrade riverine systems. Often "job blackmail" is used by industries to keep labor in line. They can also seem persuasive to elected officials. The job loss argument has often delayed or stopped riverine conservation efforts.

Maintaining or increasing the nation's primary production -- in agriculture, fisheries, or forestry, for example -- is the foundation of a sustainable economy. Maintaining the natural ecological and biological systems that produce those products is the fundamental step required to achieve sustainability. Protection and restoration of healthy riverine systems and biodiversity is essential, not just for the potential value of genetic resources, recreation and tourism, but also because these systems provide important ecological functions that support all economic activity and human welfare.

Markets often fail to account for environmental values such as the vital supportive role of ecological processes. Markets also often fail to reflect "option" or "existence" values -- values derived from preserving certain resources, ecological systems, and species for the option of future use or simply because the knowledge of their existence is valued.

When these environmental values are not reflected in existing market prices, they are considered external costs. Externalities are difficult to quantify because they are usually unintended and have indirect or diffuse effects. For example, degradation of the ecological processes and non-timber products of riverine-riparian ecosystems is rarely accounted for in logging activities. The loss of on-site fish habitat, the generation of off-site sedimentation that smothers downstream spawning beds or fills reservoirs, and the loss of soil due to erosion are typical negative externalities. At the same time, the economic contributions of fish and other foods produced by the ecosystem are also usually not accounted for.   Generally, neither the off-site nor the on-site external costs of such degradation is reflected in the market price of timber harvests, dams, irrigation projects, or road construction. These costs affect society at large and future generations.

Given such costs, the appraisal of net project benefits in terms of direct costs and benefits alone is a serious misrepresentation of the net economic value to society. The costs of on-site and off-site environmental impacts, including foregone net benefits of incompatible alternative uses must also be included as part of the costs of projects. It is ironic that the purpose of most environmental protection laws and regulations is to protect these "externalities" for society as a whole and for future generations. Yet, the very outcomes the laws try to produce are not measured or accounted for in measuring the "costs" of environmental protection. One author has equated this to measuring the pain of a hypodermic needle without measuring the benefits provided by the penicillin it injects.

As the lost fishery jobs in the Pacific Northwest and the lost soil productivity nationwide demonstrate, a more accurate depiction of the issues is "jobs vs. jobs" -- long-term, sustainable, river-related or river-dependent jobs, economic productivity, and communities (based on the biological surplus provided by healthy, sustainable ecosystems) vs. short-term jobs that degrade the resource.

The argument that the short-term economic gains of damaging development far outweigh the long-term benefits of protecting the systems can generally be supported only through incomplete cost/benefit analyses that ignore externalities and hidden government subsidies. The strategy of "socializing and hiding the costs while privatizing the gain" is generally the way that most dams, timber harvests, grazing, road building, urbanization, and other damaging development projects are made to appear as net economic "gains." For example, a recent draft Forest Service report on the economic impacts of protecting critical habitat for four endangered salmon stocks in the upper Columbia River basin found that if subsidies for grazing and road building were removed when their habitat was protected, the taxpayers would save money. (This study was quickly discounted by agency personnel and buried.) As the external issues and subsidies are better accounted for, riverine conservation efforts will increase in effectiveness.

All of these reasons culminate in seriously flawed riverine protection and restoration approaches and policies at all levels of government. Riverine system and biodiversity conservation remains the stepchild of the national environmental movement and lags far behind other national conservation efforts.

PART II

RECOMMENDATIONS

by

Bob Doppelt
Dr. Chris Frissell
Mary Scurlock
Charley Dewberry

CHAPTER THREE

RECOMMENDATIONS FOR A NEW COMMUNITY- AND ECOSYSTEM-BASED WATERSHED RESTORATION APPROACH

All thinking worthy of the name must now be ecological. -- Lewis Mumford

A New Approach to Watershed Restoration

The growing nationwide riverine crisis, combined with the failures of existing conservation approaches and policies to arrest the problems, leads to the inescapable conclusion that a new approach is needed to protect and restore America's riverine systems and biodiversity. The new approach must focus more on *prevention* than attempts to control or repair problems after they occur.

We recommend a new approach founded on the principles of watershed dynamics, ecosystem function, and conservation biology. The approach turns the traditional restoration approaches upside down, and, if applied, would refocus existing policies and establish new policies and programs towards community- and ecosystem-based watershed protection and restoration.

The new approach involves three interconnected components:

* The approach begins with the comprehensive protection of the remaining relatively healthy headwaters, biotic refuges, benchmark watersheds, riparian areas, floodplains, and the network of biological hot spots found in patches throughout entire riverine systems.

* Following the protective steps, restoration can begin, focused initially on securing the relatively healthy areas,

followed by expanding these areas through riparian and floodplain restoration and, eventually, linking the healthier areas to provide corridors of connectivity. Once sufficient resources are applied to accomplish these steps, the more severely degraded areas would be treated on the basis of carefully designed watershed-level restoration strategies.

* Finally, the approach requires the active participation of local communities in implementing all of these steps, stimulated in part by generating and supporting jobs in restoration technologies, river-oriented community revitalization projects and appropriate "economic conversions" that may help sustain both rivers and communities.

Watershed-level Protection and Restoration

Ecosystem-based watershed protection and restoration involves a number of components. These include the actual physical protection and restoration treatments, as well as systemwide policy alignment and coordination mechanisms. These components are discussed below.

Reexamining Assumptions: Strategy vs. Tactics

In environmental planning and management it is important to distinguish between strategies and tactics. Strategies concern the comprehensive, large-scale marshalling and allocation of resources, whereas tactics concern local, immediate, and short-term activities.[62] It is critical that tactics be directed by and congruent with an overall strategy founded on sound, contemporary scientific principles. It is also necessary that strategy be shaped by the limitations of technical capabilities.

The scientific and technical literature of riverine management inordinately focuses on tactics, with relatively little regard for the large-scale, strategic issues of conservation and ecosystem planning. The obsession with tactics and the failure to address strategic aspects of research, planning, and watershed-level restoration has led to wasted resources, misperceptions, misrepresentations of the success or failure of projects and programs, underestimation of the risk of cumulative or synergistic effects from multiple activities or projects, and ultimately the increased probability of irreversible, large-scale ecological crisis. Both the technical literature and government policies regarding riverine protection and restoration are unduly focused on techniques and tactical considerations.

Examples of tactical thinking are numerous. What constitutes an "outstandingly remarkable value" that would allow a river segment to be classified as a Wild and Scenic River? What technical chemical criteria can be applied to measure water quality? What type of log or boulder structures should be placed in-stream to restore a river? How do we get structures to remain in place? What designs for stormwater management or materials for in-stream habitat restoration are optimal? How can the costs per structure be minimized?

Relatively little attention is paid to the development of an ecologically sound guiding strategy for riverine restoration. Such a strategy must address broader questions: What processes cause habitat loss, pollution, and ecosystem dysfunction? How can these processes be reversed within already disconnected and impaired ecosystems? Are structural approaches to restoration even feasible, or are other kinds of treatment necessary? Should efforts concentrate on certain areas or be dispersed across the watershed? Which species will benefit from a given action, and will the benefit last? What is the risk that unwanted side effects could accrue from a particular set of treatments? The answers to these questions are critical and lie in the ecological and geophysical analysis of watershed ecosystems, riverine habitat, and the conservation biology of riverine and riparian biotic communities and populations.

Restoration can be defined as returning riverine systems toward pre-disturbance conditions, which existed before European colonization. To understand the healthier pre-European condition requires developing an historical template of the riverine system before the introduction of significant human disturbances. In view of this historical template, restoration treatments must focus on restoring ecosystem connectivity and on recreating natural dynamic stream elements and processes. The temporal and spatial scales of restoration efforts must be large enough to provide for these functions.

In recent decades, restoration programs for riverine biodiversity emphasized two related activities: the regulation of land use and other human activities to reduce their adverse effects on streams, and direct structural modification of riverine habitats to produce the conditions that riverine biodiversity (mostly game fish) presumably require for survival. One fundamental assumption underlying both activities has been that riverine systems consist of an extensive matrix of "good" habitat, well-endowed with abundant riverine biodiversity, and local patches of "poor," biotically sterile habitat.[63] In this view, the local disturbances caused by urbanization, clearing a farm, logging, triggering a landslide, or the channelization of a river reach are easily tolerated by what is an inherently forgiving and resourceful ecosystem. In this view of natural resources, nature possesses extraordinary and boundless powers of self-preservation. In this perspective, our role as stewards of natural resources is to prevent unscrupulous styles and inequitable or excessive rates of resource extraction and to direct human activities to change the natural environment in ways that favor the propagation and husbandry of desired species, such as game fish. This view of management assumes that we have full knowledge of what kinds of changes in natural systems are desirable for the target species. Parks, wild and scenic rivers, and other protected areas are established for purposes of preserving scenic values and unique features for human use and enjoyment, values seen as largely disconnected from the conservation and management of riverine-riparian ecosystems or biodiversity.

It is difficult in this perspective to envision that widespread and irreversible ecological degradation could result from permitting the "temporary," "regulated" and "planned" disturbances caused by human activities. Rather, recovery of fish and other forms of riverine-riparian biodiversity from such local, dispersed disturbances is presumed to begin instantaneously and to proceed independently, limited only by the rate of physical recovery of the disturbed site. Habitat "improvement" or restoration is taken to involve little more than boosting the on-site physical conditions, or treating the "limiting factor" -- spawning gravel quality, water quality, shade and water temperature, cover, or quiet water refuge -- as deemed locally necessary for the target fish species to survive and grow. Restoration is intended merely to speed the rate of inherent recovery of local conditions. Crucial underlying (but usually unstated) assumptions of this approach include assumptions that: a) disturbances are isolated and independent in their effects, and the ecosystem as a whole remains intact; b) recovery at each disturbed site proceeds independently and relatively rapidly, also independently of the site's context in the watershed ecosystem; c) a steady, unlimited supply of fish and other forms of biodiversity are available from surrounding areas to recolonize these disturbed habitats as they recover.[64]

Given these assumptions, it is understandable that managers could rationalize and endorse increased human disturbance in riverine systems by making those activities contingent on specific habitat improvement or rehabilitation techniques that are presumed to mitigate damage or, ideally, even enhance the fishery resource beyond its natural condition, should that ever be known. These concepts are deeply embedded in existing approaches to riverine regulation and planning. For example, most of the current management plans for national forests assume, with virtually no scientific documentation, that increased biological production from new artificial in-stream structure projects will more than compensate for the logging of thousands of acres of critical watershed ecosystems and the creation of millions of tons of sediment from those activities in sensitive watersheds.[65] A recent report by a panel of research scientists commissioned by the U.S. House of Representatives Agriculture and Merchant Marine Committees concluded that forest plans in the Pacific Northwest have a low likelihood of maintaining viable populations of salmon and other sensitive fishes.

In arid-land riverine systems, federal agencies commonly install artificial structures in streams that have been damaged for decades by livestock grazing.   Research has repeatedly demonstrated, however, that such projects cannot restore riverine habitat when the primary cause of the damage in arid-land systems -- grazing -- is not controlled.

The traditional paradigm allows little room for the possibility that human disturbances can have effects that permeate or resonate over large areas, cumulatively changing the dynamics of not just stream reaches over periods of years but entire watersheds and landscapes over many decades or centuries. Scientific studies of the long-term effects of human disturbances on riverine ecosystems reveal that land-use activities like logging, grazing, agriculture, urbanization, and channelization can have ecological consequences that persist for decades or centuries.[66] These activities involve permanent or persistent changes in the watershed, which are directly or indirectly reflected as changes in the riverine ecosystem. Because they caused sustained alterations of habitat structure and biological communities, often shifting them into states unlike those of the pre-disturbance condition, these activities have been termed *press disturbances.* Recovery of fish and other forms of riverine-riparian biodiversity and other aspects of flowing water structure from press disturbances most often involves time frames of at least several decades, and a return to healthy conditions may never occur in some cases. Disturbances that cause relatively instantaneous local alteration of biological communities, without persistent changes in the physical structure of the system, are called *pulse disturbances*. Examples include local chemical spills, moderate and small floods and drought.[67]

Many long-term studies on the effects of land-use activities on streams, rivers, and lakes have reported long time lags between disturbance events and the physical or biological recovery of the riverine-riparian ecosystem. Most have detected that despite initial indications of a recovery trend, at least some effects persist more than 20 years beyond the initial disturbance event. The pattern of arrested recovery strongly suggests that many land-use disturbances leave behind permanent or very long-term residual effects that essentially preclude a return to any semblance of initial predisturbance conditions, either physically or biologically.[68]

Refuge Effects

A recent review of case histories of riverine system recovery following disturbance found considerable evidence that the existence of refugia-- undisturbed habitats that provide a source of colonists to adjacent areas-- was critical to recovery.[69] In-stream systems where disturbance was widespread and where no accessible refugia remained, biological recovery was delayed or entirely precluded. Several kinds of riverine and hyporheic habitats can act as refugia, and examples have been provided of how they may function in the recovery of populations from natural catastrophe and human-caused disturbance.[70] A major characteristic of excessive logging, agriculture, channelization, dams, urbanization and other cumulative press disturbances is long-term, downstream-propagating loss of habitat diversity, which diminishes the abundance and connectivity of actual or potential refuge habitats.

One critical but increasingly rare kind of refuge is the intact watershed, one that is relatively unimpaired by human activities. These areas (also referred to as Class I or II waters)[71] harbor many sensitive species and can serve as efficient sources of colonists to downstream areas. They are the safest and most secure kind of refuge for fishes and other forms of riverine-riparian biodiversity by virtue of size, diversity of natural habitats, relative imperviousness to invasion by exotic species, and the lack of sources of human disturbance that can propagate downstream from sensitive up-slope and headwater areas. For example, in the Pacific Northwest, where many salmonid populations have been eliminated in downstream areas and where many remain fragmented from the effects of development and the introduction of exotic species or hatchery fish, headwater tributaries increasingly serve as de facto refugia for native salmonids. Undisturbed watersheds also contribute to high-quality water and provide channel conditions in downstream areas that may be important for additional native species, for soil and vegetation, and thus for the entire lotic food chain and for human uses.

Intact watersheds are not the only refuges that sustain riverine-riparian biodiversity for disturbed systems. At least two other kinds of refuge habitats are important. These (also referred to as class III waters)[72] tend to be located in downstream, low-elevation areas that have experienced a long history of human disturbance. Typically these are smaller habitats that are unusually resilient or resistant to the effects of disturbance; although fragmented, at least some of their natural diversity and function remains relatively intact. Occasionally they are habitats that have escaped severe disturbance by chance or by virtue of unusual ownership history. Estuaries and forested floodplain reaches of rivers can function as downstream refugia, providing islands of high-quality habitat for downstream-dependent species and life stages and serving as sources of colonists to upstream reaches. Also important and more widely distributed are small-scale or "internal" refuges, such as the hyporheic zone of a floodplain river reach, a floodplain wetland, a cold-water plume at a tributary mouth, or a groundwater-fed spring. Areas rich in these kinds of biological hot spots may be critical to sustaining the current complement of species, and cultivating the maintenance and propagation of such habitats will be a necessary component of a successful restoration program.[73]

Although many protected areas such as national parks and wilderness areas may function as riverine refugia, only three federal refuges have been established specifically to protect native fishes, and all are located in the Southwest.[74] The Scientific Panel on Late Successional Forest Ecosystems identified a network of watershed reserves on federal lands that, if recognized, would improve protection of key populations of at-risk anadromous fish in parts of the Pacific Northwest. The Oregon Chapter of the American Fisheries Society completed an extensive inventory that identifies habitat refugia and critical areas across the rest of the state. Areas identified in this survey include intact whole watersheds that harbor high riverine biodiversity, watersheds that contribute critically to downstream water quality, stream reaches that have relatively high degree of natural habitat complexity and native species diversity, and estuaries, lakes, and wetland complexes that are least disturbed in their region and least affected by introduced species. Many similar studies are underway.

The Traditional "Band-Aid" Approach to Restoration

Past and most proposed approaches to riverine restoration can best be characterized as "band-aid" strategies. Approaches to riverine restoration in the traditional paradigm have several distinguishing features. First, the identification and diagnosis of habitat problems tend to focus on finding patches of habitat that are amenable to predetermined, generic techniques. Many past and current programs, for example, rely heavily on installing structures such as log weirs to construct pools in streams. Planning for these projects generally focuses on identifying reaches of stream that have gradients and bank structures physically suited to the installation of such devices and that happen to be accessible to the heavy equipment needed to do the work. Little consideration is given to whether the fish community or the watershed as a whole are suited to the kinds of changes of habitat these structures are intended to induce. It is commonly assumed that all fish and biodiversity benefit equally from the plunge pool sequences created by such devices and that the construction of weir pools will compensate for the diverse changes in the ecosystem caused by human disturbance.

Evaluation of some of these projects indicates serious shortcomings. In cases where log weirs and other artificial structures achieve their physical objectives, their effects on native fish and other forms of biodiversity can be insignificant or even negative. In many cases, such structures suffer outright physical failure.[75] In other cases, the structures may stay in place, but have unintended and damaging physical side effects, such as severe bank erosion or blockages to juvenile fish migration.[76] Numerous studies suggest that the effects of such projects are inconsistent and difficult to predict. Conditions in the watershed as a whole appear to be more important than structure design in determining whether structures succeed or fail. Failure rates are especially high in severely damaged watersheds and in stream reaches where disturbances continue.[77] In some watersheds, riverine-riparian biodiversity is so widely depleted by extensive habitat degradation and other factors that few or no species are available to colonize artificially created habitats.[78] Finally, the vast majority of streams are inaccessible to heavy equipment or are otherwise unsuited to structural modification.

Put simply, traditional restoration techniques fail to address the root biological and physical causes of ecosystem dysfunction, habitat deterioration, and population decline, and they often aggravate, complicate, or add to existing problems.

Riverine restoration priorities under the band-aid strategy are typically determined by identifying the worst-degraded or ugliest-looking sites and spending all available resources to treat these areas with generic and largely cosmetic structural techniques to "bring them up to standards." Once the desired improvements have been made, further habitat-disturbing activities in the watershed can be allowed to proceed. The result is predictable: disturbances are maximally dispersed across the watershed landscape, and virtually all sites across the landscape are homogeneously degraded. The worst sites may be partially "fixed," but meanwhile disturbance-sensitive species have likely been lost throughout the riverine system. As developments are dispersed across the landscape, virtually every tributary and stream reach becomes vulnerable to management-accelerated disturbance from sedimentation and other effects that manifest when the next large storm strikes. Because no effort is made to identify and protect key refugia, the most productive and diverse habitats are subject to continued disturbance, while the most severely degraded areas (inherently the least amenable to structural improvement and, therefore, the most likely projects to fail) receive all the restoration resources. In other words, this strategy is a recipe for highly speculative efforts in degraded areas and for the degradation of undisturbed watersheds and other secure ecological refugia -- leading predictably to the cumulative extirpation of formerly abundant but sensitive species over large areas.[79] Instead of the ideal matrix of high-quality habitat with patches of disturbed habitat, we find we have created a matrix of disturbed, degraded and sterile habitats, surrounding a few tattered remnants of high-quality habitat that still support locally abundant and diverse assemblages of native species.

Although promulgated by well-meaning agencies and fishing and conservation groups, so-called "restoration" that applies "band-aid" treatments to distress symptoms rather than addressing the fundamental causes of watershed dysfunction, often leads to decreased stream health and harms other forms of riverine biodiversity, including non-game fish, aquatic insects, birds and beaver. For example, a recent report that evaluated stream restoration projects in the Upper Columbia River Basin in Oregon and Idaho over the past 10 years found that almost all efforts were ineffective, and that millions of dollars had been wasted.[80] The reasons stated were that the treatments were primarily focused on in-stream work that ignored the past and on-going damage to the upstream watershed. Hence, during high spring flows, much of the in-stream work was often washed out. Further, this approach has often helped foster the belief that restoration can and should compensate for damage to the system. Millions of dollars have been spent on these approaches only to find later that they were wasted.

Lessons From The Redwood National Park Model

A more ecologically rational model for watershed restoration may be called the "cost-efficiency" strategy which is perhaps typified by the program in Redwood Creek Basin in northern California. With the expansion of Redwood National Park in 1978, Congress funded a major program of research, planning, and monitoring to guide the restoration of extensive areas of the watershed that had been damaged by logging. A large-scale watershed-level research and monitoring program examined the causes and consequences of watershed damage and determined that reduction of sediment yield from disturbed slopes was the primary restoration intervention that could assist in restoring the watershed to more natural conditions. Because sediment sources on the slopes -- primarily road failures and slope gullying -- caused widespread channel aggradation and destabilization, park staff determined that instream structural treatments could not succeed. Continued monitoring of watershed restoration techniques on slopes and in headwater tributaries, conducted on a trial-and-error basis, allowed park staff to identify the most cost-efficient methods of reducing the delivery of sediment to downstream reaches.

In general, the effective techniques in Redwood Park were found after a careful survey and assessment of road drainage and diversion problems, resulting in the obliteration of problem road surfaces and fills, "deconstruction" of road crossings and re-contouring of disturbed slopes using heavy equipment.[81] These techniques addressed the largest potential sources of sedimentation in the basin (exclusive of large, natural landslides, difficult or impossible to control). A range of other techniques that focused on treating the more visually disconcerting sources of erosion -- surface and rill erosion and the ravel of exposed soil surfaces -- were more costly and had far less quantitative effect on the delivery of sediment to the stream system. The effects of most of these techniques were judged to be more cosmetic than ecologically significant, at least in terms of the overall loading of sediment into the stream.

The Redwood Creek program is a major step forward in that it addressed causal processes on a large scale. Nevertheless, it suffers from drawbacks, particularly from the biological standpoint. The strategy focused on the goal of reducing sediment yield park-wide, provided little rationale to focus restoration activities in parts of the watershed that play crucial ecological roles, such as refugia for native fish and other riverine organisms. As a result, park-wide activities have reduced sediment delivery to the stream system as a whole, but not by a volume sufficient to effect dramatic recovery of any portion of the stream ecosystem. Equally important, the expanded park boundaries did not include the headwater portions of Redwood Creek, and logging and other development of private lands in the upper basin have continued even as millions of dollars were spent on restoration of the lower basin. The result, as scientists predicted in 1981, has been that the new effects of logging the upper basin have offset the gains made by restoration inside the park. More important from the standpoint of riverine species, disturbance in the sensitive headwaters affects the entire main stem of Redwood Creek, leaving few or no refugia for sensitive and declining fish populations in the basin.

A New Protection and Restoration Approach: The Rapid Biotic and Ecosystem Response[82]

We suggest that a new synthesis of conservation biology, ecosystem science, and geomorphic knowledge about how watersheds and riverine-riparian biodiversity are organized can lead to a new and more successful strategy for restoring riverine systems. We call this the Rapid Biotic and Ecosystem Response Strategy (RBER).[83] The goals of the RBER strategy are to: 1) secure existing populations of riverine-riparian biodiversity, including fishes, and maintain the critical areas that support healthy riverine ecosystem functions; 2) institute recovery measures that stand the greatest chance of producing measurable improvement in the status and abundance of biodiversity and improvement of ecosystem function, in the near term; and 3) maintain options for future recovery by ensuring a secure, well-distributed, and diverse constellation of natural habitats and co-adapted populations and ensuring that local examples of natural ecosystem processes remain in place over the long term.

The strategy springs from the following conceptual principles, most stated previously:

* In-stream conditions are largely determined by processes occurring in the watershed and the riparian and floodplain ecosystems and cannot be manipulated independently of this context.

* Disturbances propagate downstream from headwater sources, and protection of sensitive headwater areas in watersheds is critical to the maintenance and recovery of riverine habitats.

* Effective restoration treatments change the underlying processes driving ecosystem deterioration and do not merely add structures or otherwise attempt to salve the worst-degraded or most visibly damaged areas. This premise requires comprehensive and rigorous research and monitoring to reconstruct a model of predisturbance conditions, to diagnose causal factors of ecosystem loss and to evaluate the effectiveness of various treatment techniques.

* Riverine habitats are naturally highly variable and patchy in space and time. Restoration must be directed, not at producing homogeneous or generic conditions, but at restoring the temporal regimes and spatial diversity of natural habitat systems.

* Protection and restoration of a well-dispersed network of habitat refuges and hot spots -- including headwater watersheds and relatively intact lower-river reaches (hot spots) -- is necessary to sustain current riverine populations and to ensure that sources of colonists exist to seed habitats that become available following natural recovery or restoration. Most current natural production of anadromous salmonids, for example, is sustained by the relatively small proportion of habitat that remains relatively undisturbed. Restoration that secures these areas from further degradation caused by past human activities and then improves these habitats will have the greatest immediate success in maintaining and increasing biodiversity.

* The current distribution and life history patterns of fish and other forms of riverine-riparian biodiversity -- largely governed by the nature and distribution of available refugia in the watershed -- determine the ability of populations to respond to future changes in habitat. Restoration that first secures existing refugia by preventing past management activities from degrading the areas and then re-establishes similar and nearby habitats that require little adjustment of life history patterns is most likely to provide the kinds of habitat critical to existing biological populations. Restoration measures aimed at re-establishing ecosystems and habitats that have been long-lost or that are a great distance from existing centers of productivity and diversity are likely to be colonized slowly, with delayed biological response. Time (many years or decades) may be required for the re-evolution of life history types suited to such ecosystems and habitats.

* Recovery of severely degraded and biotically impoverished watersheds will be a long-term process

requiring many decades. Restoration in these areas is likely to prove unsuccessful and the results unpredictable in the near-term (<10 years). Over the long term, however, restoration of severely degraded areas, if accompanied and guided by careful monitoring and iterative planning, could yield significant results.

* A most-pressing and principal function of restoration should be to proactively defuse existing "time bombs" that set up the refuge ecosystems for future or continuing damage. Although concerns have been stated about the external threats to refuges, it is equally important to address the fact that any newly established network of watershed biodiversity refuges will also inherit "internal" threats -- artifacts of previous human disturbance. Time lags exist between disturbances of headwater slopes and impacts to riverine habitat in downstream areas. Although many habitats today function as refugia, they lie in watersheds where slopes and headwaters have been damaged by human disturbances in recent decades -- for example, in formerly roadless watersheds penetrated by logging roads in the past 10-20 years. They simply have not yet experienced a major storm or similar catastrophic event that triggers the downstream cascade of impacts. Once such a catastrophic event occurs, the damage to the watershed and riverine ecosystem is done and cannot be easily or rapidly reversed. At-risk watersheds are "loaded guns" whose biodiversity is fated to inexorable deterioration unless humans intervene in a focused way to remove potential sources of disturbance and "secure" the watersheds.

* A small amount of effort in a watershed that still retains much of its natural integrity can secure far more critical resources than a very large effort in a watershed that has already been severely degraded. Therefore,

restoration should be focused where a small investment can maintain the largest amount of high-quality ecosystems, habitat, and riverine-riparian biodiversity. Few completely roadless, large watersheds exist in the United States, but those that are mostly undisturbed play critical roles in sustaining sensitive native species and important ecosystem processes. With few exceptions, even the least-disturbed watersheds have at least a small road network and history of human disturbance that greatly magnify the risk of deterioration of riverine ecosystems and habitats in the watershed. In other words, most currently functional riverine refugia are imperiled by past, recent, or proposed human disturbance. Focused restoration interventions on these sites and changes in land management plans are necessary to secure key watershed refugia. It is important to note, however, that most restoration programs, including the Clean Water Act, focus significant resources on the most degraded riverine systems rather than on those that still hold enough healthy pieces to respond rapidly to restoration.

* New policies are needed to facilitate restoration of low-elevation floodplains, wetlands, and other critical riverine habitats. Many such areas are privately owned, and a floodplain restoration policy will involve complex social and political dynamics. One way that floodplains and wetlands can be cost-effectively recovered could be by implementing policies that regulate land-use activities following large floods. Such policies should restrict and discourage channelization, revetment, debris removal, diking and draining, reconstruction or reoccupation of floodplain roads and structures, and other human activities that tend to impede or reverse the positive natural effects of flooding in floodplain rivers. Particularly in basins where sediment loads from

upstream areas have stabilized at more natural levels, such policies could allow lowland, floodplain rivers to reclaim habitat and restore natural processes without the large capital investment and engineering risks associated with massive structural projects. Fiscal resources could be devoted largely to education, the development of creative and relatively non-intrusive regulatory policies and the provision of financial incentives for floodplain and wetland disinvestment.

The RBER Approach: Begin by Protecting, Securing and Expanding the Remaining Healthy Ecosystem Areas

The first priority in the RBER strategy is to identify, protect, and "secure" the remaining healthy key biotic refuges and benchmark watersheds by minimizing the possibility that past and future activities will degrade them. Simultaneously, riparian areas and floodplains must be protected systemwide to provide healthy habitats and to eventually expand and link the healthier areas.

"Securing" any existing healthy area primarily involves using physical treatments to reduce or eliminate threats caused by past human activities upstream in the watershed. Appropriate measures to secure biotic refuges may involve reforesting unstable, steep hillsides and treating problems such as chronic sedimentation and catastrophic debris flows from roads and timber harvesting. Treating these problems generally requires heavy equipment and manual work. Thus, restoration based on initially securing the remaining biotic refuges will create a significant number of jobs nationwide.

For federal lands, clear mandates are needed that provide uniform prescriptions to all federal agencies for the protection of watershed ecosystems and biodiversity. This type of watershed protection does not require vast wilderness set-asides; it means protecting the remaining healthy headwaters, biotic refuges, benchmark watersheds, riparian areas, floodplains, and other areas vital to natural ecosystem processes and functions.

Congress typically does not like to mandate clear, protective prescriptions, but prefers instead to enact policies that establish "procedures" for agencies to follow. The National Forest Management Act (NFMA) and the National Environmental Policy Act (NEPA) are procedures more than clear directives. The deference to process over congressionally set prescriptions often has merit, in that specific resource issues are often best defined "on the ground." It is clear from our policy reviews, however, that this approach has failed to ensure effective riverine protection. The failure of the procedural approach can perhaps best be exemplified by examining U.S. Forest Service timber sales. Despite over 15 years of experience with the National Forest Management Act and National Environmental Policy Act, which theoretically should have provided better environmental protections and lowered harvest levels, national annual timber harvests have remained steady at roughly 11 billion board feet and, in many cases, have accelerated. The procedural approach has forced the agencies to become better organized. Some would say that it has also forced the agencies to become more creative in determining how to keep timber harvest levels high while meeting environmental procedural requirements. However, the procedural approach has failed to protect riverine systems and biodiversity. Clear new prescriptions are needed.

Protection must therefore extend well beyond the traditional river protection mechanisms such as the Wild and Scenic Rivers Act. Entirely new, comprehensive strategies are needed that protect watershed ecosystems, while not requiring the enactment of a new law for each acre or mile protected. Federal and state wild and scenic rivers remain important tools to protect outstanding scenic and recreational river segments, or to stop inappropriate dams when no state or federal "protected river" program exists. However, because they are so difficult to enact and are so limited in effectiveness, wild and scenic designations must be viewed as only one tool in the riverine protection toolbox. Wild and scenic designations may become more effective within the context of ecologically based watershed-level protection and restoration strategies.

On private land rivers, riverine protection should, perhaps be more narrowly applied to existing riparian buffers and undeveloped floodplains along with other biological hot spots. This emphasis is intended to reduce pollution and sedimentation caused by erosion and agricultural run-off, to protect floodways and retention basins to temporarily hold flood flows, to provide riverine habitat and open space. The protection of the remaining healthy in-stream habitat must also be accomplished by the installation of appropriate stream crossing culverts and the prevention of channelization, diking and riprapping.

To do this will require that Congress establish clear direction to federal agencies and states to support "bottom-up" local protection and restoration efforts on private lands. This must include minimum federal standards and the use of existing regulations along with a flexible package of financial incentives, funding options and technical assistance so that locally tailored protection programs evolve.

The second priority in the RBER strategy is to identify and protect other biological hot spots found throughout entire riverine systems. The hot spots may be occupied by riverine-riparian biodiversity only seasonally, but nevertheless provide critical habitat for certain life stages of biodiversity or a type of control for ecological processes within the system. This second priority is important to sustaining the present populations and current levels of ecosystem health in the watershed.

Third, potential hot spots that may be degraded, yet exist *close to* refuges or biological hot spots, would be identified, protected and restored. These areas may be readily colonized by riverine organisms as they become suitable, allowing relatively rapid biotic response to restoration activities. As these areas are restored, the geographic scope of the healthier riverine ecosystems expands.

The fourth priority is to identify and begin a long-term restoration program for what can be called "grubstake habitats."[84]

These areas are often larger mainstem downstream riverine reaches that may have historically supported abundant populations of riverine biodiversity or were important for ecosystem health but today are highly degraded. They are often found in low-elevation valleys subject to intensive agriculture and other kinds of development. We call them grubstakes, because the social, political, and economic challenges to restoring these areas are great and the expected timeframe of physical recovery and biological response is long. However, the potential for biological production from such areas is often higher than that of upstream refugia and hot spots, by orders of magnitude. Grubstake habitats, therefore, provide the best hope for restoring many of the nation's major riverine systems and regenerating biodiversity, especially productive fisheries.

All of the restoration steps must be accomplished within the context of carefully designed watershed-level recovery strategies.

Monitoring

Monitoring in the RBER approach focuses on measuring the response and trends in riverine-riparian biodiversity and the risk of degradation to the secured areas, and the cost-efficiency of treatments used.

The Advantages of the RBER Strategy

One major advantage to the RBER approach is that it focuses on prevention rather than on control or repair, and focuses treatments where they will have the greatest or fastest effect on the biological and ecological resources within the entire watershed. Another important advantage is that it fully integrates protection measures with restoration measures, rendering impotent the common perception that restoration activities can (or should) serve to rationalize or compensate for continuing or renewed degradation on-site or elsewhere in the watershed. Finally, monitoring habitat and biodiversity in the protected refugia and hot spots provides a direct and integrated measure of the program's success.

In the RBER strategy, the first step in restoration is actually protection. Only after the remaining relatively undisturbed and healthier headwaters, biotic refuges, benchmark watersheds, riparian areas, floodplains and other biological hot spots have been protected can carefully selected and planned restoration begin or be effective. In addition, without initial protection, restoration efforts are often pointless because any gains would be threatened, offset or overwhelmed by degradation elsewhere in the system. Finally, without initial protection, restoration can be socially and economically harmful; expectations are raised as people begin to believe that they are addressing problems when they are not, and millions of dollars may be spent only to find later that they were wasted.

We believe that the RBER approach can be applied to riverine systems nationwide, with a few possible exceptions, such as large-scale floodplain and wetland areas in the Mississippi Bayou and the Everglades.

Establishing Priority Systems

Given the realities of limited resources and time, a priority system must be established to provide a means of allocating human and financial resources. Priority systems require difficult choices that are certain to prove controversial. However, as stated, we believe protection and restoration of the relatively healthier watersheds and biological hot spots found within systems should be a higher initial priority than restoration of the most degraded streams. We suggest that, for long-term success, it will be necessary to reverse the traditional approach of applying most resources initially to the most degraded areas.

This does not mean that the restoration efforts on the most degraded streams should be abandoned. Minority communities are often most affected by the highly degraded rivers, and in the interest of social justice alone these areas must not be abandoned. In addition, some endangered fish and biodiversity in very degraded streams may be maintained with some level of intervention. We recommend, however, that sufficient investments must be made to ensure that protection is implemented and restoration begun on those healthier systems with the better possibility for rapid biotic responses before resources are exhausted on generally more speculative attempts at restoring the most degraded areas. It is obviously best if both can be accomplished simultaneously. Enlarging the funding- and restoration-resource pie is clearly needed to do so. However, this option is often impossible. Therefore, we must make a commitment to *preventing* further degradation of the remaining healthier systems and biological hot spots within systems before we plow resources into attempts to restore severely degraded systems.

Specific Restoration Treatments

Specific on-the-ground restoration treatments to expand and link the healthier areas should focus primarily on riparian and floodplain restoration and include both capital and labor-intensive methods. Projects should be aimed at reconnecting the stream with the floodplain and riparian areas close to the refugia and hot spots, thus providing watershed connectivity. For example, physical capital-intensive treatments that use heavy equipment generally may include: 1) connecting or preventing stream diversion problems at stream crossings; 2) preventing debris flows as a result of road failures; 3) preventing stream crossing washouts; 4) preventing road fill failures; 5) de-watering gullying systems; and 5) correcting or preventing other factors that may cause ecosystem dysfunction.[85] In addition, projects aimed at retiring dikes, levees and channelizations are also important so that natural meanders and flows are re-established.

Labor-intensive restoration can include native riparian reforestation and the restoration of natural stream channel dimensions. Many other non-structural erosion control treatments are possible, such as the proper siting and design of development projects, the establishment of flood- warning systems, and floodplain uses that are compatible with periodic flooding.

In-stream work not associated with reconnecting the stream with the riparian area and floodplain should be minimally and only experimentally used. We are extremely skeptical of the effectiveness of in-stream habitat projects, such as cabling single logs, placing gabions, rolling boulders and other structures in a channel to create pools and riffles, using tactics that are generally based on generic and standardized criteria. As previously stated, the failure rate of these projects is exceedingly high unless the upstream watershed is protected and secured. They often further degrade or incise stream channels. Finally, because they are aimed at habitat for individual species they often unexpectedly harm other riverine-riparian species rather than improve ecosystem functions.

It is important to note that the costs allocated should be equal to the treatment used; that is, if significant heavy equipment was used to build roads that now degrade a riverine system, a comparable kind of heavy equipment work will be required to remove or upgrade damaging roads. A volunteer manual work force, for example, is simply insufficient to accomplish the task. Therefore, sufficient funds must be allocated to accomplish the goals. The RBER approach will require an infusion of funds but will be much more cost effective in the long run than the existing piecemeal protection and restoration strategies that often throw money down ratholes and provide little ecological benefit.

Historical Reconstructions

No matter what restoration treatments are used, they must be designed at the landscape or watershed level. The first step in all restoration programs must be to reconstruct the historical conditions of the entire watershed to the state that existed before extensive human-caused disturbance. Historical data can be obtained from old maps, pioneer journals, aerial photos, early scientific investigations and surveys, and interviews with descendants of early settlers. In addition, soil, vegetation, and geologic maps are useful. The goal of historical reconstruction is to develop a picture of how the relatively undisturbed system functioned compared with how the system functions today. To do this, an assessment of the entire watershed is needed. Comparison with the historical record provides the first template for developing restoration goals -- returning certain areas within the system to a more natural condition. Long-term monitoring is needed to determine the success or failure of restoration efforts.

Addressing Key Problems

Restoration programs for other key problems in riverine systems may require that flows, passage, water quality, temperature and other issues be addressed. Stream flows, especially in the West, are subject to mostly archaic water laws that may have made sense when they were created but today wreak ecological, economic, and social havoc. The prior appropriation doctrine of the West must be amended and a national policy of providing adequate in-stream flows for riverine-riparian ecosystem and biodiversity recovery must be established. The acquisition and marketing of water rights for in-stream flows along with water conservation and efficiency measures by all users must be key elements of the new policy.

We caution against a singular focus on increasing in-stream flows absent from the restoration of ecosystem structure and function. A great many rivers nationwide are incised, channelized streams. The sinuosity and structural complexity of the systems have been lost, significantly reducing water-retention ability. Thus, flows tend to be higher in the spring run-off periods, and much lower in summer than in pre-disturbance conditions. Both conditions exacerbate ecological problems. During higher flows, fish and other organisms have nowhere to go for protection and can be swept downstream to perish. This is especially true for salmon and steelhead in many of the streams in the Pacific

Northwest. Degraded watershed conditions have led to lack of off-stream cover and habitat and increased stream volumes and velocities, causing high fish mortality rates at high flows. Therefore, increased flows alone may fail to restore riverine-riparian biodiversity.

For example, a recent study by the U.S. Forest Service Pacific Northwest Research Station found major habitat loss, despite a 50% increase in summer flows since 1940, in the Grande Ronde River in Oregon. During this period, the fisheries in the system have declined.

Simplification of riverine ecosystems often means that the aquatic food chain is disturbed or destroyed because channelized streams scour down to bedrock and become biological deserts. Improved stream flows without improved stream function and structure may not address food chain disturbances and, therefore, may prove of minimal value to riverine-riparian biodiversity in many systems.

Flows and fish passage are often affected by hydroelectric dams and other water impoundments. It is probably unrealistic to believe that the majority of dams nationwide may willingly be removed before time and natural forces combine to do so. However, some dams cause greater harm to riverine resources than others within the context of the whole river system. A watershed-level priority system of dams that cause the greatest impacts should be completed. The most damaging projects should be removed or significantly altered based on watershed needs. The Federal Energy Regulatory Commission (FERC) hydroelectric plant licensing and relicensing processes should mandate watershed-level assessments to determine the appropriateness of new dams and the changes (including dam removals) needed to maintain and recover the entire river system -- not just an affected segment. A national moratorium on new dam construction should be implemented until those rivers that cannot withstand more dams are identified and a national "protected river" program is enacted to set those systems off-limits to future dams.

Water quality, particularly from non-point sources, and temperature problems can best be addressed through riparian and floodplain protection and restoration. The impacts of both chronic and catastrophic sedimentation are significant, though the traditional regulatory approaches such as Best Management Practices (BMPs) and Total Maximum Daily Loads (TMDLs) fail to adequately address these issues. Even if the TMDL process worked, it would not address catastrophic landslides or changes created by large-scale natural disturbances. These events significantly alter watershed dynamics, and thus require constant readjustment of TMDLs. Only clear, definitive riparian and floodplain management directives can address these issues.

Systemwide Planning, Consistency and Policy Alignment

Effective watershed restoration also requires greatly improved system-wide policy coordination and consistency. On many rivers, 30 to 40 public agencies have programs entrained that affect the watershed. Each agency has different legislatively established missions and goals. Private landowners often operate under different sets of policies or under no policies at all. These interests fail to communicate with one another, and their activities and policies are almost never coordinated so that the integrity of the riverine system is maintained. New mechanisms are needed to move beyond the piecemeal management pattern evident on every riverine system nationwide so that systemwide planning, coordination and consistency can be realized.

Some may argue that better cooperation between agencies will lead to the type of watershed-level consistency needed. As discussed in the policy assessments found in the appendixes of this book, some fragments of interagency coordination policies do exist in NEPA and within cumulative impact requirements. These policies can and should be greatly improved. Although important and possible to achieve, however, better coordination is *not* the sole answer. Conflicting agency goals and missions, bureaucratic inertia and turf battles conspire to prevent public agencies from effectively cooperating to protect complex riverine systems and biodiversity on their own.

Some would also argue that improved cumulative impact models can address the systemwide planning and coordination needs. We want to carefully distinguish between predictive cumulative impact models and analysis. Although great advances are being made in the science and art of cumulative impact analysis, we caution against the use of predictive cumulative impact models. Technical models that predict how much more impact a system can withstand tend to be ineffective. However, it is possible to do a credible analysis of cumulative impact problems within a watershed by mapping the watershed terrain, slope and soil stability, the partial and temporal patterns of impacts from past and proposed activities, and so forth. Almost every riverine system in America is degraded relative to its predisturbance condition. The chronic disturbance caused by many activities such as forestry, road building or grazing usually occurs over a 5- to 25-year period, slowly causing chronic loss of deep pool habitat, for example. Catastrophic events set up by human disturbances also may not occur until a major natural event, such as torrential rainfall, strikes 10 to 20 years after a particular activity. Technical predictive cumulative impact models may never be effective enough to identify, let alone predict, the real long-term cumulative impacts of any proposed action or plan.

Of even greater concern is the fact that the standards or minimal threshold levels used in cumulative impact models most often have the unintended consequence of causing increased degradation, not protection. Agencies believe that a system can be degraded down to the threshold level, rather than looking at the threshold as a floor from which to increase stream health. If one riverine system is at the threshold level, and hence cannot support further encroachment, yet a nearby stream is above the threshold, development generally shifts to the healthier system, eventually degrading that system down to the minimum threshold as well.

Rather than relying exclusively on the hope for better "coordination" or the generally flawed cumulative impact models to achieve systemwide planning and consistency, policies and programs within watersheds must be *aligned*. Given the *existing* divergent agency missions and goals, effective interagency and interjurisdictional policy coordination and consistency will *never* be possible. Effective coordination and consistency will only occur when all agency missions and goals within a watershed are either administratively or legislatively aligned. This is possible through definitive congressional or administrative decree on federal lands. In watersheds with private land, the alignment will require a combined regulatory and voluntary approach.

Traditionally, public decisions are crafted by forging agreements between three groups -- elected officials, private interest groups, and the bureaucracy. Each is essentially a competing interest. A number of attempts have been made to institute effective watershed-wide planning and coordination mechanisms in mixed-basin ownerships among these three interests. Each has met with varying degrees of success. The most effective have been new, independent umbrella mechanisms that coordinate all the various interests. We call these "watershed councils" (though "task forces" or "watershed associations" are other possible names). As a new umbrella organization, the watershed council must pull together the three competing interests. The roles of the new umbrella entity should include aggregating and then aligning agency policies, facilitating the production of a watershed-wide ecological assessment, acting as an information clearinghouse, resolving interagency and interjurisdictional conflicts, funding acquisition and dispersal, monitoring action plans, monitoring fiscal responsibilities, and public education.

Although completely uniform and consistent watershed-level planning, policy alignment and communication are unlikely, the chances of achieving them can be vastly improved through these approaches.

Local Community Participation and Economic Enhancement

Finally, successful watershed restoration programs require the active involvement and support of local communities and citizens. No matter what policies exist at any level of government, they will fail without the support of local communities and citizens. Most of the daily decisions that affect riverine systems are made at the local level. It is the local communities that are most directly harmed by degraded riverine conditions (water pollution, loss of recreational opportunities, or water supply problems), and it is the local communities that will be asked to give up the most perceived economic gain to protect and restore a river. It is also only from the local citizenry that individuals may emerge to monitor and advocate for the conservation of local rivers. Hence, local communities must be actively engaged in bottom-up efforts to restore riverine systems and biodiversity.

Most riverine landowners and local communities realize that their rivers are degraded, that they play a role in the creation of those conditions, and that a healthier system is needed. However, they fear that restoration will mean loss of jobs and economic productivity. Local communities are told to change practices that degrade riverine systems but are provided little support or direction for making changes in ways that can also maintain economic vitality. Hence, local citizens often oppose conservation efforts.

Yet, a multitude of local riverine restoration efforts are under way across the nation. Generally, these can be characterized as efforts to implement restoration projects through the auspices of "Watershed Council" programs, water quality or fish restoration projects. The watershed council approach is widespread throughout the East and Upper Midwest. Many similar efforts are now sprouting up across the West, particularly in the Pacific Northwest.

The calls for help among many local citizens and communities and the proliferation of local restoration projects indicate a growing desire for action and change. However, for citizens to take charge of their own destiny and to be willing to forgo perceived economic gains requires something more than just desire. It requires empowerment, effective new incentives, the removal of disincentives, an effective implementation structures. In addition, a new focus on support for jobs in restoration technologies, river-focused community revitalization projects and ecologically compatible "economic conversions" are required to stimulate bottom-up local involvement. The goal is to generate economic and community development opportunities that enhance both the river and local communities.

As our review of state and local programs in the appendixes reveals, effective local efforts will occur only on a piecemeal basis in the absence of positive federal policies that include these elements. The nation desperately needs comprehensive, not piecemeal, restoration efforts.

Regulations Versus Incentives

There is a long-running debate between those who see regulations to control environmental degradation as the only viable option, versus those favoring the incentive approach. Regulations are clearly appropriate on government-owned lands. However, on private lands, regulations alone have failed to stem the degradation of riverine systems. In fact, both regulations and incentives are government interventions designed to influence behavior, and both are needed to restore riverine systems. The majority of riverine protection and restoration efforts will come about primarily through the combined use of incentive and regulatory instruments of government policy.

Both incentives and regulations have strengths and weaknesses. Incentives may be more effective than regulations when consumers rather than producers are engaging in damaging behavior. For example, it is very difficult to design a regulation that reduces consumer demand for products grown in ways that degrade riverine systems.

Regulations are more effective than incentives, however, when an outright legal ban is needed -- to stop cutting trees in riparian areas, for example. Regulations are also more effective when the need is to reduce degrading activity very quickly. Incentives usually take longer to introduce, and the reaction to them is usually slower.

Incentives generally have a clear advantage over regulation in their motivational effect. Regulations tend to produce little motivation to reduce damaging activities below the permitted level and often generate resentment. Regulations rely on the threat of penalties which, if not assessed, can prove hollow and build even greater resentment. Further, regulation does not often change the underlying economic incentives that may be driving the degradation. For example, cheap water may drive the over-appropriation of many streams, and simple regulation of water use will not change the fundamental motivating factor.

Incentives, however, encourage constant innovation to save money or reap benefits -- practices very important to restoring riverine systems. For the most part, incentives are believed to be more efficient in reaching restoration targets. However, evidence indicates that for this to be accurate, incentives need to be accompanied by a great deal of persuasion and public education about the existence and methods of use of the incentives.

Incentives also tend to be more "libertarian" than regulations -- an important consideration when dealing with private lands. While regulations can mandate certain behaviors, incentives simply encourage them, thus leaving the freedom to choose. This different perception of regulations and incentives makes incentives more politically viable in many cases.

On the other hand, incentives by their nature allow for some degradation to occur, and hence can be viewed as "licenses to degrade." By trying to encourage change through incentives as opposed to outlawing degradation, the activity is allowed to continue, putting an explicit price on riverine systems. Yet, regulations can also be viewed as licenses to degrade unless absolutely no degradation is allowed. Any degradation standard above zero is effectively a license to degrade up to that amount.

In summary, because problems and needs vary, a combination of both incentives and regulatory mechanisms will be necessary to protect and restore America's private land riverine systems and biodiversity. Some degrading activities must be stopped rapidly and definitively while at the same time the basic motivations to degrade must be changed and long-term, bottom-up restoration programs encouraged.

THE BASIC COMPONENTS OF EFFECTIVE BOTTOM-UP PROGRAMS AND POLICIES

A number of conditions are, therefore, required to effectively support and catalyze successful local bottom-up private-land riverine restoration programs.

First, a mechanism must be established to empower local communities, and to develop links between a wide diversity of interest groups to become engaged in bottom-up watershed restoration programs: Watershed restoration on private lands requires bottom-up community efforts that cannot be imposed from the top down. Local programs require flexibility, creativity and adaptation to meet local conditions and needs. Bottom-up involvement requires a careful new delineation of federal, state and local government roles and responsibilities. The federal and state governments can and must provide incentives for landowner participation, grants, loans, and in some cases, direct funds to assist in restoration. Incentives to foster coalitions between disadvantaged groups and those concerned about riverine health are also needed. Local citizens must be encouraged to become involved in the process of planning and implementing restoration strategies. This requires that government provide flexibility and the capability for local citizens to use the incentives in adaptable ways. Yet, government must make it clear that restoration is a state and national priority by providing minimum standards and enforceable criteria. When multiple ownerships and jurisdictions exist within a watershed, as stated earlier, a new citizen-driven umbrella planning, decision-making and communication mechanism will most often be needed to coordinate the efforts. Again, the non-profit watershed council approach appears to be the best strategy available.

Second, sufficient technical and financial support must be provided to produce independent scientific assessments and watershed restoration recommendations: A sound scientific base is required upon which to craft restoration goals and options. All too often restoration efforts lack this vital scientific grounding. When this occurs, many evolve into useful "social" projects, yet they cannot be considered restoration programs. The scientific watershed assessments must include a variety of options for meeting restoration goals. Each option should include a biological risk assessment so that the pros and cons of each choice can be accurately weighed. The assessments must be developed free from political or economic pressure. Most local communities lack the capability of developing these on their own, especially for large watersheds with multiple jurisdictions. However, with the proper types of technical assistance and funding, these assessments can be completed. If consultants are hired and monitored directly by the watershed council, they can often do much of this work. A note of caution however: If a government agency rather than the watershed council hires and monitors the consultant, all too often the majority of available funds go into a big budget "black hole" and very little helpful information or actual dollars may ever be applied on the ground. This strategy cannot be a gravy train for consultants -- the work and funding must get out to the field and into the hands of local citizens.

Third, scientific information and risk assessments must be freely and fully distributed: The people's right to participate must be backed up by the people's right to know. The decision-making process must be visible, open to the public, and free from interference from special economic interests.

Fourth, the process must have built-in accountability and long-term monitoring: Decisions and on-going management must be monitored to ensure that the recovery strategies are fully implemented and effective and that a constant feedback loop exists.

Fifth, assistance must be provided to educate the public and provide new economic and community development options: Mechanisms must be provided to help educate the public, to identify and provide local jobs in restoration technologies, to stimulate compatible community revitalization projects and to assist with appropriate "economic conversions." Educational programs can include school system and adult awareness programs. It is vital to create an awareness of the connection between local economic development practices and riverine degradation, of the jobs and economic opportunities already lost, and of the increased direct and indirect financial costs incurred by communities as a result of riverine degradation.

This awareness needs to be coupled with an awareness of the social and economic benefits of restoration. For example, the physical and labor-intensive work of restoration may provide a short-term (3-10 year) influx of family-wage jobs. River-oriented community revitalization projects and "economic conversions" provide longer-term opportunities to develop sustainable economies and healthier rivers. Such awareness often elicits interest in new economic and community-development options.

Many types of labor-intensive jobs in restoration may be available. As previously stated, a draft estimate of the job potential available by restoring key watersheds in the Pacific Northwest to protect at-risk salmon found that 20,000-30,000 person-years of employment were possible to treat potential chronic and catastrophic sedimentation problems caused by forest roads, restore riparian areas and re-establish large woodjams at ecologically appropriate sites. Almost all of these jobs would involve heavy equipment work that would thus provide "family wage" jobs to communities hard-hit by timber supply cutbacks.

"Economic conversions" may include methods that will "stop the leakage" of local dollars out of the community through practices that also restore the river. For example, both local dollars and in-stream flows may be saved through improved irrigation practices and municipal water conservation that cuts electric costs paid to utilities outside of the community. Efforts to use less water-and-energy consumptive, alternative agricultural crops may provide greater profits for farmers and improve stream health. New products, or increased production of existing products that do not degrade a river provide other vital conversion options.

Once new opportunities are identified, local communities need support to implement the projects and to develop new local businesses, including the necessary infrastructure, training and support for local entrepreneurs, access to capital, and market development.

To ensure that the conditions exist to empower local bottom-up river restoration programs, new federal policies must provide the following:

> *An enabling legislative framework that gives bottom-up riverine restoration policies and programs the force of law.* Statutory directives are needed that provide clear legislative intent and a set of minimum federal standards so that effective local restoration action plans can be implemented. This framework is also needed to strengthen the powers of the judiciary to ensure compliance.

> *Clear and uniform directives to federal agencies.* Directives are needed to ensure that the law is followed, to mandate that agencies participate in developing aligned and consistent riverine system-wide recovery strategies, and to provide sufficient long-term fiscal and human resources to the agencies so that they fully and effectively implement and monitor the policies.

> *A flexible package of incentives, training and technical assistance.* Whatever incentives and financial supports are provided must be packaged to allow for flexible,

locally tailored use. Policies that create river conservation cost-sharing between landowners and local, state and federal governments must be a part of this incentive package. Preferential treatment in state and federal grant, cost-sharing, and technical assistance programs to local citizens and organizations involved in restoration are also needed. Property and income tax incentives may also be part of the mix.

Mandated state or federal consistency clauses that require federal agency actions to be consistent with restoration goals may be one of the most important incentives required to elicit the support and involvement of state and local governments. The Federal Consistency Clause of the Coastal Zone Management Act, which allows states to have a voice in or veto power over federal projects, is one example of such an incentive.

* *The removal of disincentives for voluntary local participation.* The greatest disincentives are the real and perceived threat of loss of landowner and local government control and lost economic opportunities. Landowners, citizens and local officials often see restoration efforts as indictments of their past management, or as limiting economic outputs. Many people also fear that government involvement will result in inflexible regulations and the accomplishment of state or national interests to the detriment of local concerns. Finally, there is the persistent stereotype that government agencies are condescending toward landowners and local officials or will use the appearance of consensual decision-making processes to forward or legitimize their own agency agendas or personal careers. To prevent such conflicts, policies are needed that prevent top-down approaches and catalyze bottom-up citizen-driven planning and implementation. Policies must also encourage local, not

government nominations of rivers for restoration, and preserve local autonomy while encouraging local, state, and federal partnerships.

The result of these combined factors may help catalyze bottom-up restoration programs that lead to the adjustment of existing local economic practices and to the creation of new job and community revitalization options that sustain both the river and local communities. Previously unknown, creative, new approaches to both community development and riverine restoration may be stimulated.

Community-based watershed restoration programs must become central organizing focuses of new programs and policies nationwide.

CHAPTER FOUR

RECOMMENDATIONS FOR NEW NATIONAL RIVERINE POLICY GOALS AND STRATEGIES

It is clear that a top-level strategic federal initiative is needed to arrest the decline of riverine systems and biodiversity nationwide and to catalyze comprehensive community and ecosystem-based watershed restoration programs. Although it would be ideal to use existing federal statutes and programs to meet this need, we conclude that this will not be sufficient. A number of new federal policy goals and strategies are needed. This chapter discusses these goals and strategies. Their implementation requires new federal policies. We propose three new federal policies, which are discussed in chapters five, six and seven.

A new federal emphasis on rebuilding the nation's infrastructure will certainly be important to building a healthy national economy. However, not just the human-built infrastructure must be repaired. It is imperative that we restore the natural ecological infrastructure if we are to have any hope of long-term social or economic health. Watershed restoration programs can be designed and the initial steps implemented within a very short time, and these programs would provide many benefits. The short-term benefits of ecosystem-based watershed restoration can be readily and visibly apparent, such as erosion control, bank stabilization and sediment reduction, and job creation for dislocated workers and other disadvantaged groups. The long-term benefits will be even more important and apparent -- improved water quality and lower water treatment costs, increased stream flows and lower irrigation costs, revitalized fisheries, healthier aquatic and natural food chains, increased recreational benefits, and the creation of new environmental technologies and jobs.

To reap these benefits, however, the Administration and Congress must establish the following goals and strategies:

A Coordinated Strategic National Watershed Restoration Initiative

A new, top-level, strategic federal initiative is needed to cut through the inertia, turf battles, and conflicting federal agency missions, goals and policies to catalyze comprehensive watershed protection and restoration efforts nationwide. Without elevating the issues to a high national level and marshalling significant resources in a coordinated way, protection and restoration efforts will fail.

A Single Department to Coordinate and Lead National Efforts to Protect and Restore Riverine Ecosystems and Biodiversity

Given the plethora of fragmented and narrow policies found throughout federal agency mandates, it is clear that a unified effort will require the leadership of a single department. This department will need the requisite policy-making authority to align policies and ultimately to review and monitor watershed restoration action plans. One option could be to reinstate the Water Resources Council originally authorized under the Water Resource Development Act of 1965. The program was dissolved by President Reagan. The Water Resources Council consisted of the Secretaries of Agriculture, Interior, and Army and the Director of the Office of Management and Budget. However, the Council had no real policy-making authority and consequently was fraught with conflicts between agencies over fiscal matters and other issues. We conclude that this is not an appropriate direction to take.

At this time we conclude that the Environmental Protection Agency is best equipped to provide the necessary overall federal leadership, though specific new programs can be managed by agencies such as the USDA Soil and Water Conservation Service under a new mission. The EPA is already charged with the responsibility of implementing the Clean Water Act, which applies to every body of water in the nation, and is staffed with watershed scientists, aquatic ecologists, and other scientists and engineers. The EPA also administers community-based grant programs, including the Section 319 nonpoint-source program, the National Estuary Program, and the Near Coast Program. We make this recommendation with the knowledge that problems exist within the EPA. We hope that the new administration will elevate the EPA administrator to a cabinet-level position and empower the Secretary to be a strong advocate for the environment, with the ability to mandate policy alignment and coordination between federal agencies.

Should improvements fail to materialize within the EPA, however, it may be necessary to empower the Department of the Interior or to create a new National Biological Restoration Department, which would have clear authority to coordinate and align federal agency policies and to set clear and effective protection and restoration standards. We believe that responsibility must be vested in a federal department with clear policy-making authority, not an advisory council.

An Expanded National Goal Built Upon the Existing Goal of the Clean Water Act

We propose the formal adoption of the following goal: "To restore and maintain the chemical, physical and biological integrity of the nation's waters, *and the natural ecological integrity of riverine-riparian ecosystems and biodiversity.*" (Italics would be the new words added to the Clean Water Act.)

This goal establishes a new public resource -- riverine-riparian ecosystems and biodiversity. The riverine-riparian ecosystem is the network of streams and riparian systems within a given watershed. Riverine biodiversity includes all biological species that depend on the riverine ecosystem, in part or in full, for survival.

The definition of natural ecological integrity shall include species composition, diversity, and functional organization comparable to that of the natural habitat of the region under conditions of aboriginal influence. The definition shall also be based on the principles of connectivity, natural variability, and on the capacity of the ecosystems to self-repair after disturbances.

Explicit Definition and Protection of Riverine-Riparian Ecosystems and Biodiversity to Prevent Rather than Attempt to Control or Repair Problems

New statutes must explicitly define riverine-riparian ecosystems as a public resource so that the ecological processes contributing to the health of those systems are protected. Protection of riverine-riparian ecosystems will, in turn, provide maximum protection for those subcategories of resources and uses that depend on a healthy watershed, such as fish and other forms of riverine biodiversity. Thus an emphasis will be placed on prevention rather than control or repair.

To define and protect riverine-riparian ecosystems and biodiversity as a public resource provides legal protections similar to those afforded other noncommodity resources, such as recreation.

The definition and protection of riverine-riparian ecosystems is also important because, for the first time, Congress will establish definite legal rules that apply to watershed ecosystem protection. Despite the fact that Congress has repeatedly invoked the term watershed in federal land management and resource protection statutes since the 19th century, it has not adequately defined the values or resources to be protected, nor has it enacted specific prescriptions to guide the management of the watershed resource. As a result, watershed has been the forgotten multiple use in legal contemplation. Without a statutory definition of watershed or a specification of the values that the term encompasses, watershed management by federal agencies will never be realized.

Because of their importance in the maintenance and restoration of water quality, riparian areas deserve the attention wetlands currently receive under the Clean Water Act. Wetlands and riparian areas are functionally similar: They both contribute to groundwater recharge and discharge, sediment stabilization, flood attenuation, water quality, habitat, climate moderation, shoreline protection and recreation.

Federal land-management policies must definitely recognize the importance of riverine-riparian ecosystems. The crucial role of riparian areas has already been recognized by some federal land-management agencies and by the EPA.

Clearly defining riverine-riparian ecosystems as a new resource also makes sense because it will finally merge contemporary science with federal policy. Despite recent advances in congressional legislation affecting water quality, the major advances in lotic ecology over the past 25 years are not well-reflected by either existing criteria for the assessment of riverine-related resources or the management policies or practices that follow from them.

This proposal is consistent with the EPA's recent conclusion that good science should govern all levels of water resource policy.

Uniform, Consistent Standards for All Federal Land Management Agencies

Although many federal land managers under current law may have the authority to promulgate consistent, ecologically defensible riverine management standards, it is within managers' discretion not to do so. In practice, inconsistent management standards have resulted in the loss of riverine-riparian biodiversity and in degraded in-stream water quality and quantity. Ideally, the best way to address these issues on federal lands would be to consolidate management of all federal lands within a watershed into a single agency. Although inconceivable to some, the overlapping and fragmented nature of land ownership, agency mandates, and management practices is exceedingly costly to the taxpayer and makes effective watershed restoration without single agency oversight difficult, if not impossible. If agency mergers are not possible, then uniform, consistent and aligned standards are needed.

Uniformity: One major problem with current federal planning and management is its lack of uniformity. Although formal land- planning requirements have increased for all federal land- management agencies in recent years, the lack of specific statutory standards for riverine management has resulted in a wide divergence of management policies, both within and between federal land-management agencies.

For example, planning and management of national forests lacks consistency among various forests. As one investigator discovered, "planning criteria, indicators for measuring resource values, modeling assumptions, and analytic procedures varied substantially among forests, such that direct quantitative comparisons between plans are of only limited value." Likewise, standards and guidelines for riparian management varied considerably among forests. For example, the Willamette (Oregon) and Shasta-Trinity (California) National Forests adopted guidelines recommending no-cut buffers averaging 100 to 200 feet and ranging up to 400 feet on all class I, II and III streams, while the Mt. Baker-Snoqualmie and Olympic National Forests (Washington) allow extensive logging in all riparian areas, with few restrictions to prevent total stand removal. Few plans provide any protection at all for non-fish bearing streams, ephemeral streams, or headwater streams, despite their important contributions to the downstream environment. Moreover, only a minority of the 156 national forests have developed management plans and standards specifically for riparian areas.

In the BLM, although a national policy of riparian improvement has been announced, very few area plans have been revised to implement this policy. In September, 1990, the BLM published its Riparian-Wetland Initiative for the 1990s, which established a goal of restoring "proper functioning condition" to 75% or more of the riparian acreage managed by the BLM by 1997.

Unfortunately, as the plan notes, the status of more than 79% of the total riparian acreage (5.7 million acres) on BLM lands is unknown.   All BLM state offices have riparian management documents, but their actions have not been incorporated into the BLM's resource management plans, which are the agency's basic land use plans.

Specificity in Federal Land-Use Plans: History has demonstrated that federal land-management agencies tenaciously guard their discretion with the result that many land-use plans promulgated pursuant to statute are too general to provide meaningful limitations or standards for subsequent management decisions.   However, such general, ineffectual land-use plans are often upheld as consistent with statutory requirements because the language of the land use planning statutes failed to place any concrete limitations on agency discretion.

Although many policy areas should logically be administered pursuant to broad delegations of authority, the maintenance and recovery of riverine-riparian ecosystems and biodiversity should be governed by good science, not individual manager's discretion.

Enforceability: The few specific riparian area management guidelines that do exist are not formally developed as agency regulations. Rather, they appear as manual provisions or technical guides, neither of which are binding on the agency or legally enforceable by affected parties.

The Willamette National Forest, for example, has developed a technical document entitled the *Riparian Management Guide*, which is generally acknowledged to contain the most contemporary, scientifically defensible riparian protection guidelines in the Forest Service.   However, this document contains no directives that are binding on the agency.   Rather, the document was prepared to assist in implementing the Standards and Guidelines of the Willamette National Forest Land and Resource Management Plan for Riparian Management Areas. Because it is an informally developed document, not subject to the notice and comment procedures of the Administrative Procedures

Act, the *Riparian Management Guide* lacks the force and effect of law and is not, therefore, enforceable against the agency in court.

The establishment of uniform protection standards for all permanent and intermittent fish-bearing and non-fish-bearing streams, headwaters, floodplains, refugia and biological hot spots across all federal lands is needed because they would establish clearer direction for and public oversight of federal land management. Increased legislative oversight is also consistent with democratic principles. More detailed planning guidelines reduce parochial influences on federal land-use decisions and reduce the risk of undue informal influence by government officials or private interests. By the same token, planning processes permit increased public participation by citizens as well as local and state governments in federal decisions, contributing greatly to the public welfare.

Inter-agency policy alignment and consistency to manage at the watershed level: Although a number of federal statutes address interagency coordination, agencies are nevertheless authorized to act primarily on their own statutory goals and mandates and internal agency priorities. The mere existence of discretionary authority to reduce conflicts between various federal programs has not lead to the full exercise of that authority. Again, the most ideal way to resolve this issue would be to consolidate management of all federal lands within a watershed into a single agency. In lieu of this it appears that agencies must have precise legislative language that provides uniform goals and consistent mandates from which to proceed. That fact calls for legislation or administrative direction that requires agencies to align their missions, goals and management policies within individual watersheds. This strategy would provide specific directives to use the same data-gathering resource definitions and standards and decision-making criteria, for the protection and restoration of riverine-riparian ecosystems and biodiversity.

Aligned and consistent standards would help strengthen many existing federal policies: Clear new uniform standards would be consistent with the stated objective of the Clean Water Act: to "restore and maintain the chemical, physical, and biological integrity of the Nation's waters," and to control water pollution on a watershed-by-watershed basis. As defined in the House Public Works Committee report on the Act, Congress's use of the term "integrity" recognized the importance of preserving natural ecosystems rather than simply improving water quality in an isolated sense.

Aligned and uniform standards are needed to finally recognize congressional intent that the objectives of the Clean Water Act should be attained by managing water resources on a watershed-by-watershed basis. Such standards would also be consistent with congressional intent to manage for the wider goal of watershed protection under other statutes, including the Federal Lands Policy and Management Act, the Forest Service Organic Act of 1987, the National Forest Management Act, the Taylor Grazing Act of 1934, and the Public Rangeland Improvements Act of 1978. These statutes, which affect land management in the national forests and on BLM public lands all use the term watershed and appear to recognize it as a distinct public natural resource. Although the term is not specifically defined in any statute (including the Clean Water Act), one scholar has concluded that watershed is "legislative shorthand for the vegetation systems that regulate and stabilize water quantity while protecting water quality and land integrity. Watershed constitutes both the elements comprising the ecosystem -- soil, water, flora, and fauna -- and the resource relationships within the ecosystem."

Ecosystem and Watershed Level Planning by All Federal Agencies

A report on the Forest Service planning process by the Office of Technology Assessment (OTA) recommended that planning be done at the ecosystem level. We believe this should apply to all federal agencies and to all new and existing federal programs.

The OTA specifically recommended that Congress should:

* require the Forest Service to expand its forest planning inventory and analytical base, which now focuses on the timber resource, to include necessary information and models on all resources, such as natural ecosystem conditions

* require the Forest Service to set targets for ecosystem conditions in forest plans and RPA planning

* improve public involvement

* expand the use of geographic information systems to better understand resource interactions

* require monitoring as a distinct responsibility, including an annual monitoring report with public participation review

All federal agencies and programs should be required to implement these policies at the watershed level.

A Comprehensive Ecosystem-Based Watershed Protection Program For All Federal Land Management Agencies

The program should mandate the rapid identification and protection of the best remaining headwaters, biotic refuges, benchmark watersheds, riparian areas and biological hot spots found throughout river systems.

These areas must be identified through whole watershed assessments and be fully protected. Protecting these areas will place an emphasis on prevention of further degradation rather than on attempts to control or repair problems once they occur.

Establish a System of Watershed Biodiversity Management Areas: A nationwide system of refuges on federal lands for at-risk riverine biodiversity must be established. We call these Watershed (Riverine) Biodiversity Management Areas. They would include entire key watersheds (primarily smaller tributaries) that are already impacted by developments but still house the remaining healthier habitat for the widest diversity of species. Being already partially developed, they will often need active restoration interventions to secure their existing health status.

Establish a Nationwide System of Benchmark Watersheds: Benchmark Watersheds are the remaining ecologically intact whole watersheds that are not impacted or encroached by development. These watersheds provide the control areas needed for scientifically valid research and monitoring programs to determine long-term variation and trends in ecosystem health and populations. They should be designated in all ecological regions of the country and include all stream orders within the region. Both the Watershed Biodiversity Management Areas and Benchmark Watersheds would be identified through whole-watershed assessments.

Protect Riparian Areas and Identify and Protect Biological Hot Spots: In addition, riparian areas and the other biological hot spots found throughout riverine systems must be identified and protected, using full watershed assessments.

Significantly, the concept of watershed-level, at-risk salmon refuges, along with ecologically-based riparian area and floodplain protection, was recently incorporated into the proposals of the congressionally convened Scientific Panel on Late Successional Forest Ecosystems. The panel adopted a "key watershed" protection strategy and identified 137 watersheds in the Pacific Northwest from the Cascade Mountains to the ocean, where the long-term survival of at least 90 stocks of at-risk salmonids (trout, steelhead, salmon, and char) could be protected on federal lands while simultaneously addressing the habitat needs of the northern spotted owl and old-growth forests. Subsequently, the U.S. Forest Service developed a Scientific Analysis Team (SAT) report that was submitted to Judge William Dwyer as part of the requirements of the court case involving the northern spotted owl. Section 5K of the SAT report also delineates the concept of watershed refugia as "key watersheds," while proposing ecologically-based riparian protections for permanent and ephemeral streams.

A Comprehensive, Ecosystem-Based Watershed Restoration Program that Initially Focuses on Securing, Expanding and Linking the Remaining Healthy Ecosystems and Habitats

Congress must develop a national watershed restoration policy that includes clear and carefully developed restoration priorities, approaches and implementation mechanisms. The policy must explicitly require the integration of protection efforts with restoration by focusing restoration, initially, on securing the relatively healthy headwaters, biotic refuges, benchmark watersheds and riparian areas. Following the elimination or reduction of the threats to the remaining healthier areas, the emphasis should be placed on restoring the areas that link these remaining healthy areas, thus eventually expanding them and merging them (rather than initially prioritizing the most degraded or worst-looking sites). Where there are no relatively healthy habitat areas upon which to anchor restoration, riparian and floodplain restoration should be the highest priority. Congress must require that restoration be implemented at the watershed (landscape), ecosystem, and genetic levels, and that restoring watershed and stream ecosystem function, rather than individual segments or species, be the restoration goal.

Bottom-Up Private Land Watershed Restoration Programs that Foster Ecologically Sustainable Development

New bottom-up, locally-driven private-land restoration programs are needed that create local jobs in restoration technologies and river-oriented community revitalization projects and support appropriate agricultural crop and other types of economic conversions. The programs must use a combination of regulatory and non-regulatory approaches, with appropriate incentives to foster participation in restoration. Regulatory approaches are needed to set and enforce minimum standards for restoration nationwide and particularly where voluntary, non-regulatory efforts do not work.

A Moratorium On New Dam Construction, A National "Protected River" Program, and a Process to Prioritize, Remove, and Alter the Most Damaging Dams and Water Projects Within River Systems

The nation's river systems have been dammed, diverted and channelized beyond their carrying capacity -- a process that has made our use of riverine systems for hydroelectricity non-sustainable. To begin to address these problems, Congress must establish a nationwide moratorium on new dam construction and require the identification of those rivers or river segments that should be permanently set off-limits to future hydroelectric or other water projects. A number of states and regions have already established these kinds of protected river programs. The Northwest Power Planning Council's Protected Area Program, for example, set over 40,000 miles of rivers off-limits to future hydroelectric projects in the Pacific Northwest, and the Federal Energy Regulatory Commission subsequently adopted this as a comprehensive hydroelectric plan under Section 10(a) Federal Power Act requirements. This type of system may be helpful even to developers who will have some security in knowing that a project proposed in a non-protected area may avoid a blizzard of opposition that would run up costs and possibly delay construction for years. The national moratorium on new hydroelectric projects and the creation of a nationwide protected river program should be top priorities within the National Watershed Restoration Initiative.

In addition, watershed-level dam assessments should be complete for each river system within a state. From these assessments, a priority list can be developed indicating which dams cause the greatest biological damage within the system.

After careful economic and ecological analysis, those dams at the top of the list that can be dismantled should be. Those that need to have their operations changed to meet biological needs system-wide would be identified. States can use these watershed hydroelectric plans to meet the comprehensive plan requirements of Section 10(a) of the Federal Power Act. Congress should mandate that FERC accept these programs under Section 10(a) requirements of the Federal Power Act as comprehensive, statewide hydroelectric plans.

A Periodic "State of the Nation's Rivers" Report and a Data Bank on the Conditions and Trends of Riverine Systems and Biodiversity

A comprehensive assessment and report on the current conditions of the nation's riverine systems and biodiversity should be completed. The report should be produced by a high-level, independent scientific body. It should be similar in style and scope to the National Wetlands Report. The report should not necessarily be a mile-by-mile evaluation. Instead, the report should focus on aggregating the conditions and trends of water quality and quantity, riverine-riparian ecosystems, fisheries, and other forms of riverine-riparian biodiversity nationwide.

Timeliness is of the essence in developing an accurate understanding of the current conditions of the nation's riverine-riparian ecosystems and biodiversity. A "State of the Nation's Rivers" report should be completed every five years to provide benchmarks and future goals on the nation's drive to maintain and restore these vital systems and species.

To obtain the information required to produce the reports, a national rivers data bank is needed. The data bank should integrate the many river inventories and assessments across the country, reinforce inventory efforts already under way in the BLM and the U.S. Forest Service and lead to the acquisition of sound biological data. The National Biological Service proposed by the

U.S. Department of the Interior may be an appropriate agency to handle such a task.

Stable Long-Term Funding and Sufficient Financial and Tax Incentives for Riverine Restoration

For decades Congress has provided subsidies and tax breaks that have helped support the process of developing the nation's rivers. Much good has come from this development. We now realize, however, that river development has far outpaced the conservation required to maintain healthy functioning ecosystems and biodiversity. Consequently, an equal amount of federal subsidies, financial and technical incentives, and direct long-term funding is now required to restore the nation's riverine systems and biodiversity so that they can provide ecological, economic, and social benefits for future generations. The massive river development that has occurred nationwide would not have been possible without federal subsidies and incentives. Effective restoration will not be possible without this same level of commitment. These must be viewed as investments today that will yield benefits in the future.

Many funding options exist. A great deal of money can be found within existing government programs, though, as with existing policies, they tend to be fragmented and most often spend money on "band-aid" approaches and projects. These funds need to be coordinated, better targeted and marshalled to apply to priority watersheds in more effective ways. Existing funds are available from sources such as EPA grant-in-aid, the 1990 Farm Bill, Soil and Water Conservation Service grants and many others. These agencies should administer their existing grant programs to support local citizen watershed councils and bottom-up watershed restoration action programs.

Further, many federal agency budgetary processes need to be restructured to support watershed management and restoration. Some agency budgets, such as that of the U.S. Forest Service, rely on timber receipts that maximize budgets based on resource (timber) extraction. Restoration will probably never be truly possible on those lands given this type of budgeting. These budgets must be restructured so that agency funding, and, therefore, the incentives provided to local resource managers are not connected to resource extraction.

Given the scope of the problems and needs, existing public dollars will not be enough. New revenues will also be required. New revenues can include sources such as mitigation trust funds from existing hydroelectric projects. As a condition of relicensing hydroelectric projects, the Federal Energy Regulatory Commission (FERC), should require the license holder to establish such accounts. The strategy is already being applied successfully in a number of FERC relicensing procedures.

In addition, new private funding sources may be available. Local banks, for example, could become involved by establishing community development restoration loan funds. Individuals would deposit targeted funds in the bank much as they would into any interest-bearing account. The bank would use the money to loan to riverine restoration or compatible economic development projects. Investors would be pleased that their money is used for "green" investments, banks would make money and loan funds would be available for restoration projects. This concept has already been used successfully by South Shore Bank of Chicago, and by their spin-off organizations to promote community development. Plans are underway to initiate a pilot project of ecological development banking in Willapa Bay in southwest Washington state.

Finally, and perhaps most importantly, we recommend that Congress establish a National Watershed Restoration Trust Fund to provide a long-term funding source. The trust should be a free-standing budget account. One revenue option to fund the trust may be to create a river or fisheries restoration stamp program similar to the very successful U.S. Fish and Wildlife Service's Duck Stamp program. Although the details of establishing a restoration trust fund are complex, the National Research Council has already proposed this option in their report entitled *Restoration of Aquatic Ecosystems*. We support the National Research Council's proposal and believe that effort must begin to create the Trust Fund in the immediate future.

Improvements to Existing Federal Riverine Policies to Support the Proposed New Protection and Restoration Goals, Strategies and Policies

The assessments in the appendixes of this book reveal numerous strategic and tactical flaws in existing federal and state riverine policies and programs. We believe that the Administration and Congress must take the steps needed to improve these programs and policies in ways that support the proposed new goals and strategies. We also hope that the states will seek to improve their riverine policies.

It is important to remember, however, that fixing the problems with existing policies will not, alone, ensure the protection and restoration necessary for America's riverine systems and biodiversity. As we hope to have made abundantly clear, fundamental changes are needed in the underlying assumptions of existing riverine protection and restoration approaches and policies, and entirely new approaches, implementation mechanisms and policies are needed.

In the next three chapters, we recommend three new federal policies that we believe can help catalyze a new national strategic community and ecosystem-based watershed protection and restoration initiative.

CHAPTER FIVE

RECOMMENDATIONS FOR FEDERAL LANDS

Immediate Needs on Federal Lands

To implement many of the proposed new national restoration goals and strategies on federal lands, we recommend that a comprehensive umbrella policy be enacted to apply to all federal land management agencies. A uniform act is needed to bring all federal riverine management policies and programs into alignment.

At present, federal land management agencies have no clear or consistent congressional mandate to maintain or restore riverine systems and biodiversity at the ecosystem and watershed levels. On the contrary, most policies serve to further degrade riverine systems and to drive riverine-riparian biodiversity toward extinction.

The Pacific Rivers Council established a National Rivers Policy Scientific Committee composed of some of the nation's leading freshwater ecologists and fishery biologists. The committee was charged with identifying the specific scientific directives needed to protect and restore federal land riverine-riparian ecosystems and biodiversity. In addition, we established a separate committee of more than 20 scientists who assisted in the development of the Rapid Biotic and Ecosystem Response restoration strategy. Based on the work of these committees and our own extensive research, we make the following recommendations:

The Federal Lands Watershed Management Act (FLWMA)

The FLWMA is intended to establish a new national policy to protect and restore riverine-riparian ecosystems and biodiversity at the watershed level as a primary management goal on federal lands. It, therefore, allows only those management activities that

89

do not compromise the integrity of riverine-riparian ecosystems and biodiversity.

Riverine-riparian Ecosystem and Biodiversity Protection and Restoration Rules and Standards

Riverine-riparian ecosystems should be defined so that in most riverine landscapes the stream channel and riparian ecosystem will delimit the surface of alluvial formations. The major exception would be areas of Pleistocene glaciation, where the upper boundary would be established at the 100-year flood level or would extend to the boundary of the alluvial formation if consistent with subsurface hydrology or hyporheic zones. Especially in small headwater streams, the riverine-riparian ecosystem will extend upslope to include the zone of vegetative inputs of leaves, needles and wood in the riverine-riparian ecosystem as well as the zone contributing shade. The objective in delineating this area is to capture the longitudinal, lateral, and vertical dimensions of connectedness.

Riverine-riparian biodiversity should be defined as all native aquatic and riparian organisms and species that depend upon riverine-riparian ecosystems for survival, in part or in whole. Native riverine-riparian biodiversity and their habitat shall be maintained at the ecosystem, species and genetic levels across all federal lands.

Biological hotspots should be defined as smaller habitat patches that provide vital ecological and biological functions for a riverine system. Biological hotspots within federal land riverine systems shall be identified, using a watershed assessment. It should be the top management priority to fully protect these areas by any and all means from degradation caused by past or future development activity.

The following standards are necessary to prevent further degradation and to maintain the ecological integrity of riverine-riparian ecosystems and biodiversity on federal lands:

* *Timber harvest.* Timber harvesting should be prohibited except where it can be shown that it enhances the ecological integrity of the riverine-riparian ecosystem. This restriction would be placed on permanently flowing, seasonally flowing and intermittent streams and their associated riverine-riparian ecosystems. No timber harvesting should be permitted on sites that have locally unstable soils.

* *Salvage logging.* Salvage logging should be prohibited in riverine-riparian ecosystems, including the harvest of blow-down salvage, except where necessary for human health or safety.

* *Large woody debris management.* No removal of large, downed woody debris should be allowed in any riverine-riparian ecosystem or stream channel, except where necessary for human health or safety.

* *Road and bridge design and location.* Roads and bridges should be designed to minimize their impact on the riverine-riparian ecosystem. New road construction within 100-year floodplains should be prohibited to prevent fragmentation of the riverine-riparian ecosystem. All roads should be constructed and maintained (including culvert cleaning and placement) so that they minimize required modifications of water routing (surface and subsurface) and prevent or minimize additions of sediments (direct and indirect) to streams. The timing of road and bridge construction should be determined primarily to minimize possible disturbance. A watershed-level plan for phased road removal should be implemented for existing roads within riverine-riparian ecosystems. Priority should be given to removing roads that currently or potentially may fragment or degrade riverine-riparian ecosystems.

Reconnecting flowing water with the floodplain should be a top road restoration priority. This should be accomplished by replacing or adding new culverts, removing roads, and other appropriate measures where possible.

* *Grazing.* Grazing should be prohibited in riverine-riparian ecosystems, especially in designated riverine biodiversity management areas and benchmark watersheds and in biological hot spots. Where not eliminated, grazing should be restricted to specific seasons and certain levels to ensure that adequate grass, herb, tree, and shrub vegetation is constantly maintained, because vegetation is a major determinant of bank stability, soil conditions, nutrient loading and water balance. Areas significantly degraded by grazing should be fully rested and protected from grazing and restored to complete ecosystem health before any further grazing is considered.

Upland Management Rules and Regulations

Although upland management must be watershed- and biome-specific, new upland management policies should be developed to protect against major changes in watershed hydrology or sedimentation delivery rates. The policies must ensure that the frequency and magnitude of erosion processes are not substantially altered. Specifically, the managing agencies should identify areas not suitable for logging, road building, grazing or mining in their watershed assessment and management plans. The standard for what would constitute "substantially altered" needs to be determined ecologically. Areas that meet these criteria should be withdrawn from development activities. Decisions should err on the side of safety to prevent elimination of future options.

Drought Management Rules and Regulations

Riverine management practices should not be modified during periods of drought.

Flood Management Rules and Regulations

After flooding of riverine-riparian ecosystems and floodplains, reconstruction of previously existing development should be prohibited on federal lands. Floods should be viewed as natural ecological occurrences that enhance the riverine-riparian ecosystems, not as catastrophes. Consumptive water resources management shall not be altered during periods of flooding.

In-stream Flow Management Rules and Regulations

Federal land management agencies should take all actions necessary to ensure that in-stream flows are adequate to meet the needs of native riverine-riparian species and stream functions and processes. Such actions would include, but not be limited to, the establishment of permanent in-stream water rights.

In-stream flows should be maximized to the extent practicable through conservation measures that should include, but not be limited to: the use/reuse of "graywater"; the coordination of water and land use policies with other federal agencies and with private parties; the pricing of water at market value; all other practical legal and administrative remedies.

On-going Monitoring Program and Evaluation Rules and Regulations

Riverine management programs should be evaluated on the basis of continuous monitoring, so that the scientific and tactical assumptions underlying such programs are periodically reassessed. Such evaluation should consider at least the following:

* The short- and long-term effectiveness of the programs
being evaluated over time, based on the analysis of long-
term data sets as well as traditional methods, such as
field surveys.

* Historical and current baseline and inventory
information, including, but not limited to biological
criteria, chemical criteria, in-stream water temperature,
physical and hydrological criteria.

The goal of this program is to ensure the analysis of
information through a common currency of communication and to
recognize biological criteria as the most sensitive and important
criteria, while retaining the use of water chemistry, temperature,
and physical/hydrological criteria.

Rules and Regulations to Establish a Nationwide System of Watershed Biodiversity Management Areas and Benchmark Watersheds

Watershed Biodiversity Management Areas should be
defined as watersheds that may already have been entered and
impacted but nonetheless house the remaining relatively healthy
habitat for at-risk and sensitive riverine-riparian species, and
relatively healthy ecosystems. Benchmark Watersheds shall be
defined as those remaining undisturbed watersheds that are a
remnant of ecological conditions existing before European
colonization.

Key watersheds on federal lands nationwide should be
identified and protected as Watershed Biodiversity Management
Areas and Benchmark Watersheds as follows:

* Watershed Biodiversity Management Areas and
Benchmark Watersheds should generally include the
entire watershed but will be no less than the stream
channels and the entire riverine-riparian ecosystem on

permanent and ephemeral streams with associated uplands, floodplains, wetlands, and hyporheic zones.

* The sole management goal for Watershed Biodiversity Management Areas and Benchmark Watersheds should be the maintenance of riverine and riparian habitat and ecological elements and processes (biological integrity).

* Watershed assessments, riverine habitat "gap analysis," and historical reconstruction techniques should be used to identify the Watershed Biodiversity Management Areas and Benchmark Watersheds.

* Management activities in Watershed Biodiversity Management Areas should be limited to those practices that are known to result in increased ecosystem and species health. Benchmark Watersheds should receive the highest degree of protection afforded to federal lands. Road building, timber harvesting, grazing, mining and any and all other types of encroachment should be prohibited within Benchmark Watersheds.

* A Watershed Assessment should be completed within each Watershed Biodiversity Management Area. The assessment should identify and prioritize existing and potential threats to the biological integrity of the watershed, and restoration goals. Roads should be progressively removed within the Watershed Biodiversity Management Areas and a program established to improve road drainage and prevent damage from existing or future road construction. Other threats should be treated and eliminated.

* Watershed Biodiversity Management Areas and Benchmark Watersheds should be spaced geographically to ensure maximum riverine-riparian species

recolonization and to ensure an appropriate representation of approximations of pre-European stream conditions. Each must be large enough to function as an independent biological unit.

* Benchmark Watersheds should be used as research and monitoring sites to detect long-term chronic problems such as acid precipitation and climate change and changes in ecosystem status over time.

Riverine-riparian Ecosystem and Biodiversity Restoration Rules and Regulations

Riverine-riparian ecosystems and biodiversity should be restored on all permanent and intermittent streams on federal lands.

* A watershed-level assessment should be used to determine restoration priorities.

* Restoration should be based on a long-term, whole-system perspective rather than on restoring single species or other discrete segments within a riverine system.

* Restoration interventions should initially focus on fully protecting and securing key refugia (watershed biodiversity management areas, Benchmark Watersheds) riparian areas and biological hot spots from degradation caused by past or future management actions and on expanding and linking these areas before other restoration efforts proceed.

* Restoration of stream ecosystem processes (e.g., reconnecting the flowing water with the riparian ecosystem and floodplain and allowing the stream to

flood and repair itself, where possible) should be the primary management goal.

* A detailed restoration action plan to expand and link the key refugia (Watershed Biodiversity Management Areas and Benchmark Watersheds), riparian areas and biological hot spots should focus on riparian and floodplain restoration, on road removal, displacement, upgrading or maintenance, in-stream flow improvements, and on other strategies to restore stream ecosystem function. In-stream structures not aimed at recreating natural stream processes should be used only as a last resort, and then only on an experimental basis.

* Restoration plans should include the identification and assessment of the relative impacts of dams, diversions and other water projects within the system.

* Restoration plans should be designed to minimize the need for future human support.

* The introduction or use of exotic plants or species should be prohibited, and the cost of exotic species removal should be calculated and carried out where feasible.

* Native materials should be used for restoration, whenever possible.

* Restoration management plans and goals shall be established around the flood scale (for example, 10 years, 100 years).

* Water policy and land-use development should be coordinated with water availability within a basin to restore sufficient flows to critical areas. (Conservation of

water and use/reuse of graywater should be promoted;
in-stream water rights for native species should be a
priority, based on the natural flow required to reconnect
the surface water with the riparian area so that
regulation of in-stream flows reflects the needs of native
species and stream functions and processes, such as
channel morphology).

Watershed Assessments and Historical Reconstruction

Watershed-level assessments and historical reconstruction
should be completed before any restoration plans are developed or
treatments are initiated. An understanding of the complete system
and conceptual reconstructions of the natural riverine-riparian
ecosystem are necessary to successfully assess the condition of
riverine systems and biodiversity, to monitor them or to
implement restoration programs. Without these reference points,
maintenance and restoration policies will lack a biologically
meaningful context. The historical reconstructions will function as
baseline standards and comparisons for the health and biological
integrity of riverine systems.

* Watershed assessments should begin at the landscape
level and then move to the tributary and stream-reach
level. This effort involves documentation, both spatially
and temporally, of ecological processes and status and
trends and identification of the critical ecosystem
components, control points, and other areas of high
priority (such as areas of greatest connectivity, refugia,
and biological hot spots) throughout the watershed.

* Historical models should be constructed, based on all
available information, from early natural history writings,
surveys of aquatic organisms, early scientific studies,
historical journals, cadastral surveys, well-drilling
records, and snagging and beaver-trapping records to

up-to-date aerial photos, soil maps and so forth. In addition, information can be obtained by assessing and comparing ecologically similar Benchmark Watersheds. The historical information should then be integrated with research on current stream ecosystem community structure and functional processes and synthesized into conceptual frameworks.

* Comparisons can be made with the current state of the riverine systems to provide the context for developing watershed-specific restoration policies and setting treatment priorities. In cases where gaps in the protection afforded critical organisms or biological communities are identified, for example, areas that need to be added to the protection system can be determined.

Dam and Water Project Rules and Regulations

The degradation of riverine-riparian ecosystems and biodiversity caused by dams and water projects within watersheds should be reduced or eliminated and future problems avoided, through the following policies:

* An Environmental Impact Statement for the entire watershed should be prepared for all systems with potentially damaging dams. After full public interest and National Environmental Policy Act reviews, the Environmental Impact Statement shall identify the relative impacts of each project and display a range of alternatives to resolve the problems.

* A priority list of other projects, including, but not limited to, check dams, levees, dikes, riprap and channelizations that cause the greatest ecological or biological impact or that are incompatible with federal land riverine protection or restoration goals, shall be

established for each riverine system on federal lands. Water projects on the top of the priority list with the greatest damaging impacts shall be slated for removal or significant alterations. Existing projects not prioritized for removal shall be repaired, readjusted, rewound or retrofitted or in other ways modified to protect and restore ecosystem integrity and biodiversity based on watershed-level needs. Diversions should be minimized and/or progressively retired. Congress should require that the Federal Energy Regulatory Commission accept the systemwide watershed plan as a comprehensive plan under Section 10(a) of the Federal Power Act, and Congress should prohibit the Federal Energy Regulatory Commission from issuing licenses on reaches designated as protected areas.

* A moratorium on new dam construction should be instituted on all federal lands. The moratorium shall remain in effect until a program is established to permanently set specific river systems or segments off-limits to future hydroelectric or dam construction projects on federal lands. All riverine systems on federal lands shall be assessed to determine which systems, segments, or tributaries should be permanently withdrawn from future water impoundments. Once completed, Congress should prohibit the Federal Energy Regulatory Commission from licensing or building in protected areas. Congress shall provide similar mandates to the Bureau of Reclamation and Army Corp of Engineers for federal water projects.

Mining Rules and Regulations

The existing legal priority status given to mining within or near riverine-riparian ecosystems, floodplains, and toeslopes should be removed. Mining should be allowed only after full National

Environmental Policy Act and public interest reviews are concluded which determine that no adverse impacts on riverine-riparian ecosystems and biodiversity will occur and that the mine will produce a paying quantity of minerals.

Inter-agency and Inter-jurisdictional Watershed Policy Alignment

All federal land management agencies should uniformly align their policies and cooperatively manage watersheds with all other federal land managers within an affected watershed to meet protection and restoration goals. Federal agencies should also align policies and cooperatively plan and manage with state and private interests within an entire riverine system, provided that no federal land riverine system policy will be modified to provide less protection than is required under the FLRMA.

Alignment should include, but not be limited to, the following: resource definitions; data gathering, watershed assessment and historical reconstruction techniques, procedures and standards; riparian area, floodplain, biological hot spot, headwater and upland management protection and restoration prescriptions, standards and guidelines; and, monitoring standards and procedures. Planning, management and monitoring must be performed in cooperative, uniform methods at the whole-watershed level.

Initial Implementation of the Federal Lands Watershed Management Act

We propose that the policies described above be implemented initially on federal lands throughout the Pacific Northwest. Over 200 anadromous salmonids (trout,steelhead, char, and salmon) and over 750 of 1100 native fish total are at risk of extinction, and watershed ecosystems are highly degraded regionwide. At the same time, the region is certain soon to protect critical habitat for the Northern Spotted Owl and other species on the west side. Similar protections may follow on the east-side of the region. Implementing the new federal-land riverine policies in conjunction with the impending protection for these species will provide a more structured and integrated land protection and management scheme.   It would also allow the policies to be refined, if needed, before application to federal lands nationwide.

CHAPTER SIX

RECOMMENDATIONS FOR PRIVATE LANDS

The National Watershed Registry

To implement the proposed new goals and strategies for private (non-federal) lands, we recommend a new federal policy to support the numerous existing local riverine restoration efforts and to catalyze new bottom-up efforts nationwide. Although improvements in the Clean Water Act may help address non-point pollution through regulatory approaches, much more is required for riverine systems flowing through private lands. Restoration of the structure, functions and processes of riverine systems and the full complement of biodiversity is required. Further, bottom-up community involvement must be fostered for citizen-based planning, project implementation, monitoring, and stream inventorying. Finally, direct and indirect job and community benefits must be provided at the local level for those involved in restoration. A community-based approach is needed to stimulate these programs.

We propose that a National Watershed Registry (NWR) program be established, administered by the Environmental Protection Agency (EPA) or the USDA Soil and Water Conservation Service (SCS), that would provide financial support, incentives and technical assistance to stimulate bottom-up local participation in watershed restoration programs. The National Watershed Registry would not require the enactment of separate laws for each river included. The program could be enacted as an amendment to the Clean Water Act, or as a new legislative Act.

Administration

Nomination Process and Criteria: Inclusion in the NWR would be accomplished through a nomination process similar to the National Register of Historic Places.

103

Rather than having the EPA or SCS pick priority rivers, nominations by local governments or private citizens or interest groups, with subsequent state government approval, would be required for inclusion in the National Watershed Registry. Each river would undergo two assessment processes. Local governments would assess the degree of local support for petitions and forward them to the state for review. Each state may determine which office will review the petitions, though the agency that addresses Clean Water Act compliance would be the most logical in many cases. After the state approves the nomination, a petition would be sent to the EPA or SCS. The EPA or SCS would then assess the river on the basis of National Watershed Registry criteria and determine whether the state and a sufficient number of local governments are committed to taking reasonable action to maintain and restore the river. Qualifying rivers would then be added to the National Watershed Registry by publication in the Federal Register, an administrative process. No Act of Congress would be required.

A competitive nomination program that gives added weight to petitions that include the involvement of economically disadvantaged communities and to areas with strong local support should be used as the baseline criteria for inclusion in the National Watershed Registry. This prioritization system may help stimulate coalitions between river activities and disadvantaged or low-income communities. Non-profit fish or river advocate organizations, for example, may band together with Native American tribes or depressed farming communities to develop a proposal to restore rural rivers in a manner that may restore fisheries and create immediate employment in restoration work.

As criteria for eligible rivers, the National Watershed Registry Program could use rivers that have contiguous federal land components with restoration plans that may be under way (under the Federal Lands Watershed Management Act), state 305(b) Water Quality Reports required under the Clean Water Act, or endangered fishery inventories, for example. However, criteria would not be limited to these.

Some may argue that the EPA is not the most appropriate agency to handle such a program, favoring instead the Soil and Water Conservation Service (SCS) or the National Park Service and its Rivers and Trails Technical Assistance Program. Each agency has its advantages and disadvantages, and each would probably be a good choice to manage the National Watershed Registry program in some areas. As stated previously, however, at this point we believe the Environmental Protection Agency is the most appropriate agency, though strong consideration should be given to SCS. The EPA enforces the Clean Water Act, and the National Watershed Registry would be a natural extension of growing watershed planning programs and their community-based grants programs, including the Section 319 non-point source program. The EPA also has a somewhat broader perspective than the Park Service (which is primarily focused on wild and scenic rivers and recreational issues), and the Park Service is not universally welcome in some areas of the country (especially portions of the West). The SCS, however, has a long and successful history and is much more adept at dealing with private land owners. It may therefore be more appropriate on rural rivers.

The National Register of Historic Places represents a good model for administration of the National Watershed Registry. It is overseen at the federal level by the Advisory Council on Historic Preservation. The council reviews properties for consistency with federal designation guidelines and oversees the implementation of state programs. Further, each state has a state historic preservation officer who coordinates implementation at the state level and provides project review. Most local planning agencies have specialists on staff to coordinate the historic preservation process and review potential historic sites, districts or ensembles.

The National Watershed Registry would use a similar administrative structure. As part of designation as a river on the National Watershed Registry, minimum protection and restoration standards would be developed by the EPA. However, specific standards would be established and administered by the state program. These standards would be flexible enough to be applied to the particular system and would be implemented at the local level. The program would not apply to federal lands.

Local Watershed Councils and Watershed Restoration Action Plans: Once accepted into the National Watershed Registry, a local non-profit Watershed Council would be established, composed of key private landowners, residents, citizen organizations, concerned citizens and river advocates. Local, state and federal elected officials and agencies may participate or serve in an advisory role.

The watershed council would be responsible for developing and implementing a watershed restoration action plan, and for coordinating and aligning management policies along the river. In addition, if local communities so desired, the watershed council would be responsible for helping to identify and develop new jobs in restoration, river-oriented community revitalization options, and appropriate economic conversions that can help restore the river and sustain local economies.

The first steps would be to complete an historical reconstruction and a watershed assessment to identify the problems within the system. A series of options to address the problems would be developed, including biological risk assessments. A watershed restoration action plan would then be chosen by the watershed council. The plan would consist of the specific goals, implementation procedures and timetables to address the needs and problems identified. The plan would identify all existing local and state authorities and tools that could be used, such as voluntary agreements, land leases, trades or purchases, the adoption of county river-zoning ordinances, and others. The plan would also prescribe the specific funding resources and fiscal incentives needed for successful implementation. To ensure that federal agencies and consultants do not use up the majority of funds in planning, the contracts for this work would be distributed by the watershed council and the planners would report directly to the citizen council. State and federal agencies may help prepare or review proposed plans to ensure their scientific validity.

Inclusion in the National Watershed Registry would trigger federal and state involvement to produce a comprehensive hydroelectric and water project assessment. This may be accomplished through a system-wide environmental impact statement to assess the problems caused by all dams and water projects. Segments or entire systems to be permanently set off-limits to future projects would be identified. The water projects causing the greatest damage would be identified, and a systemwide strategy would be developed to alter the operations of the water projects. Congress would mandate that these plans meet the comprehensive plan requirements of Section 10(a) of the Federal Power Act for hydroelectric projects. This should provide incentives for many states to participate.

Planning criteria and technical and financial incentives: The National Watershed Registry would use planning criteria based on riverine-riparian ecosystem attributes (100-year floodplains, riparian ecosystems, refugia, and hot spots) rather than on any fixed corridor width. As such, it would have a narrower focus than the proposed federal-land policy. This strategy is intended to help allay fears of a huge federal "overlay" zone. Management based on physical or biological attributes is less arbitrary from an ecological perspective than a fixed corridor width, though a local community could initially establish any management parameters with which they feel comfortable. Initial inclusion would not necessarily require that an entire riverine system be nominated. Acting through the state program, the EPA could use incentives to encourage the eventual inclusion of the entire riverine system. Such a system would help encourage local efforts to proliferate and expand.

A state/federal consistency clause that requires the federal government to act in a consistent manner with respect to the restoration action plan would be included. Implementation remains locally controlled, subject to annual or tri-annual review by the EPA to determine if the goals have been met. Should the goals fail to be met, the river may fall out of the National

Watershed Registry system, and the local communities would lose all of the incentives.

Once included in the National Watershed Registry, funding and technical assistance for planning and implementation would be provided to the watershed council from the EPA, the National Park Service's Rivers and Trails Technical Assistance Program, the U.S. Soil and Water Conservation District and other federal and state programs. A strong financial incentive for individual landowner participation and support may be the adoption of a voluntary conservation goal and certification model. If landowners accepted conservation goals set by the Action Plan for their land, a memorandum of understanding and a conservation certificate would be granted. The landowner would use the certificate to obtain tax credits or to qualify for federal or state conservation grants. States may choose to nominate all rivers within their state wild and scenic river programs, thus providing stronger protection against inconsistent federal actions, more certainty regarding future hydroelectric development, and federal assistance in developing watershed restoration action plans for those rivers.

Minimum federal standards: The EPA would establish a set of minimum riverine-riparian standards to be applied to any National Watershed Registry river. A starting point may be some variation of the standards we have proposed in the Federal Lands Watershed Management Act. For example, floodplain restoration standards should include the removal or modification of outdated, unused or inappropriate levees, dikes, or channelizations so that stream flows can reconnect with the riparian and floodplain ecosystem.

Inter-Agency and Inter-Jurisdictional Communication and Policy Alignment: The watershed council would establish a procedure for policy alignment, on-going management coordination and interagency communication within the river system. The U.S. Soil Conservation Service's Coordinated Resource Management planning program may offer a public/private partnership model that could be used as a starting point.

Provisions for memoranda of understanding between city, county, state, and federal agencies would provide an administrative basis for interjurisdictional action plan development and implementation.

Local economic and community enhancement: As stated, it is important that watershed restoration be administered in a manner that stimulates and enhances local social benefits and economic opportunities.

Local citizens should be employed in the restoration work. Appropriate river-oriented community revitalization projects should be identified and initiated. Crop conversions to less water- and energy-intensive produce, and other types of economic conversions, should be a high priority. To meet these needs, we recommend that no more than 10% of the funds allocated for the program be used for administrative purposes and that at least 70% of the funds be allocated to on-the-ground projects (the remainder to planning, mapping, etc.).

The watershed council could choose from a menu of federal tax incentives and economic development grants to stimulate the local economy, consistent with the action plan. This process would be similar to that used to stimulate urban economic development, except that the incentives would be provided in a manner that allows flexibility to meet local needs.

A key responsibility of the watershed council would be to develop an assessment of the relationship of existing economic practices to riverine health. Following this, the watershed council may help local communities identify and develop new job and business options. The economic development plan can be as extensive as the community desires as long as it is consistent with and enhances the watershed restoration action-plan goals and programs.

A Case Example: the Azure River

To provide an example of how the National Watershed Registry may work, let's use the fictional Azure River. The Azure is a representative western river system 45 miles long, with a 40% public land, 50% private land, 5% Native American and 5% state and county land mix. The local Native American community is economically depressed, and many local communities, once dependent on timber and mining, are also economically distressed. The Azure is popular for fishing, boating, and hiking and once was a popular bird resting site on the Pacific Flyway. Yet the water quality and quantity, wetlands, fisheries, and scenic values are degrading, and endangered fish populations have been identified.

Concerned local citizens would try to generate sufficient support from the Native American community and a few local city councils and/or county commissions within the watershed to petition the state for inclusion of the Azure in the National Watershed Registry. The knowledge that the criteria for inclusion may favor coalitions with economically disadvantaged groups may help local fisheries and conservation groups to work closely with the Native American tribe and the depressed communities.

The state concurs that the Azure qualifies for inclusion in the National Watershed Registry, and petitions the EPA or SCS. The state may choose to seek agreement from some previously defined minimum number of local governments within the watershed before forwarding the petition. Thus, concerned citizens have to organize an educational campaign to be successful. However, they have to succeed at getting only local and state level nominations, not a new act of law, and no congressional action is required.

In addition to the potential restoration jobs and community revitalization benefits, many reasons may motivate local communities to seek inclusion in the National Watershed Registry. The financial and tax incentives may prove enticing. Local communities may desire to improve the conditions of the Azure without overbearing government control. They may fear what the potential filings of endangered species petitions for at-risk fish or riverine-riparian species might bring, or may fear that opposition to the National Watershed Registry might trigger more-intensified and elevated efforts for national wild and scenic river protection, or some other more restrictive protection mechanism. As proposed, the National Watershed Registry did not flatly prohibit dams or other federal water projects. If this were a key concern, citizens would have to pursue state or federal wild and scenic river status.

Once included in the National Watershed Registry, a watershed council is formed composed of landowners, Native Americans, interest groups, river and fish advocates and the business community. Federal land management agencies are required to participate in the advisory council to the watershed council and to amend their land management actions to be consistent with the local watershed restoration action plan, as long as it did not require less protection than would exist on federal lands. A watershed assessment of the conditions of the Azure River system is then developed along with a historical reconstruction of how the system functioned before significant human impacts. These may be completed by subcontract with a private firm after consensus by the watershed council. Funds for the assessments were provided through the technical assistance programs of state and federal agencies.

The watershed assessment leads to a determination of the system's needs and to a series of options to address the problems along with biological risk assessments for each option. Problems and potential solutions for dams and water projects are identified as well.

The watershed council then initiates a public education process. They hold a one-day watershed symposium to develop local awareness of the early history and ecological conditions of the Azure, the current role of the river in the local economy, existing problems and the potential solutions. A public decision-making process is then used to determine which option to choose and implement as the restoration action plan. This process may require six-to-twelve months (or more) as communities grapple with the hard realities of restoring the Azure.

The restoration action plan determines that the headwaters and riparian areas on federal lands are the anchors to the existing health of the fisheries and water quality and quantity. A few small, undeveloped floodplains and hot spots, including certain cold-water springs, are also found to be important on private lands. The plan identifies the creation of wetland habitat and decreased runoff from the forest and farmlands as top priorities. Further, the plan targets one old dam for potential removal and recommends that two dikes and channelizations be retired to allow for better in-stream flow for fish and wildlife. The federal land restoration program creates 50 family-wage jobs over a five-year period, primarily in heavy equipment work to retire or improve roads that are threatening the remaining healthy areas. The Watershed Council works to ensure that local workers are trained and hired for these jobs. Short-term contracts are also given to local firms to address problems caused by the dikes and channelizations.

Fencing of riparian areas and timber and grazing restrictions within riparian areas are proposed. Tax advantages and grants for fencing and training in new grazing techniques are provided to willing private land owners in return for protecting riparian areas on their land. After a contentious process, the county then establishes new development setback-zoning ordinances to protect riverine-riparian ecosystems from future home building intrusions. The watershed council and non-profit groups successfully negotiated conservation easements, and a few lands are purchased from willing landowners to convert specific floodplain areas back to floodways and wetlands. The local communities, working with state agencies, intervened in the Federal Energy Regulatory Commission relicensing process to seek amendments to the operation of the two existing dams, based on a systemwide strategy, and to seek removal of the older dam. The state includes the Azure in its comprehensive statewide hydroplan, thus providing insurance against future hydroelectric projects.

Upon realizing that direct job, community revitalization and economic benefits are possible, the watershed council petitions for inclusion as a watershed conservation and development zone. The federal government provided tax incentives and economic development grants to help stimulate community projects consistent with the restoration action plan. For example, implementing agricultural and municipal water conservation measures helps save water pumping and purification electrical and maintenance costs, reducing the flow of dollars to utilities based outside of the watershed and leaving more water in the stream for fish, wildlife and recreation. Small businesses such as specialty food products, bed and breakfasts, Native American craftspeople and other businesses are provided assistance to expand. Soon, the word spreads about the broad commitment the communities of the Azure River watershed have made to restoration, thus drawing increased public attention, new businesses, and probably increased tourism (a double-edged sword that the community will have to decide how to deal with). The community commitment also helps invigorate the local citizens, who are now proud of their efforts. The social and economic multiplying effect of these actions within local communities is significant.

Conclusions

The National Watershed Registry is certain to provide less protection than designation options, such as state or federal Wild and Scenic River designation. However, it would serve as a vital program to support, initiate and coordinate local efforts, to develop new coalitions between diverse interests, and to create new restoration technologies and jobs. Thus, the program may help nurture larger, more comprehensive efforts. It is probable that many rivers nationwide would ultimately be included and that many of the vital ecological and biological resources would receive much greater attention than at present. For the first time, local citizens concerned about their rivers would have a tool available to mobilize their community and begin conservation efforts. Avoiding the need for a separate legislative act, along with the preservation of local autonomy, may stimulate many requests for inclusion.

This strategy is certainly not the only new policy required to meet the needs of riverine-riparian ecosystems and biodiversity on private lands nationwide. However, it would fill a significant gap in existing policies and provide a much less costly and time-consuming method of conserving those river systems that local citizens deem to be important.

CHAPTER SEVEN

RECOMMENDATIONS FOR A COMPREHENSIVE SOLUTION

The National Riverine and Riparian Conservation Act

Ultimately, to fully implement the proposed federal goals and strategies, a new comprehensive federal policy called the National Riverine and Riparian Conservation Act (NRRCA) is needed to protect and restore riverine systems and biodiversity on every river mile nationwide. The strategy must combine both regulatory and non-regulatory approaches. This goal may seem unattainable at present. However, we believe that the implementation of the proposed National Watershed Registry and Federal Land Watershed Management Act will lead to a growing awareness of the national riverine crisis and to the creation of a broadening and diverse new constituency for rivers. This can eventually make the goal of comprehensive protection and restoration a reality.

The National Riverine and Riparian Conservation Act would focus on three predominant issues: riparian area and floodplain protection and restoration, system-wide policy alignment and the resolution of problems caused by dams and water projects. The NRRCA would help directly generate jobs in restoration and community revitalization projects and support appropriate economic conversions. It would apply to all riverine systems, just as the Clean Water Act applies to all waters. The Act would not require any type of congressional designation process. The federal government will provide all states with minimum standards, technical assistance and incentives for the development and administration of state National Riverine and Riparian Conservation Act programs.

Because the concept of the National Riverine and Riparian Conservation Act combines many of the components of the Federal Lands Watershed Management Act and the National Watershed

Registry, many of the specifics will not be repeated here. The key points, however, bear repeating.

Clarifying the Goal: The National Riverine and Riparian Conservation Act would establish the new national goal as stated in chapter four:

"To restore and maintain the chemical, physical, and biological integrity of the nation's waters and the natural ecological integrity of riverine-riparian ecosystems and biodiversity."

Congress would also define riverine-riparian ecosystems and biodiversity as a new public resource.

Accomplishing the Goal: To accomplish the new national goal, a new federal National Riverine and Riparian Protection program would be established that required each state to implement the following:

* Prioritize riverine systems statewide in need of treatments based on a set of standards and criteria established by the federal National Riverine and Riparian Conservation Act Program; the priority list would begin with those systems that hold a sufficient degree of ecological health to provide a reasonable chance of rapid biological and ecological improvements.

* Implement watershed restoration action plans for all riverine systems and river miles in the state, beginning with the priority riverine systems.

* Align and coordinate all levels of governmental and nongovernmental policies and management programs for each system on a watershed-wide basis.

* Identify riverine systems or segments statewide that, for biological, ecological, recreational or other reasons, should be permanently set off-limits to future

hydroelectric or water project development; in addition, states would prioritize on a watershed-level basis dams and water projects that cause the greatest impacts and that, therefore, should be considered for removal or alteration.

* Establish local jobs in restoration technologies, community revitalization projects and appropriate economic conversions for communities affected by riverine degradation and/or restoration programs.

Implementation Mechanisms

Administration: The NRRCA Program would oversee the development and implementation of state programs, help align and coordinate the many federal policies and programs addressing riverine resources, and supervise federal grants to state programs. The federal program would also be responsible for evaluating state programs and would have the authority to withhold federal funds if states fail to meet the national program standards. Strong federal leadership is required to oversee 50 separate National Riverine and Riparian Conservation Act programs consistently. As with the National Watershed Registry, at this time we believe the program should be operated under the auspices of the EPA in a process similar to the Clean Water Act. However, should the EPA fail to become a department with cabinet-level status, to be empowered with clear policy-making authority or to improve its overall operations, thought must be given to empowering the Department of the Interior, or to establishing a new federal Biological Restoration Department.

Statewide assessments and prioritization: As a first step, states would be required to assess and prioritize all riverine systems statewide within five years of the enactment of the Act, using full watershed-level assessments. Using biological monitoring and the assessment of biological endpoints, the watershed assessments would provide a critique of the conditions and trends of the riverine-riparian ecosystem and native biodiversity. Thus, the assessment would identify both at-risk and healthy systems and riverine-riparian biodiversity. From these assessments a priority list of riverine systems that may respond most effectively and rapidly to restoration treatments would be established.

The most degraded streams with little or no remaining native biodiversity or healthy habitat would be at the lower end of the list, and systems that hold potential for broader and quicker responses to restoration would be at the top of the list.

Rivers high on the priority list and already included in the National Watershed Registry would be given sufficient time to implement effective restoration plans before the more regulatory approach is applied. This prioritization approach may help stimulate interest in including other riverine systems in the National Watershed Registry program to avoid direct National Riverine and Riparian Conservation Act regulatory impacts. Initially, then, the National Riverine and Riparian Conservation Act would target those priority riverine systems not included in the National Watershed Registry.

As previously stated, there are problems with initially prioritizing the areas with the best chances for rapid biotic recovery. Again, the goal is to distribute and target resources so that further degradation to the remaining healthier areas, which serve as anchors to species and ecosystem health, is prevented. Protecting and expanding these areas will often greatly assist in the restoration of the more degraded areas.

Comprehensive hydroelectric plans: Based on those assessments, the segments, tributaries, or entire riverine systems that should be withdrawn from consideration from future hydroelectric or water project development would also be identified. The state program office would compile statewide findings and establish the state "protected rivers" program and a comprehensive statewide hydroelectric plan.

Watershed councils and watershed restoration action plans: Each state would develop and oversee the implementation of Watershed Restoration Action Plans for priority riverine systems. To accomplish this, each state may establish watershed restoration commissions to establish clear statewide definitions, standards and procedures consistent with federal National Riverine and Riparian Conservation Act standards. Where sufficient local interest exists, the state would establish local watershed councils composed of all key interest groups, including river advocates, non-profit organizations, major landowners and others concerned with the priority systems. The watershed councils would be responsible for developing, implementing, and monitoring the watershed restoration action plan.

A system-wide Environmental Impact Statement would be completed by the state, with federal agency assistance, to display options to address the problems caused by the prioritized dams and water projects. The Environmental Impact Statement would fully display all options for addressing the problems, from a "non-action" alternative to alternatives that recommend total removal of projects. Complete ecological and economic assessments for each alternative would be completed, to fully account for and identify external and subsidized costs of the existing project.

The preferred alternative would become a key component of the watershed restoration action plan. The action plan may, therefore, slate the highest priority dams and water projects for decommission or removal and others for major adjustments to suit the objectives of the action plans. The state would decree the watershed restoration action plan to meet Section 10(a) Federal Power Act system-wide comprehensive plan requirements and would be empowered to deny 401 Clean Water Act permits for hydroelectric projects on these systems.

The restoration action plan would use the Rapid Biotic and Ecosystem Response restoration strategy. Specific restoration treatments would be aimed at reconnecting the flowing water system with the riparian area and floodplain, at retiring dikes, channelizations, and levees, and at reestablishing native riparian vegetation. All of the work would be completed within the context of a full watershed-level strategy.

Minimum federal standards: Federal standards would establish a baseline for the maintenance of all forms of riverine-riparian biodiversity, thus moving beyond the limited focus of maintaining habitat just for endangered species.

The standards proposed in the Federal Lands Watershed Management Act are a starting point for determining these NRRCA standards. Riverine-riparian ecosystems are so degraded on private lands nationwide that the primary emphasis will need to be placed on restoring some percentage of riparian health by a specific date. We suggest that a good target would be to restore 50% of native riparian vegetation on each priority system statewide within 10 years. While the National Watershed Registry may primarily rely on incentives to encourage citizen actions, the NRRCA would combine a regulatory and non-regulatory approach by utilizing fines and other definitive mechanisms to ensure effective and timely implementation. For example, citizen suit provisions should be extended to violations which include authorization for civil penalties. In addition, federal farm business and other development subsidies should be eliminated should be eliminated on priority riverine systems until and unless state and local governments and citizens implement a recovery strategy.

Planning, technical and financial incentives: Once a watershed council is established on a priority riverine system, the Environmental Protection Agency and many other federal, state, and local sources for funding and technical assistance would be provided to help develop and implement a restoration action plan.

To ensure federal consistency, federal agencies would be subject to a federal consistency doctrine requiring all their actions to be consistent with state program goals and with each riverine restoration action plan.

The program would provide Riverine Resource Recovery Grants to be used for the protection or restoration of specific riverine and riparian areas that are designated as critical because of their biological or ecological values. To foster local landowner participation, a cost-sharing federal riverine restoration trust fund would be developed. This program would encourage local landowners to implement projects designed to protect and restore riverine-riparian ecosystems on their properties.

The National Rivers Data Bank and the "State of the Nation's Rivers Report"

The National Riverine and Riparian Conservation Act would establish the river data base report described in chapter four. This component could and should be established in some form in the immediate future. Inclusion in the National Riverine and Riparian Conservation Act is proposed in case the program has failed to materialize prior to the enactment of the Act.

Riverine data acquired through watershed assessments would be integrated into state and then the national rivers data base. The watershed assessment process should provide baseline information on the historical and existing conditions of riverine-riparian ecosystems and biodiversity. A complete historical reconstruction should be developed to provide an accurate template for restoration, along with benchmarks to evaluate success in reaching action plan goals over time. Definitions and data collection criteria and processes would be standardized by the federal National Riverine and Riparian Conservation Act program. A report on the status and trends of the nation's riverine-riparian ecosystems and biodiversity would then be produced based on this information every five years.

Watershed Biodiversity Management Areas and Benchmark Watersheds

The National Riverine and Riparian Conservation Act would establish a nationwide system of Watershed Biodiversity Management Areas and Benchmark Watersheds on private lands nationwide. The program would identify and establish mechanisms to protect these areas. Protection can be accomplished through land trades and acquisitions, acquisition of conservation easements, or voluntary Memoranda Of Understanding. The sites would be identified through the system and statewide watershed assessments. (Watershed Biodiversity Management Areas and Benchmark Watersheds would be established on federal lands through the Federal Lands Watershed Management Act.)

A National Moratorium on New Hydroelectric Project Construction and the National "Protected Rivers Area" Program

A nationwide moratorium on new hydroelectric licensing would be established. The moratorium would remain in effect on a state-by-state basis until each state had determined which river segments or systems are to be permanently set off-limits to future hydroelectric and water projects. Once a state protected-area program is established, submitted and accepted by the Federal Energy Regulatory Commission as the Statewide Comprehensive Plan under Section 10(a) of the Federal Power Act, the moratorium may be lifted within the state.

Inter-agency and Inter-jurisdictional Policy Alignment

The NRRCA program would require federal and state agencies to align their policies within watersheds. The state Watershed Restoration Commissions would facilitate the alignment of state and local policies within watersheds.

A key task of the watershed council would be to aggregate and then align all policies and existing management programs and plans within the local watershed. Federal agencies would already have aligned their policies on federal lands under the Federal Lands Watershed Management Act. State, local and private land policies would then also be specifically amended and aligned. An on-going communication and conflict resolution process would be established to ensure that future management decisions are consistent with the restoration action plan. The state and federal National Riverine and Riparian Conservation Program would review the action plan to ensure that alignment and coordination mechanisms are effective.

Local Economic Development and Community Enhancement

In a process similar to that used in the National Watershed Registry, the watershed council could request that its river be designated a Watershed Conservation and Development Zone. Tax incentives and economic development grants would then be provided to stimulate the local economy. Such incentives should be provided only if they are consistent with the restoration action plan. This process would be somewhat similar to that used to stimulate urban economic development, though again greater flexibility would be built in.

A key responsibility of the watershed council would, therefore, be to help local communities identify and develop new community revitalization options. The community and economic development efforts can be as extensive as the community desires, as long as they are consistent with restoration action plan goals and programs.

Conclusions

The National Riverine and Riparian Conservation Act is certain to be viewed as immensely complicated and controversial, even unattainable. Some may argue that amending the Clean Water Act to more effectively address non-point pollution will address these issues sufficiently. Improvements in the Clean Water Act will certainly be a great help. However, much more is needed. The identification, protection and restoration of headwaters, biotic refuges, benchmark watersheds, riparian areas, floodplains and biological hot spots systemwide are required. The maintenance and recovery of riverine-riparian biodiversity, along with interagency and inter-jurisdictional policy alignment, and dam and water project restoration are also needed, yet these are issues that the Clean Water Act will probably never address.

Many will argue that the National Riverine and Riparian Conservation Act is a new form of national land-use planning and that the riparian protection requirements will constitute a form of "takings." This is not the case. Basin-wide land-use plans are not needed, or even desirable, to protect and restore the more narrowly defined critical riverine-riparian ecosystems and biodiversity within private land riverine systems. The Clean Air Act, Clean Water Act, and wetlands policies were also once considered "pie in the sky," yet they eventually became law. The economic, social and ecological losses to the nation as a result of riverine degradation have already been significant. We cannot allow this trend to continue. As a nation we must take the steps necessary to stem future losses and to restore these critical systems. We must initiate a new age of community- and ecosystem-based watershed restoration nationwide.

CHAPTER EIGHT

CONCLUDING THOUGHTS ON ENTERING THE WATERSHED

This book contains recommendations that we hope will help initiate comprehensive protection and restoration of America's riverine systems and biodiversity. We realize they are certain to be controversial; some will view them as unattainable. Indeed, implementing these policies will require a significant change in our assumptions and an expansion of our thinking about riverine systems and biodiversity. To help with this process we close by summarizing some of the key issues that we believe the nation must address to successfully initiate a new age of community- and ecosystem-based watershed restoration.

First, we must fully acknowledge the severely degraded state of riverine systems and biodiversity nationwide and make a national commitment to change this: Almost 50% of America's streams do not meet water quality standards once biological criteria are considered, and multitudes of fish populations and other riverine species are already extinct or at risk of extinction. Less than 2% of America's river miles remain of sufficient quality to even qualify for national wild and scenic river protection. This means that few or no effective policies exist to protect the remaining 98% of America's river miles and the untold numbers of riverine-riparian species that have been lost. No truly effective restoration policies exist at any level of government. The general public and the majority of elected officials do not yet realize the severity of the problems or the bankruptcy of existing approaches and policies. The nation cannot begin to change policies and practices until we fully acknowledge the seriousness of these problems.

Riverine systems must no longer be defined as renewable energy and water resources: Given the severely degraded conditions nationwide, it is clear that society's use of riverine systems for energy and water production has not been sustainable. Most people, however, continue to think that rivers can serve these functions indefinitely. Unlike wind or solar resources, riverine systems cannot help produce energy without significant adverse biological impacts. Rivers may provide a long-term source to power turbines, but the ecosystems that produce the water and support the biological processes and species within the system are destroyed in the process. The nation's rivers are already over-dammed, vastly over-appropriated and their ecosystems dangerously simplified. Widespread ecosystem and biodiversity breakdowns have resulted. We long ago exceeded the renewable use capability of the nation's riverine systems.

Larger numbers of riverine systems must be addressed simultaneously and comprehensively: One of the primary reasons why riverine degradation far outpaces protection is that the most effective existing protection mechanisms require separate legislative acts for each river or group of rivers protected. Even then they generally address only isolated stream segments. This approach will simply never meet the needs of the nation's riverine systems and biodiversity. Policies that stimulate comprehensive protection and restoration without new laws for each river mile are essential because of the sheer number of riverine systems and species at risk nationwide.

Current assumptions, strategies, management practices and policies must be redesigned from the stream segment and single species focus to the watershed (landscape), ecosystem and biodiversity perspective: Maintenance and recovery of riverine systems and biodiversity cannot be accomplished by focusing on discrete river segments or individual species. By definition, this approach fails to address the way riverine systems and biodiversity are composed and function. America's critical riverine problems cannot be solved with just a wild and scenic river here, or a stream restoration project there (though these strategies may become more effective when applied within the context of larger watershed-level restoration strategies). The temporal and spatial scale of riverine protection and restoration efforts have been too narrow to be successful. Unless they are linked with protection of headwaters, biotic refuges, Benchmark Watersheds, riparian areas, floodplains and other critical biological hotspots within the entire riverine landscape, isolated protected segments or restoration sites are physically and biologically vulnerable.

Some would argue that we lack sufficient knowledge about the way watersheds work to implement ecosystem-based strategies. We suggest that even if no further research were done, we currently have the knowledge and skills necessary to do a vastly improved job of conserving riverine resources at those levels. What stands in the way are, primarily, organizational and bureaucratic turf issues, inertia and lack of political will. We must acknowledge that science will never know all there is to know. Science is a process, not an end point. Rather than allowing the unknown to paralyze us as more systems and species disappear, we must apply the best of what we know today -- while, at the same time, providing wide enough management "sideboards" to allow for change and for what we don't yet know. This means we must not plan for riverine systems to operate near the limits of their capacity.

Local investment in river conservation must be encouraged: Without the active involvement of local communities and citizens, efforts to maintain and restore riverine ecosystems and biodiversity will ultimately prove ineffective. Incentives must be provided to foster local participation, and disincentives must be removed. To gain local support, riverine conservation must move beyond the focus on purely wild rivers and encourage the development of local jobs in restoration technologies, community revitalization projects and appropriate economic conversions that lead to the sustainable use of riverine systems. At the same time we must fully protect the remaining few wild river areas and the best scenic and recreational areas. Riverine restoration costs landowners and local governments money. Financial incentives are crucial in gaining local landowner and government support. Ideally, river restoration should compare favorably with road maintenance or parks development in local economies. Opportunity costs from capital investments or revenues foregone from the loss of other development need to be balanced. This presents a particularly important challenge to the river conservation movement, a challenge that takes us well beyond the stream channel.

Stable, long-term funding must be provided: For comprehensive riverine recovery and sustainable economic development efforts to prove successful, stable sources of long-term funding are required. Federal agencies will need long-term budget incentives to stimulate cooperation and to allocate top-level staff and resources. Restoration action plans will require funds for planning, implementation and long-term monitoring. A multitude of existing funding sources may be used as part of the overall short-term funding package. As concern about the federal budget deficit grows, however, it seems increasingly important to establish a separate, free-standing, long-term riverine restoration funding source. The National Research Council recommended that Congress establish a National Aquatic Ecosystem Restoration Trust Fund. We believe this is the most appropriate long-term solution. The fund would be a separate budget account created by Congress and would be treated during the budgeting process in the same way as other trust funds.

Accounting procedures must be expanded: Riverine degradation is generally a function of flawed economic policies. Most damaging development fails to take the long-term external environmental costs into account, or the impacts on direct or indirect riverine-dependent jobs and long-term economic benefits. Analyses that take these factors into account often reveal abundant red ink. Our nation sinks billions of dollars into highly degrading (usually pork-barrel) projects that create short-term jobs in one sector but that ultimately eliminate long-term jobs and economic benefits elsewhere and for future generations. Riverine development accounting procedures must be expanded so that project costs are identified up front and calculated as part of the cost of projects, not incurred by distant communities or future generations.

Sustainability and restoration must be clearly defined: The National Science Board estimates that as many as half of all living species may disappear in the next few decades, and aquatic species are disappearing at a faster rate than terrestrial species. If accurate, time is of the essence in securing sustainable levels of riverine-riparian biodiversity. Yet, establishing those levels of success is difficult. We know that future generations will need ample supplies of timber, clean water and topsoil. We also know that these resources are the product of the biological "surplus" that healthy, sustainable ecosystems provide. But we don't know the numbers of biological species or the levels of ecosystem integrity that will be required to sustain ecosystems or human life. Is preservation of one fish species sufficient, or must all fish populations with genetic variations be preserved? Is it enough to preserve populations in one river system while allowing populations to go extinct elsewhere? Is ecosystem sustainability defined by the "products" that can be produced over time, or does the definition extend to the ecosystem that is resistant to stress and maintains its elements and processes over time? We often hear the angry questions raised about what is to be conserved, how much, and for whom.

It is certainly ecologically insufficient to preserve a single species or even just one population of a species. We propose that the most critical measure of sustainability is whether a riverine ecosystem is free of "distress symptoms" and can self-repair after disturbances. One key indicator of this is whether native riverine-riparian biodiversity survive in large natural landscapes throughout their historic range. This means that we must maintain native riverine biodiversity at the ecosystem, species and genetic levels. We also propose that questions of the levels of "natural ecological capital" required to accomplish this goal cannot be answered. Therefore, we assume that because we do not know, we must protect the remaining fragments of healthy riverine habitat and ecosystems and all populations of biodiversity across their historic range to hedge our bets for the future. Many riverine-riparian species are already at the brink of range-wide or regional extinctions. It is morally, economically and ecologically untenable to allow the nation's surviving riverine systems and biodiversity to further degrade or go extinct on our watch.

A commitment to prevention rather than repair or control is required: If we have learned anything in the management of riverine systems it is that early steps to prevent problems are much cheaper and clearly more effective than those aimed at repairing or controlling the problems once they occur. Efforts to prevent problems can be achieved most often through slight adjustments in the overall scheme of things, whereas efforts to control existing problems often cost many times the price of prevention and are much less, if at all, effective. Many, if not most impacts on riverine systems and biodiversity are, in fact, irreversible because of the cascading effects through the riverine food chain.

Much scientific research and many management practices and policies have aimed primarily at determining the amount of stress and disturbance a riverine system can withstand before collapse. Little research and few policies have focused on determining strategies to prevent disturbance and maintain and restore ecosystem health. This pattern must be reversed. Strategies to prevent disturbances and restore ecosystems must become a high-priority research and management focus and a top national political priority.

Finally, and most important, we must rapidly implement the comprehensive protective measures and the separate but connected set of recovery actions described in this book: The remaining relatively healthy headwaters, biotic refuges, Benchmark Watersheds, riparian areas, floodplains and biological hot spots found throughout river systems provide the ecological capital and genetic seed stock required for restoring systems and biodiversity for future generations. The identification and protection of these areas is the pivotal first step and the fundamental building block for all subsequent restoration efforts. Restoration efforts that precede such protection will always be threatened by degradation elsewhere and will hence be rendered ineffective. This critical point is most often ignored. Even the recent National Research Council report on restoration of aquatic ecosystems ignored this fundamental point.

Protection for these areas alone is insufficient to reach the long-term goal of recovery for America's riverine systems and biodiversity. Long-term restoration strategies must be rapidly implemented. These strategies must focus initially on securing, expanding and linking the relatively healthy areas whenever possible rather than on initially restoring the most degraded areas. Although protection alone is not sufficient, it is absolutely necessary if we are to hold any hope of implementing or reaching longer-term restoration goals.

We believe that restoring America's riverine systems and biodiversity is an investment, not a make-work program. It is an investment in the natural infrastructure that supports our human-built infrastructure, our lives and the lives of the species and systems on which we depend. The goal is to yield future ecological, social and economic benefits that warrant incurring costs now; setting out to accomplish this goal provides the added benefit of generating restoration jobs and economic benefits now.

To initiate a new era of comprehensive riverine restoration in America will require acknowledging that significant trade-offs must be made between what is typically considered short-term economic growth and long-term ecological sustainability. Our democratic system is best set up to address narrow time frames, while ecological sustainability must be considered over much longer periods. This reality will force us to make tough choices.

It is in our self-interest to protect and restore America's riverine systems and biodiversity. It is also our moral obligation. The stakes are high. Let us hope that our nation can muster the courage to meet the challenge.

APPENDIXES

THE FAILURE OF EXISTING
RIVERINE PROTECTION AND RESTORATION
POLICIES AND PROGRAMS

by

Mary Scurlock
Debbie Gilcrest
Bob Doppelt

APPENDIX A

RIVERINE MANAGEMENT ON FEDERAL LANDS UNDER EXISTING RESOURCE PROTECTION AND MANAGEMENT STATUTES

If we are to preserve and restore the vast majority of America's riverine systems and biodiversity we must begin with and demonstrate leadership on the federal lands, where a significant number of the nation's riverine systems begin. This is especially true in the West. Federal stewardship permits immediate and comprehensive protection for these critical systems.

This section assesses the strengths and weaknesses of the statutes which currently affect the ecological integrity of federally managed riverine systems and biodiversity. Statutes protecting specific resources include the Wild and Scenic Rivers Act, which targets a few, selected "free-flowing rivers"; the Clean Water Act, which protects the "Nation's waters"; and the Endangered Species Act, which attempts to protect "the ecosystems upon which endangered species and threatened species depend." Federal regulation of water resources developments and mineral resources are also discussed. The last two parts of the section briefly analyze the nexus between state and federal water law and the special case of regional watershed management under the Northwest Power Act.

OVERVIEW OF FEDERAL LANDS

Approximately 30% of the United States' land base of 2.3 billion acres is administered by federal civil and defense agencies.[86] About 91% of this land, 627 million acres, is managed by four agencies: the Department of Agriculture's Forest Service (U.S.F.S.), and the Department of Interior's Bureau of Land Management (B.L.M.), Fish and Wildlife Service (F.W.S.), and

National Park Service (N.P.S.). The Forest Service manages 28%; the Bureau of Land Management manages 39%; the Fish and Wildlife Service manages 13%; and the National Park Service manages 11%. The Department of Defense administers most of the remaining 9% of federal lands.[87]

As a result of early treaties and land settlement laws, most of the federal lands are located in the western United States: approximately one-half of the federally administered land is located in Alaska and more than 90% of the remaining federal lands are located in the eleven western states. Alaska and Nevada have the most federal land (81% and 79% respectively), while Connecticut and Iowa have the least (.4% each).[88]

It is estimated that over 60% of the average annual water yield in the eleven western states flows from federal lands[89] and about 96% of the population of the eleven western states is dependent upon water from these lands.[90] Of the western federal lands, the National Forest and National Park lands are most often located at higher elevations and have the greatest water yields: About 88% of the water from federal lands is produced from forest lands, and about 9% from park lands.[91] In general, the BLM lands are more arid than those of the other federal agencies: The BLM lands produce only about 3% of the water yield from public lands. Together, the lands under the administration of the USFS, the NPS and the BLM produce an estimated 99.4% of the water yield from federal lands in the western states.[92]

THE NATIONAL WILD AND SCENIC RIVERS ACT OF 1968

The National Wild and Scenic Rivers Act (WSRA)[93] was passed in 1968 to protect the "free-flowing condition" of "certain selected, outstandingly remarkable" rivers, and "to protect the water quality of such rivers." To date, the Wild and Scenic program has designated 151 river segments, comprising 10,378.85 miles of river in 33 states.[94]

The Wild and Scenic Act has been somewhat effective in protecting certain values on segments of designated rivers on federal lands. It is a very important tool in protecting key scenic and recreational river segments from viewshed damage and other development. Despite the fact that the Act is now almost 25 years old, this program is just now coming into its own. The Oregon Omnibus Wild and Scenic Rivers Act of 1988 provided a new model for simultaneous, multiple-river designations which is being emulated by other states. Consequently, the Act should protect more and more river segments over time. With some amendments to the existing Act or to its administrative implementation, the WSRA could prove even more effective.

However, as will be discussed, the Wild and Scenic River program is of limited value to comprehensively protect or restore riverine systems and biodiversity nationwide. Its primary strength is its ability to protect outstanding recreational and scenic segments and corridors on federal lands.

Purposes of the Act: The National Wild and Scenic Rivers Act creates a system for designation and preservation of free-flowing rivers through private, state or federal land. Under the Act, federal land management agencies must manage designated rivers within their jurisdiction for the primary purpose of preservation.[95] Through the WSRA, Congress declares it to be:

> the policy of the United States that certain rivers of the Nation which, with their immediate environments, possess outstandingly remarkable scenic, recreational, geologic, fish and wildlife, historic, cultural, or other similar values, shall be preserved in free-flowing condition, and that they and their immediate environments shall be protected for the benefit and enjoyment of present and future generations. [96]

The overall objective of the Act is to complement the "established national policy of dam and other construction at appropriate sections of the rivers of the United States" with "a policy that would preserve other selected rivers or sections thereof in their free-flowing condition to protect the water quality of such rivers and to fulfill other vital national conservation purposes."[97] Various provisions of the Act combine to set forth the following values as purposes of the Wild and Scenic system: maintenance of scenic views and aesthetic values; protection of fish and wildlife, preservation of geologic, historic and cultural assets; promotion of recreational uses, such as fishing and whitewater rafting; protection of water quality; preservation of the free-flowing character of the rivers for the benefit of present and future generations.[98]

The Act expressly recognizes that an adequate supply of water is necessary to accomplish the purpose of preserving the free-flowing condition of designated rivers, thereby establishing a federal water right for federal lands containing designated river segments.[99] The Act also appears to preempt state water law to the extent that state water law conflicts with the stated purposes of a designated river.[100]

Designation, classification of system components, corridor boundaries and management areas: Designation generally occurs in one of three ways.[101] First, Congress may enact legislation which deems a river worthy of study for possible WSRA protection. During the Congressional study period, when a study of the subject area is prepared by either the National Park Service or other federal agency,[102] the area is subject to a moratorium on water resources development projects. After receiving the study report, the President submits a recommendation to Congress, which may then decide whether to protect the river section.

Second, Congress may designate a river segment through legislation without an official study. Federal agencies such as the BLM or the Forest Service identify rivers eligible for inclusion in the system through federal land-planning processes and complete "suitability" studies, and then they make recommendations to Congress.

The third and least utilized designation procedure provides for inclusion through state initiative with the Interior Department's concurrence.[103] This method requires states to identify and develop conservation plans for qualified rivers before requesting that the Secretary of the Interior designate the rivers.

Regardless of which designation process is followed, to be eligible for protection a stream must be "free-flowing"[104] and the "related adjacent land area" must possess at least one "outstandingly remarkable scenic, recreational, geologic, fish and wildlife, historic, cultural, or other similar value."[105] Designated rivers are classified according to the Act's criteria for three "classifications":

> * "Wild river areas" are those "rivers or sections of
> rivers that are free of impoundments and
> generally inaccessible except by trail, with
> watersheds and shorelines essentially primitive
> and waters unpolluted."[106]

> * "Scenic river areas" comprise a less restrictive
> classification, which includes rivers or river
> segments that "are free of impoundments, with
> shorelines or watersheds still largely primitive
> and shorelines largely undeveloped, but accessible
> in places by roads."[107]

> * "Recreational river areas" are the least restrictive
> category and include "those rivers or sections of
> rivers that are readily accessible by road or
> railroad, that may have some development along
> their shorelines, and that may have undergone
> some impoundment or diversion in the past."[108]

Although permitted by the definition, the Act clearly does not require, nor speak to, the designation of an entire watershed or river system, though it does permit it. The term "river" is defined broadly as any "flowing body of water or estuary or a section, portion, or tributary thereof, including rivers, streams, creeks, runs, kills, rills, and small lakes" and encompasses

headwater reaches.[109] Ephemeral (intermittent) streams, critical
to watershed functions, are not specifically included, although
there has been one instance in which an ephemeral stream has
been recommended for inclusion in the Wild and Scenic
system.[110] In practice, Congress generally designates mainstem
river segments.

Theoretically, there is a one-quarter mile "interim" boundary
set during the study phase of the designation process, which
should result in a recommended boundary that is determined on
the basis of the needs of identified river-related resources.
However, in practice, many final boundaries approximate the
quarter-mile interim boundary, regardless of whether this
boundary reflects the ecologically critical riparian area.
Furthermore, although corridors may be wider than a quarter-mile
in places, the Act places a strict upper limit on the land area which
may be included as part of the management area for a
congressionally designated river: The average acreage per river
mile may not exceed 320 acres.[111] State-designated segment
boundaries may not be so limited.[112]

The protected values of a designated river corridor may be
determined either by Congress in a designating statute and
legislative history, or by a federal agency-management plan.
Managing agencies are required to cooperate with other agencies
in managing designated rivers. This duty requires more than mere
consultation, and conflicting agency positions must be
resolved.[113]

Specific management directives and agency discretion:
Designated segments flowing through federal lands are primarily
administered by the federal agency already having jurisdiction
over the area.[114] The Act generally requires that designated
rivers be administered to emphasize the protection of "aesthetic,
scenic, historic, archaeologic, and scientific features,"[115] and these
values are reflected in the management plans which each
administering agency is required to promulgate.[116] Wherever
other conservation statutes apply -- such as governing wilderness

areas, parks and refuges -- the "more restrictive" provisions dominate.[117]

The Act grants broad authority to each federal agency with jurisdiction over land that contains or adjoins a component river, ordering that they "shall take such action respecting management policies, regulations, contracts, plans, affecting such land . . . as may be necessary to protect such rivers in accordance with the purposes of [the Act]."[118] The most specific directive to federal agencies requires that "particular attention shall be given to scheduled timber harvesting, road construction and similar activities which might be contrary to the purposes of this chapter."[119] It is left to the managing agency to decide what constitutes "particular attention" to these activities. The agencies are generally permitted to take any actions reasonably consistent with the requirement that the identified values of river segments be "protected and enhanced."

Although much is left to the discretion of federal managers, the language of the Act provides the following management prohibitions:

> * "The Federal Energy Regulatory Commission
> [FERC] shall not license the construction of any
> dam, water conduit, reservoir, powerhouse,
> transmission line, or other project works . . . on or
> directly affecting any river which is designated . .
> . as a component of the national wild and scenic
> rivers system."[120] This is an absolute prohibition
> against licensing "on or affecting" a component
> river. It is irrelevant whether a project does not
> demonstrably affect the particular values for
> which the river was included in the system.[121]
>
> * "[N]o department or agency of the United States
> shall assist by loan, grant, license or otherwise in
> the construction of any water resources project

that would have a direct and adverse effect on the values for which such river was established."[122]

* Mineral development under unperfected mining claims is subject to the regulation by the applicable government department and those restrictions of the WSRA which withdraw all minerals located in and along the banks of designated rivers on federal lands. Claims perfected prior to designation of a river segment are subject only to existing mineral leasing and mining laws. However, land within one-quarter mile of each bank of "wild" rivers is specifically withdrawn from the operation of mining and mineral leasing laws.[123]

Aside from these three directives, decisions about particular uses of a component river segment on federal land remain largely within the discretion of the relevant federal agency. Following established principles of administrative law, courts will give "considerable weight" to that department's construction of the statutory scheme it has been entrusted to administer.[124] Courts will uphold an action if the challenged decision "represents a reasonable accommodation of conflicting policies that were committed to the agency's care by the statute . . . unless it appears from the statute or its legislative history that the accommodation is not one that Congress would have sanctioned."[125]

To some degree, inclusion in the Wild and Scenic River System has the potential to affect federal activities outside the river corridor which could adversely impact the outstanding values of a designated segment. The Act explicitly instructs federal agencies with jurisdiction over adjacent lands to take all actions necessary to protect designated rivers in accordance with the Act's purposes. These provisions seem to imply that any activity which harms the outstanding values which lead a river to be designated may be prohibited by the managing agency.[126]

This duty to protect designated river segments has been held to impose a "continuing obligation" on federal agencies to protect both water quantity and water quality.[127] Moreover, in *Wilderness Society v. Tyrrel*, the first case to challenge Forest Service management practices under the WSRA, the court enjoined a federal salvage timber sale beyond a corridor boundary because it found the sale would harm water quality within the designated area.[128] The court further found that the Act's requirement that managing agencies consult with the Environmental Protection Agency ("EPA") and state water pollution control authorities[129] means that managing agencies must comply with EPA and state recommendations on proposed activities affecting water quality on designated rivers.[130]

It is still unclear whether other courts will adopt or uphold the *Tyrrel* court's holdings. To date, the potential water-quality-protection authority demonstrated by *Tyrrel* has not been realized. In addition, the extent to which the WSRA provides authority to limit activities on private lands has not been judicially tested. The term "enhanced" has meant different things to the federal agencies involved. Some interpret it to mean developing the recreational opportunities within a Wild and Scenic River without great regard for ecological impacts. Therefore, because the statute's management guidelines are so general, special provisions designating a specific river segment remain the best means of controlling land management practices.[131]

In sum, the managing federal agencies have a great deal of discretion to decide how to "protect and enhance" the values of a particular river segment and to decide when a particular use does "not substantially interfere with the public use and enjoyment of these values."[132] No agency action could be successfully challenged in court under the WSRA unless the agency's judgement were shown to be clearly inconsistent with congressional intent.[133]

Joint departments of interior and agriculture guidelines and internal agency policies: In 1982 the Departments of Interior and Agriculture promulgated guidelines to assist them in managing river corridors. These guidelines include the following interpretations of the Act:

> * The guidelines state that the Act's command to "protect and enhance" and give "primary emphasis" to the protection of "aesthetic, scenic, historic, archaeologic, and scientific features" is "interpreted as stating a nondegradation and enhancement policy for all designated river areas, regardless of classification. Each component will be managed to protect and enhance the values for which the river was designated, while providing for public recreation and resource uses which do not adversely impact or degrade those values. Specific management strategies will vary according to classification but will always be designed to protect and enhance the values of the river area."[134]

> * "Agricultural and forestry practices should be similar in nature to those present in the area at the time of designation. Generally, uses more intensive than grazing and hay production are incompatible with wild river classification. Rowcrop production and timber harvest may be practiced in recreational and scenic river areas. Recreational river areas may contain an even larger range of agricultural and forestry uses. Timber harvest in any river area will be conducted so as to avoid adverse impacts on the river area values."[135]

The guidelines do not add significantly to the broad language of the statute, although they explicitly limit the purposes and goals of management plans. Notably, the Act's "protect and enhance" mandate is interpreted as stating a "nondegradation and enhancement policy," while providing for uses which "do not adversely impact or degrade" the values for which a river was designated. No standards for determining adverse impacts or degradation to river values are stated.

The agricultural and forestry practices guideline merely states that "more intensive" uses than grazing and hay production are "generally" (but not de facto) incompatible with wild river classification, leaving it up to the agencies to decide when these activities are appropriate and under what conditions. Criteria are not identified for determining whether an activity causes "adverse impacts" on river area values.

Significantly, the statute and its implementing guidelines indicate that the values intended to be protected by river management plans are limited to those values deemed outstanding during the designation process. It is important to note that these values do not necessarily include the full range of ecological values and processes inherent in riverine-riparian ecosystems and biodiversity.

In addition to the joint guidelines, the Forest Service has adopted internal policies, as has the Bureau of Land Management.[136] To their credit, the Forest Service policies prohibit tree harvest in wild river corridors except where required to clear trails, protect hikers or control fire. However, the same policies permit cattle grazing, despite what appears to be a clear conflict between grazing and the specified values of a "wild" river. With reference to this inconsistency, one critic notes that the managing agencies have kindled a conflict by using the same guidelines to determine the suitability of a river and what to permit in it after it is designated. The conflict arises when a river has an existing structure or use that is incompatible with the characteristics of protected rivers but does not disqualify the river from inclusion in the system. Thus, management of the river in accordance with the Act may require removal of an existing structure or discontinuance of an existing use although designation was permitted despite the incompatibility.[137]

In practice, federal agencies have permitted activities within river corridors which are inconsistent with the protection and enhancement of the values for which the river was included in the system. For example, on the Grande Ronde and John Day "wild" rivers in Oregon, grazing is permitted to continue in riparian areas.

The result has been the destruction of riparian vegetation, the degradation of fish habitat, water pollution and the widening of stream channels.[138]

Federal water rights expressly reserved: Consistent with its goal of maintaining rivers in free-flowing condition, the WSRA expressly claims unappropriated water in amounts and flow levels necessary to fulfill the purposes of the Act:

> Designation of any stream or portion thereof as a national wild, scenic or recreational river area shall not be construed as a reservation of the waters of such streams for purposes other than those specified in this [Act], or in quantities greater than necessary to accomplish these purposes.[139]

This provision establishes a water right which may be quantified under state law and asserted directly against other public or private water users. However, this water right cannot be used to limit land use activities unless they directly interfere with the full exercise of the federal governments's right established under the Act. Although water rights are established under the Act, however, there is no clear requirement that a federal land manager take any particular action to establish or enforce these rights. Hence, in reality, whatever authority really exists to establish sufficient instream flows is rarely used or enforced.[140]

Federal agencies are only now beginning to quantify the amounts of water reserved under the Act, and there are only a few claims which have been successfully quantified and asserted.[141]

Pre-existing private rights protected: Like most other statutes constraining the use of federal land for environmental reasons, the WSRA protects private rights which flow from a federal license or contract predating the Act. Nothing in the Act may "abrogate any existing rights, privileges or contracts affecting Federal lands held by any private party without consent."[142] Thus, only those pre-existing uses not conducted under federal license or contract may be prohibited on the grounds that they substantially interfere with river corridor values.

The Act's protection for pre-existing rights has eroded its effectiveness in protecting many river corridors. Of particular concern are the numerous federal grazing permits on Western rivers. On the positive side, federal agencies do have the authority to place conditions on grazing permits which specify seasonal use, set forage consumption limits and prohibit grazing in riparian areas, but only to the extent that such conditions do not "abrogate" a permittee's rights.[143] Furthermore, the Act provides agencies the authority to take any action necessary to protect river corridors after grazing permits expire.

National Rivers: A few, select rivers have been protected pursuant to special acts of Congress, outside of the official National Wild and Scenic Rivers framework. The concept of a "National River" was introduced by the Missouri chapter of the Nature Conservancy and resulted in the designation of the Current River, and its tributary, Jack's Fork, as the first National River system in 1964. National River status has been conferred only rarely since then. For example, the Buffalo River in Arkansas was designated in 1972, the South Fork of Tennessee's Cumberland River was protected in 1974, and West Virginia's New River Gorge became a national river in 1976.[144] More recently, certain stretches of several other rivers and streams have been granted protection under legislation creating special recreation areas. These include, among others, the Mississippi National River and Recreation Area in Minnesota,[145] the San Pedro Riparian National Conservation Area in Arizona,[146] and the Gila Box Riparian National Conservation Area, also in Arizona.[147]

The protection afforded these national rivers is substantially greater than that provided under the Wild and Scenic Rivers Act because wider land areas along the rivers are preserved. In the case of the Current and Buffalo Rivers, where most of the watershed is protected, these rivers are relieved of the usual circumstance under the WSRA, where the "protected" area remains subject to the adverse effects of upstream management practices.[148]

Conclusions

The Wild and Scenic Rivers Act Is Not an Effective Tool to Comprehensively Protect or Restore Riverine Systems and Biodiversity on Federal Lands Nationwide

Although Becoming Increasingly Effective, The WSRA's Focus Is Primarily Limited to River Segments Which Have Not Been Significantly Degraded: The Wild and Scenic Act has proven somewhat effective at protecting the scenic and recreational values within most designated river segment corridors and at preventing dams once a river is designated. However, the WSRA does not specifically recognize the inherent value of protecting the ecological functions or biodiversity of a riverine system, either in the Act's designation criteria, classification system, boundary system, or management plan criteria. The statutory scheme focuses on "select" river segments which have "outstandingly remarkable value" and which have not been significantly degraded -- a very small subset of all rivers (less than 2% nationwide).[149] This is not to say that these "outstanding" segments should not be protected--they should be, and Wild and Scenic designation is one method to achieve this.

The Act's emphasis on "select" river sections has resulted in a program which primarily benefits rivers in western states -- especially California, the Pacific Northwest and Alaska. As of 1992, only about 10% of river miles protected under the WSRA were east of the Mississippi.[150] However, the full potential of this program is only now being realized; in 1992 alone, 26 river segments were added.[151]

There are many positive attributes of the Act that can be built upon and utilized. We are likely to see many more river segments added to the system over time. If future designations are situated within the context of river system-wide protection and recovery strategies, the program would increase its value and importance in protecting riverine systems. Unfortunately, even if implemented to its full potential, the focus on "outstanding rivers" is too limited to do much to resolve the overwhelming crisis facing the nation's riverine systems and biodiversity.

Protected Areas Are Limited To Arbitrarily Designated Corridors: Most often, protection for riverine systems and biodiversity cannot be effectively accomplished unless the elements and processes within the entire watershed are addressed. Congressionally designated rivers are restricted to an average protected corridor one-quarter mile on each side of the actual river, or to a maximum average of 320 acres per river mile.[152] Unfortunately, these statutorily restricted boundaries do not require inclusion of all ecologically important parts of the watershed ecosystem.

The Wild and Scenic Rivers Act does not recognize the unique hydrogeologic characteristics of a river system. Because a river is a function of its watershed, protecting a segment of a river system, by definition, does not address riverine ecosystem processes. Adjacent river areas beyond one-quarter mile from each river bank may only be studied for inclusion "if their inclusion could facilitate management of the resources of the river area."

The WSRA Lacks Specific Management Directives: The WSRA gives broad discretion to federal agencies in the development of management plans for designated rivers, requiring only that plans contain such provisions as are "necessary" to "protect and enhance" the values which caused the river to be designated, and other uses may be permitted if they do not "substantially interfere" with public use and enjoyment of these values.

Management decisions about whether to allow particular uses of Wild and Scenic rivers and how to regulate those uses are almost exclusively within the discretion of the agency with jurisdiction. As a result, component rivers segments are not subject to consistent standards for river management. Therefore, designated sections of the same river managed by different federal agencies may have different management plans due simply to jurisdictional differences.[153]   Even where management plans do not appear significantly different on their face, the broad discretion accorded agencies can lead to discrepancies in implementation which cannot always be logically attributed to segments' characterization as wild, scenic or recreational.

The federal managing agencies have also failed to use their full authority under the Act to benefit river corridors. A prime example is the underutilization of the Act's provision for instream flows in quantities necessary to accomplish the purposes of the Act. Another example is the fact that the federal government has never exercised its authority to condemn state-allocated water rights.[154]

In sum, designated riverine segments often are not managed consistently between federal agencies or even between management units within the same federal agency: In the Forest Service, both wilderness and non-wilderness forest policy is made at the forest level; BLM plans vary between districts and other planning units; wildlife refuges and national parks are managed individually. Further, statutes applying to all agencies, such as the Endangered Species Act, may further complicate the management of any of these areas for species-specific reasons.

The WSRA Provides No Authority, Standards, Mechanisms or Incentives to Restore Degraded Riverine-Riparian Ecosystems: Although the Act focuses on riverine segments which are not significantly degraded, almost all designated riverine corridors suffer from some degree of degradation or flow alteration and are influenced by degraded areas upstream or downstream from the designated segment. From an ecological perspective, healthier areas outside the protected section may often be the most important to protect, even to maintain the protected section. Degraded areas may require restoration in order to maintain the healthier areas. As written, the WSRA does not provide federal authority to restore dammed, drained, polluted, or simplified riverine ecosystems to a healthier, more natural state -- although it does not forbid such projects.[155] Without a clear mandate, including standards, mechanisms and incentives for restoration, the Act has done, and will do, little to promote the restoration of degraded riverine-riparian ecosystems and biodiversity.

The Act Does Not Require Policy Coordination and Alignment Throughout The River System: In general, the Wild and Scenic Rivers Act has not been broadly invoked by federal land managers to protect contiguous riverine systems on federal lands. Agencies generally have also not used the Act to exercise their authority over riverine management on lands beyond their jurisdiction. For example, the water rights for component river segments are not routinely enforced or otherwise used to protect the river system.

Furthermore, the WSRA provides inadequate authority to regulate activities on private lands, such as timber harvest and road building, which adversely affect the component river segment. However, such authority could be implied from the language of the Act.

It has been suggested by at least one scholar that the WSRA requires amendment because it fails to: a) grant direct agency authority to regulate or prohibit activities on private lands surrounding designated areas which threaten to adversely affect the values protected by designation of river segments flowing through federal lands; b) expressly direct federal agencies to take actions necessary to fulfill the purposes of the WSRA, including the issuance of regulations, commencement of litigation and assertion of the federal water rights expressly granted in Section 13(c) of the Act; and c) include an express private right of action to enforce the statute which augments the enforcement powers of the agencies and the Department of Justice against private individuals and other agencies.[156] Without policy coordination and alignment within the entire river system, even the limited protection provided for a segment by the Wild and Scenic Act is often in jeopardy.

The Designation Process is Often Long, Inefficient, Costly and Controversial, and Requires a Separate Act of Congress For Each River Segment or Group of Rivers Protected: While it does not take a new congressional law for every human activity that degrades a river, a new federal law is required for every Wild and Scenic River segment protected. Fears of federal management and the fact that the designated segment and corridor are generally withdrawn from most detrimental land use practices generates considerable opposition to most designations. Hence, the designation process for most rivers takes years and requires large campaigns and expenditures of funds. Often the most controversial segments must be dropped from consideration to pass multiple river segment bills, leaving some of the most important segments unprotected. The process has time and again proven too time-consuming and cumbersome to protect all the rivers that require protection on federal lands. Only one designation option does not require an Act of Congress. The procedure allows the Governor of a state to request designation directly to the Secretary of the Interior. There are also many problems with this mechanism as will be discussed in Appendix C.

Protection of Pre-existing Rights Requires That Federal Managers Continue to Permit Ecologically Damaging Activities: The Act's protection of pre-existing uses authorized under federal licenses and contracts has eroded its effectiveness in protecting many river corridors. Grazing is of particular concern on many western rivers, where numerous grazing rights pre-date designation.

THE CLEAN WATER ACT

The Clean Water Act[157] (CWA) is the nation's primary mechanism for protecting and improving water quality. The broad purpose of the Act is "to restore and maintain the chemical, physical and biological integrity of the Nation's waters,"[158] and its thrust is to declare unlawful the unregulated discharge of pollutants into all waters of the United States.[159] The main strength of the Clean Water Act is its comprehensive, nationwide approach to water-quality protection which requires federal, state and local governments to act cooperatively for the achievement of common goals.

In practice, the CWA has proven reasonably effective in reducing chemical pollutants from point sources. However, it has failed to protect river ecosystems and biodiversity from the insidious degradation caused by nonpoint-source pollution. It also has not yet proven effective at addressing the multiple factors causing riverine ecosystem "simplification." This is because the CWA is not successful in addressing land management practices such as timber harvesting, roadbuilding, grazing, agricultural practices and urbanization which destroy riparian areas, floodplains and biological hot spots and which change the physical structure of the system and the biological complexity of the waters through increased sedimentation and pollution. Over thirty percent of the nation's rivers, streams, and estuaries still fail to meet existing chemical water quality standards. According to the Ohio EPA, when biological criteria, including biodiversity, are taken into account, almost 50% of water bodies nationwide may be sub-standard.[160] It is now clear that the CWA has failed to realize its potential as a comprehensive, proactive directive to adequately protect riverine systems from degradation.

The most crippling limitations of the Act are: 1) It emphasizes permitting processes which are, by nature, primarily reactive rather than proactive; 2) it emphasizes traditional water quality criteria to measure water body health; 3) administrators of the Act have failed to enforce a "no degradation" standard to maintain the quality of waters flowing through federal lands, and; 4) the Act does not regulate all ecologically related portions of a riverine system; for example, the "dredge and fill" program applies only to "wetlands" and does not protect many riparian and floodplain areas and inadequately applies to many others. Riparian areas are arguably intended to be protected by the Act because of their connection to the biological integrity of rivers and streams. However, without a clear Congressional statement of intent to include riparian areas in the Act's definition of "navigable waters," it appears unlikely that the CWA will ever provide the level of riparian, floodplain, and hyporheic zone protection required to ensure the future ecological and biological integrity of riverine-riparian ecosystems on federal lands, or on non-federal lands, for that matter.

Purpose, structure and goals: In 1972, Congress expanded and strengthened the 1948 Federal Water Pollution Control Act, creating what is now commonly referred to as the Clean Water Act (CWA).[161] The stated purpose of the CWA is "to restore and maintain the chemical, physical, and biological integrity of the Nation's waters."[162] The overly optimistic and still unmet goals of the Act are to eliminate the discharge of pollutants into "navigable waters" by 1985 and to achieve water quality levels adequate for the "protection and propagation of fish, shell fish and wildlife and . . . for recreation in and on the water. . . by July 1, 1983."[163]

The Act makes the states and the EPA jointly responsible for identifying and regulating both point and non-point sources of pollution. Point sources are controlled by a permit-based program, while non-point sources are approached with a management strategy. The Act's framework thus allows for both environmental quality (water quality standards) and technology-based (e.g. Best Management Practices) approaches to water pollution control. Each state is required to develop and adopt water-quality standards which enumerate the designated uses of each water body as well as specific criteria deemed necessary to protect or achieve the designated uses.[164]

Under the CWA, federal agencies are required to comply with both the point and nonpoint-source components of state water pollution control standards and plans:

> Each . . . . agency of the federal government (1) having jurisdiction over any property or facility, or (2) engaged in any activity resulting, or which may result in the discharge or runoff of pollutants, and each officer, . . . shall be subject to, and comply with, all Federal, State, interstate, and local

requirements, administrative authority, and process and sanctions respecting the control and abatement of water pollution.[165]

The requirement that federal agencies comply with water quality standards constitutes a significant constraint on agencies' management discretion. Especially for those agencies operating under a commodity-oriented interpretation of the "multiple-use, sustained-yield" philosophy (i.e. the U.S. Forest Service and the Bureau of Land Management) compliance with the strictures of the CWA often requires the agencies to reconcile patently conflicting management objectives.

State water-quality standards; chemical and biological measures required: The CWA requires states to develop and implement water quality standards in accordance with Environmental Protection Agency (EPA) regulations and guidance. State water quality standards programs are required to integrate three components: 1) a designation of uses for all state waters;[166] 2) criteria to meet those uses;[167] and 3) an antidegradation policy for waters that meet or exceed the criteria to meet existing uses and for "outstanding national resource waters."[168]

In order to comply with the CWA, state water quality standards must, theoretically, include indicators of the health of ecological habitats and the level of biological diversity. The use of biocriteria is generally authorized by the stated objective of the Act -- to restore and maintain chemical, physical and biological integrity.[169] Also, the Act specifically provides that state criteria to meet designated beneficial uses must include both numeric standards for quantifiable chemical properties and "narrative criteria or criteria based upon bio-monitoring" where appropriate to protect beneficial uses and serve the purposes of the Act.[170] The Act's "interim" water quality goal, which includes the provision of water quality adequate for the protection and propagation of fish, also supports the use of biocriteria because propagation necessarily includes the full range of conditions required to support reproducing populations of aquatic life and the non-aquatic life which depends on healthy aquatic systems.[171]

As defined in the Act, the term "biological monitoring" means:

> the determination of the effects on aquatic life, including accumulation of pollutants in tissue, in receiving waters due to the discharge of pollutants (A) by techniques and procedures, including sampling of organisms representative of appropriate levels of the food chain appropriate to the volume and the physical, chemical, and biological characteristics of the effluent, and (B) at appropriate frequencies and locations.[172]

Under current EPA regulations, water-quality management planning is focused on priority water-quality issues and geographic areas. This process requires the development of Total Maximum Daily Loads (TMDLs), which sets the amount of pollution that may be allowed while still complying with water-quality standards.[173] Theoretically, states will allocate among each point and non-point source the total load of each pollutant that may be introduced into a water body without exceeding standards.   These allocations are implemented through the issuance of permits for point sources and the prescription of Best Management Practices for non-point sources.[174]   State Water Quality Management plans are required to identify priority point and non-point problems, consider alternative solutions and recommend control measures.[175]

In some cases, it is clear that the designation of beneficial uses and water quality standards to protect them places strict limitations on federal land uses. For example, the Bull Run Special Management Area in the Mount Hood National Forest (Oregon) constitutes the main water supply for the City of Portland, and municipal water supply is a designated beneficial use. As a result, the Forest Service has somewhat reduced (though not eliminated) logging in the adjacent area, and has also prohibited public entry as a means of complying with state water quality standards.[176]

Pollution control; point source reduction: The pollution control provisions of the CWA apply to the "navigable waters" of the United States, which are defined as "the waters of the United States, including the territorial seas."[177] Judicial interpretation of the term "navigable waters" has established the inclusion of areas saturated by groundwater that produce wetland vegetation, or "wetland" areas. The term has also been interpreted to include all waters with a "direct hydrological connection" to surface waters.[178]

Under the Act, the National Pollutant Discharge Elimination System (NPDES) permitting program regulates the discharge of pollutants into navigable waters from "point sources." The CWA defines a "point source" as:

> any discernible, confined and discrete conveyance, including but not limited to any pipe, ditch, channel, tunnel, conduit, well, discrete fissure, container, rolling stock, concentrated animal feeding operation, or vessel or other floating craft, from which pollutants are or may be discharged. This term does not include agricultural stormwater discharges and return flows from irrigated agriculture.[179]

The provisions of NPDES permits may be specifically enforced by the EPA, authorized state agencies and by private citizens.[180] It is a condition of all NPDES permits that the permittee comply with discharge limits based on the use of "best technology" and with discharge monitoring and reporting obligations, among other requirements.

Through the NPDES program, great strides have been made in limiting a wide range of point source effluents, including stormwater runoff from industrial activities and larger municipalities. The program has been most successful in reducing conventional chemical pollutants from factories and sewage treatment plants through large capital outlays by industry and municipalities.   However, it has generally failed to respond adequately to water quality threats from toxics discharges and diffuse pollution sources related to population growth.

Pollution control; non-point source reduction: The pollution problems that remain even after the drastic improvements made in point source controls clearly demonstrate that the nation's most significant, long-term water-quality problems are caused by non-point sources.

Nonpoint sources are regulated under Section 208 of the Act,[181] which requires states to designate planning agencies on an areawide basis and requires these agencies to identify bodies of water where water quality objectives are not being met.[182]   In areas where non-point pollution is identified as the reason objectives remain unmet, the planning agency is directed to devise a strategy of either voluntary educational programs or state regulation to control the problem.[183]   State regulatory strategies must define "Best Management Practices" (BMPs) for specific land uses, and, though these practices may be either voluntary or mandatory, the state is required to demonstrate to the EPA's satisfaction that these practices will be implemented so that compliance with state water quality standards is achieved.[184] States are given two incentives for entering into this difficult planning process: 1) The EPA can revoke state authority to issue point-source permits if the state fails to prepare an acceptable non-point plan,[185] and 2) the EPA can withhold federal funding for wastewater treatment facilities.

EPA regulations further require that state Water Quality Management plans describe specific regulatory and non-regulatory programs, activities and BMPs selected to control non-point pollution and protect designated beneficial uses.[186]   Regulatory programs are required where they are necessary to attain or maintain a designated use, or where a non-regulatory program is otherwise inappropriate.[187]   BMPs must always be identified for silvicultural activities.[188]   In some cases (especially where other federal statutes contain water quality protection provisions, such as the Wild and Scenic Rivers Act), states may choose to implement management plans though agreements or Memoranda of Understanding with federal agencies.[189]

The 1987 amendments to the Clean Water Act included stronger nonpoint-source control provisions, primarily in Section 319[190]. The new language has had the significant effect of broadening the range of federal activities which are subject to state review and comment, thereby effectively increasing the accountability of public land managers for water quality protection. Secondly, the amendments suggest that Federal agencies must accommodate state concerns without allowance for technological or economic feasibility.[191] Section 319 also allows states to challenge federal projects on the basis of their own consistency analysis, through which a state determines whether a project will comply with its own standards, BMPs and procedural requirements -- a process which provides a new federal legal handle for third party enforcement of water quality standards against nonpoint-source polluters where such pollution is not exempt under state law.[192]

In effect, Section 319 allows states to demand full evaluation and disclosure of water quality impacts and places increased emphasis on the in-stream biological effects of proposed activities rather than on BMP utilization and water-column chemistry. Significantly, the amendments seem to impose a more site-specific planning approach, requiring states to develop and implement their management programs on a "watershed-by-watershed basis" to the maximum extent practicable.[193] As amended, there is no question that states with ample authority to alleviate nonpoint-source pollution. To date, however, there have not been ample enough resources and political will for the EPA and the states to significantly step up their non-point control efforts.

Although the CWA does not provide specific authority to enforce water quality standards against non-point sources, all polluters -- including federal land management agencies -- are nonetheless required to attain state water quality standards[194] Federal agencies are further subject to the provisions of the Act requiring that federal facilities comply with state requirements.[195]

The scope of the limitations posed by state nonpoint-source regulations for federal land managers was the subject of *Northwest Indian Cemetery Protective Ass'n v. Peterson*, which applied state nonpoint-source pollution standards to rainwater runoff caused by roadbuilding and timber harvesting in the Blue Creek unit of the Six Rivers National Forest in California.[196] The district court found that state standards for turbidity and sedimentation would be violated by the Forest Service's proposed road and timber harvest plan.[197] On appeal, the Forest Service argued that it was not bound by the state standards because the California Environmental Protection Agency had accepted its BMPs as adequate to meet water-quality standards.[198] The court rejected this argument, stating that state approval of a BMP is no substitute for compliance with water-quality standards because BMPs merely serve as guidelines to meet those standards and are not a substitute for actual compliance.[199]

Thus, just as point sources must comply with the effluent limitations in their NPDES permits, nonpoint sources of pollution must comply with state water-quality standards. Unfortunately, in many instances, the water-quality standards which apply do not adequately measure the types of pollution caused by non-point runoff.

Wetlands regulation and riverine protection on federal lands: It is now generally recognized that wetlands, which include swamps, marshes, bogs, estuaries and similar areas, play a key ecological role in groundwater recharge, waste disposal, flood control, wildlife reproduction and the general maintenance of ecological diversity. Section 404 of the CWA, which establishes a permit requirement for dredging and filling in navigable waters, is the nation's primary wetlands protection law.[200] Based on the CWA definition of "navigable waters" as "waters of the United States," judicial interpretation has established that the scope of Section 404 extends to non-navigable tributaries[201] and even to areas saturated by groundwater that produce wetland vegetation.[202] This program is primarily administered by the Army Corps of Engineers ("Corps"), pursuant to guidelines developed by the EPA.[203] Section 404 constitutes an exception to the Clean Water Act's general prohibition against the pollution of waterways and to the NPDES program.

Corps permitting authority under section 404: Because the Corps is highly decentralized, Section 404 program management and administration is delegated to its 36 district engineers and 11 division engineers. All permit applications must undergo a "public interest review," during which interested parties may comment on a project's reasonably foreseeable adverse impacts and its benefits.[204] Importantly, the Corps is not limited to the consideration of water quality; it must also consider wetlands values, conservation, economics, aesthetics, general environmental concerns, historic values, fish and wildlife values, flood damage prevention, land use, navigation, recreation, water supply, water quality, energy needs, safety, food production, and, in general, public needs and welfare. A permit will be granted unless the Corps determines that the project is contrary to the public interest - - a rather lofty determination for a district engineer to make.[205]

In addition to individual dredge and fill permits, the Corps issues "general" permits, depending on the type and size of the proposed project. General permits must be conditioned on a determination that the permitted activities are similar in nature and will "cause only minimal adverse environmental effects when performed separately, and will have only minimal cumulative adverse effect[s] on the environment."[206] In addition, general permits must follow certain "management practices" "to the maximum extent practicable."[207] In all, the regulations specify fourteen conditions which must be met for any general permit to apply, including a requirement that the fill must not "disrupt the movement of those species of aquatic life indigenous to the water body."[208] Activities usually authorized under general permits include: some navigational aids, bank stabilization, bridge building, minor road crossing fills and the placement of fish and wildlife harvesting devices.

General permits may be nationwide or limited to a particular geographic area or region. National permits are issued by the Chief of Engineers through the rulemaking process. To date, the Corps has issued 26 nationwide permits. Such permits may not include any activity which:

* is close to public water supply intakes

* is located in concentrated shellfish production areas

* jeopardizes endangered or threatened species or modifies their habitat

* significantly disrupts the movement of indigenous aquatic species

* contains toxics

* is located in a designated or proposed wild and scenic river, or impairs reserved tribal rights[209]

The requirement that no general permit may be issued unless the applicant demonstrates that an endangered or threatened wildlife species will not be affected has the potential to prevent projects which directly or indirectly affect habitat on federal lands. In *Riverside Irrigation District v. Andrews*,[210] the Tenth Circuit upheld the Corps' denial of a permit to dam and divert a stream due to the potential adverse impact on the habitat of an endangered bird many miles downstream, stating that the Corps must consider indirect, downstream effects of proposed projects.[211] Protection of habitat on federal lands is particularly important because the federal lands encompass a significant portion of the critical habitat identified for threatened and endangered species listed to date.

In some instances, the Corps is authorized under its regulations to permit an activity without formal permits via letters of permission and regional general permits. Such informal permission may be granted if the district engineer determines that a proposal would be minor, would not have a significant impact on environmental values, and is not expected to meet appreciable opposition. In these circumstances, concerned agencies are notified without general public notification.

Some federal projects may be entirely exempt from the Section 401 permitting process, though still subject to NEPA and other applicable reviews.[212] Such projects must be entirely planned, financed and constructed by a federal agency and must meet the applicable guidelines, as demonstrated by an Environmental Impact Statement submitted to Congress. This section has been invoked infrequently.[213]

If the Corps or the EPA finds that a project does not comply with permit requirements, either agency may take enforcement action against the violators. Such action may include civil, criminal or administrative penalties.

Nationwide Permit 26: Nationwide Permit 26 (NWP 26) is believed to have a significant negative impact on riverine-riparian ecosystems. Nationwide Permit 26 authorizes "discharges of dredged or fill material into waters above the headwaters and isolated waters, so long as the work does not fill or substantially adversely affect more than ten acres of such waters."[214] Fills that will adversely affect between one and ten acres must be preceded by a pre-discharge notification to the Corps, but no reporting at all is required for fills of less than one acre.

The EPA regulations define "headwaters" as the point on a non-tidal stream at which the average annual flow is less than five cubic feet per second.[215] District engineers may establish headwaters as the point at which a flow of five cubic feet per second is attained or exceeded 50% of the time. The headwaters analysis is critical because it determines whether an individual permit or a nationwide general permit, which is subject to more lenient environmental review, is required.[216] It is estimated that about 17 million acres of wetlands and 40-50,000 annual discharges are authorized by general permits in headwater areas,[217] many of which are covered by NWP 26.

The federal resource agencies generally agree that the NWP program contributes significantly to the loss of valuable wetlands and riparian areas. This is especially true in arid California, where a high percentage of the remaining wetlands meet the isolated or headwaters criteria of NWP 26 because many riparian corridors have less than the requisite five cubic feet per second annual flow.[218] As a result, substantial lengths of critical riparian habitat fall within the authority of NWP 26, and these losses are not (and, probably cannot) be offset by mitigation.

Unfortunately, due to the structure of the permit there is a significant lack of data on the actual individual or cumulative impacts of NWP 26, which has made the task of determining the permit's legality nearly impossible.[219] The program requires no notification for fills of less than one acre, and only inadequate review procedures where it is required.[220]

The federal resource agencies and state authority over wetlands: Although the Corps is responsible for issuing or denying dredge and fill permits, other federal agencies and the individual states are also involved in implementing the wetlands program. The primary agencies involved are the Environmental Protection Agency (EPA), the National Marine Fisheries Service of the Department of Commerce (NMFS), and the Fish and Wildlife Service of the Interior Department (FWS).

The Act requires that the EPA work jointly with the Department of the Army to develop guidelines for the selection of sites for disposal of dredged or fill materials.[221] The EPA may veto a decision by the Corps to issue a permit to fill a wetland whenever it determines that such filling constitutes a discharge which "will have unacceptable adverse effect on municipal water supplies, shellfish beds and fishery areas, wildlife, or recreation areas."[222] The EPA is also responsible for construing the term "navigable waters" and for interpreting the scope of exemption from the Section 404 program.[223]

Pursuant to the Fish and Wildlife Coordination Act,[224] the NMFS and the FWS are authorized to make advisory comments on permit applications and to report possible permit violations. The Corps is required to give full consideration to these recommendations in evaluating a permit, and such comments may serve as the basis for modifying, conditioning or denying a permit. When another agency disagrees with a permit decision made by a Department of the Army district engineer, the agency may request higher level review within the Department of the Army.[225]

States may assume responsibilities which directly affect the issuance of dredge and fill permits. For example, states are required to issue a water quality certification or waiver (under the Section 401 authority discussed below) before the Corps can issue a dredge and fill permit. Also, if a state with a federally approved program under the Coastal Zone Management Act (CZMA)[226] files a timely objection to an applicant's consistency certification, the Corps is precluded from issuing that permit, unless the Secretary of Commerce determines that the proposed activity is either consistent with the objectives of the CZMA or in the interest of national security.[227]

Under some circumstances, states may assume limited responsibility for issuing dredge and fill permits.[228] To date, however, few states have indicated an interest in doing so.

EPA wetlands guidelines: The EPA wetlands guidelines state that "no discharge of dredged or fill material shall be permitted if there is a practicable alternative to the proposed discharge that would have less adverse impact on the aquatic ecosystem."[229] In addition, "no discharge of dredged or fill material shall be permitted which will cause or contribute to significant degradation of the waters of the United States."[230]

The EPA currently defines wetlands as:

those areas that are inundated or saturated by surface or groundwater at a frequency and duration sufficient to support, and that under normal circumstances do support, a prevalence of vegetation typically adapted for life in saturated soil conditions.[231]

The EPA and the other resource agencies have taken the position that the Corps does not exercise its full range of authority to protect wetlands under several key provisions of the official regulations and guidance.[232] The primary areas of interagency disagreement involve how to assess the cumulative impacts of individual permit decisions, how to weigh alternatives to development in wetlands and how to delineate wetlands boundaries.[233] Since the scope of the program's implementation is a function of these interpretations, the existing program could be broadened considerably were the Corps to change its views.

Section 404 implementation issues: As mentioned, the EPA 404(b)(1) guidelines prohibit the issuance of a permit if there are "practicable alternatives" to the proposed project. The guidelines further require that all permitted discharges reflect "appropriate and practicable steps" to minimize adverse impacts of the discharge on the aquatic ecosystem. Practicability is determined by cost, existing technology, and logistics in the context of the project's overall purposes. Under the Guidelines, practicable alternatives would include alternative sites not owned but which could be obtained or otherwise utilized. According to Corps guidance, practicability would be determined by what is reasonable in light of the applicant's wishes and capabilities and by the need for or purpose of the proposal.

While the resource agencies would apply practicable alternatives as a threshold test and basis for permit denial, the Corps rarely uses this as a basis for denial because it relies primarily on applicants' own determinations of what alternatives are practicable.[234] Furthermore, the Corps tends to look only at short-term, rather than long-term economic benefits of a proposal, and does not perceive any alternative as practicable if it is not reasonable from the applicant's standpoint.[235] As a result, permits are granted under Section 404 which dilute the Clean Water Act's water-quality goals with economic interests.[236]

The resource agencies and the Corps also differ on their view of the EPA Guidelines defining "cumulative impacts" of proposed project. The guidelines define cumulative impacts as changes in aquatic ecosystems that are attributable to the collective effect of various individual discharges of dredged and fill material. The guidelines presume that these effects may be predicted to some reasonable, practical extent. In the administration of the Section 404 program, however, the Corps has not developed a consistent method of determining cumulative impacts, i.e., no standard criteria are considered. Therefore, cumulative impacts are assessed on a project-by-project basis.

The Corps' tendency has been to assess impacts based on the surrounding land uses. For example, if a few acres of wetlands remain in an already largely agricultural area, then their conversion will not have a significant effect on the existing hydrology of the area. However, if the subject wetland area is one of a few remaining wetlands in an entire regional drainage, then its destruction could be considered to have significant cumulative impacts. Without improved standards and data collection to assist in cumulative impacts assessments, these determinations will remain largely within the Corps' discretion.[237]

The agencies have also differed in their application of the wetlands delineation criteria, with the Corps taking the narrower view. As a result, wetlands determinations sometimes differ by thousands of acres.[238] The EPA has taken the position that Clean Water Act jurisdiction extends to all wetlands which constitute potential migratory bird habitat, regardless of whether a particular wetland is adjacent to other waterbodies.[239] The Corps has been determined to make jurisdictional deliberations on a case-by-case basis, relating each area to interstate commerce.[240] Some of these tensions have been resolved by a 1989 Memorandum of Understanding in which the Corps agreed to fully implement EPA guidance.[241]

It is important for the protection of riverine-riparian ecosystems that the most expansive definition of wetlands be applied, because it is more likely that non-wetland riparian areas will be protected.

Jurisdictional limitations on Corps authority; riparian areas not included in wetlands definition: Regardless of the fact that many riparian areas are functionally identical to wetlands, wetlands and riparian areas are generally considered to be physiographically distinct for regulatory purposes.[242]

Generally speaking, "wetlands" and "riparian areas" describe ecosystems with comparable values and functions; they both contribute to groundwater recharge and discharge, sediment stabilization, flood attenuation and water quality and provide habitat, climate moderation, shoreline protection and recreation. However, Section 404 includes only "wetlands" within the definition of waters of the United States for Clean Water Act purposes. The Act's protection of wetlands, therefore, does not include the many riparian areas and floodplains which are not also wetlands. The most significant omissions of riparian areas occur in arid regions, where riparian areas and floodplains have the same values and functions as wetland riparian areas in more rainy regions.[243]

Basically speaking, riparian areas are vegetation areas within and are hydrologically connected to the waterway and/or their flood plains. These areas are characterized by plant and animal species different from the immediately surrounding terrestrial upland areas.

An area qualifies as a wetland under the federal wetlands delineation manual if it exhibits evidence of three mandatory criteria: 1) hydrophytic vegetation; 2) hydric soils; and 3) wetland hydrology. Under these technical criteria most riparian areas and floodplains are excluded because they lack typical hydric soils or hydrology.[244]

Broad statutory exemptions: The scope of the wetlands permitting program is further limited by the Act's broad exemption of the following activities from regulation:

* "Normal agricultural, silvicultural or ranching activities, such as plowing, seeding, cultivating, minor drainage, harvesting for the production of food, fiber, and forest products, or upland soil and water conservation practices."

* Activities "for the purpose of maintenance, including emergency reconstruction of recently damaged parts, of currently serviceable structures, such as dikes, and bridge abutments or approaches and transportation structures."

* Activities "for the purpose of construction or maintenance of farm or stock ponds or irrigation ditches, or the maintenance of drainage ditches."

* Activities "for the purpose of construction of temporary sedimentation basins on a construction site which does not include placement of fill material into the navigable waters."

* Activities "for the purpose of construction or maintenance of farm roads, or temporary roads for moving mining equipment, where such roads are constructed and maintained, in accordance with best management practices, to assure that flow and circulation patterns and chemical and biological characteristics of the navigable waters are not impaired, that the reach of the navigable waters is not reduced, and that any adverse effect on the aquatic environment will otherwise be minimized."

* Discharges resulting from any activity with respect to which a state has an approved, areawide, waste-treatment program under section 208(b)(4), and meeting the requirements of that section. These activities are also exempted from regulation under Section 301 (a)

(effluent limitations), and Section 402 (NPDES permit program) of the Act, except for effluent standards or prohibitions under section 307 (Toxic and pretreatment effluent standards).

These extremely broad exemptions are explicitly narrowed only by provisions disallowing exemptions for discharges of dredge or fill material "incidental to any activity having as its purpose bringing an area into a use to which it was not previously subject, where the flow or circulation of navigable waters may be impaired or the reach of such waters be reduced."[245]　In other words, "new uses" which reduce flow or impair water circulation may not be exempt.

Further limitations on the Corps' jurisdiction over activities affecting wetlands derive from the Act's language which extends regulatory authority only to the placement of "dredged and fill" material in U.S. "waters." As a result, activities that do not directly deposit substantial dredged or fill materials, such as clear-cutting existing riparian or wetland forests, ditching which drains wetlands, and some plowing, have been interpreted by the Corps as being outside the scope of the Corps' regulatory mandate. The EPA noted an example of such an activity in a 1986 report:

> . . . the nagging problem of destruction [of wetlands] by draining continues . . . . Section 404 only grants authority to regulate filling activities. Much of the wetland destruction in Nebraska occurs through draining. Thus, without regulatory authority, all we can do to attempt to stop such activities is to increase public awareness of the value of these wetlands and appeal to landowners to preserve the wetland.[246]

In sum, it is legal to dredge, drain and dig ditches or large holes through and in a wetland without a permit if none of the resulting dirt, mud or sand is actually deposited in the wetland from which it was removed.[247]   It is estimated that about 80 percent of wetlands losses involve draining and clearing inland wetlands for agricultural purposes.[248]

State water quality certification and riverine protection: Under Section 401, the CWA grants states the authority to veto federal licenses or permits where the proposed activity may cause discharges to regulated waters in violation of state water quality standards.[249]   Examples of federal permits and licenses requiring state certification include: NPDES permits; Section 404 permits (both general and individual); permits for activities regulated by the Sections 9 and 10 of the Rivers and Harbors Act; hydroelectric licenses required under the Federal Power Act; and permits for discharge-related activities under the licenses issued by the Nuclear Regulatory Commission. Certification processes differ from state to state, with some states participating early enough in a project's development to have an impact on determining alternatives and mitigation possibilities.[250]

States must act to grant or deny certification within a reasonable time (not to exceed one year) after a request is received, or certification authority will be deemed to have been waived. Where a state does act, denial of certification effectively prohibits the federal permitting or licensing agency from issuing the permit or license. Some analysts have characterized state certification authority as the "sleeping giant" of water quality and wetlands protection because the full potential for state control over federal activities has not been realized.[251]

With regard to the protection of riverine systems and their associated riparian areas, the certification program probably has the most impact as it relates to wetlands and NPDES permits. However, it is important to note that because the current definition of wetlands often excludes riparian areas and floodplains, states do not have jurisdiction over federal permitting activities affecting these areas. Moreover, state law and water quality regulations usually do not protect riparian areas or floodplains either, though a few states have included riparian areas in their definitions of "waters of the state" for purposes of water quality standards enforcement.

The Clean Water Act's antidegradation mandate, EPA regulations and state implementation: The CWA is the source of an "antidegradation" mandate which has the potential to provide powerful water quality protection. Based on the Act's directive that the quality of the nation's waters should be "maintained," the EPA promulgated an "Antidegradation Policy" which requires each state to adopt and implement a three-tiered antidegradation program to protect water quality.[252]

The EPA's antidegradation policy[253] may be summarized as follows:

* States must act to ensure that all "existing instream water uses" and the level of water quality "necessary to protect the existing uses" must be "maintained and protected." This is the minimum level of protection applicable to all waters in the nation.

* States must further protect existing water quality for high quality waters, i.e., those where the existing quality exceeds "levels necessary to support propagation of fish, shellfish and wildlife and recreation in and on the water." Exceptions may be allowed for limited degradation after public involvement, but only if existing uses are still "fully" protected. Exceptions must be based on evidence that lower water quality is necessary to accommodate important economic or social development in the local area.

* States must, without exception, maintain the existing quality of those high quality waters which comprise "an outstanding National resource, such as waters of National and State

parks and wildlife refuges and waters of
exceptional recreational or ecological significance."
This standard provides the highest level of
protection, and no degradation of existing water
quality is allowed except to accommodate
temporary and short-term changes. Under no
circumstances may allowable short-term or
temporary changes "alter the essential character or
special use" which made the water an
Outstanding National Resource Water.[254]

As interpreted by the EPA, the antidegradation policy
applies to both point and non-point sources and the exception for
degradation of high quality waters is intended to apply in rare and
"extraordinary circumstances," where the proponent of the
degrading activity carries a "very high" burden of justification.[255]
The EPA has also stated that the policy must be applied to all
parts of a water body segment, meaning that the degradation of
stream tributaries is not allowed even if the main stream segment
is unaffected.[256]

The antidegradation regulation could provide a very high
level of protection to riverine systems on federal lands if the "no
degradation" standard were applied to all systems running
through National Parks, forests, refuges and BLM public lands, as
well as to all Wild and Scenic Rivers. Unfortunately, the EPA has
only recently become serious about enforcing its antidegradation
regulation. As a result, few states have actually implemented a
"no degradation" standard for those waters on federal lands which
would appear to qualify as "Outstanding National Resource
Waters."[257] Furthermore, the EPA has not interpreted its
regulation to *require* the designation of any particular water as an
ONRW, leaving such designation entirely within states' discretion.
Therefore, the EPA will not intervene to designate waters as
outstanding national resource waters under state antidegradation
programs.[258]

Conclusions

The Clean Water Act is Ineffective at Protecting and Restoring Riverine Ecosystems and Biodiversity

The Act Has Failed to Eliminate or Significantly Reduce Nonpoint-Source Pollution: Polluted runoff is the primary cause of water pollution in rivers and streams nationwide. In 1988, the states reported that, of the waters they had assessed, 30% of river and stream miles were not healthy enough to support fishing and swimming. The major causes for this impairment were agricultural runoff (55%), logging (8%) and urban and construction runoff (14%).[259]   Mining and grazing impacts were also significant. In Florida, all the headwaters of the Peace River drainage were severely impaired by runoff from abandoned phosphate mines.[260]   In Oregon, officials classified over 1000 miles of the John Day River Basin as severely impaired due, in large part, to grazing (as well as logging) practices.[261]

These problems persist in large part because the EPA has consistently failed to enforce states' nonpoint pollution control mandates. For example, there has been very weak enforcement of the Act's requirements that states implement their Water Quality Management plans under Section 208,[262] and, where implemented, the Act has consistently failed to result in federal land management plans which ensure adequate protection of riverine-riparian ecosystems and biodiversity on federal lands. In addition, the EPA has generally failed to seed or obtain any federal financing for State implementation of Section 319 nonpoint-source planning requirements.[263]

Another part of the problem is that many state water quality standards are not strictly enforceable against nonpoint-source polluters because most states do not use their discretion to provide independent enforcement authority against these sources in their programs.[264] Landowners (private or federal) cannot be prosecuted directly under the CWA for violating state water quality standards. Rather, when standards are exceeded, the EPA (or affected party) must act to compel the state to take corrective measures by strengthening management prescriptions in BMPs or by writing specific discharge limitations into a permit.[265]

"Best Management Practices" Fail to Ensure Compliance With Water Quality Standards: In order to balance competing demands on resources, the BLM and the Forest Service have emphasized the use of "Best Management Practices" (BMPs) as controls on non-point pollution from timber, grazing, mining, recreational development and other uses of the federal lands rather than on compliance with standards.[266] Theoretically, the use of BMPs will ensure that water-quality standards are met without unduly restricting resource use and production. However, BMPs suffer from chronic deficiencies which have led to continued water quality problems on federal lands.

Problems faced by the Forest Service provide prime examples of the results which can be expected from overemphasis on BMPs in water quality planning. First, the agency fails to recognize that in many physical settings even the most stringent BMPs will not act as expected to protect streams, especially when placed individually within the watershed landscape.[267] For example, the chronic sedimentation and catastrophic blowouts caused by logging roads is virtually unavoidable on unstable steep terrain, though the effects generally remain unseen for years after the road is built.[268] These circumstances, as well as those where adverse effects can only be avoided at unacceptable cost, call for prevention through development prohibitions, not futile attempts to manage the level of stress to the system to control problems after they occur. It is the location of harvests and roads and the underlying geology and soils, as well as the size of the affected area, that will determine water quality impacts, not the engineering methods used.[269] Prevention, not "doing one's best" to manage these areas, is the key. Using what may be the 'best management practices" does *not* constitute meeting the law.

To date, national forests have consistently failed to exclude water-quality-sensitive lands from timber management, despite the availability of land use planning tools to do so.[270] Moreover, the

Forest Service does not adequately consider the water quality impacts of logging on nonfederal lands when scheduling its projects. These problems have led to plans which permit logging in areas where BMPs cannot prevent significant erosion and water-quality degradation.[271]

Besides being inadequate in many physical settings, another problem with BMPs is that even where they could work they are improperly or incompletely implemented.[272] One study of BMP implementation showed that most cases where BMPs had been substantially violated involved "ineffective streamside management zones."[273]

The biggest limitation of BMPs is that even if correctly implemented to meet state water-quality standards, they do not guarantee protection of riparian areas, floodplains and biological hot spots that are critical for riverine-riparian ecosystems because current water-quality standards do not measure degradation of these important components of the riverine-riparian ecosystem. It is now clear that the use of BMPs on upland areas does not guarantee stream protection. For example, many streams in the logged watersheds of Idaho's National Forests where BMPs were considered to have been properly implemented have suffered up to a 75% loss of fishery production potential.[274] This problem leads us to the next limitation of the Clean Water Act as currently implemented -- the inadequate use of standards which reflect the biological functioning of an ecosystem.

As Currently Implemented, There is Inadequate Utilization of Biological Criteria: Surface water monitoring and evaluation of biological integrity under the Clean Water Act has historically been dominated by non-biological measures of chemical and physical water properties.[275] This traditional emphasis on the quantification of chemical and physical parameters is reflected in the majority of water-quality standards developed to date. Many states have simply failed to develop biological criteria (numeric or narrative), despite the Act's clear intent to develop standards which actually reflect the health of ecological habitats and the level of biological diversity.

Not only is water chemistry just one limited indicator of riverine-riparian ecosystem health, but this approach alone fails to detect the majority of water-quality standard violations, which are transitory, and depend for their efficacy on intensive monitoring, which is usually lacking. Even when violations are detected, appropriate corrective actions may not be taken because: 1) it is difficult to directly attribute violations to specific upland activities, and 2) periodic exceeding of standards, e.g., turbidity, fails to measure cumulative damage to riverine resources.[276]

Like compliance with BMPs, compliance with traditional water-column criteria should not be an end in itself. Traditional water-chemistry criteria is totally inadequate to protect riverine-riparian ecosystems because the real point of water quality protection should be to protect the biological and ecological integrity of streams. Therefore, criteria should also be used which are based on riverine and riparian species and habitat. These types of criteria are not only better indicators of stream health, they will necessitate coordination between regulatory and resource management agencies.[277]

The inadequacy of traditional chemical measures was demonstrated in a recent study which compared the abilities of chemical water-quality criteria and biological criteria to detect impairment to aquatic life through ambient monitoring in Ohio. The result was that of the 645 waterbody segments analyzed, biological impairment was evident in 49.8 percent of the cases where no violations of chemical water-quality criteria were observed.[278]

Biological criteria are important because they are specifically related to the unique characteristics of a particular water body. Although all surface-water types exhibit functional similarities with regard to ecological community function, the biological integrity of a given site is dependent upon its physical habitat and the organisms that thrive there. Different surface-water types, and different habitats within a surface-water type may contain unique assemblages of species. Therefore, different surface-water types may require different habitat-assessment techniques adapted to the unique characteristics of the subject water body.[279]

Recent EPA guidance to the states has emphasized the use of narrative and biological criteria[280], and biological criteria have become the focus of recent battles over a state's right to deny certification of hydropower projects under Section 401 of the CWA. The Act's intent to address the ecological aspects of water quality require the consideration of all elements which comprise riverine systems, including aquatic life, wildlife, wetlands and other habitat, vegetation, and hydrology. Relevant water-quality issues include the toxicity and bioaccumulation of pollutants; the diversity and composition of aquatic species; entrapment of pollutants in sediment, stormwater and nonpoint-source impacts; habitat loss; and hydrologic changes.[281]

Although the existing CWA requirement that federal agencies comply with state water-quality standards comprises a substantive constraint on the land use activities of federal land managers, the development of biocriteria will further limit agency discretion and more effectively protect riverine-riparian ecosystems and biodiversity on federal lands.

Wetlands and Riparian Areas Are Not Protected Under the Act, Despite Their Important Role in Maintaining Biological Integrity: Under the Clean Water Act, normal farming and draining, grazing and logging may occur in or directly affect wetlands without constraint. In fact, the Act has so many loopholes and exemptions that most wetlands can be legally eradicated. Because these unregulated activities cause most of the wetlands losses each year, it is clear that Section 404 does not effectively protect most wetland areas, although many of these areas are crucial to maintaining the health of riverine-riparian ecosystems both on and off federal lands.

One of the biggest problems with the current wetlands program is that it actually permits the destruction of significant amounts of riparian land under general permits, especially Nationwide Permit 26. In certain arid regions such as California, a high percentage of the remaining wetlands meet the isolated or headwaters criteria of NWP 26 because many riparian corridors have less than the requisite five cubic feet per second annual flow.[282] Consequently, substantial stretches of critical riparian habitat on smaller stream reaches fall within the scope of NWP 26.

Even worse for riverine systems, Section 404 regulates only "wetlands," the definition of which does not include the many riparian areas and floodplains which are not also wetlands. Therefore, even if all activities in wetlands were regulated under the program, the Clean Water Act's wetlands program would not adequately protect riverine-riparian ecosystems on a whole watershed basis.

In order to adequately protect riverine systems and biodiversity, the Act needs to be amended to expressly recognize, as the EPA has done, that healthy riparian areas are critical to the maintenance and restoration of the chemical, physical and biological integrity of watercourses -- the goal of the Clean Water Act and its implementing programs.[283] Protection of riparian areas and floodplains are crucial to the health of river systems because of their valuable contributions to habitat for riverine and terrestrial species, channel and bank stability, flood storage and peak flow attenuation, groundwater recharge and discharge, and aesthetics. Many of these functions, like bank stability, relate directly to improved water quality measurements for traditional indicators such as suspended solids and turbidity.[284]

The EPA Has Not Enforced The Nondegradation Mandate, and States Retain Discretion to Determine Criteria for Outstanding National Resource Waters: Until recently, the federal antidegradation regulations and their application to nonpoint-source pollution in particular have been the least enforced components of water pollution law.[285] Enforcement of the antidegradation regulations could provide a large measure of protection for riverine-riparian ecosystems on federal lands if: 1) they are applied effectively to both point- and nonpoint sources, and 2) the standard is enforced for "high quality" water bodies on federal lands and/or these water bodies are designated as

Outstanding National Resource Waters and subjected to a strict nondegradation standard.

Even where the EPA has begun to require states to implement an antidegradation policy, the EPA has interpreted its nondegradation regulation to require only that states devise some process by which Outstanding National Resource waters may be designated and protected. States have not been required to designate any particular waters, regardless of whether such waters have already been established as outstanding public resources by inclusion in other federal conservation programs under other federal statutes, such as the WSRA (which establishes its own nondegradation policy), and the Parks and Refuge System Acts.[286]

State Implementation of the Act is Incomplete: The EPA has not effectively enforced the requirement that states develop new water quality standards, Total Maximum Daily Load Allocations, or water quality-based controls. The primary reason for this failure appears to be a lack of resources to carry out the monitoring and analysis required to determine where standards are being violated and by whom. As a result, many agencies lack the information required to identify TMDLs and waste load allocations.[287] Some states have not even specified the designated uses for their waters in detail and have failed to develop either narrative or biological criteria.

Furthermore, some state water quality standards, both numerical and narrative, exempt logging, grazing and other non-point sources. Others liberally allow temporary variances from, or modifications to, otherwise applicable water quality criteria for non-point sources.[288]

Implementation of the Clean Water Act Has Not Resulted in Widespread Coordinated Management of Riverine Systems on a Watershed Level: At long last, the Environmental Protection Agency has formally recognized the Clean Water Act's failure to function at the watershed level in its 1991 initiative entitled "The Watershed Protection Approach."[289] The watershed protection framework builds on numerous recent efforts around the country to protect and restore water quality by developing site-specific, interdisciplinary programs focused on whole watersheds, with the EPA document focusing on those watersheds where human health concerns and ecological assessments indicate the strongest need for pollution control. By adopting this framework, the EPA acknowledges that most past and many current efforts to improve the nation's waters suffer from an overemphasis on traditional water quality parameters, an approach that does not adequately address ecological function or habitat, cumulative impacts from multiple types of pollution or the need for all levels of government to be involved in cooperative decision-making for holistic management of watershed resources. Not only is this approach socially and ecologically sound, such an approach is consistent with the nonpoint-source provisions of Section 319 of the CWA which was part of the 1987 amendments.

The "Watershed Approach" indicates that the EPA is committed to reorienting federal, state and local governments to meet water-quality goals by managing whole watersheds, and that it will provide support (technical and otherwise) for the development of cooperative watershed management plans which consider cumulative chemical, physical and biological effects of human impacts watershed-wide. Although this initiative is still in the early stages, Regional offices are expected to develop regional action plans in the near future. Hopefully, the EPA's involvement in locally-driven watershed protection efforts could vastly improve management of riverine systems on federal, state and private lands.

THE ENDANGERED SPECIES ACT OF 1973

Because of its emphasis on the protection of habitat and ecosystems, the Endangered Species Act[290] ("ESA") appears to provide potentially powerful, albeit "backdoor" protection for riverine-riparian ecosystems with endangered biodiversity. However, the ESA alone does not accomplish ecosystem-based management of federal riverine lands, primarily because it was not intended as a proactive land management statute. Rather, it is a mechanism for federal intervention, which is triggered only after severe ecosystem degradation has occurred, the result of which is the endangerment of one or more identified species. Unfortunately, even after the Act is triggered by the near extinction of a species, the federal agencies responsible for administering the Act have still tended to focus narrowly on the affected species, rather than on the entire ecosystems of which their identified "critical" habitat may be just a part.

Overview of the Act

The ESA attempts to stave off extinction of "endangered" and "threatened" species by preventing both the "taking" of individuals and the destruction of critical habitat. An endangered species is "any species which is in danger of extinction throughout all or a significant portion of its range."[291]   A species is threatened if it is "likely to become an endangered species within the foreseeable future through all or a significant portion of its range."[292]   The Act is jointly administered by the Secretaries of Interior and Commerce; the Fish and Wildlife Service (FWS) takes jurisdiction over terrestrial and native freshwater species and the National Marine Fisheries Service (NMFS) is responsible for listings of marine species, including anadromous salmonids, such as salmon, searun trout and steelhead.

The language of the ESA focuses strongly on the protection of habitat and "ecosystems." Section 2 of the Act, which sets forth purposes and policy, names habitat protection ahead of species protection, stating that the purposes of the ESA are "to provide a means whereby the ecosystems upon which endangered species and threatened species depend may be conserved, [and] to provide a program for the conservation of such endangered and threatened species . . . ."[293] Both the Act's legislative history and agency policy support the primacy of ecosystem conservation in interpreting the ESA.[294]

Other sections of the ESA explicitly protect habitat by: 1) providing for the designation and acquisition of "critical habitat";[295] 2) requiring federal interagency cooperation to "insure that [agency action] is not likely to . . . result in the destruction or adverse modification of [critical] habitat";[296] and 3) prohibiting significant habitat modification as a form of "taking."[297]

The ESA is unique among federal statutes in that it puts science first, and implementation of the ESA clearly requires a solid foundation of ecological knowledge. Section 4 requires the FWS and NMFS to determine "critical" habitat for the maintenance and recovery of endangered species; Section 7 requires that the impacts of human activities on species and habitat be assessed; Section 9 prohibits acts leading to the loss of individual members of an endangered species.

The critical habitat approach: The original ESA failed to define "critical habitat," leaving it to the agencies to determine which and how much habitat should be managed as critical. The FWS and the NMFS proceeded to promulgate joint regulations defining critical habitat broadly, restricting any action which could be expected to result in a reduction of the numbers or distribution of a species of sufficient magnitude to place the species in further jeopardy, or restrict the potential and reasonable expansion or recovery of that species, and expressly stating that the term "critical habitat" should *not* be restricted to the habitat necessary for a minimum viable population.

Unfortunately, as a result of the agencies' broad interpretation, Congress amended the ESA in 1978 to provide a narrow statutory definition of critical habitat and to create a critical habitat designation process.[298] These amendments specified that critical habitat must be determined "on the basis of the best scientific data available and after taking into consideration the economic impact, and any other relevant impact, of specifying any particular area as critical habitat."[299] By introducing a balancing approach, the amendments were intended to prevent the designation of areas as critical habitat without considering impacts on land use and development interests.[300] The approach ensures that all remaining habitat of a listed species need not be protected to comply with the Act.

As now defined, "critical habitat" is an area occupied by a threatened or endangered species "on which are found those physical or biological features (I) essential to the conservation of the species"; and, (II) which may require special management consideration or protection.[301]   This statutory definition differs from that used by biologists in that the statute emphasizes "conservation"[302] and limits designated areas to those needing special management attention.[303]

The FWS regulations further narrow the definition of critical habitat by requiring the Secretary to "focus" only on those "*principal* biological or physical constituent elements . . . that are essential to the conservation of the species," rather than the full range of habitat requirements.[304]   The elements identified as "primary constituent elements" must be listed with the critical habitat designation.[305]

Thus, as currently written, the ESA and its regulations limit the geographic scope of critical habitat, directing in Section 3 that "critical habitat shall not include the entire geographic area which can be occupied by the . . . species," unless the Secretary determines otherwise, and habitat not currently occupied by the species may only be designated as critical "upon a determination by the Secretary that such areas are essential for the conservation of the species."[306] For species such as native freshwater fish, and especially anadromous fish, this is inadequate protection.

Of course, the designation of some critical habitat is better than no habitat at all. Theoretically, the Act requires that critical habitat should be designated "to the maximum extent prudent and determinable" at the same time a species is listed. In practice, however, critical habitat is rarely designated, and has been identified for only one-fifth of all listed species.

Interagency cooperation under the Endangered Species Act: Section 7 of the ESA prohibits **any government action** that may jeopardize a listed species or adversely modify its critical habitat:

> Each Federal agency shall . . . insure that any action authorized, funded, or carried out by such agency . . . is not likely to jeopardize the continued existence of any endangered species or threatened species or result in the destruction or adverse modification of habitat of such species which is determined by the Secretary . . . to be critical . . . .
> [307]

The same section authorizes the action agency, on its own initiative, to consult with the Secretary of the Interior to accomplish the "no jeopardy" and "no adverse modification" goals. The action agency must conduct a biological assessment of the endangered or threatened species in the area of a proposed project as soon as the Secretary is advised that such species "may be present."[308]   After consultation, the Secretary is directed to provide a written opinion to the action agency "detailing how the agency action affects the species or its critical habitat," and recommending "reasonable and prudent alternatives" when jeopardy or adverse modification is found.[309]

It is clear from the statutory language and the legislative history that the section 7 prohibition is meant to apply both to actions which "jeopardize" the species and actions which "adversely modify" critical habitat.   However, the regulations effectively reduce this dual mandate to a single "no jeopardy" standard.[310] The regulations provide that "destruction or adverse modification" means "alteration that appreciably diminishes the value of critical habitat for both the survival and recovery of a listed species . . . "[311] This means that destruction or adverse modification cannot be deemed to occur unless the species is put in jeopardy.[312]

The result of the regulatory interpretation is that some species, especially those with wide natural ranges such as anadromous fish, could face severe habitat loss before a FWS "jeopardy opinion" will issue.   Because the intent of the Act is clearly habitat protection, not merely population protection, the regulatory interpretation is open to attack as contrary to clear congressional intent.[313] This issue remains to be litigated.

Prohibition on taking as prohibition against habitat modification: Under Section 9 of the ESA no "person" may "take" any endangered species. This section applies both to federal action and to private conduct. According to the legislative history, the prohibition on taking explicitly encompasses "every conceivable way in which a person can 'take' . . . any fish or wildlife."[314] The term "take" encompasses "harm"[315] which is defined in the regulations as "significant habitat modification or degradation which actually kills or injures wildlife by significantly impairing essential behavioral patterns, including breeding, feeding or sheltering."[316]

As a result, Section 9 also prohibits adverse modification of critical habitat because such modification amounts to a "take."[317] However, as under current interpretation of Section 7, no taking will be found unless there is "significant impairment to that habitat,"[318] an interpretation which seriously limits habitat protection under Section 9.

Caselaw demonstrates that endangered species act listings do not always protect habitat: The case of *Pyramid Lake Paiute Tribe v. United States Department of the Navy*,[319] applies and defines the affirmative conservation duty imposed on agencies by Section 7 of the ESA.[320] This case demonstrates that, despite the facially absolute terms of the ESA, the Act does not guarantee habitat protection for endangered species.

Pyramid Lake involved a Navy land-leasing program which also leased appurtenant water rights. A Paiute Tribe claimed that the water diversion used to irrigate Navy land threatened the cui-ui, an endangered fish. The tribe also argued that the diversion of water from the river caused habitat modification that impaired cui-ui spawning capabilities, thereby working a Section 9 taking.

The Ninth Circuit upheld the FWS "no jeopardy" finding, stating that unless new information is brought to bear a FWS jeopardy opinion will not be held arbitrary or capricious under the Administrative Procedures Act's standard of review.[321]

Furthermore, the Court found that federal agencies have wide discretion to decide how their conservation duties are fulfilled, and they may not be compelled to implement proposed alternative actions if they do not have a significant effect on the specific conservation goals.[322] In *Pyramid Lake,* since the FWS had already made a supportable "no jeopardy" finding with regard to the subject diversion, the agency was not required to adopt any particular conservation-promoting plan unless it could be shown that such a plan had a "significant" effect on the amount of water diverted from the river.   Additionally, the court held that no agency action will be considered a taking under Section 9 unless it is demonstrated that habitat degradation is a direct result of the agency action.[323] On the facts at hand, the Navy's action was not the only diversion of water from the stream in question, so the causal effects on spawning could not be conclusively attributed to their diversion.

We note that the outcome of *Pyramid Lake* may have been different if the Navy land in question had been designated as critical habitat.[324] No fish species has ever recovered sufficiently under the ESA to be removed from the list.   Rather, their extinction serves this function.

Water rights and the Endangered Species Act: When a species is listed under the ESA, the lead federal agency is required to issue a biological assessment and "jeopardy" opinion whenever an action in which the federal government is involved "may affect" a listed or threatened species. If an action will jeopardize a listed species or its habitat, the lead agency must provide mitigation measures for, or alternatives to, the proposed activity.

As a matter of law, the ESA supersedes most other federal laws and policies.[325] Given this, it is still unclear whether state water law and water rights are immune from ESA regulation. Caselaw under the Clean Water Act suggests that if the lead agency is careful to couch its regulation in language which conditions how a right may be exercised, then ESA priorities will prevail.[326] *Riverside Irrigation District v. Andrews*[327] involved the downstream impacts of a reservoir on whooping crane wetlands habitat in Nebraska. A Corp of Engineers' decision to require a Section 404 permit was challenged on the basis that the Corps had no authority to regulate water quantity. A federal district court held that approval of the irrigation district's reservoir under an interstate water rights compact did not limit subsequent regulation of the project under the Clean Water Act, which imposed conditions on how a water right may be exercised. Significantly, the USFWS had issued a finding that the reservoir would jeopardize crane habitat and had imposed conditions on water use during peak flows.

Policies enunciated by courts to date demonstrate substantial deference to ESA requirements. In *Carson-Truckee Water Conservancy District v. Clark*,[328] the long-standing water right application of a water district was denied by the BOR based on the need to provide instream flows for threatened cutthroat trout and on Indian water rights in Pyramid Lake. *Pyramid Lake Paiute Tribe of Indians v. United States Dept. of Navy*[329] upheld leases and water rights utilization as consistent with the ESA, but here the USFWS had approved the leases without findings of adverse effects on an endangered species.

Although the extent of potential water resources regulation under the Endangered Species Act is still unclear, the caselaw indicates that the ESA does authorize diminution of existing water rights through regulation. Consistent with this view, a federal district court in California recently held that the exercise of valid water rights for irrigation constituted a "taking" of an endangered salmon species in violation of Section 1538 of the ESA.[330]

There are several legal arguments which may be made to limit the ESA's regulation of water rights. First, since water rights can be protected as real property, it may be argued that interference with them works a taking which requires compensation. A second argument is that since rights to water are derived from statehood acts ratified by Congress as part of admission to the union, ESA regulation violates the constitutional scheme dividing federal and state powers. Third, some argue that interstate water compacts are protected from abrogation by other federal laws. The most powerful of these arguments is that, in certain cases, water rights regulation under the ESA may require compensation. An examination of the takings law derived from wetlands regulation provides some information as to when conditions imposed on water rights under the ESA are likely to be compensable. However, a full discussion of these issues is beyond the scope of this book.

The potential impact of ESA listings on water use and riverine-riparian ecosystem protection is perhaps best illustrated by (1) the listing and potential listing of Columbia and Snake river salmon runs in the Pacific Northwest, which are highly impacted by federal dams; and (2) the plant, fish and waterfowl listings of species dependent on water from the Sacramento and San Joaquin Rivers, which feed the Bureau of Reclamation's giant Central Valley Project in California.

In the case of the Pacific Northwest salmon, in order to avoid tearing out dams or dramatically changing the power production of the vast Bonneville Power Administration hydrosystem, power users on the Columbia River system have identified increased water flows as the solution to a declining salmon population. At the same time, most conservationists believe that although the curtailment of irrigation and other water uses may alleviate some threats to salmon, the dams, hatcheries, overfishing, habitat, and riverine ecosystem problems represent significant and perhaps irreversible threats to the species. The ESA may prove vital to ensuring that minimally sufficient flows exist for salmon and to invoke the "takings" clause on federal projects. However, the prospects for salmon maintenance and recovery under the ESA appear slim at best, and the Act should be considered a last ditch effort to save riverine species on the brink of extinction.

Conclusions

The Endangered Species Act is not an effective tool to proactively or comprehensively protect and restore riverine systems and biodiversity nationwide.

As Implemented, the Endangered Species Act Focuses More on Individual Species than on Habitat and Ecosystem Protection: As the field of wildlife management has evolved, habitat management has become the central concern and "ecosystems" have become the predominant unit of analysis.[331] If properly implemented, ecosystem-based management yields the following benefits:

* A wide range of biological diversity[332] is preserved.

* The entire support system and habitat upon which a targeted species depends is protected, including the need for a large, contiguous habitat space.

* Managers are forced to take an ecological, long-term view of species survival.

* Scarce public resources are more efficiently used to prevent the extinction of individual species.[333]

However, the ESA alone fails to accomplish ecosystem-based protection or restoration for federal riverine systems because:

Implementation of the ESA Has Concentrated On Protection of Individual Species Rather Than on Watershed Protection of Habitat, Ecosystems and Biodiversity: Despite the ESA's mandate to protect "the ecosystems upon which endangered species and threatened species depend," implementation of the Act has concentrated on the protection in individual species rather than the protection of habitat and ecosystems. One example of this is the Fish and Wildlife Service's fusion of the Act's prohibitions against "jeopardy" and "adverse modification of critical habitat," such that it makes a single determination when analyzing proposed federal actions. In practice, the ESA is applied species-by-species and project-by-project, regardless of the fact that the listing of a single species is a clear indicator that an entire ecosystem is in trouble.[334] The recent listing of four anadromous fish stocks in the Columbia River system is clear evidence that an entire riverine system has broken down, yet effective, watershed-wide recovery strategies have yet to be pursued.

Riverine-Riparian Ecosystems are Only Addressed Through the Designation of Critical Habitat for Particular Species: There are certain problems implicit in the ESA's emphasis on "critical habitat" which detract from the Act's stated "ecosystem" approach. First, the term "critical habitat" implies that Congress accepted a scientifically erroneous assumption that species may be protected from extinction by preserving small populations on small pieces of habitat.[335]   This assumption ignores the fact that species preservation depends on the concept of "Minimum Viable Populations."[336]   Second, as in the case of anadromous salmonids, critical habitat may not be easily delineated -- an excuse the agencies have used more often than is justified when failing to designate critical habitat.

As now defined, the critical habitat for a species need only encompass those areas deemed "essential" to the "conservation" of a species and/or which require "special management." In most cases, this does not include the entire ecosystem, of which the listed species is a part. Thus, the Act will only protect entire ecosystems where it is determined that a particular endangered species requires such protection. As a result, the cumulative destruction of habitat which occurs when riverine-riparian ecosystems as a whole are degraded often goes without remedy under the ESA until impacts on a particular species are identified.[337]   In effect, riparian areas will be protected only if they are actually designated as "critical habitat." To date, habitat has been designated for only one-fifth of all listed species nationwide.

The ESA Was Not Intended to be a Proactive Federal Land Management Statute, and is Only Triggered After Significant Degradation Has Occurred to An Ecosystem: The most obvious reason that the ESA fails to comprehensively protect riverine-riparian ecosystems and biodiversity through proactive management is that it was intended by Congress merely as a safety net to preserve endangered species and their "critical" habitat. The Act is triggered only when a species becomes endangered, at which point ecosystem degradation has probably reached critical levels.

However, to the extent that riverine species are now listed or are eligible for listing, the ESA alerts federal and private parties to severely degraded riverine systems. Perhaps one of the greatest benefits of the recent listings of four anadromous fish in the Columbia River System is that affected parties are motivated to avoid further listings on the Columbia or on other regional rivers. Because these listings have impacted numerous economic interests (public and private utilities, irrigators, commercial fishermen, sport fishermen, Native Americans) over a wide geographical area, it has become painfully clear that the ESA is not the ideal vehicle for proactively managing watersheds and their resources. Not only will millions of dollars be spent litigating implementation of the Act, but ultimately the implementation process will be far more costly to river users than "prevention" and ecologically and biologically sensitive river management would have been.

With the number of candidate species increasing daily, it is time to act decisively to conserve riverine ecosystems and watersheds. As the Director of the Pacific Region of the FWS recently remarked, federal and state agencies must heed the warnings embodied in the recent ESA listing and fully use their authorities to conserve ecosystems by forming partnerships with local governments, non-governmental organizations and private citizens. "The Endangered Species Act should be used as a safety net only after everything else has been tried and failed."[338]

FEDERAL HYDROELECTRICITY AND WATER IMPOUNDMENT LICENSING AUTHORITY

Despite the existence of independent statutory grants which authorize the federal land management agencies to make land use decisions within their respective jurisdictions, external agencies may have the ultimate decision-making authority with regard to dams and hydroelectric projects. Frequently federal land managers' authority overlaps or is superseded by that of the Federal Energy Regulatory Commission (FERC), the Army Corps of Engineers (Corps), or the Bureau of Reclamation (BOR).

In general, the mandates and policies of each of these agencies have not been effectively interfaced with the land use planning efforts of the public land management agencies. This is only partly the fault of the land management agencies themselves -- much of the problem derives from independent statutory grants of authority given to FERC, the Corps, and the BOR over decisions which have significant impacts on federally managed lands. Overall, the agencies with final authority over dams and hydroelectric projects have focused their environmental impact analyses too narrowly, virtually ignoring impacts on the larger riverine systems and biodiversity which they so deeply affect.

Current trends within some of the land management agencies to assert themselves to prevent or modify dam projects are encouraging. However, dam and hydroelectric planning is still not integrated into a watershed management process which protects riverine systems and biodiversity. Under existing law, the detailed facts of each dam, reservoir or hydroelectric project will determine which agencies have regulatory authority and which substantive standards must be met, without adequate regard for the cumulative impacts of projects on a watershed basis.

Non-federal dams and the Federal Energy Regulatory Commission: Except in a very few circumstances, the construction and operation of non-federal hydroelectric projects is regulated by the Federal Energy Regulatory Commission ("FERC"). Although FERC operates under a legal framework which was intended to protect natural resources and recreational values, the frequency with which FERC licenses are challenged by parties seeking to protect these interests clearly demonstrates that the Commission overwhelmingly favors hydroelectric power production.

FERC is created by the Federal Power Act (FPA), and is the only licensing agency for non-federal water resources projects on the nation's navigable waters.[339] The Commission is authorized to issue hydroelectric licenses "for the development, transmission, and utilization of power across, along, from, or in any of the streams or other bodies of water over which Congress has jurisdiction . . . or upon any part of the public lands and reservations of the United States."[340] "[T]he public lands and reservations" include national forests, BLM lands, national wildlife refuges and hatcheries, and Indian reservations, but do not include national parks or national monuments.[341] FERC has interpreted this exemption narrowly, choosing to exercise jurisdiction over national recreation areas and over new hydroelectric projects at existing federal dams within parks.

Aside from the Federal Power Act provisions discussed below, FERC's approval authority is limited by obligations under other federal environmental laws, including the National Environmental Policy Act, the Clean Water Act, the Endangered Species Act, the National Wild and Scenic Rivers Act and the Pacific Northwest Electric Planning and Conservation Act (Northwest Power Act).[342] For example, under Section 401 of the Clean Water Act, a FERC application requires state certification that the project will meet state water-quality standards from the state in which the project is located.[343]

FERC "public interest" and "equal consideration" review: The basic standard for FERC decisions to allow hydroelectric development is set by Section 4(e) of the FPA: The Commission must review applications based on what it determines to be "desirable and justified in the public interest."[344] The Supreme Court has interpreted this standard broadly, requiring FERC to consider "all issues relevant to the public interest, including future power demand and supply, alternate sources of power, the public interest in preserving reaches of wild rivers and wilderness areas, the preservation of anadromous fish for commercial and recreational purposes, and the protection of wildlife."[345] Due to the broad array of factors deemed relevant to the determination of the public interest, the Commission has been permitted to emphasize power development over river protection in most of its decisions.[346]

As a result of FERC's continued endorsement of power production over environmental values, the Electric Consumers Protection Act of 1986 (ECPA) was passed to reinforce the environmental protection provisions of the FPA. The ECPA added specific provisions which require increased scrutiny of riverine impacts, including: (1) an amendment to Section 4(e) of the FPA to require that FERC accord *"equal consideration* to the purposes of energy conservation, the protection, mitigation of damage to, and enhancement of fish and wildlife (including related spawning grounds and habitat), the protection of recreational opportunities, and the preservation of other aspects of environmental quality;"[347] and (2) an amendment to Section 10(a) to expressly require "the adequate protection, mitigation, and enhancement of fish and wildlife," and to include the other purposes referred to in the ECPA's amendments to Section 4(e) of the FPA. Under the standard "reopener" clause contained in all licenses, a FERC license may be amended if a request is made by FERC, the licensee or an interested party. The reopener condition reserves FERC's right to make "reasonable modifications" in order to protect fish and wildlife.[348]

Even prior to its amendment by the ECPA in 1986, courts interpreted Section 10(a) of the FPA to require an evaluation and resolution of conflicting needs *before* a FERC license could be issued. FERC must balance the respective needs for power, energy alternatives, impacts to fish and wildlife and other national resources, the preservation of wild rivers and wilderness areas, the maintenance of natural beauty and the preservation of historic sites.[349] FERC is also compelled to include licensing conditions for the protection, mitigation and enhancement of fish and wildlife.[350] These conditions must be based on recommendations from the NMFS, the FWS and state fish and wildlife agencies.

Thus, the Commission may deny licenses to accommodate environmental concerns, which could include the protection of water quality, riparian and aquatic habitat, national park resources and so forth.[351]   In practice, FERC almost always fails to condition or deny licenses for projects with significant adverse environmental impacts.[352]

The comprehensive planning requirement: Section 10(a) of the FPA also requires FERC to find that a project is "best adapted to a comprehensive plan for improving or developing a waterway or waterways" for hydroelectric generation and "for other beneficial water uses, including recreational purposes."[353]   This provision requires two things: 1) that the Commission prepare a "comprehensive plan" for use and development of the river in the context of each project application -- a requirement that has been generally ignored;[354] and 2) that the Commission consider the proposal's consistency with existing state or other federal comprehensive plans.

The Commission has taken the position that it need not prepare written plans for river basins to satisfy the comprehensive planning requirement and that it may simply make its decision based on the evidence presented at FERC proceedings.[355] However, recent court decisions have overturned Commission licenses based on deficient comprehensive planning. One court has stated that Congress intended the Commission to conduct "coordinated study and comprehensive planning along an entire river system" which would ensure that project impacts are determined on a system-wide rather than a local basis.[356] If this could ever become reality in a meaningful way, hydropower projects could be assessed, planned and modified much more effectively.

With regard to comprehensive plans not developed by FERC, the ECPA amendments require the Commission to consider "the extent to which" the project is consistent with an existing comprehensive plan "for improving, developing, or conserving a waterway or waterways affected by the project."[357] This appears to mean that it must at least consider plans developed by states and by any agency established pursuant to federal law with authority to prepare such plans.

The Commission's official interpretation of its obligations to consider existing "comprehensive plans" recognizes a wide variety of plans, stating that plans are cognizable if (1) an authorized federal agency or state prepared the plan; (2) the plan qualifies as a "comprehensive study of one or more of the beneficial uses of a waterway or waterways," (3) the plan describes the standards, data and methodology upon which the plan is based, and (4) the plan has been filed with the Commission.[358] Although it is uncertain whether FERC's "consideration" of "the extent to which" a project is "consistent" with these plans requires complete compliance with the plans, it is clear that this provision requires some deference to resource management plans established by any of the federal land management agencies, and authorizes FERC to deny any hydropower project which conflicts with a recognized plan, absent compelling circumstances.

Authority of the land management agencies over FERC: In general, any party or agency to a FERC licensing must make substantial affirmative efforts to ensure that its views are considered by the Commission during the licensing process. Like any other interested party, federal land management agencies must formally intervene in FERC proceedings by filing a motion or petition for intervention in order to get their views on the record. If an affected party fails to intervene, it will not have standing to appeal an objectionable decision.[359]

However, under certain circumstances, the land management and fishery agencies have the right to specify mandatory license conditions.[360] Under Section 4(e) of the FPA, licenses for hydro projects on a federal reservation[361] are to be issued "only after a finding by the Commission that the license will not interfere or be inconsistent with the purpose for which such reservation was created or acquired."[362] The Act also states that such licenses "shall be subject to and contain such conditions as the

Secretary of the department under whose supervision such reservation falls shall deem necessary for the adequate protection and utilization of such reservation."[363] *Thus, the Commission must accept and implement any conditions deemed "necessary" by the supervisory land management agency.* As the Supreme Court has observed, however, this is not an absolute veto power, since the agency's conditions must be reasonably related to the goal of protecting the reservation, and it is up to the courts to judge what is reasonable.[364] Moreover, the Supreme Court has limited the scope of the agencies' conditioning authority to the geographical boundaries of the specific reservation involved. In other words, although a federal reservation which is downstream from a hydro project may be adversely affected by the project, no Section 4(e) conditions may be applied.[365]

To date, the Commission has denied several hydroelectric applications on the basis of inconsistency with federal land management objectives on reserved lands. For example, in *Re Rainsong Co.*, FERC rejected an application based on its finding that a project would deviate from an applicable Forest Service policy against road construction and logging in a "special management area" within the Olympic National Forest.[366]

Land managers' right-of-way authority: Under the Federal Land Policy and Management Act, the USFS and the BLM may grant "rights of way" for "systems for generation, transmission, and distribution of electric energy."[367] In the past, this authority has not been construed to give independent authority to these agencies to reject hydroelectric proposals, and FERC has taken the position that no such authority exists, due to preemption by the Federal Power Act.[368]

Authority of the fish and wildlife agencies: The fish and wildlife agencies have authority under the Federal Power Act to impose mandatory terms and conditions on three types of projects: 1) conduit projects at existing constructions for agricultural, municipal or industrial purposes;[369] 2) small hydroelectric projects at existing dams which use natural water features and have a generating capacity of less that 5 megawatts;[370] and 3) hydroelectric projects involving new dams or diversions where the developers seek benefits under the Public Utility Regulatory Policies Act of 1978.[371]

For these types of applications, the Commission *must* consult with the FWS, the NMFS and the local state fish and wildlife agency, and *must* include in any approval order "such terms and conditions" as any of these agencies "determine are appropriate to prevent the loss of, or damage to," fish and wildlife resources.[372] The agencies have used this broad discretion to devise terms and conditions which require minimum stream flows below dams and the installation of fish passage facilities, among other requirements.

The Commission also has a more general mandate under Section 10(j) of the FPA to consult with fish and wildlife agencies about their recommendations for fish and wildlife protection for all types of hydroelectric proposals.[373] However, these consultations do permit FERC to reject agency recommendations. The Commission may determine that recommended conditions are "inconsistent with the purposes and requirements" of the Federal Power Act or with "other applicable law," in which case it must resolve the conflict, "giving due weight to the recommendations, expertise, and statutory responsibilities" of the concerned agencies.[374]

If the Commission fails to adopt all or part of a recommended condition, it must make specific findings that the purposes of the FPA or other applicable law are contravened, *and* that the conditions imposed by the Commission comply with its mandate to adequately and equitably protect, mitigate damage to, and enhance fish and wildlife (including related spawning grounds and habitat) affected by the project.[375]

In recent years, challenges to FERC approvals have solidified the agency's obligation to fully evaluate and resolve fish and wildlife impacts as well as to consider alternative project operations *before* licensing.[376]

FERC consultation with other agencies: The ECPA amendments to the FPA now require the Commission to consider the recommendations of all federal and state agencies and Indian tribes that have jurisdiction over any resources which may be affected by a proposed hydroelectric development. Section 19(a)(2)(B) directs the Commission to consider the recommendations of all agencies with authority over "flood control, navigation, irrigation, recreation, cultural and other relevant resources of the State in which the project is located and the recommendations (including fish and wildlife recommendations) of Indian tribes affected by the project."[377] However, FERC retains the discretion to reject any proposed terms and conditions.[378]

The federal dam operators -- the Bureau of Reclamation and the Army Corps of Engineers: The Bureau of Reclamation ("BOR") and the Army Corps of Engineers ("the Corps") are both authorized to construct and operate multiple-purpose dams and reservoirs pursuant to various statutes. The extent of federal land managers' control over these dams and reservoirs varies with each project's specific authorizing legislation, individual local circumstances and the degree of interagency cooperation.[379]

The Bureau currently operates 355 storage reservoirs and 254 diversions dams and provides water to about 10 million acres of land in 17 western states.[380] Corps projects are primarily devoted to flood control, navigation and power generation, and these projects exist throughout the country.[381] In some cases, FERC may interact with these agencies where nonfederal hydropower projects occur at Bureau or Corps dams.[382]

Dams and parks: Within the National Park System, the National Park Service is obligated to administer all lands and waters so as to protect park values and resources.[383] Moreover, the 1921 Federal Power Act (FPA)[384] amendments prohibit new hydroelectric projects in national parks and monuments:

> no permit, license, lease, or authorization for dams, conduits, reservoirs, powerhouses, transmission lines . . . within the limits, as constituted, March 3, 1921, of any national park or national monument

shall be granted or made without specific authority
of Congress.[385]

There is some question as to whether this prohibition
applies to components of the park system which are not technically
"national parks or monuments," such as National Recreation Areas
and National Rivers.[386] The Park Service has taken the view that
the General Authorities Act of 1970, subjecting "all areas within the
National Park Service" to "the various authorities relating to the
administration and protection of areas" administrated by the
Service, extends the FPA prohibition to all park system
components. FERC has taken the narrower view that the FPA
prohibition applies only to parks and monuments proper. On this
basis, FERC has approved hydroelectric projects within the
boundaries of National Recreation Areas.[387]

Another problem facing the NPS is the uncertain
jurisdiction over dams and hydroelectric projects which predate the
creation of a particular park or which were specifically authorized
by Congress. Disputes over primary regulatory authority have
arisen when these dams come up for relicensing. One such
dispute involves the Gines Canyon Dam on the Elwha River in
Washington State's Olympic National Park -- a controversy which
could result in federal action to remove an operating dam for the
first time in history.

Like other federal land management agencies, Park Service
authority over areas outside park boundaries is limited to the
presentation of recommendations to federal dam operators and
regulators -- even where the proposed activity threatens to
adversely affect park values and resources.

Relicensing: A chance to correct past mistakes?: A FERC
license is valid for fifty years.[388] At the end of this period, the
project requires a new license and is subject to a completely new
licensing procedure under current law.[389] Despite the fact that
there is no legal distinction between the original licensing and the
one that takes place prior to the expiration of an old license, this
process is commonly referred to as "relicensing."

Hundreds of FERC licenses are now expiring nationwide, with most expiration dates prior to 2000. The new license applications will be subject to the amended Federal Power Act's requirement that FERC give "equal consideration" to the project's effect on non-developmental goals -- including fish and wildlife and other aspects of environmental quality -- as well as power and development goals such as navigation, irrigation, flood control and water supply.

If past actions are any indication, FERC will, by and large, continue to give the minimum protection legally allowed to non-developmental interests. As the Commission has recognized, the law does not require it to balance competing uses of a river "so each gets equal benefits from a project." Rather, the Commission simply needs to act, based on a record which includes an evaluation of all aspects of a development, including arguments from all sides. Of course, the Commission still has the discretion to determine which aspects of a resource are most critical to the public interest.[390]   With the aggressive participation of environmental interests and many state and federal resource agencies, however, there is reason to believe that some significant improvements will be made to existing operations through the relicensing process. These improvements are likely to be based on limited "mitigation" goals which fall far short of full restoration of rivers at the watershed level to a close approximation of their natural state. There appears to be no significant effort to assess the cumulative impacts on rivers with multiple dams or to adjust the operations of each, based on watershed-level needs.

Relicensing on the Elwha River -- will a precedent be set for dam removal?: No federal action, administrative or legislative, has ever required the removal of an operating dam for environmental reasons. However, recent events surrounding the relicensing of two dams on the Elwha River on the Olympic Peninsula in Washington State indicate that where the environmental havoc wreaked by a dam is not clearly outweighed by economic and social benefits, FERC and the federal land managers may now be willing to consider dam removal as a viable option.

Two dams built on the Elwha River in 1913 and 1926 pose insurmountable barriers to anadromous fish. These dams have led at least ten species of wild fish to the brink of extinction, violated Indian treaty rights and caused severe and expensive downstream erosion problems. Yet these same dams produce power for a single pulp mill. When the dams' owner applied for a new permit, FERC was required under the current Federal Power Act to determine whether the dam was in the public interest and to assess the value of the fishery.[391] In making this determination, the Commission has released a draft environmental impact statement which includes dam removal as one of four alternatives for restoring fish runs on the Elwha. Pending issuance of the final EIS, Congress is now considering statutory removal of the dams.[392] Congress failed in 1992 to successfully address the issue.

Conclusions

FERC Generally Uses Its Authority to License and Relicense Projects that Degrade Riverine Systems and Biodiversity

Federal Land Managers Have Limited Control Over Hydropower Development: Federal land managers have limited control over hydropower development affecting land within their jurisdiction. Although they may impose mandatory conditions on projects within reserved lands, they may not veto a project FERC is determined to approve. Similarly, the resource agencies (NMFS and the FWS) may prescribe the construction of fishways at FERC-licensed hydropower projects, but they do not have the power to override a FERC decision not to license at all.

In the final analysis, FERC still has the discretion to decide that a project's developmental benefits outweigh its environmental costs, and as long as a licensing decision is based on substantial evidence it will withstand legal challenge.[393] As a result, riverine systems and biodiversity continue to be degraded through issuance of FERC licenses for projects that do not protect these resources.

The hope is for significant changes in most projects on federal lands through the relicensing process.

The FERC Licensing and Relicensing Process Does Not Adequately Consider Cumulative Impacts Through the Entire River System When Approving Individual Projects: Despite the FPA's "comprehensive planning" requirements, the licensing process for dams and hydropower projects does not adequately consider the cumulative impacts of such projects on the integrity of the affected riverine system and biodiversity. Further, the impacts of multiple dams within a river system are rarely weighed, nor are new licenses or relicensing criteria based on a systemwide assessment of problems within the system or on the identification of priority projects that cause the greatest damage within the system. Under current law, FERC's analysis is generally limited to the environmental consequences of the specific proposals, without accounting for imminent actions not yet before it or outside its jurisdiction.[394]

There is No Effective Mechanism for Excluding Dams and Hydropower Projects From Specific Riverine Systems or River Segments Based On Their High Biological Importance: In general, there is no effective mechanism for excluding dams and hydropower projects from specific rivers or river segments based on their high biological importance or their relationship and effect on areas of special importance. A nationwide riverine system assessment and "protected area" program is needed to identify and protect rivers which are unsuitable for damming and hydropower development due to their ecological and biological characteristics.

This process would be similar to the "Protected Area" Program adopted by the Northwest Power Planning Council in the Pacific Northwest, which identified river segments that would be off-limits to future hydroelectric works, based primarily on fish and wildlife values. The NWPPC program was developed as a "comprehensive plan" under Section 10(a) of the FPA. A new national process to assess the impacts of all dams within specific river systems nationwide is also needed so that the most damaging projects can be prioritized. The dams causing the greatest problems within a river system should then be removed or significantly modified.

THE NORTHWEST POWER ACT AND THE COLUMBIA RIVER BASIN: AN ATTEMPT TO RESTORE AN ENTIRE RIVERINE SYSTEM

The Pacific Northwest is unique in that seventy percent of region's electricity is generated by hydroelectric dams, many of which are on the Columbia River and its principal tributary, the Snake. While the immense energy capacity of the Columbia River system has long been the envy of water- and energy-poor regions of the country, hydroelectric development has had devastating effects on the biological functions and species of the entire riverine system. Riparian areas have been inundated, water levels fluctuate wildly, wetlands have been drained, streams have been channelized, fish passage has been severely impaired, shorelines have been riprapped and vegetation has been cleared for powerlines.

Primarily as a result of flow alterations and blockages caused by the hydrosystem, by the late 1970s the legendary anadromous fish runs of the Columbia (estimated at 10 to 16 million fish per year) had dwindled to the point that the NMFS and the FWS were studying the need to list upriver runs under the Endangered Species Act. Today, only a few hundred thousand naturally spawning fish return to the Columbia each year. Four species have been listed as federally threatened or endangered.

Partly in response to the imminence of ESA petitions, in 1980 Congress passed the Pacific Northwest Electric Power Planning and Conservation Act ("Northwest Power Act").[395] The Northwest Power Act rejected project-by-project evaluation of environmental impacts in favor of a program which must, to the greatest extent possible, address the entire 258,000 square miles of the thirty-one watersheds in the Columbia River basin.[396] In order to achieve this goal, the Act created an independent regional planning body, the Northwest Power Planning Council ("the

Council") comprised of representatives appointed by the Governors of Washington, Oregon, Idaho and Montana. In addition to energy conservation and efficiency goals, the Council was required to "protect, mitigate and enhance" the fish and wildlife damaged by the hydrosystem, with specific emphasis on the improvement of flows and on providing bypass systems at major dams.[397]

The legislative history of the Act indicates that Congress intended the Council to consider fish and wildlife resources "on a par" with other river uses as a "co-equal partner" with hydropower.[398] The Council is also required to choose energy resources that minimize the total cost of providing energy services, with environmental costs included in the calculation of total cost. Positive biological results are given priority over economic considerations: minimum economic cost alternatives are favored only where biological goals are also attained, and[399] the fish and wildlife agencies' and tribes' recommendations must be given "due weight" in making programmatic decisions.[400]

Interstate regional riverine system planning under the Northwest Power Act -- success or failure?: The Council has attempted to improve fish passage, while also developing fish production and harvest management strategies. However, the Council also recognized in its 1987 plan that real improvement of the fish runs would not take place without coordinated, system-wide planning. A systemwide plan has now been established by the integration of individual plans for each of the thirty-one distinct watershed within the larger Columbia Basin. However, the plan has failed to lead to effective implementation.

In 1988 the Council approved the creation of its "Protected Areas Program," which designated 44,000 miles of stream reaches on which future hydroelectric development is now severely restricted. These areas were designated on the basis of the Council's determination that hydropower development would cause unacceptable harm to critical fish-spawning grounds or wildlife habitat.[401]

The Protected Areas Program is a great step forward. Its effectiveness is still in question, however, because it has no legal power to absolutely prohibit future hydroelectric development. Rather, the Federal Power Act requires only that federal agencies such as FERC give the program "due consideration" "to the fullest extent practicable. The Program is also limited to the extent that it designates stream reaches outside the Columbia Basin -- such as those near Puget Sound and on the Oregon, Washington and California Coasts -- where FERC, the BOR and the Corps may act without hindrance by the Northwest Power Act. This limitation permitted FERC to recommend construction of the now defunct Salt Caves Hydroelectric Project on a designated protected area, the Upper Klamath.

What should be done to protect and restore the Columbia Basin's riverine systems and biodiversity?: The Columbia River system is so heavily developed with hydropower that it is unlikely ever to be restored to any semblance of its natural state. However, it is time for past mistakes to be ameliorated, and there are changes which can be made to operation of the hydrosystem which will vastly improve the odds for anadromous fish. The stickiest issue seems to be that fish require increased instream flows at precisely those times when hydropower demand is at its seasonal low -- during the spring and summer.

But changing hydrosystems operations through flow alteration and retrofitting to improve fish passage is not enough to stop degradation of riverine-riparian ecosystems on the federal lands in the Columbia Basin. The federal lands managers have a responsibility to make substantial changes in their land use practices because over fifty percent of the remaining fish habitat in the basin is on federally managed land.[402] The Forest Service must reduce the sedimentation and loss of large woody debris that has caused an average 60 percent loss of large pools on streams in national forests over the past fifty years.[403] Grazing reforms are critical: some analysts believe that current grazing practices are the single greatest source of habitat degradation in the Snake River Basin.[404]

These changes must be accompanied by energy marketing, rate and contract adjustments which minimize barriers to increasing flows as well as costs. Regionwide, fishery management -- harvest, hatchery and supplementation practices -- will also have to change to protect weak and wild stocks. Existing habitat must be protected and degraded habitat restored. Water law reforms must be promoted to ensure increased instream flows, including the use of trust water rights, water marketing, user fees and aggressive enforcement of existing water rights.

Conclusions

The Northwest Power Act Has Not Yet Created Fundamental Change in the Columbia River System

The Northwest Power Planning Council has been most successful in protecting riverine areas from future hydroelectric development and in procuring funding for mechanical fish bypass systems at Army Corps dams on the mainstem Columbia and Snake Rivers.[405]   However, hydrosystem operations have continued without significant alteration or restoration of the riverine systems or species affected. Although an exhaustive analysis of the problems encountered by the Council is beyond the scope of this book, a few observations about the process are offered below.

Under Its Current Mandate, the Northwest Power Planning Council Has Proven Ineffectual in Compelling Significant Changes to the Hydrosystem and in Federal Land Management Practices: The Northwest Power Act's vision for a regionwide remedial plan in which fish and wildlife must be given "equitable treatment" in the planning and operation of the hydrosystem provide some hope for at least the partial recovery of the Columbia River ecosystem and biodiversity. It was anticipated that the Council planning process would require federal dam operators, the states, the numerous river users and affected interests to act collectively to improve the condition of the river system -- primarily by providing the instream flows necessary to ensure passage of juvenile fish to the ocean. To date, however, the

Council's Columbia Basin Fish and Wildlife Program, now in its fourth phase of development, has failed to resolve the "fish-power" conflict. It now looks as though the courts will ultimately be responsible for doing what the Council has not, in the context of pending lawsuits under the Northwest Power Act, the Endangered Species Act and other applicable law.

Specific problems with the Act and its implementation include:

* The Council has not deferred to the judgment of the fish agencies and tribes in developing its policies.[406] Rather than taking the more expeditious approach of depending on the existing expertise of federal and state resource agencies and the tribes to provide biological information upon which to build its Program, the Council has insisted on doing its own protracted analysis of agency and tribe proposals. Alternatively, the Council has rejected recommendations based on their perception that there is inadequate biological justification. This approach has been unnecessarily slow and has resulted in an ineffectual position with regard to the crucial issue of increased spills to increase fish passage over dams.

* Federal water managers, such as the Army Corps, have refused to implement the Council's spill requirements, arguing (not without basis) that they are not legally required to do so.[407]

* The Council has not aggressively enforced its Program, particularly with regard to flows.[408] To date, the Council's authority to enforce its own Program has been fully tested, permitting federal dam operators to pick and choose which provisions of the fish and wildlife program they will enforce. Enforcement is crucial in the face of refusal by water managers such as the Army Corps of Engineers to implement the Council's program.

Unfortunately, the Council has assumed the role of mediator between fish and power interests rather than acting as an advocate for its restoration program.[409]

* The Act's enforcement provisions are ambiguous, requiring agencies merely to take the program "into account at each relevant stage of their decision-making processes" to the extent practicable.[410]

One authority has proposed specific amendments to the Northwest Power Act which would require Council deference to the biological expertise of the fish agencies and tribes, clarify the enforcement provisions of the Act to require that all agencies act consistently with the Council's program, include fuel switching from electricity to natural gas as a conservation measure, in part to facilitate attainment of biologically required fish flow, and affirm that "equitable treatment" for fish and wildlife imposes a separate, independent obligation on federal water managers outside the Council's program.

The Northwest Power Act Does Not Focus on Restoration of Natural Riverine Systems or Biodiversity: The Northwest Power Act puts fish and wildlife habitat on a par with hydroelectric and other value of the Columbia River system, but it does not specifically identify natural riverine systems as a resource worthy of protection for its inherent value.   Even assuming that fish and wildlife habitat were actually accorded the parity it was intended to receive under the Act, there is no clear mandate to protect and restore riverine system elements and processes as a priority over other uses.

Drastic action is necessary to preserve the remaining relatively intact riverine systems, many of which are on federal lands. However, in the face of increasing pressure to maximize hydropower to meet regional needs, federal agencies appear unlikely to give these areas the protection they deserve unless they are singled out and clearly given priority over other regional resources.

MINING AND RIVERINE PROTECTION ON FEDERAL LANDS

This section examines much of the law governing minerals extraction from federal lands. We have concluded that: 1) Although the 1872 hardrock mining law has been narrowed and remedial legislation has placed some environmental safeguards on mining practices, hardrock mining remains a significant cause of riverine degradation. Due to the mining industry's continuing political power in Congress, any significant amendments to the 1872 law do not appear imminent, and mining practices reforms should be integrated into comprehensive riverine protection legislation; 2) Despite the major reforms contained in the Surface Mining Control and Reclamation Act, coal mining continues to cause damage to riverine resources; (3) Protection for long-held mineral rights on federal lands also threatens sensitive riparian areas, and 4) The BLM and the Forest Service do not fully use their authority to protect riverine systems from mining damage.

The General Mining Law of 1872: The General Mining Law of 1872[411] governs all hardrock mining for gold, copper, lead, uranium, and other metals on public lands. This law, known as the "Hardrock Act," established the now infamous policy of giving metallic ores from federal lands to all those who can find them at minimal or no cost -- essentially giving mining favored status over other uses of public lands. The law allows individuals or corporations to look for minerals on federal lands and stake claims. Each 20-acre claim may be maintained if the claimant spends at least $100 annually to "develop" the site.

If a miner proves that a deposit can be economically recovered, the law further allows the claim to be "patented," a process which leads to full ownership. Depending on the type of claim, the fee for acquiring federal land is $2.50 or $5.00 per acre. As of 1990, about 1.2 million claims covering 35 million acres were held by 160,000 corporations and individuals. About 3.5 million acres have been patented and transferred to private ownership.[412]

The Mineral Leasing Act of 1920: Federal mining law underwent a major change in 1920, when Congress passed the Mineral Leasing Act of 1920.[413] The 1920 Leasing Act exempts certain minerals from regulation under the 1872 Hardrock Act. The 1920 Act allows prospecting and development of non-hardrock minerals under leases or permits. Minerals leasable under the 1920 Act include the fossil fuel minerals (oil, gas, oil shale, coal, native asphalt, bituminous rock, and solid and semi-solid bitumen); and the fertilizer and chemical minerals (phosphate, potash, sodium, and in a few states, sulphur).[414]

In the 1920 Act, Congress authorized the Secretary of Interior to lease the applicable minerals at the Secretary's discretion and to attach conditions to the leases in order to protect public resources and the public interest. In effect, the Leasing Act ended miners' open access to these valuable minerals.

Under the 1920 Act, the leasing and development of federally-owned onshore oil and gas reserves are subject to more federal control than they were under the 1872 Mining Act. Oil and gas leases are primarily located on national forest and BLM lands which are available for such development, except in designated wilderness areas. National parks are specifically excluded from lease issuance under the Mineral Leasing Act, but National Recreation Areas (also administered by the Park Service) are not.

The impacts of oil and gas exploration and development include forced shifts in wildlife migration patterns due to human presence and the siltation and pollution of streams due to roadbuilding and development-related construction. Pre-development exploration may involve frequent helicopter flights over remote areas as well as the detonation of numerous explosive charges. Where seismic tests indicate energy reserves, exploratory drilling begins, necessitating the construction of roads and the operation of drill rigs. In addition to the disruption of wildlife migration caused by road traffic and the erosion of newly moved earth in watersheds, there is the additional risk of stream pollution from accidental spills of drilling materials. Where exploration results in full-blown commercial development, the impacts are longer-term and more severe. These impacts derive from grading for drill pads, installation of pipelines for collection and shipment and electrical lines for powering equipment.

The decision to issue a lease is discretionary with the Secretary of the Interior,[415] whose role is delegated on a day-to-day basis to the BLM. Wildlife and environmental values may provide the basis for rejection of a lease application, in addition to other "public interest" values. Under the 1920 Act, the Secretary of the Interior had equal authority over national forest lands, despite the fact that surface resources are managed by the Department of Agriculture's Forest Service.[416]

On "acquired lands" held by the Forest Service or any other agency, the consent of the appropriate department to lease issuance must be procured -- a requirement which gives the Forest Service virtual control over leasing decisions in some cases, primarily on Eastern forests. Yet, on "public domain" national forests, the Forest Service originally had only advisory powers -- except to the limited extent that land planning and management authority overrode Interior's leasing authority.

This situation changed with the passage of the Federal Onshore Oil and Gas Leasing Reform Act of 1987,[417] which elevated the Secretary of Agriculture to a position equal to the Secretary of the Interior with regard to leasing in national forests.[418] Thus, the Forest Service gained statutory authority to determine whether leases will be issued on national forest lands and was directed to regulate all surface-disturbing activities conducted pursuant to any lease. Another important aspect of the 1987 Reform Act was that it emphasized reclamation of land disturbed by leasing.[419]

The 1920 Act originally included certain other minerals which are now governed under other laws. "Common varieties" of minerals, such as sand, stone, gravel, pumice, and cinders, are governed by the Materials Disposal Act of 1947,[420] as amended by the Common Varieties Act of 1955.[421] All minerals, including hardrock minerals but not including the "common varieties," which are located on federally acquired lands are subject to lease under the Acquired Lands Act of 1947.[422] Federal geothermal resources are leasable under the Geothermal Steam Act of 1970.[423]

Because of the different laws governing certain types of minerals, the minerals found on federal lands are usually divided into three groups: locatable (hardrock minerals subject to the 1872 Hardrock Act); leasable (fuel and fertilizer minerals, as well as all minerals of acquired lands); and salable (common varieties).[424] Although coal is leasable under the Leasing Act of 1920, specific requirements for coal were tightened by the Federal Coal Leasing Amendments of 1975.[425]   Moreover, all coal strip mining operations are now subject to an important reclamation law passed in 1977.

The Surface Mining Control and Reclamation Act of 1977: The Surface Mining Control and Reclamation Act of 1977[426] primarily addresses the environmental impacts of coal mining, although the mining of other minerals is also addressed. The Act's goal is to establish a "nationwide program to protect society and the environment from the adverse effects of surface coal mining operations."[427]

The SMCRA establishes environmental protection performance standards for mining operations. Under its reclamation guidelines, all strip-mined land must be reclaimed, and reclamation plans must be approved prior to the starting of new mines.[428]   In effect, the Act provides for the restoration of lands damaged by strip mining before 1977 and the prevention and repair of damage from subsequent operations.

The SMCRA applies to surface coal mining operations on both public and private lands. Although much of the SMCRA addresses coal mining practices on the private land holdings in the Eastern United States, some provisions are specifically directed at the impacts of coal mining and reclamation on federal lands. The most important of these provisions is Section 522,[429] which provides for the designation of lands as unsuitable for some or all types of surface coal mining and prohibits mining in certain sensitive areas. This provision is of particular importance to federal land managers because it prohibits strip mining after 1977 on lands in national parks, wildlife refuges, trails, wilderness, and wild and scenic river system units.[430] Coal mining in national forests is also prohibited unless: 1) it is not incompatible with other resource values, or 2) it is incident to underground mining or takes place on unforested Western lands and is otherwise consistent with applicable land-management statutes.[431]

The prohibitions of Section 522 are expressly made "subject to valid existing rights." The intent of this provision is to avoid takings of private property requiring compensation and increasing the federal costs of SMCRA's implementation. The provision has been interpreted to exempt operators who demonstrate a good-faith attempt to apply for all necessary permits by SMCRA's effective date.

According to SMCRA criteria, the Secretary of the Interior may declare lands unsuitable for mining based on a mandatory review of federal lands or in response to a petition from any party who would be adversely affected by coal mining in a particular area. The Secretary is also authorized to review federal lands to determine suitability for mining minerals other than coal, and is required to conduct such a review at the request of a State governor or private party.[432]

Unsuitability determinations may be based on findings that: 1) the operation would be incompatible with state or local land use plans or programs; 2) mining will result in significant damage to historic, cultural, scientific or aesthetic values and "natural systems"; 3) mining will adversely affect long-range land or water productivity; or 4) mining could endanger life or property.[433] Designation as unsuitable under Section 522 does not require a showing of irreparable or permanent damage to other resources or values. Rather, the damage to a particular interest must be "significant."[434]

In sum, SMCRA requires mining companies to restore land and water affected by mining and acid mine drainage. In most cases, conditions must be restored to their pre-mining uses, though ecologically this is almost impossible to achieve. In addition, a federal tax on coal provides funds to restore lands abandoned before the Act's effective date, as well as to identify and set aside lands unsuitable for mining in the future. Lands will be identified as unsuitable for mining based on their high value for other uses, including habitat for rare or endangered species. However, SMCRA's success has been limited. Although the SMCRA unsuitability procedures do provide an opportunity for the protection of watershed-related resources, the scope of this protection is largely within the discretion of the Secretary of the Interior. Moreover, neither the reclamation requirements in SMCRA nor the 1987 Leasing Reform Act even apply to hardrock mining and the terrible dangers it poses for America's rivers.

Mining regulation by the BLM and the U.S. Forest Service: The BLM is primarily responsible for the administration of all subsurface and mineral resources on all federal lands, though its task is accomplished with the assistance of the other federal agencies. Pursuant to the National Environmental Policy Act (NEPA),[435] the BLM consults with the agency responsible for managing the surface resources whenever the exploration, development or production of subsurface resources will "significantly affect" the environment or surface land and resources.

Under FLPMA, the BLM has the authority to prevent "unnecessary and undue degradation" of public lands from any activity within its jurisdiction, including mining. As discussed above, this provision has not been extensively exercised to bar damaging activities from riparian areas, which would protect the integrity of riverine-riparian ecosystems.[436]

Because both the 1872 Hardrock Act and the 1920 Leasing Act granted all management authority for covered activities to the Department of Interior, the Forest Service originally had little control over effects of hardrock mining or mineral leasing in the national forests. In fact, the Forest Service's 1897 Organic Act permitted not only mining in the forest reserves, but also gave miners free access to timber and stone which they needed for their mining operations.[437]

However, under the Acquired Lands Act of 1947, the Department of Interior could issue leases only after approval by the agency in charge of management of the subject lands.[438] Moreover, under the Materials Disposal Act of 1947, which governed the sale of common variety minerals, the Forest Service was given authority over deposits of such minerals located within national forest lands.[439] As a result, the Forest Service enjoys greater control over subsurface activities within the national forest system.

Congress passed the Surface Resources Act in 1955 in an attempt to fight certain abuses of the 1872 Hardrock Act. Claim areas located by miners after the 1955 Act were no longer subject to exclusive possession by the miners. In effect, the Act allowed the Forest Service to finally manage the surface resources of national forest lands for multiple uses. Thus, the Forest Service was in a much better position to fight excessive mining practices in order to protect other resources, such as recreation and wildlife.[440]

Although minerals were not one of the resources listed for management by the Forest Service in the Multiple Use Sustained Yield Act 1960,[441] MUSYA was significant in the development of mineral regulation because it recognized that some uses should be limited, or even prohibited, in certain areas.[442]

Relying on its authority under these various acts, the Forest Service promulgated regulations in 1974, which require all mining operations to be conducted in such a way as to minimize adverse environmental effects on the national forest surface resources.[443] Forest Service regulations now play a major role in managing mining and mineral leasing on forest lands.[444]

Some of these regulations involve complete withdrawal of certain forest lands from mining activities, but usually lands are withdrawn from hardrock mining only.[445] Withdrawals from mineral leasing are rare because the land and surface resources can usually be protected with lease stipulations. However, where leasing would be incompatible with existing or planned uses, withdrawal may be possible. Thus, lands may be withdrawn for special uses, including uses as scenic and botanical areas, public recreation areas, or riparian zones.[446]

Under the SMCRA, national forest lands which are determined to be unsuitable for surface coal mining must be withdrawn from entry.[447] Lands deemed by the Forest Service to be unsuitable are thus withdrawn by the Department of Interior. In addition, the Department of Interior may condition or deny mineral leases based on the specific characteristics of the subject land.[448] However, such decisions depend on the discretion of the agency officials, who may be subject to numerous political pressures from industry lobbyists, and, hence, the system is dubious, at best.

NFMA safeguards: Another significant element in the regulation of minerals on forest lands involves Forest Service planning. As amended by the National Forest Management Act (NFMA) the Rangeland Renewable Resources Planning Act (RPA) requires the Forest Service to prepare integrated plans for each unit of the national forest system which reflect all "proposed and possible actions."[449] These plans are required to consider the suitability of lands for resource management and provide for methods to identify special conditions or situations which are hazardous to the various resources and to determine the relative hazards of alternative activities.[450]

Therefore, because unit planning in the national forest system is intended to consider the environmental effects of all resource-related actions on forest lands, it must evaluate those involving oil and gas. Where the effects of oil and gas development could not be mitigated in certain areas (such as riparian areas, wetlands and floodplains), these findings should be included in unit plans. Existing oil and gas leases must also be consistent with land management plans under NFMA, so such plans must specify known leasing actions in enough detail for internal consistency to be determined. Subsequent decisions by the Secretary of Interior must also be consistent with such plans.

A further safeguard on leasing is provided by the NFMA provisions requiring that "any road constructed . . . in connection with a . . . lease shall be designed with the goal of reestablishing vegetative cover on the roadway and areas where the vegetative cover has been disturbed."[451]   However, the impacts of road construction on riverine-riparian ecosystems can be significant and revegetation alone does not resolve the problems.   The NFMA implementing regulations further require an examination of the relationship between nonrenewable resources (such as minerals) and renewable resources and the need for mineral exploration and development in the planning area.[452]

As outlined above, the Forest Service has made various efforts to protect surface resources from damage due to mining, such as: regulating hardrock mining; including stipulations in mineral leases; enforcing reclamation and environmental protection requirements; and proposing that certain areas be withdrawn from mineral activity.   Frequently, though, the agency has conducted its environmental analyses only after mineral activity has begun. Consequently, the Forest Service has often failed to develop sufficient data, relating to such concerns as wildlife and hydrology, before land use decisions are made.[453]

Although the NFMA planning regulations present "the potential of providing each national forest with an overall picture of present and anticipated mineral development and of its effects on the other surface resources," it is unlikely to happen, due to obstacles such as the vast amount of surface area involved, the high number of individual mining claims, inadequate surface reclamation techniques, and perennially insufficient funding.[454] As a result, forest plans currently fail to adequately integrate minerals and leasing concerns into the management of other forest resources, and are likely to continue to do so.[455]

State and local programs affecting the environmental impacts of mining: In addition to federal statutes and regulations, miners must also comply with various state laws, which in some cases may be stricter than their federal counterparts.[456]

Of the eleven western states in the continental United States, eight have hardrock mining reclamation requirements.[457] These states require mine operators to submit reclamation plans for approval before mining operations begin. The laws of these states also require state inspectors to examine mine sites for reclamation compliance during the mining operations. These states also have authority to require mine operators to post a bond or financial guarantee to ensure reclamation.[458]

The other three western states[459] have no reclamation requirements. However, many states, including these three, do have laws and regulations to assist state officials in controlling the impacts associated with hardrock mining that could affect water quality, air quality, or hazardous waste disposal.[460] In particular, water quality laws of various western states encompass the restoration of streams affected by mine drainage and related point sources of pollution. In some cases, community programs focused on protection of environmental quality may also encompass mining impacts on local rivers and streams.[461]

The need for reforms in the 1872 Hardrock Act: Under the 1872 Hardrock Act, there is no requirement that federally owned hardrock mine lands be restored to pre-mining conditions when the ore runs out. Yet mining generates vast amounts of groundwater pollution and hazardous waste.

Approximately 424,000 acres of federal land are currently unreclaimed as a result of hardrock mining operations in the eleven contiguous western states.[462] About two-thirds of the unreclaimed areas relate to abandoned, suspended, or unauthorized mining operations. While the cost to reclaim this land has been calculated at about $284 million, much more will ultimately be needed in light of the fact that the remaining one-third of that land is currently being mined and will also need reclamation.[463]

No specific fund exists for cleaning up old hardrock mining sites. There is some money available from the abandoned mine land reclamation fund (AML) established under title IV of SMCRA. Between 1974 and 1988, five states, Colorado, Montana, New Mexico, Utah, and Wyoming, spent about $2 million from this fund to reclaim federal land damaged by hardrock mining.[464] Although the main goal of the AML fund is to promote reclamation of areas adversely affected by coal mining operations, funds may be used in some cases to reclaim non-coal sites that endanger human life and property, constitute a hazard to public health or safety, or degrade the environment. In addition to AML money, Montana, Utah, and Wyoming spent another $849,000 for hardrock reclamation on federal lands. These state funds originated in fines and fees the states impose on mine operators for reclamation purposes.[465]

In addition to state-led reclamation in certain areas, many mining sites are now listed as federal Superfund hazardous waste sites under the Comprehensive Environmental Response, Compensation and Liabilities Act of 1980 (CERCLA).[466] In fact, approximately one-tenth of the sites on the National Priorities List of sites urgently needing cleanup with Superfund moneys are mining-related sites.[467] Because mining waste sites typically span extremely large areas, the problems are typically much larger and more complex than in an average Superfund site.[468] The two largest Superfund sites in the country are mining sites: a 120-mile stretch of the Clark Fork River in western Montana, and the Burke mine in the Coeur d'Alene region of Idaho.[469]

Not only do these mining waste sites encompass massive areas, but they also contain massive amounts of waste. Mining in the United States creates 30 billion tons of solid waste per year (including mining for coal, metals and building stone), more than any other waste producer group except agriculture.[470]

Moreover, 800 million tons of that annual waste is classified as hazardous by EPA standards.[471] Environmental contamination from mining includes acid mine drainage, dissolved toxic metals (arsenic, cadmium, copper, lead, zinc), cyanide, and mercury in surface and ground waters.[472] Heavy metals pollution causes huge fish kills and destroys aquatic life in miles of streams downstream from problem mine sites.[473]

Many critics of the 1872 Act have tried for years to abolish or reform the Act. Most have argued for the passage of a law to regulate hardrock mining which would encompass many of the elements of the 1920 mineral leasing law. They argue that the location system under the 1872 Act presents numerous problems, including the facts that it provides no financial return to the federal government, it does not allow for sufficient environmental management, and it discourages comprehensive planning.[474] The major advantage to legislation based on the mineral leasing model is that federal agencies would have increased control over mining activities through the issuance of prospecting permits. With greater federal control over mineral development planning, agencies will be more likely to force miners to operate in compliance with established land use goals.

Better mineral planning is crucial because a mining company's ability to control toxic wastes released by mining operations depends a great deal on the specific site location. According to the EPA, "site selection for the mine, as well as its associated beneficiation and waste disposal facilities , is the single most important aspect of environmental protection in the mining industry."[475] As it stands, the 1872 Hardrock Act gives the miner, not the public or regulatory agencies, control over mine location, the most important factor in the environmental impacts of mining.

Finally, although many of the worst sites of mining pollution pre-date many environmental laws,[476] future and current mining operations will continue to threaten riverine-riparian ecosystems and biodiversity. In recent years, mining larger and lower-grade ore deposits has become economical through the development of chemical milling technology and large scale equipment. These new operations pose a significant threat because such operations generate an even higher volume of waste per unit of product than traditional mining operations did.[477]

Conclusions

Mining Remains a Major Threat to the Health of Riverine Systems and Biodiversity

New Riverine System and Biodiversity Protection Policies are Needed Regardless of Reforms to the 1872 Hardrock Act: Although the reclamation requirements in SMCRA and in the 1987 Leasing Reform Act have helped lessen the damage done from the mining and drilling of coal, oil, and gas, the legislative attempts to protect land and water do not even apply to hardrock mining and the terrible dangers it poses for America's riverine systems and biodiversity.

Obviously, the 1872 Hardrock Act should be replaced with new mineral development policies. However, because the crisis facing riverine systems and biodiversity is reaching significant proportions, we cannot wait for reform of the 1872 Act. Rather, new policies are needed to integrate minerals policies with the protection of other riverine resources on all federal lands. If Congress is ultimately able to pass new legislation to protect the nation's riverine systems and biodiversity from mining operations, such legislation may also help facilitate international agreements aimed at protecting rivers from pollutants caused by mining and other activities in neighboring countries.[478]   Perhaps the most insidious reason that targeting the 1872 Act is an inadequate strategy for reducing mining pollution facing the nation's rivers relates to the basic political reality in Washington. Calls for reform have echoed through the halls of Congress for years, but real changes to the 1872 Act appear to be not a great deal closer now than they were several decades ago. In the 102nd Congress, the mining reform movement has been led by Sen. Dale Bumpers, (D-Ark.) and Rep. Nick Joe Rahall II, (D-W.Va).[479] However, these congressional members are likely to meet the same fate as many of their predecessors, who were unable to pass any major reform legislation in face of the fierce opposition from the powerful mining lobby.[480]

Coal Mining Still Causes Considerable Damage to Riverine Systems Despite SMCRA: SMCRA requires mining companies to restore land and water affected by mining and acid mine drainage to their pre-mining uses. However, because such restoration is often ecologically impossible to achieve, meaningful riverine protection cannot take place unless sensitive riparian areas are protected from mining impacts altogether. SMCRA's program to identify and set aside lands unsuitable for mining should therefore be implemented to the fullest extent possible to protect riverine-riparian ecosystems based on their intrinsic value as fully functioning systems, rather than solely based on their value as fish or wildlife habitat for rare or endangered species or other values identified by SMCRA as worthy of protecting. To date, the Department of the Interior has not fully utilized SMCRA unsuitability procedures to protect riverine-related resources, although full protection appears to be within the discretion of the Secretary.

Federal Land Managers Have Not Fully Used Their Authority to Prevent the Degradation of Federal Land Riverine Systems from Mining: Although the BLM has the authority to prevent "unnecessary and undue degradation" of public lands from any activity within it jurisdiction, including mining, this provision has not been used to bar damaging activities from riverine-riparian ecosystems. Moreover, both the BLM and the Forest Service have the authority to completely withdraw certain lands from mining activities, but usually lands are withdrawn from hardrock mining only and complete withdrawal from mineral leasing is rare. Theoretically, the land and surface resources can be protected with lease stipulations, but these stipulations are not always effective to protect riverine resources.

Furthermore, the Forest Service has frequently conducted its environmental analyses only after development activity has begun. The agency consequently often fails to develop sufficient data relating to such concerns as wildlife and hydrology before minerals-related land-use decisions are made.[481] With consideration for the overall picture, etc. (through surface area involved) the Forest Service has been unable to meet its obligations under NFMA planning regulations to manage the high number of individual mining claims, inadequate surface reclamation techniques and perennially insufficient funding.[482] Overall, forest plans currently fail to adequately integrate minerals and leasing concerns into the management of other forest resources.[483]

STATE LAWS AFFECTING FEDERAL-LAND RIVERINE SYSTEMS AND BIODIVERSITY

State Wetlands Programs and Riparian Areas

Although few states to date have assumed primacy for administration of dredge and fill permits under Section 404 of the Clean Water Act, most states have programs which regulate wetlands and some riparian areas. These programs may be part of broader regulatory programs, such as coastal zone management programs implemented under the Coastal Zone Management Act or water quality certification programs under Section 401 of the CWA. Alternatively, some states have enacted laws which specifically address the regulation of activities in wetlands and riparian areas.[484]

More than one-half of the 50 states have their own wetlands programs, but many of these states protect only coastal wetlands -- leaving inland wetlands to federal regulators.[485] As of 1985, one observer said that "no state west of the Mississippi has adopted a comprehensive wetland or riparian habitat protection program for public or private lands, unlike the coastal states which have all adopted some protection for their coastal wetlands and 11 eastern states which have adopted freshwater protection statutes."[486] Exceptions include Oregon, which has adopted statewide planning guidelines for some riverine lands as well as a state tax incentive program,[487] and Washington, which includes inland shorelines as part of its coastal-zone protection program.[488]

Inland wetlands, which are closely associated both physically and biologically with riparian areas, constitute the majority of wetlands remaining in the lower 48 states. Therefore, the states' general omission of these areas from their wetlands and riparian programs is significant indeed.[489]

In response to the inadequacy of federal law to protect wetlands, some states are now acting to protect inland wetlands, which is also good for riparian areas. For example, in February 1991, the Wyoming legislature passed the Wyoming Wetlands Act, which declares that "all water, including collections of still water and waters associated with wetlands within the borders of this state are property of the state," and found water to be one of the state's most important natural resources which must be protected for the overall public welfare of the state.[490]

In general, however, riparian areas are regulated as part of a shoreline, watercourse or forestry program "buffer strip" rather than as a distinct resource to be protected.[491]   As a result, definitions of riparian areas are less common than definitions of wetlands.   For example, in Alaska a riparian area is regulated under the state Forestry Practices Act as a 100-foot corridor along a watercourse. In Connecticut, riparian areas are regulated according to local discretion under state standards, but only as they relate to watercourses and floodplains.   Kansas regulates riparian areas through its statewide water plan in terms of vegetation and associated wildlife areas.   Arizona defines riparian areas through executive order as a larger area which encompasses wetlands and is determined by the aquatic and terrestrial ecosystems dependent upon surface and groundwater.[492]

State Water Resources Law

Ever since Congress enacted the Reclamation Act of 1902, establishing a major program of water storage and distribution, the United States has generally agreed to abide by state laws relating to the control, appropriation, use or distribution of water.[493] Thus, although they may be influenced by federal requirements, federal and private rights to water are governed by state law. Congress has repeatedly deferred to state water allocation systems in the creation, administration and enforcement of water rights[494]. This deference is demonstrated in the Wallup Amendment, now codified in the Clean Water Act:

> It is the policy of Congress that the authority of each State to allocate quantities of water within its jurisdiction shall not be superseded, abrogated or otherwise impaired by this chapter. It is further the policy of Congress that nothing in this chapter shall be construed to supersede or abrogate rights to quantities of water which have been established by any State. Federal agencies shall co-operate with State and local agencies to develop comprehensive solutions to prevent, reduce and eliminate pollution in concern with programs for managing water resources.[495]

Because state law has primacy in water resources allocation, the federal government is required to seek appropriation for water just like any other legal person.[496] The federal government explicitly consented to the jurisdiction of state courts in adjudication of water rights under the McCarran Act.[497]

Generally, water rights in the West are governed by the doctrine of prior appropriation, which allocates water rights based on the basic principle of priority: "First in time, first in right." This principle has its source in the 1867 Mining Law, which allocated both water and mining rights according to the same theory. Those who first appropriated water to a beneficial use hold the "senior" right and have a superior claim to the available water from a particular source in times of shortage. Water rights are appurtenant in perpetuity to the land on which they were first put to use, unless they are altered through state administrative procedures, or by the operation of forfeiture laws which deem the right to have been abandoned after periods of nonuse.

Historically, water rights in the Eastern states were governed by common law principles of riparian rights, in which the ownership of land adjacent to streams or bodies of water gives the landowner the right to make reasonable use of natural flows. The riparian owner's right is subject both to the availability of water and to the reasonable use by other landowners similarly situated. Rights to water are litigated between the parties using the procedural rules governing quiet-title action for real property.[498]   Today, some western states have integrated elements of riparian law into their statutory water laws.

Both eastern and western states have enacted permitting or registration requirements applicable to the use of both surface and groundwater.   With certain exceptions, these requirements generally apply to all water uses above established threshold quantities, including water uses claimed by Native American tribes and the federal government.   A number of states have also established minimum stream flows, lake levels and groundwater levels. The establishment of minimum flows may be accompanied by a statutory definition of beneficial use which includes instream uses.

An extensive discourse on the problems inherent in the water rights allocation systems of the various states is beyond the scope of this paper. This assessment is limited to the impact of state law on federal water rights for federal lands.

The most significant developments for federal water rights have been: (i) the establishment of federal reserved water rights under the "Winters Doctrine," (ii) the enactment of the Federal Power Act which gave the federal government a dominant role in licensing dams and hydroelectric facilities (Section IV above) ; (iii) the designation of river-dependent species as threatened or endangered under the ESA, which imposes independent limits on water use (Section III above); (iv) the imposition of permit requirements on cities and other water purveyors under the Clean Water Act (Section II above); and (v) the designation of federal Wild and Scenic Rivers, which prevents water resources developments (Section I above). The doctrine of federal reserved water rights is discussed below.

State law and federal implied water rights: Winters' Doctrine: Although state law remains a primary authority over federal rights to water, courts have interpreted federal law to establish a larger role for the federal law in the determination of federal water rights.

Winters v. United States[499] established an implied federal reserved water right for federal land reservations, such as Indian reservations and national forests. This water right is limited to the water necessary to serve the purposes of the original reservation.[500] Federal reserved rights have been extended to national monuments,[501] and, by analogy, to other federal reservations, including national parks, national wildlife refuges, stockwater ponds and springs.[502]

Federal implied reserved water rights are limited. Significantly, they have been rejected for wilderness areas[503] despite the fact that a federal court held in 1985 that wilderness designation included a reserved water right.[504] Reserved water rights have also been rejected for BLM land not expressly reserved, and for other federal land withdrawals, including public land orders for grazing districts under the Taylor Grazing Act, unless an express claim for water is made.[505]

The implied reservation doctrine may be used to protect federal lands from detrimental upstream uses whenever water necessary to effect the purpose of reserved lands is threatened. For example, in *Cappaert v. United States*[506], the Court held that the United States had priority to water over upstream users because a downstream national monument contained fish that depended on the water and one of the purposes of the monument was preservation of the fish. However, in *United States v. New Mexico*, the Court held that the doctrine did not apply to wildlife preservation on National Forest lands, because the sole primary purpose on these lands is to preserve timber supply and watersheds, and the secondary purpose of wildlife preservation cannot be used to trigger the doctrine.[507]

Even where an implied reserved water right does exist, however, absent express statutory direction to an agency, there is no federal duty to assert this right against other water users in state adjudications.[508]   As a result, reserved rights often go unrecognized.

In sum, although many of our federal lands are entitled to reserved water rights, these rights have been infrequently asserted by the managing agencies.[509]   As a result, riverine-riparian ecosystems on federal lands have suffered. Furthermore, current judicial interpretations of implied reservation law denies reserved rights to many federal lands, including wilderness areas. Express statutory reservation of water rights for wilderness and other areas may, therefore, be necessary to protect flows in these critical areas.

Conclusions

State Laws Fail to Fill Gaps Left by Federal Statutes

State Wetlands Programs Omit Many Riparian Areas: Because most state wetlands programs omit inland wetlands, which are closely associated with riparian areas (and which constitute most of the remaining wetlands in the lower 48 states), these laws fail to adequately protect riverine and riparian areas.

Water Rights for Federal Lands: Express Reservation Needed to Ensure Adequate In-Stream Flows: Although many federal lands are entitled to reserved water rights, which could ensure sufficient instream flows to protect riverine resources, such rights are not always used to the full extent of the law. To their credit, federal agencies (particularly the Park Service), have become somewhat more vigilant in identifying and asserting their rights as competition for the resource increases. However, because there is no clear federal duty to assert these rights, and because the extent of implied rights is both limited and subject to a factual showing, the express reservation of specific rights would be in the best interest of preserving riverine systems and biodiversity on the nation's federal lands.

APPENDIX B

RIVERINE SYSTEM AND BIODIVERSITY MANAGEMENT BY THE FEDERAL LAND MANAGEMENT AGENCIES

This section analyzes how the primary managers of federal lands protect riverine systems and biodiversity under their authorizing statutes. The Department of Agriculture's Forest Service is discussed in Part I and the Department of Interior's Bureau of Land Management is discussed in Part II. Part III is a brief discussion of the "multiple use" principles utilized by the Forest Service and the BLM and why they fail to result in watershed-level planning by either agency. The protection of riverine resources under Interior's National Park Service (NPS) and Fish and Wildlife Service (FWS) is discussed in Parts IV and V respectively. Part VI briefly discusses the potential for riverine ecosystem protection in the Wilderness System, and Part VII reviews statutory provisions for interagency coordination and the consideration of cumulative impacts in federal land management.

UNITED STATES FOREST SERVICE MANAGEMENT OF RIVERINE SYSTEMS AND BIODIVERSITY

The Forest Service has what would appear to be ample authority to manage forest lands for the protection of riverine systems and biodiversity based on several statutes and executive orders:

> * The Organic Act of 1897 gives the Forest Service authority to manage for the purpose of preserving "water flows," as well as to furnish a continuous timber supply

* The National Environmental Policy Act requires the agency to identify the environmental impacts of its planned activities on riverine resources

* The Multiple Use and Sustained Yield Act (MUSYA) requires that the Forest Service manage "watershed" and "fish" resources as equally valuable resources with outdoor recreation, range, timber, and wildlife[510]

* The National Forest Management Act prohibits timber harvest where "watershed conditions" will be "irreversibly damaged" or where "water conditions or fish habitat" will be "seriously" or "adversely affected,"[511] and also requires the Forest Service to manage fish and wildlife habitat to maintain well-distributed, viable populations of existing native fish species throughout the national forests system

* Two Executive Orders on "Floodplain Management" and "Wetlands Protection" require the Forest Service to manage development on floodplains to minimize future damage, which includes the protection and improvement of riparian areas and to recognize that healthy riparian areas may have the same values found in wetlands, such as species diversity and hydrologic values

* The Clean Water Act requires all federal agencies to comply with all federal, state, and local water quality standards, and the Forest Service has signed individual memoranda of agreement with several state water quality agencies in which it agrees to meet or exceed state water quality protection standards

However, a review of the current situation reveals that despite explicit directives in the NFMA and the MUSYA to manage for all renewable resources -- including "watershed," and fish habitat, as well as timber harvesting standards -- the current implementing regulations and informal Forest Service policies fail to guarantee protection for riverine-riparian ecosystems, watersheds or their floodplains in national forests. Further, the Forest Service has failed to promulgate specific rules regarding the protection of fish habitat and riverine biodiversity despite the mandate to do so in the NFMA. Although some actions affecting riverine-riparian ecosystems and biodiversity pursuant to current regulations and policies appear to conflict with the language of NFMA, such actions have generally been upheld as within Forest Service discretion. Directives under NEPA, the Organic Act and Executive Orders also fail to protect the biological integrity of riverine systems, because they do not contain explicit standards for the protection or restoration of riparian areas, hillslopes, floodplains, and other biological hot spots found throughout river systems. The limitations of the CWA have been previously discussed.

Non-NFMA U.S. Forest Service mandates

The Organic Administrative Act of 1897: The Organic Administrative Act of 1897[512] created the National Forest System and declared that the national forest lands of the United States "shall, as far as practicable, be controlled and administered in accordance with the following provision," which reads, in relevant part:

> "No national forest shall be established, except to improve and protect the forest within the boundaries, or *for the purpose of securing favorable conditions of water flows,* and to furnish a continuous supply of timber for the use and necessities of the citizens of the United States."[513]

The Organic Act entrusted the forest reserves to the Secretary of the Interior, but the Transfer Act of 1905 transferred forest administration to the Department of Agriculture, where it remains today.[514]

Essentially, the Organic Act authorizes the President to establish national forests for the dual purposes of (1) securing "favorable conditions of water flows," and (2) "to furnish a continuous supply of timber." Although the Act sets some strict limits on timber harvesting, the statute provided no forest management guidelines. While the Organic Act appears to provide a clear mandate to protect watersheds, the reality is that subsequent policies have rendered the original mandate almost meaningless. While the phrase "securing favorable conditions of water flows" has escaped judicial scrutiny, top legal scholars have argued that these words are the same as "watershed."[515] They have further argued that Congress was more concerned with protecting watersheds in National Forests than timber supply. However, Supreme Court cases have denied the Forest Service's arguments that minimum in-stream flows to protect aesthetic, recreational and fish values were reserved to the United States within a National Forest.

Regardless, there is still potential for the application of the Organic Act to protect riverine systems and biodiversity. In *United States v. Jesse*, the Colorado Supreme Court accepted the Forest Service's argument that in-stream flows were essential to "secure favorable conditions of water flows" under the Organic Act.[516] Some legal scholars have argued that this case could potentially implicate not only in-stream flows but also the physical structure of the stream channel as part of watershed protection.

The Multiple-Use, Sustained Yield Act of 1960: Although the Forest Service Organic Act of 1897 emphasized timber supply, watershed protection, and general forest preservation, the Forest Service has always managed for a wide range of uses, including recreation, livestock grazing, wildlife and, later, wilderness.[517] The Multiple Use Sustained Yield Act of 1960 ("MUSYA")[518] formally established a multiple-use policy on the national forests by stating "outdoor recreation, range, timber, watershed, and wildlife and fish" shall be subject to multiple use management.[519]

Congressional intent was to give each of the listed resources equal status in the eyes of federal resource managers.[520] Specific requirements of the Act directed the Forest Service to develop formal district and regional "Multiple-Use Planning Guides" and district-wide Management Plans. Many aspects of this planning mechanism have been carried forward into present-day planning under the National Forest Management Act (NFMA)

The MUSYA (and its more limited 1944 precursor) created no new authority; it simply confirmed the Service's authority to continue doing what it had been doing for decades. The terms of the Act supplement and refine the Organic Act but do not supersede it.[521] Although the more specific terms of the NFMA tend to supplant the Act's general standards, the NFMA clearly reaffirms the multiple-use, sustained-yield policy as the fundamental basis of forest planning and management. As the Public Land Law Review Commission concluded in 1970, the vaguely defined concept of "multiple use" has "little practical meaning as a planning concept or principle."[522] The definition of "sustained yield" is also open to interpretation and leaves many critical questions unanswered. For example, how large a reference area is used to determine whether the sustained yield of timber is being achieved? Are yields from extra-forest private and federal lands to be considered? What time unit should be used to determine sustainability for a particular resource?

The specific provisions of the MUSYA are further discussed in the section entitled "Watershed as a Multiple Use." Suffice it to say here that the MUSYA provides scant guidance to Forest Service land managers and was largely a symbolic piece of legislation designed to provide explicit authority for recreation and other uses for which prior authority was unclear or nonexistent. The Act had the additional effect of statutorily condoning existing Forest Service policies and of retaining the Forest Service's traditionally broad administrative discretion in managing the forest system.

National Environmental Policy Act: The National Environmental Policy Act[523] is an umbrella statute which applies to certain actions of the federal government and generally embodies public trust principles with regard to preservation of the environment for future generations. NEPA declares "a national policy which will encourage productive and enjoyable harmony between man and his environment; to promote efforts which will prevent or eliminate damage to the health and welfare of man; to enrich the understanding of the ecological system and natural resources important to the Nation; and to establish a Council on Environmental Quality."[524]

Courts have interpreted NEPA to establish judicially enforceable obligations which require all federal agencies to identify the environmental impacts of their planned activities. Within the Forest Service, the passage of NEPA in 1969 increased the importance of planning almost immediately, primarily because a number of agency initiatives were judicially blocked on the basis that they failed to comply with NEPA. As a result, the Forest Service began to focus on NEPA compliance at the forest planning level.[525]

Although NEPA has been successfully used by conservationists to provide the procedural grounds for injunctions against roads and timber sales affecting watersheds,[526] NEPA is a limited legal tool because it forces only the disclosure of consequences of federal actions, not actual protection itself. Therefore, any agency action for which an agency writes a sufficiently thorough Environmental Impact Statement (or Environmental Assessment) cannot be judicially challenged on substantive grounds. The significance of NEPA in accomplishing watershed-level management of the federal lands is discussed further in Section VII.

The Forest and Rangelands Renewable Resources Planning Act: In 1974, Congress enacted the Forest and Rangelands Renewable Resources Planning Act (RPA)[527] which, for the first time, required agency-wide strategic planning. The RPA emphasizes Congressional oversight of the Forest Service by requiring extensive reporting and formulation of a recommended Renewable

Resource Program. The RPA requires planning at the national, regional, and individual forest levels.

In effect, the RPA has been amended by and merged with the National Forest Management Act (NFMA), which reduced Forest Service management discretion by creating a comprehensive planning process with detailed forest-by-forest planning provisions, but preserved the agency's traditional management independence.

Planning and riparian management under the National Forest Management Act of 1976: The Forest Service is currently responsible for the management of the 191 million acre National Forest System (NFS). Each national forest ranges in size from 400,000 to 3,000,000 acres and is comprised of four to nine ranger districts.

The National Forest Management Act[528] ("NFMA") provides a comprehensive planning framework for management of the National Forest System through the development of management plans for individual forest units. The Act's primary focus is to establish land and resource management planning, ostensibly in order to achieve the effective use and protection of renewable resources and a balancing of uses on forest lands. Although non-NFMA legal authorities also govern management for recreation, range, watershed and wildlife purposes in national forests, most planning for these resources is now conducted as part of the general NFMA planning process.[529] The NFMA planning process is also refined by the procedural requirements of the National Environmental Policy Act, but NFMA imposes greater public participation requirements.

As discussed below, the express language of the statute provides direct legal authority for development of a Forest Service-wide riparian management policy in Section 1604(g)(E), which provides that timber harvests shall not be conducted if watershed conditions will be irreversibly damaged or unless protection is provided for streams from "detrimental changes which are "likely to seriously and adversely affect water conditions or fish habitat."[530] However, the only codified regulation implementing these provisions is a directive in the Forest Service regulations requiring forest managers to be guided, generally, by a 100-foot "riparian management zone" from the edge of a water body, within which land uses may not degrade water quality or fish habitat.

General planning structure and unit planning: In general, of the four federal land management agencies the Forest Service is the most accomplished and sophisticated land planner. Not only does the Forest Service have a longer history of land-use planning, but the NFMA provides a more comprehensive and specific planning mandate than do statutes which govern the other agencies. By 1988, the Forest Service had promulgated the 10-year Forest plans required by the statute for each of the 156 National Forests, and the implications of these plans for the riverine-riparian ecosystems affected by them are just now becoming apparent.

The forest planning process is primarily concerned with establishing allowable timber harvest levels and harvesting modes, and actual planning decisions often rely on computer programming models.[531] NFMA contains numerous limitations on timber harvesting, including standards restricting harvest in certain areas and limits on how much timber may be cut in any given period. Procedural and substantive criteria limit the approval of clearcutting.[532]

At the general planning level, the NFMA requires the development of four types of planning documents, which were also required under the RPA: 1) an Assessment, every ten years, which describes the renewable resources in all the national forests,[533] 2) a Program, every five years, which proposes planning objectives over the next 45 years for all Forest Service activities;[534] 3) an annual Report which evaluates actual forest activities in relation to Program objectives; and[535] 4) a Presidential Statement of Policy every five to ten years which frames budget requests, as well as annual explanatory statements when such budget proposals fail to request adequate funds to achieve the objectives of the Statement of Policy.[536]

The national objectives of the Program are essentially "filtered" through the Statement of Policy, and each region and each forest within the region is expected to meet certain of the Statement goals in the regional and forest plans.[537] However, the

Statement itself is not binding, and local District Rangers retain wide discretion to determine how Statement goals shall be met by individual forest plans. The Forest Service regulations implementing NFMA describe the planning process as "iterative," in that "information from the forest level flows up to the national level where in turn information in the RPA program flows back to the forest level."[538]   Statements of Policy serve as general parameters, with the regional and local plans setting definite standards and goals upon which actual management decisions are based.

Forest unit planning occurs in three stages: 1) planning regulations meeting statutory guidelines are promulgated in conjunction with scientific specialists; 2) unit plans are drafted and refined in accordance with the regulations and with the Statement of Policy, and 3) plans are revised at set minimum intervals.

Unit planning begins with the development of a continually updated comprehensive inventory of all National Forest System lands and resources by the Secretary of Agriculture.[539]   The stated goal of the unit planning process is to "form one integrated plan for each unit," which is amendable only with public participation and which must be revised at least every fifteen years, or as warranted by "significantly changed" conditions.[540]

In promulgating plans, the Secretary of Agriculture is instructed to coordinate with all state, local, and other federal agencies and to use a "systematic interdisciplinary approach" which provides for public participation at all stages, including a hearing prior to plan adoption.[541]   Plans are also required to comply with the multiple use and sustained yield objectives of earlier legislation, the most prominent of which is the MUSYA of 1960.[542]

Statutory directives for riparian and floodplain management: As already mentioned, protection of "watershed," which necessarily includes riparian areas and floodplains, is specifically addressed by NFMA: The statute provides in Section 1604(g)(E) that timber harvests shall not be conducted *unless*:

(i) . . . soil, slope or other watershed conditions will not be irreversibly damaged . . . [and]

(ii) . . . protection is provided for streams, streambanks, shorelines, lakes, wetlands, and other bodies of water from detrimental changes in water temperature, blockages of water courses, and deposits of sediment, where harvests are likely to *seriously and adversely affect water conditions or fish habitat.*[543]

As discussed below, the only codified regulation implementing these provisions is a directive in the Forest Service regulations requiring forest managers to be guided, generally, by a 100 foot "riparian management zone" from the edge of a water body, within which land uses may not degrade water quality or fish habitat. Thus, under the Forest Service's regulations and implementing forest plans, "serious" or "adverse" effects may not be considered to have occurred until after considerable damage to the resource has been done.

The NFMA also purports to preclude timber harvest in situations where necessary to preserve biodiversity or on "unsuitable" lands: 1) In managing fish and wildlife habitat, statute requires the Forest Service's regulations to specify land management guidelines which "provide for diversity of plant and animal communities";[544] and 2) Management plans are required to identify marginal lands deemed "unsuitable for timber production," based on "physical, economic, and other pertinent factors" where "resource protection or reforestation cannot be ensured on such lands."[545]

At the time NFMA was passed, there was some confusion over the extent to which the statute was intended to impose substantive limits on Forest Service authority over water resources. For example, the Senate sponsor of a competing bill perceived the NFMA as providing the agency with "the complete authority to harvest timber in any manner it desires with little or no protection for soils, nutrients, aesthetics, wildlife, watershed protection or slope condition."[546] As one legal commentator observes, NFMA's language arguably sets forth a "statutory charge," not "enforceable standards," because, ultimately, the statute relies primarily on the agency's professional expertise to decide how the charge will be implemented.[547]

Regardless of whether NFMA's watershed protection provisions are labelled as "standards," they are nonetheless enforceable against the Forest Service to the extent that they enunciate non-discretionary agency duties.

Forest planning regulations specifically pertaining to the protection of water and riparian areas: Forest plans must comply with the NFMA implementing regulations,[548] which are codified at 36 C.F.R. Part 219. The statute sets forth reasonably detailed criteria for the content of the planning regulations, including NEPA compliance and clearcutting standards requirements.[549] Each nontimber resource is also briefly addressed in the regulations. The listed nontimber resources are wilderness, fish and wildlife, grazing, recreation, minerals, cultural and historical values, "natural" areas, and plant and animal diversity.[550] Consistent with the statute's directives, the stated purpose of the regulations is to ensure that forest plans "provide for multiple use and sustained yield of goods and services from the National Forest System in a way that maximizes long-term net public benefits in an environmentally sound manner."[551]

The focus and substance of the forest planning regulations were largely determined by the fact that the immediate precipitating force behind the NFMA was the injunction against clearcutting which came out of *West Virginia Div. of Izaak Walton League of America, Inc. v. Butz* in 1975.[552] As a result, the regulations concentrate on where, how and how much timber is to be cut from the national forests. Planning for nontimber surface resources, including riparian and floodplain management, is to a large degree determined by limitations on timber production -- despite the fact that the NFMA repeatedly directs that the forests be managed for "multiple use" of renewable resources.[553]

The regulations do, however, state general management guidelines for the protection of riparian areas:

> * *Riparian Areas*. Special attention shall be given to land and vegetation for approximately 100 feet from the edges of all perennial streams, lakes and other bodies of water. This area shall correspond to at least the recognizable area dominated by the riparian vegetation. No management practices causing detrimental changes in water temperature or chemical composition, blockages of water courses, or deposits of sediment shall be permitted within these areas which seriously and adversely affect water conditions or fish habitat. Topography, vegetation type, soil, climatic conditions, management objectives, and other factors shall be considered in determining what management practices may be performed within these areas or the constraints to be placed upon their performance.[554]

> * *Soil and water*. Conservation of soil and water resources involves the analysis, protection, enhancement, treatment, and evaluation of soil and water resources and their responses under management and shall be guided by instructions in official technical handbooks. These handbooks must show specific ways to avoid or mitigate damage and maintain or enhance productivity on specific sites. These handbooks may be regional in scope or, where feasible, specific to physiographic or climatic provinces.[555]

These regulations are intended to comply with the NFMA mandate requiring the Forest Service to "insure" that timber will not be harvested unless "protection is provided for streams, streambanks, shorelines, lakes, wetlands, and other bodies of water from detrimental changes in water temperatures, blockages of water courses and deposits of sediment where harvests are likely to seriously or adversely affect water conditions or fish habitat."[556] However, the actual implementation of this provision for individual forest plans or permit requests depends on the Forest Service's interpretation of what constitutes "serious and adverse" effects on water conditions and fish habitat. Clearly, the current NFMA regulations provide little guidance here. They vaguely provide that "special attention shall be given to the 100 feet on either side of perennial streams" and then repeat the NFMA provision that "serious and adverse" effects shall not be allowed to occur as a result of activities in these riparian areas.[557] Even if no logging were permitted in the 100-foot riparian area (which the regulation does not require) it is unlikely that all streams would be protected -- especially those in steep headwater areas.

The minimum viable populations requirement: The regulations also attempt to comply with the NFMA "adverse effects" on fish habitat directive by claiming that adverse effects have not occurred wherever "minimum viable" fish populations are maintained.[558] However, the Forest Service typically fails to distinguish between fish species and individual fish stocks (or populations) in implementing its "minimum viable population" regulation. Failure to manage or protect stocks allows the agency to claim a species may be "maintained" within one river segment, forest, or state, while many genetically distinct stocks are completely eradicated in other parts of the forest, state or region. As a result, the "minimum viable" test does not preserve substantial amounts of habitat on an ecosystem basis, and the "minimum viable" threshold often permits considerable sedimentation and fish habitat loss to occur under particular forest plans.[559] As a result, this regulation only constrains habitat management where a fish species is at or near endangered status. For healthier fish populations, the regulations specifically address only riparian area management,[560] and agency guidance merely gives preferential consideration to riparian-dependent fish habitat in cases of user-conflict, otherwise calling only for "coordinated management" to prevent, mitigate or compensate for habitat losses.[561]

Thus, although this regulation may provide some protection for endangered and threatened species, healthier fish populations receive no assurance under a "minimum viable" test that existing habitat levels will be maintained. For example, during the promulgation of a 1986 plan for the Boise National Forest, the Secretary's office stated that fish habitat need only be maintained in that condition which would support "minimum viable" fish populations, and that planning for higher protection was merely "discretionary."[562] This interpretation seems at odds both with the NFMA mandate and with the Clean Water Act's requirement that state water quality standards be met by non-point polluters, including timber harvesters.[563]

These and other problems with Forest Service implementation of their statutory duties have recently prompted a coalition of environmental groups to level a Service-wide legal challenge against existing forest plans in the Pacific Northwest on the basis that the plans fail to insure the prevention of "serious and adverse" effects on "water conditions and fish habitat" under 16 U.S.C. § 1604(3)(E)(iii).[564] Furthermore, as defined ecologically, riparian areas are often wider than 100 feet from streams and nothing in the regulations specifically addresses floodplains, which are most often wider than 100 feet and critical to ecological functions, or other important biological hot spots.

"Marginal Lands" narrowly applied: Forest Service regulations dilute the NFMA's "marginal lands" provisos by requiring land to be identified as not suited for timber production where "technology is not available to ensure timber production from the land without irreversible damage to . . . watershed conditions."[565] Since "irreversible damage" may only be found where mitigating technology is "not available," marginal lands designations turn on the determination of whether technology is "available." This narrowing construction of the NFMA directive to

exclude lands from timber production has been upheld on judicial review.[566]

We note that although it would make sense to consider steep slopes and other factors contributing to soil instability as "physical" or "other factors," the current planning regulations dilute the applicability of the marginal lands provisions considerably. As a result, the agency has excluded very little of its land from timber production under this provision. The Forest Service's actual application of the regulation is demonstrated by the following:

> * Some local planners have interpreted the regulations not to require that the damage prevention technology actually be available for use on the subject site. Rather, they deem it sufficient that such technology exists and is available somewhere.[567]

> * The Forest Service Manual provides that "economic efficiency is not a factor in the determination of physical suitability."[568] As a result, agency policy does not require planners to consider whether a given harvest method (for example, helicopter logging) is economically feasible.

> * In response to the many landslides that have occurred in the Northern Region (Montana and Idaho), the agency has defined "irreversible" damage as landslides greater than one acre in size, thereby excluding most landslides in the region from the NFMA provision.[569]

In sum, the Forest Service's planning regulations discussed above are not only ecologically inadequate to protect riverine-riparian ecosystems and habitat, they may also be legally inadequate to comply with the watershed protection requirements of NFMA.

Minimum management directives: The Forest Service informally developed nonstatutory standards called "minimum management directives" for resource protection in 1986. The directives address each of the subjects listed in § 219.27 of the regulations: resource protection, vegetative manipulation, silvicultural practices, riparian areas, soil, water and biological diversity. The authority for directives derives from the regulations on "resource integration requirements" for forest planning, which state:

> The minimum requirements· for integrating individual forest resource planning into the forest plan are established in §§ 219.14 through 219.26 of this subpart. For the purposes of meeting the requirements of § 219.12(c) [preparation of planning criteria], additional planning criteria may be found in the guidelines for managing specific resources set forth in the Forest Service Manual and Handbooks.[570]

Since the planning regulations are too general to provide non-discretionary management standards, the Service has purportedly developed MMRs to interpret the planning regulations, claiming that these requirements do constitute non-discretionary standards.[571] Thus, minimum management requirements are ostensibly derived from and are identical to the regulatory provisions addressing various resources.[572] The directives are intended to provide national direction and to ensure consistency in forest planning under NFMA and its implementing regulations.[573] Current MMRs include, for example, interpretation of the regulations' requirement that the Forest Service give "special attention" to areas within 100 feet of streams.[574]

In practice, individual national forest managers have interpreted "special attention" differently: some completely eliminate timber harvests from the 100-foot corridor, some allow harvests on extended rotations and others simply place increased emphasis on logging standards.[575] On the whole, the directives do not appreciably constrain forest-level management decisions in matters of riparian protection.

Forest Service Manual provisions: The National Forest Service Manual (FSM) defines riparian areas somewhat more broadly than do the federal regulations. As stated in the Forest Service Manual, riparian areas are defined as:

> Geographically delineated areas with distinctive resource values and characteristics that are comprised of the aquatic and terrestrial ecosystems.[576]

This provision recognizes that riparian areas should be determined ecologically, and the Manual goes on to state that these areas should be managed "in the context of the environment in which they are located, recognizing their unique value."[577] Managers are further required "to give preferential consideration to riparian dependent resources when conflicts among land use activities occur."[578]

We note that Manual provisions may be amended by regional policy supplements which can place different emphases on riparian and floodplain policy in a particular region.[579] For example, the FSM from the Forest Service Region I (November 1983) supplements the national riparian management guidance as follows, with an emphasis on the use of interdisciplinary teams to meet policy goals:

> * FSM 2526 recognizes that: "Riparian areas in the Forests of the Northern Region sustain life, attract people and produce resources greatly disproportionate to their size."
>
> * FSM 2526.02 establishes that "the objective of riparian area management is to protect, maintain, and improve the management of riparian areas by recognizing their

inherent biological, visual and physical values, as well as selective commodity values."

* FSM 2526.03 sets two Region I riparian management policies: "(1) preserve and enhance productivity through maintenance and improvement of dependent resources (high water quality, fish, certain wildlife and vegetation); and (2) utilize independent resources (i.e. timber, forage, minerals, and certain recreation) so they do not adversely affect dependent resources." These policies are to be accomplished through project-level plans for desired riparian conditions, BMPs and interdisciplinary implementation processes.

* FSM 2526.046 requires the Regional Forester to develop a "procedural guide for the description, inventory, analysis, protection and improvement of riparian areas."

* FSM 2526.04c requires the Forest Supervisor to 1) delineate all existing riparian areas and describe current and desired conditions for identified independent resources in riparian areas; 2) ensure that interdisciplinary teams evaluate projects, describe desired future riparian conditions, develop management objectives and develop or update project plans. This section also includes a provision stating that management activities shall "encourage improvement as well as protection of riparian areas," such as: planting or encouraging indigenous riparian vegetation, streambank stabilization, "controlling surface erosion within the riparian ecosystem," re-establishing water tables, and initiating habitat improvement projects.

* FSM 2526.04d requires the District Ranger to develop management guidelines/project plans for specific sites and to convene interdisciplinary teams.

* FSM 2526.12 requires riparian inventory and analysis, and 2526.13 states that BMPs shall be defined by journeyman hydrologists and/or soil scientists and incorporated into all project designs in riparian areas.

Forest Service Region 6 (Oregon and Washington) supplementation to the FSM (June 1987) emphasizes the identification of the riparian area based on site-specific characteristics:

* FSM 2526 defines streamside management units (SMUs) as perennial and intermittent streams "and an adjacent area of varying width where practices that might affect water quality, fish and other aquatic resources are modified to meet water quality goals for each class of streams." Ephemeral streams are not included in SMUs, but the Manual urges the application of "satisfactory land management practices along these streams."

* FSM 2526.05 defines stream classes, types and classification procedures.

* The Region 6 FSM provisions rank streams in Classes I-IV, depending on their significance for domestic use and fish habitat. BMPs are to be applied to all streams, and forests are encouraged to establish specific water quality goals where state standards are not "appropriate" for non-point sources. Specific management goals are set for each class of stream. We note that management criteria which give less protection to streams which do not themselves bear fish are dangerous because managers may ignore the fact that smaller streams may flow directly into fish-bearing streams, delivering silt and debris caused by logging and roadbuilding in upper stream reaches.

Although many of the Forest Service Manual provisions noted here conceptually encourage the protection of riparian areas and floodplains, in practice they provide only limited guidance for the management of riverine systems, and do not constitute specific land management standards or binding, enforceable regulations.[580] Rather, they are used to guide forest managers in devising specific project and land management plans for individual forests. Further, there is not even a "guideline" to stimulate the identification and protection of riverine refugia or watershed/biodiversity reserves. The end result of these generic guides is that the Forest Service management fails to protect riverine-riparian biodiversity and does not accomplish needed restoration.

Enforceability of NFMA mandates and Forest Plans: Despite the fact that forest plans are subject to statutory requirements and are legally binding, when combined with the wide discretion accorded the Forest Service by the NFMA and the MUSYA, judicial review of forest plans has generally resulted in deference to Forest Service judgments. This means that even though the statutes appear to provide ample authority for full protection of watershed resources and riverine-riparian ecosystems, it would be very difficult to challenge any particular Forest Service action on the basis that they did not comply with NFMA's mandate.

However, two cases involving judicial review of agency decisions made under pre-NFMA plans are significant because of their relation to water quality: *National Wildlife Federation v. United States*[581] and *Northwest Indian Cemetery Protective Association v. Peterson*[582].

In *National Wildlife Federation v. United States*,[583] plaintiffs claimed that a Forest Service clearcutting plan violated pre-NFMA guidelines, which were substantially similar to those which became part of NFMA. One claim was that the clearcutting would seriously injure fisheries within the forest, therefore violating the guidelines' requirement that clearcutting must protect water resources and fish habitat -- a provision which parallels the current NFMA requirement at 16 U.S.C. § 1604(g)(3)(F)(v) stating that clearcuts must be "consistent with the protection of soil, watershed, fish, wildlife . . ."[584] Another claim was that the proposed cut was not silviculturally essential, as required by a provision in the guidelines -- a provision which parallels the NFMA requirement at 16 U.S.C. § 1604(a)(3)(F)(i), that clearcutting be used only where it is "determined to be the optimum method."[585]

Ultimately, although the court found that the guidelines which plaintiffs invoked were judicially enforceable, the court decided that the plaintiffs had presented insufficient evidence to show that serious injury to fisheries or other natural resources would ensue from the proposed cut and accepted the Forest Service's determination that clearcutting was silviculturally essential. For rivers, the most positive finding of this case was that the Forest Service could not sell timber in an area prone to mudslides, and where the sale would affect fish habitat, without preparing an EIS.[586] The case thus established a requirement for project-level NEPA review in unstable riparian areas and steep slopes.

In *Northwest Indian Cemetery Protective Association v. Peterson*,[587] the Forest Service proposed timber sales and road construction in an area susceptible to water pollution through siltation. The district court found that construction of a proposed road would cause significant slope failure and loss, and that the existing EIS was deficient because it failed to adequately discuss the probable impacts of the proposed agency action. However, the court made clear its position that NFMA provisions constitute broad policies rather than prescriptive standards, stating that "like the Multiple Use, Sustained-Yield Act, the NFMA requires that national forest lands be managed with due consideration given to environmental values . . . . Here, the balancing of competing values struck by the Forest Service . . . was not so insensitive to environmental concerns that it violates the NFMA."[588] The district court's findings were ultimately upheld by the Ninth Circuit Court of Appeals,[589] striking a blow to parties interested in enforcing the watershed protection provisions of NFMA against the Forest Service.

Northwest Indian is also significant for watershed protection because it illustrates the substantive limits placed on federal land managers by the Clean Water Act.[590] The court found that state non-point source water pollution standards must be met by the proposed action, and that such compliance is not automatically demonstrated by a statement that "Best Management Practices" will be complied with.[591] Therefore, if implementation of a proposed plan will violate state water-quality standards, the plan may be enjoined on these grounds alone.[592]

Few cases have been decided directly under NFMA plans. Perhaps the most important case under a NFMA forest plan to date is *Citizens for Environmental Quality v. United States* (the *"Rio Grande"* case), the first case involving a full analysis of NFMA planning requirements.[593]   In *Rio Grande*, environmental organizations challenged the land use plan for the Rio Grande National Forest in Colorado. These organizations primarily objected to the designation of certain lands as suitable for timber production. Although the court agreed with the Forest Service on most issues, the court sided with the environmentalists on NFMA planning issues and ordered the cessation of increased timber harvests until the identified problems were corrected. Thus, the agency was forced to go back to the drawing board on several major plan issues, including its use of FORPLAN, the computer model used to project timber harvests.

The *Rio Grande* plaintiffs also attacked forest service planning methodologies and the resulting land-use plan on nine separate grounds, many of which the court upheld. The court's disposition on at least two of these claims bears directly on riparian management standards under NFMA:[594]

> * Unstable soils. The Forest Service claimed that no
> lands should have been removed from timber production
> due to unstable soils because its regulations allow
> harvest where technology is available to correct
> watershed damage.[595] The court rejected the
> environmentalists' claim that physically unsuitable land

should be removed from the timber production inventory completely, finding that temporary watershed damage is allowable if it is not irreversible, and that post-plan site-specific studies could determine unsuitability.[596] However, because the Forest Service failed to identify or explain the available technology, the court required the agency to modify its plan in light of specific technological applications.[597]

* Plan amendment after post-plan landslides. The environmentalists argued that landslides occurring after plan approval require the reevaluation of soil stability assumptions and, therefore, plan amendments. The court agreed with the Forest Service that even though the NFMA provides that plans "shall" be revised "when the Secretary finds conditions in a unit have significantly changed," the implementing regulations interpret this language to make plan amendment discretionary.[598]

In summary, the few cases to date involving forest plans promulgated under the NFMA indicate that Forest Service actions are likely to be subject to greater scrutiny for substantive and procedural compliance than were earlier plans because there is simply more law to apply in conducting judicial review. However, courts are still likely to resort to de minimis review and deference to agency interpretations in order to preserve agency management discretion.

Current USFS national riparian/wetlands management policy: Recently, the Forest Service has made efforts to improve its management of riparian and wetland areas, primarily through the issuance of more executive policy documents which set general goals and strategies. However, these documents are general and do not provide any additional clear technical guidance on how riparian, floodplain, and wetland areas are actually to be managed or how statutory and regulatory requirements should be interpreted.

The Forest Service first issued a national riparian management policy in 1980, which appeared as a section in the National Forest Service Manual. Each region then issued its own manual supplements or "action plans" based on the policy. In 1986, the USFS revised its original policy to omit areas in the 100 year floodplain which are not perennial streams, such as ephemeral drainages.[599]

In 1989, the Chief of the Forest Service called for forest regions and individual forests to develop a schedule for improving 75 percent of the unsatisfactory riparian areas by 2000. Apparently, this result caused the ranks to request additional funding, which has not yet materialized.

In the fall of 1991, the Chief issued a two page document entitled "Riparian Management: A Leadership Challenge." This document called for increased agency efforts to: 1) "adjust activities and uses affecting riparian areas to achieve, over a reasonable period of time, consistency with existing forest plan standards and guidelines"; 2) "strengthen and clarify forest plan standards, where needed, to protect riparian areas and wetlands"; and 3) "implement regional riparian strategies and develop forest action plans that respond to the national strategy and our [RPA] commitment." The Chief stated his belief that these activities could take place with available resources.

Six Goals and five Strategies were also stated and may be summarized as follows:

Goals:

* Improve 75% of "unsatisfactory" riparian conditions to meet forest plan standards by 2000, and the remaining 25% by 2010

* Design future activities and current uses to avoid the degradation of "healthy riparian areas" and "wetlands"

* "Strengthen regional guidance and incorporate additional standards and direction in forest plans, as necessary, to sustain the health of riparian areas that are affected by mining, recreation, wildlife and domestic livestock, off-road vehicles, roads, and other activities"

* Assist and advise landowners via cooperation with State Foresters and the [Soil Conservation Service] to identify, manage and improve riparian areas and to sustain "riparian productivity"

* Continue riparian and wetland research

* Begin riparian demonstration projects on all ranger districts by fiscal year 1992

Strategies:

* Use an "integrated approach" to implementing forest plan riparian area and wetland standards

* Set on-the-ground national, regional, and forest goals: e.g., "to meet forest plan riparian condition standards by the end of the forest planning period"

* Establish a "priority action program" in each region using the forest plan process, to improve riparian conditions through integrated resource management of "whole watershed basins"

* "Complete a forestwide inventory of riparian area conditions and ecological health by the year 1995

* "Develop broad-based support for a strategy that energizes people, promotes innovation, supports entrepreneurial spirit, builds on success through

networking, provokes appropriate change in perspective, and recognizes those that accept the challenge"

Although these types of general policy directives are encouraging, they do not constitute specific, legally binding standards and procedures for the management of river systems on the national forests. Rather, riparian management standards are still determined at the forest level. As a result, "each National Forest's plan varies in the thoroughness of its efforts to "protect, manage, and improve" riparian areas."[600] Further, there are not even general policy directives to catalyze the identification and protection of riverine refugia or watershed/riverine biodiversity refuges.

Significantly, there is no national guidance (other than the arbitrary 100-foot standard in the NFMA regulations) as to what constitutes a "riparian area."

Executive Orders pertaining to Forest Service management of riparian areas: Executive Order 11988 on "Floodplain Management" and Executive Order 11990 on "Wetlands Protection" were issued on May 24, 1977. EO 11988 requires the Forest Service to manage development on floodplains so as to minimize future damage. This implies the protection and improvement of riparian areas.[601] EO 11990 recognizes that healthy riparian areas may have the same values found in wetlands, such as species diversity, hydrologic values.

Both of these orders provide authority for the protection of floodplains and riparian areas as priorities in management of forest lands. However, floodplain management and protection is still discretionary and there is no national guidance as to what constitutes a floodplain or hyporheic area.

Riparian management on Alaskan forest lands: Congress has imposed additional riparian management standards on forest system lands in Alaska through the Tongass Timber Reform Act,[602] which amends the Alaska National Interest Lands Claim Act (ANILCA).[603] This bill reduces timber production targets, eliminates the annual road-building appropriation, requires renegotiation of two long-term timber contracts, authorizes the USFS to choose harvest sites and sizes, and establishes a minimum 100-foot buffer along major anadromous fish-bearing streams.[604]

While a positive step, the 100-foot buffer is still not an ecological definition of riparian areas. As the National Marine Fisheries Service recognizes, the 100-foot buffer policy addresses only a minimum buffer zone width, and in some cases a wider zone will be necessary to protect fisheries resources.[605] As with the 100-foot riparian "special attention" area on other forests, the implementation of the 100-foot buffer requirement on the Tongass has been inconsistent and has not provided adequate protection for river ecosystems.[606]

Clean Water Act requirements and memoranda of agreements with state agencies: Like all federal agencies, the Forest Service must comply with federal, state, and local water-quality standards under the Clean Water Act. In addition, the Forest Service has signed individual MOAs with Idaho, Oregon, and Washington in EPA Region 10. In these agreements, the Forest Service generally agrees to meet or exceed state water-protection measures. Additional obligations may also be entailed. For example, in Idaho the Forest Service may be audited by the Idaho Division of Environmental Quality. In Oregon, the agency has agreed to meet or exceed the stream protection measures of the Oregon State Forest Practices Act, which in itself is almost totally devoid of effective riverine and riparian protection regulations.[607]

The requirement that the Forest Service comply with the standards promulgated under the Clean Water Act imposes perhaps the most substantive of all existing legal limitations on federal land management. On its face, the specific resource protection goals of the CWA appear to conflict with the multiple use principles of the NFMA and the MUSYA. The Forest Service, however, takes the position that these statutes are not incompatible because water quality need only be controlled "to the extent feasible," given the competing demands of its various statutory mandates.[608] In accomplishing this balancing feat, the Forest Service has emphasized the development of "Best Management

Practices" which are intended to control potentially detrimental, commodity-oriented land uses so that water quality standards can be met. The limitations of the BMP approach to water quality protection on federal lands have been previously discussed.

Minerals and forest management: Mining on the federal lands has been previously discussed. In sum, national forest lands overlay large quantities of both "leasable" minerals (such as coal, oil, gas, and geothermal steam) and "locatable" minerals (such as uranium, chromium, gold, and silver). The Forest Service's minerals program purports to ensure that these resources are developed only as compatible with the management of surface resources, including water, fish and wildlife. In administering its minerals program, the Forest Service cooperates with the BLM, which is the lead administrative agency for all energy and mineral resources on all federal lands. Minerals removal requires the completion of environmental analyses and the issuance of lease permits or mining claim permits. The Forest Service is also responsible for administering operating plans designed to minimize the off-site impacts of mining activities.[609]

Conclusions

Forest Service Policies, Rules and Regulations are Inadequate and Ineffective to Protect or Restore Riverine Systems and Biodiversity

The Forest Service operates under statutory directives which in theory require direct watershed management on forest lands. First, the Organic Act and the MUSYA require the USFS to manage for "favorable conditions of water flows" while considering the sustained yield of multiple uses, including "watershed," in all resource allocation decisions.[610] Second, under the NFMA, timber harvests are supposedly restricted under certain circumstances: (1) in areas where harvests are "likely to seriously or adversely affect water conditions or fish habitat, "[611] and (2) on "marginal" or unsuitable lands whenever resource protection cannot be "insured," e.g., where "irreversible" watershed damage would occur.[612] On their face, these provisions appear to provide some protection for riverine-riparian ecosystems and biodiversity.

In practice, however, these provisions have failed to provide adequate protection for riverine resources on national forests for the following reasons:

Existing Directives are Too Broadly Stated: The directives for watershed management imposed by the Organic Act and the MUSYA are too broad to constitute enforceable substantive "standards" against particular management activities. Rather, they constitute policy guidelines within which the Forest Service has retained ample discretion over the management of lands under its administration. More specific guidance is needed to constrain Forest Service discretion so that riverine-riparian ecosystems and biodiversity are consistently protected -- even when balanced against the exploitation of commodity resources.

The Forest Service has Narrowly Interpreted its Charge Under NFMA to Provide Limited Protection for Riverine-riparian Ecosystems: Although the broad language of the NFMA requires that individual forest plans prevent timber harvesting in all cases where it will "seriously or adversely affect water conditions or fish habitat," the regulations tend to narrow the recommended protected area to an arbitrary riparian "zone" which consists of the 100 feet on either side of streams or surrounding lakes.[613] It appears that in promulgating the regulations, the agency's scientific advisory committee concentrated on protection of narrowly defined riparian areas, although the NFMA does not limit the protected area in this way. Rather, timber harvesting on non-riparian erosive toe slopes can seriously detract from water quality and fish habitat. These areas should be protected in forest plans.

Specifically, the regulations contained in 36 C.F.R. Part 219 which pertain to the management of riparian areas do not adequately protect riverine systems because "riparian areas" are effectively limited to 100 feet from the edges of perennial streams or that area which is dominated by "riparian" vegetation. In fact, riparian areas are most often much wider than this 100-foot corridor and include floodplains. Floodplains, hyporheic areas and ephemeral streams are not included, nor are headwaters and other upland areas which are significant components of riverine ecosystems. Significantly, roadbuilding and timber harvest along intermittent and ephemeral streams can adversely affect downstream seasonal and perennial streamflows and fish habitat, primarily through sedimentation, warming of water temperature and energy content.

Notably, FSM 2526.05 defines riparian areas as "geographically delineated areas with distinctive resource values and characteristics that are comprised of the aquatic and riparian ecosystems," but this definition does not provide for the scientific location of riparian areas or set specific management standards. Moreover, its legal status is that of internal agency guidance rather than that of an enforceable regulation.

The Forest Service Regulations Do Not State a Clear, Nationally Applicable Riparian Area Management Policy: Even within the arbitrarily selected riparian area, there are no strict constraints on forest plans. Rather, this area must be given "special attention," and soil and water conserved so that "permanent" impairment of the productivity of the land does not occur.[614] This gives wide latitude to individual forests in coming up with their forest plans. Often, specific timber sales, roadbuilding and other activities "shave away" at even this arbitrary riparian area setback.

There Are No Policy Statements, Standards, Rules or Guidelines that Even Mention the Need to Identify and Protect the Remaining Healthy Biotic Refugia, Benchmark Watersheds and Biological Hot Spots: To its credit, the Forest Service has recognized the dire need for restoration on many of the river and streams within its jurisdiction. However, current Forest Service policy, at all levels, fails to recognize the unique value of the remaining, relatively undisturbed watersheds, biotic refugia and biological hot spots that still remain in riverine systems within the National Forest system. These areas must be identified and protected to provide the natural capital needed to maintain and restore the systems.

Identification and protection of these areas is important because most of the remaining relatively healthy riverine habitat for many entire riverine systems is on federal lands, especially in the West. Hence, the federal lands will "carry the weight" of long-term maintenance and recovery efforts until habitat restoration on contiguous private land sections downstream takes effect. This was the dramatic conclusion drawn by the Scientific Panel on Late Successional Forest Ecosystems, a panel of four scientists empowered by the Agriculture and Merchant Marine Committees of the U.S. House of Representatives. The so-called "Gang of 4" released a report in October 1992 that identified 14 overall options to manage west-side forests in Oregon, Washington and northern California. Also included was a "watershed and fish habitat option," which identified 137 key watershed reserves on federal lands in need of protection to maintain at least 90 endangered salmon populations. Their justification was that the federal lands held most of the remaining healthier habitat for these salmon, and that the 137 watersheds needed protection and restoration to maintain viable populations, given the degradation of private-land riverine habitat.[615] The "watershed option" also included ecologically defined riparian area protection proposals across the landscape on federal lands, a ban on new roads in roadless areas and other ecological protections.

The Minimum Viable Population Requirement is Inadequate to Protect Fisheries and Other Forms of Riverine Biodiversity: The regulations require forest plans to provide sufficient habitat to "maintain viable populations" of fish.[616] These provisions are intended to ensure that fish habitat is managed to ensure the continued existence of threatened and endangered species throughout their range. These regulations have the potential to provide significant protection for habitat within river ecosystems, and, consequently, fish populations.

However, because the Forest Service typically fails to distinguish between fish species and individual fish stocks (or populations) in implementing this regulation, the agency is permitted to claim a species may be "maintained" within one river segment, forest, or state, while many genetically distinct stocks are completely eradicated in other parts of the forest, state or nation. Thus, the "minimum viable" test does not speak to the preservation of substantial amounts of habitat on an ecosystem basis and has been interpreted to set a threshold for habitat destruction rather than protection, permitting considerable sedimentation and riverine habitat loss to occur under particular forest plans.[617]   Although this regulation may provide some protection for endangered and threatened species, healthier fish populations and other forms of riverine biodiversity receive no assurance under the regulations that existing habitat levels will be maintained, and riverine-riparian ecosystems, as a whole, are not protected.

Marginal Lands Narrowly Applied: Although the NFMA requires timber harvests to be prohibited on "unsuitable" or "marginal" lands on the basis of "physical, economic, and other pertinent factors,"[618] the current planning regulations authorize the identification of marginal lands only where "technology is not available to ensure timber production from the land without irreversible damage to . . . watershed conditions."[619] As a result, the agency has interpreted its marginal lands mandate narrowly, and has excluded very little of its land from timber production under this provision, with dire consequences for watershed-related values.

Because the Forest Service Manual provides that "economic efficiency is not a factor in the determination of physical suitability"[620] the agency does not require planners to consider the economic feasibility of a particular harvest method, which allows many inappropriate ones to go forward with dire consequences for watershed-related values.

Furthermore, the agency has defined "irreversible" damage as landslides greater than one acre in size, thereby excluding many landslides in the region from the NFMA provision.[621] This policy is indefensible from an ecological perspective, since landslides of any size bury critical spawning beds, increase sediment flows that fill in deep pools and, in general, can cause significant and often irreversible damage to delicate riverine-riparian ecosystems.

Riverine Management Varies from Forest to Forest: Largely because the forest planning regulations do not set stringent riparian protection standards nationwide, the management of riparian areas varies considerably from forest to forest. Although some forests, such as the Willamette and the Shasta/Trinity forests have used their management discretion to propose reasonably protective management guidelines, others, such as the Umpqua, Siuslaw and Siskiyou National Forests in Oregon, have extremely lax and ineffective proposals from the scientific perspective.

Pursuant to a 1987 National Policy Statement, the Forest Service announced its intent to maintain and enhance fishery resources through the "balanced consideration" of all resources in forest planning and management, resulting in healthy riparian areas and aquatic ecosystems.[622] At this point, however, without a significant infusion of resources to accomplish these goals, as well as the promulgation of clear implementing rules and standards, such statements do little to slow the continued degradation of riparian areas and biodiversity on national forests.

A Directive for Watershed-wide Assessments and Management of Riverine Systems and Biodiversity is Lacking: Under current law, there is no mechanism to ensure that the condition and trends of riverine systems and biodiversity under Forest Service management be assessed, planned, monitored and documented on a watershed basis. The efforts of several Forest Regions and Research Stations to develop and publish methods to inventory and classify riparian areas is a start, and should be unified and funded through new legislation. The Chief's 1991 Riparian Management Strategy calls for the completion of a "forestwide inventory of riparian area conditions and ecological health by the year 1995," but no additional funding for this purpose was allocated.

However, riparian areas and other riverine resources should be assessed not only in terms of the forests. An entire river-system-wide assessment is required to determine the role that federal land habitat and ecological processes play in maintaining and recovering the conditions of the entire system. Generally, most cumulative impacts caused by forest activity such as increased sedimentation have the greatest impact on the lower end of the river system--which are generally on private lands, not federal forest lands. Without river system-wide assessments, most cumulative impact analysis are meaningless. Further, as the Scientific Panel on Late Successional Forests found for public lands in the Pacific Northwest, system-wide assessments are needed to determine the role that healthier federal land habitat and riverine areas ecosystems may play in ensuring the maintenance of fish and other forms of riverine biodiversity systemwide.[623]

BUREAU OF LAND MANAGEMENT RIVERINE SYSTEMS AND BIODIVERSITY MANAGEMENT

According to the Bureau of Land Management ("BLM"), "riparian-wetland areas" constitute 8.8 percent of the 270 million acres administered by the agency, or approximately 23.7 million acres.[624] This amounts to 180,000 miles of riparian-wetlands in Alaska and the 11 contiguous western states, and includes smaller tracts in Minnesota, Alabama, Arkansas, Florida, Louisiana, and Mississippi. The BLM has recently devoted increased verbiage and some resources to problems of riparian degradation, but specific management regulations for the protection of riverine-riparian ecosystems have not been developed at the national level.

The statutes governing land management under the BLM are generally less specific than those governing the Forest Service. The multiple use provisions of the Federal Land Policy and Management Act ("FLPMA") and the watershed provisions of the Public Rangelands Improvement Act ("PRIA") appear to prohibit BLM approval of activities which harm watershed values. However, these laws fail to impose hard constraints on riparian management, because they do not sufficiently limit agency discretion, and thus permit the BLM to sacrifice watershed values in favor of other resources.[625]

The most serious threats to the integrity of riverine systems and biodiversity on BLM lands derive from: 1) timber and roadbuilding operations on the BLM's revested Oregon and California lands; 2) livestock grazing; 3) mining and mineral leasing; 4) water diversion; and 5) intensive motorized recreation.[626] Because the watershed damage from overgrazing by cattle, sheep and horses and from timber operations on the Oregon and California lands constitute the most widespread threats to riverine systems on BLM public lands, this analysis will concentrate on those activities.

Federal Land Policy and Management Act of 1976: The Federal Land Policy and Management Act of 1976[627] ("FLMPA") grants the BLM its general administrative authority, sets general management guidelines and focuses specifically on several resources and tracts. Although Section 1712, which addresses agency planning, neglects to include any requirements for plan schedules, procedures or content, other provisions of the statute do require that management actions and priorities must be consistent with land use plans.[628]

FLPMA was intended to institute formal, systemwide land use planning on BLM public lands. However, the language of the statute does not provide enough clear planning guidance to effectively focus the BLM's planning efforts. As one analyst observes, the result is that "[t]he overall planning picture on the BLM public lands is . . . one of confusion."[629] As of this writing, the BLM is still in the process of implementing FLPMA's directive that the agency plan for all its lands.

Substantive planning requirements under FLPMA: Although FLPMA states nine mandatory criteria for plan development and revision[630], the statute contains only a few clear, land-use planning requirements. First, the Secretary of Interior must prepare and maintain a continuing inventory of all public lands and resources.[631] Second, the Secretary must "give priority" to the designation and protection of "areas of critical environmental concern" (ACEC) in developing and revising land use plans.[632] Third, such plans must "provide for compliance with applicable

pollution control laws."[633] A fourth provision requires the BLM
to "take any action necessary to prevent unnecessary or undue
degradation of the [public] lands."[634]

Other FLPMA planning requirements, all contained in
section 1712 (c), are even more general and require the Secretary
to do the following:

> * use multiple use and sustained yield principles, as
> defined elsewhere in FLPMA and in other law
>
> * "use a systematic interdisciplinary approach to achieve
> integrated consideration of physical, biological, economic
> and other sciences"
>
> * rely on available inventories of "public lands, their
> resources and other values"
>
> * consider both existing and potential future land uses
>
> * "consider the relative scarcity of values involved and
> the availability of alternate means (including recycling)
> and sites for realization of those values"
>
> * weigh the long-term against the short-term benefits
>
> * coordinate federal land use plans to be consistent with
> other federal, state, local and tribal plans to the extent
> "practical," as determined by the Secretary, and "provide
> for meaningful public involvement" of state and local
> officials in the federal land-use planning, regulations, and
> decisions.

The available caselaw involving BLM land-use planning
indicates that courts are unwilling to carefully examine the above
provisions in order to derive effective standards of review. As a
practical matter, BLM compliance with these standards is difficult

to challenge because both the courts and the Interior Board of Land Use Appeals (the BLM's administrative review body) will defer to agency-planning judgments. "Consequently, unless the judiciary takes a harder look at the BLM planning process than it has so far, the agency will be free to choose its own schedules, its own priorities, its own methods and its own topics."[635]

Enforceability of BLM plans: Once promulgated, FLPMA clearly intends that BLM land-use plans be binding. Although the importance of planning is mentioned in several other provisions, the main provision regarding the effect of planning is contained in Section 1732(a), which provides that:

> the Secretary shall manage the public lands in accordance with the land use plans developed by him under section 1712 of this title when they are available.[636]

The Secretary is authorized to issue management decisions which implement BLM plans under Section 1712(e). Management decisions are subject to reconsideration, modification, or termination, pursuant to the standards of the land-use plan involved.[637] Certain major management decisions that completely eliminate a principal use on 100,000 acres for two years or more must be submitted to Congress for legislative veto consideration.[638] Special planning provisions apply to the review of termination of existing withdrawals.[639]

In appeals of plans addressing specific resources or conflicts, the Interior Board of Appeals will not reverse or remand unless the record clearly discloses arbitrariness or error.[640] However, courts have consistently rejected BLM programmatic decisions made without guiding land-use plans.[641]

FLPMA procedural requirements: FLPMA states two mandatory procedural requirements: 1) public involvement and participation,[642] and 2) the use of "a systematic interdisciplinary approach to achieve integrated consideration of physical, biological, economic and other sciences."[643] In practice, the BLM has been unable to comply with the interdisciplinary planning requirement, due to lack of resources for resource specialists and other experts.[644] Further planning requirements set forth in the BLM planning regulations have been accurately described as "vague to the point of opaqueness."[645]

In general, the Resource Management Planning (RMP) process involves nine steps, starting with issue identification and ending with monitoring and evaluation.[646] As required by the regulations, each plan is accompanied by an Environmental Impact Statement (EIS) and a Record of Decision.[647] Since the BLM has not established standard procedures for public participation in the development of planning standards and criteria, the only means of protesting a plan is an appeal to the Director of the BLM.[648]

Because BLM planning is completely decentralized, RMPs need not conform to any national model with regard to promulgation procedures or substantive content.[649] As a result, planning varies among districts and the resource being planned for.[650]

FLPMA's intent to restore degraded riparian areas: FLPMA defines "Areas of Critical Environmental Concern" (ACECs) as "areas within the public lands . . . where special management attention is required to protect and prevent irreparable damage to important . . . fish and wildlife resources or other natural systems or processes."[651] This general definition leaves ample discretion with the agency in designating ACECs. Although agency guidance has accepted that riparian zones easily fall within the statutory definition of an ACEC because of their significance as natural systems and for fish and wildlife resources, the BLM has not promulgated regulations which specifically protect "riparian zones" or "riparian ecosystems" as ACECs.[652]

Due to the vagueness of the statutory language about ACECs, it would be difficult to challenge the BLM's compliance with the statutory mandate. There is no caselaw to date which has examined the meaning of the directive requiring the Secretary to "give priority" to the designation of ACECs. It is clear, however, that giving priority to ACECs means something more than mere "consideration."[653]

It is also clear that FLPMA does not require the BLM to prohibit grazing-caused riparian-zone degradation, though the statute anticipates that the BLM would act to restore riparian areas. The Act declares that "a substantial amount of the federal range is deteriorating in quality and that installation of additional range improvements could arrest much of the continuing deterioration."[654]   Based on this declaration, Congress went on to direct that fifty percent of all grazing fee receipts be available for "on the ground" range rehabilitation, protection and enhancement and suggested that such projects include seeding and reseeding, fencing, water development and fish and wildlife habitat enhancement.[655]

We note that FLPMA regulations no longer require local agency managers to conform all grazing permits with land use plans.   Rather, managers may "modify" permits if monitoring shows a failure to meet plan objectives.[656]

Planning to protect water quality under FLPMA: Perhaps the most concrete requirement in FLPMA requires BLM land management plans to "provide for compliance with applicable pollution control laws, including State and Federal air, water, noise or other pollution standards or implementation plans."[657]   This requirement reinforces the applicability of state water-pollution-control schemes promulgated pursuant to the Clean Water Act.[658]

Nonpoint-source pollution from forestry, grazing, roadbuilding, and mining may be the most widespread pollution problems faced by BLM planners.   Since the Clean Water Act's Section 313, requiring federal compliance with nonpoint-source pollution standards, has been interpreted to include rainwater runoff caused by roadbuilding and timber harvesting,[659] it seems clear that all BLM activities which cause runoff (including grazing and mining) must comply with water-quality standards.   Thus, state water-quality standards, if enforced, are a potentially powerful check on the otherwise broad BLM discretion over land and resource management.   However, as discussed previously, the

Clean Water Act has failed thus far to adequately protect the watersheds on the BLM lands from nonpoint-source pollution.

The failure of the CWA to effectively control nonpoint-source pollution, caused by improper grazing, timber harvest, roadbuilding, mining and certain recreational activities, is partly due to the states' incomplete implementation and enforcement of the nonpoint-source control provisions of the CWA. One specific problem is that BLM plans often claim they are adequate to ensure compliance with water quality standards, but when actually implemented they are not. For example, a specific timber cut may cause a landslide despite the BLM's belief, and the plan's claim, that the management practices used would avoid such an event. In such cases, states rarely have the resources to undertake formal enforcement action against the agency and citizens have no remedy under the CWA because the pollution is not being caused by a point source.

BLM management policies: Current BLM planning regulations[660] interpret each of the BLM's ten multiple-use objectives. The objectives most pertinent to riparian areas are fish and wildlife development and utilization and watershed protection. The "domestic livestock grazing" objective of multiple use is termed entirely in terms of forage production: *"(a) Domestic livestock grazing.* Management of public lands for domestic livestock grazing involves the protection, regulated use and development of forage producing public lands and the management of livestock (cattle, sheep, horses, and goats) use to obtain a sustained yield of forage."[661] Similarly, the "timber production" provision speaks only of obtaining "a sustained yield of forest products."[662]

The fish and wildlife regulations direct that "management of public lands for fish and wildlife development and utilization involves the protection, regulated use, and development of habitat on public lands and waters to obtain a sustained yield of fish and wildlife and provision and maintenance of public access to fish and wildlife resources."[663] Unlike the Forest Service planning regulations which speak to "minimum viable populations," of native vertebrates, this regulation is too vague to be meaningful, because it requires only that management shall "obtain a sustained yield of fish and wildlife resources."

The watershed protection regulations state that watershed management "involves the protection, regulated use, and development of any public lands in a manner to control runoff; to minimize soil erosion, siltation and other destructive consequences of uncontrolled water flows; and to maintain and improve storage, yield, quality and quantity of surface and subsurface waters."[664] Again, this language does not pose any real management constraint for the protection of riparian areas, floodplains or hyporheic zones. Specific management steps are not prescribed to control runoff, erosion and siltation, or to "maintain and improve" the quality of surface waters, although any such practices must meet the requirements of the Clean Water Act.

The Oregon & California (O & C) lands: The Oregon and California ("O & C") lands comprise 2.6 million acres in Western Oregon, and are a major source of federal timber.[665] These lands were originally public domain which was reconveyed and revested to the United States from grants made to private concerns for construction of the Oregon and California Railroad and the Coos Bay Military Wagon Road. Although the O & C lands were originally intended for private agricultural development, the O & C Act of 1937[666] provided that the lands would be retained for timber production under the Department of the Interior. Other management purposes included "protecting watersheds, regulating streamflow, and contributing to the economic stability of local communities and industries."[667] The Act also provided that timber management was to be based on the "principle of sustained yield"[668] -- the earliest instance of mandated sustained-yield management on federal timberlands.

On the ground, these lands have been the most heavily logged of all federal lands. Destruction of natural ecosystems has been especially severe because the BLM lands are configured in a checkerboard pattern, interspersed with even more heavily logged industrial timberlands. Today, most of Western Oregon's public and private timberlands are scarred by roads and clear-cuts, with forests primarily comprised of second-growth trees under 40 years old.

Since 1990, however, the BLM has been involved in an unprecedented unified planning effort in Western Oregon which promises to radically improve riparian management on the O & C lands.[669]   Six planning districts have simultaneously released draft Resource Management Plans.[670] This process has attempted to respond to the following major issues: timber production practices; old growth forests; habitat diversity; special status species habitat; special areas; visual resources; stream, riparian and water quality protection; recreation resources (including wild and scenic rivers); land tenure and rural interface areas. The Director of the BLM's Oregon office has characterized the planning efforts as a conceptual revolution in forest management which he hopes will put the BLM on course to protect ecosystems and biological diversity.[671]

If implemented, the preferred alternative plans identified by the six BLM districts would establish riparian management areas along perennial streams and other streams that carry fish and protect natural functions. Within these areas, no timber harvest would normally occur, although exceptions would be made if selective harvest of hardwoods were deemed necessary to achieve diversification, or if road construction and yarding corridors were necessary to facilitate timber harvest outside the riparian management area. According to the BLM draft plans, the width of resource management areas would be determined by on-the-ground riparian vegetation and stream characteristics. Thus, the management area would be approximately one and a half times the width of riparian areas, or even wider on smaller fish-bearing streams.   Although these plans promise limited protection for ephemeral or intermittent streams, the establishment of ecologically sound riparian management practices on these six BLM districts could set an important example for other BLM lands.

Other positive aspects of the proposed plans for riverine-riparian ecosystems include: the establishment of 793,000 acres as old-growth management areas; the designation of a reduced acreage as suitable for timber production (41%) and a policy stating that new roads will be kept to a minimum; the establishment of special status areas to prevent deterioration of threatened and endangered species habitat; the improvement of fish habitat and the recommendation of eleven rivers as suitable for designation under the Wild and Scenic Rivers Act.[672] In sum, under the new plans, riparian management areas, ACEC's and wild and scenic river miles will double or triple.

Only time will tell if the proposed plans will actually improve the management of riverine-riparian ecosystems and biodiversity on the O & C lands. Their success may be limited by resources, since it is not yet clear whether the BLM plans will be fully funded to implement and monitor these more labor intensive land management policies. However, the drastically improved ecological sensitivity demonstrated by the draft plans signifies a radical shift in policy toward increased sensitivity to ecosystem-level concerns at considerable political cost. The BLM is prepared to defend the plans in lawsuits certain to be brought by timber interests and counties (whose timber receipts will be cut by 50%) on the basis that the plan's reduced timber cuts violate the O & C Act. Hopefully, if Oregon BLM meets these challenges, its unified planning effort will be duplicated by other BLM districts with similar concerns.

Current riparian management policies/plans: At the national guidance level, the BLM unofficially defines a "riparian area" as "an area of land directly influenced by permanent water," and excludes from this definition "such sites as ephemeral streams or washes that do not exhibit the presence of vegetation dependent upon free water in the soil."[673] "Wetland areas" are defined as those areas meeting the definition of wetland areas in the current "Federal Manual for Identifying and Delineating Jurisdictional Wetlands."

These definitions exclude many riparian areas which lie beyond the "direct influence" of "permanent water," including those associated with intermittent streams and many headwater reaches which are critical to the healthy functioning of riverine-riparian ecosystems.

There is now increased BLM attention to the health of stream ecosystems, with the agency calling for increased appropriations to cover riparian and wetland management positions. However, at the national level the agency has not provided district managers with concrete land management directives.[674] Rather, pursuant to a 1987 Policy Statement, "[t]he objective of riparian area management is to maintain, restore, or improve riparian values to achieve a healthy and productive ecological condition for maximum long-term benefits."[675]

The goals and strategies enunciated under the most recent BLM document, "Riparian-Wetland Initiative for the 1990s," are as general as the 1987 policy statement, calling for: 1) the restoration and maintenance of riparian-wetland areas "so that 75 percent or more are in proper functioning condition" by 1997, i.e. having "an advanced ecological status," except where "resource management objectives would require an earlier successional stage"; 2) the "protection" of riparian-wetland areas and associated uplands through "proper" land management and the avoidance **or** mitigation of negative impacts; 3) the acquisition/expansion of key areas; 4) an information/outreach program; and 5) improved partnerships and cooperative restoration and management processes.[676] At present, the agency has classified riparian-wetland areas together as either "meeting agency objectives," "not meeting objectives," or "unknown." As of 1990, 18% of these areas were meeting objectives, 3% were not meeting objectives, and the remaining 79% were of "unknown" status.[677] Clearly, this is not an effective program. Further, there is no clear definition of "key areas" and hence no method of identifying or protecting critical riverine refugia or watershed reserves.

These goals and strategies were not accompanied by formal agency rulemaking or proposed standards to guarantee maintenance and guide restoration, nor have funds been appropriated to implement them.

The BLM's Alaskan riparian lands: The BLM Alaskan lands face special riparian management problems, primarily due to the large amount of riparian area involved. According to the BLM, about 90%, or 6,563,000 acres of all riparian lands managed by the BLM are in Alaska. Because there is so much Alaskan riparian land, the EPA observes that "public and private land managers in Alaska often perceive alteration of riparian vegetation as insignificant relative to the total acreage."[678] Mining causes much of the riparian damage on Alaskan BLM lands, mostly due to the fact that the Mining Law of 1872 effectively makes mineral extraction the highest priority land use. Therefore, riparian management is often limited to mitigation or rehabilitation rather than focusing on riparian protection.[679]

Grazing and riparian degradation on BLM and Forest Service rangelands: Especially in the West, grazing has been a traditional use of federal lands which was completely unregulated until the 20th century. For example, not until 1911 did a court hold that the Forest Service had the right to regulate grazing.[680] Grazing is the direct cause of large amounts of nonpoint-source water pollution, causes the loss of riparian vegetation, and continues to have a major adverse impact on the integrity of riparian areas, including floodplains. Because much of the law governing public rangelands applies to both the Forest Service and the BLM, range-related directives will be discussed together in this section.

According to the BLM and the Forest Service, riparian areas represent about one percent of the over 250 million acres of federally owned rangeland.[681] The BLM currently allows grazing on about 159 million acres under grazing permits (inside grazing districts) and leases (outside grazing districts) in 16 western states.[682] The Forest Service estimates that it manages 102 million acres in 10,387 range allotments in 36 states -- about half the land area of national forests.[683] Overall, the federal lands provide 13 percent of the nation's Animal Unit Months (AUMs), and about 17 percent of all livestock forage.[684]

Rangeland management: Livestock grazing on these lands is subject to several statutes that requiring multiple use/sustained yield principles to be used in range planning. These statutes include: 1) the Public Rangelands Improvement Act of 1978,[685] which states national rangeland policies applicable to the USFS and the BLM; 2) the Federal Land and Policy Management Act,[686] which requires the Secretary of the Interior to develop, maintain and revise land use plans for the BLM public lands; 3) the Forest and Rangeland Renewable Resources Planning Act of 1974,[687] which requires the Secretary of Agriculture to develop, maintain and revise land and resource management plans for the national forests that provide for multiple uses and sustained yield of the forests' products and resources.

Federal rangelands are divided into approximately 31,000 grazing allotments with an average size of 8,500 acres each. In addition to large-scale planning documents, each agency must prepare permits and management plans to define how grazing will be carried out on each grazing allotment. A permit may be issued to one or more permittee with conditions specifying the number and type of livestock allowed, the duration of use, and the amount of forage which may be eaten. Permits are valid for a maximum of 10 years, and may be altered or suspended by the permitting agency if range conditions are being degraded. In 1991, the agencies collected a fee of $1.97 per animal unit month (AUM)[688] from each permittee. The number of acres required to provide one AUM ranges between about six and 22 acres, depending on the location of the rangeland.[689]

The individual allotment plans which have been prepared for many of the grazing allotments add to the basic conditions in grazing permits by describing how grazing will be conducted to meet the various multiple-use objectives, including watershed, and fish, and by detailing the implementation of specific "range improvements" required to meet these objectives.[690]

Prior to 1976, grazing was governed by the Taylor Grazing Act of 1934.[691] In 1976, these grazing policies were supplemented and modified by FLPMA, which applies to rangelands managed by both the Department of Agriculture and the Department of Interior, which defines grazing permit terms and sets up grazing advisory boards. FLMPA was based on Congressional findings that "a substantial amount of the federal range is deteriorating in quality and that installation of additional range improvements could arrest much of the continuing deterioration."[692] This finding is supported by the allocation of 50% of all grazing fee receipts for range rehabilitation, protection and enhancement, including seeding, fencing and fish and wildlife habitat restoration.[693]

FLPMA amended several features of the Taylor Act. Most significantly, the statute tried to reduce the influence of grazing interest groups on BLM policy by (1) limiting the role of grazing advisory boards and (2) requiring the agency to provide the public with an opportunity to "comment and participate in the formulation of plans and programs relating to the management of the public lands."[694] These public participation requirements have weakened the hegemony of grazing interests over BLM planning and expanded the agency's constituency. However, the lack of concrete, enforceable riparian standards in either FLPMA or the subsequently enacted Public Rangelands Improvement Act of 1978 (PRIA)[695] has handicapped the ability of new, environmentalist BLM constituencies to effect programmatic range policy change.[696]

Grazing and riparian management are also addressed by PRIA, which also covers both Forest Service and BLM public lands. Grazing concessions are granted according to a permit system.[697] PRIA is the primary authority over BLM grazing practices, stating that the goal of range management "shall be to improve the range conditions."[698] In PRIA, Congress emphasized the manifest threats of grazing on watershed and aquatic habitat.[699] However, although PRIA instructed the Forest Service to inventory range conditions and trends, range improvement was not set forth as a management priority for national forests as it was on the BLM public lands.[700]

The legislative history of PRIA demonstrates a Congressional finding that deteriorated range conditions were caused by overgrazing permitted under the Taylor Grazing

Act.[701] Through PRIA, Congress declared that "vast segments of the public rangelands are . . . in an unsatisfactory condition."[702] PRIA went on to associate deteriorated range with soil loss, desertification, increased siltation and salinity, reduction of water quantity and quality, loss of fish and wildlife habitat, increased surface runoff and flood danger, and the potential for undesirable long-term local and regional climatic and economic changes.[703] Several of these conditions are directly caused by the degradation of riparian zones, especially degraded water quality, loss of fish habitat, and desertification.[704] PRIA gave special attention to the rehabilitation necessary "to restore a viable ecological system that benefits both range users and the wildlife habitat."[705]

Despite this language, however, PRIA's riparian protection mandate appears to have made little difference. The main problem is that Congress erred in failing to give the BLM clear range improvement priorities and regulations. For example, PRIA defines "range improvement" as

> any activity or program on or relating to rangelands which is designed to improve production of forage; change vegetative composition; control patterns of use; provide water; stabilize soil and water conditions; and provide habitat for livestock and wildlife. The term includes, but is not limited to, structures, treatment projects, and use of mechanical means to accomplish the desired results.[706]

On its face, this definition is too broad to be meaningful because there are no real goals set for restoration of the naturally functioning riparian area. Furthermore, Congress did not specifically mention riparian areas, floodplains or biological hot spots in either FLPMA or PRIA, leaving to BLM discretion the priority, method and scale of riparian and floodplain protection projects. Allotment Management Plans need not consider resources other than "range" and the rather vague goal of "range improvement."[707] Finally, there is no mention of the need to identify and protect the remaining healthy riparian areas, riverine refugia or watershed/riverine biodiversity refuges.

Also inadequate is FLPMA's provision at Section 1732(b) that "the Secretary shall, by regulation or otherwise, take any action necessary to prevent unnecessary or undue degradation of the land." Although it would seem that the long-term degradation caused by overgrazing of the public lands would qualify as "unnecessary" or "undue," the vagueness of the multiple-use/sustained-yield principles which guide BLM and Forest Service land management has continually allowed the agencies to sacrifice watershed values in favor of commodity values such as grazing. This is true despite the fact that, theoretically at least, the multiple-use/sustained-yield portions of FLPMA limit the use of a resource to that level which does not permanently impair the productivity of other resources. It is undisputable that overgrazing has damaged watershed resources, riparian areas and riverine-riparian biodiversity on vast areas of the BLM's western lands.[708] However, as discussed below, damage caused to one resource by overuse of another has not, to date, succeeded as a basis for judicial relief.[709]

Caselaw confirms inadequacy of statutory mandate to protect riparian resources from grazing abuses: The wide berth of BLM discretion under FLPMA and PRIA was judicially acknowledged in *Natural Resources Defense Council v. Hodel*.[710] In *Hodel*, the plaintiffs asserted that past overgrazing on a BLM planning area in Nevada had caused degradation of the range and that both FLPMA and PRIA required the agency to reduce livestock use in that area. The court subsequently found that four of the area's allotments were overgrazed by livestock, and eight were overgrazed by both livestock and wildlife. Nevertheless, the court declined to conclude that either FLPMA or PRIA required the BLM to reduce livestock use in order to rehabilitate the range.

The Court's reasoning was that the statutes' declarations of goals and policy could "hardly be considered concrete limits on agency discretion." Therefore, the Court deferred to the BLM's assertions that methods other than livestock reduction would improve range conditions, stating:

> "Although I might privately agree with plaintiffs that a more aggressive approach to range improvement would be environmentally preferable, or might even be closer to what Congress had in mind, the Ninth Circuit has made it plain that "the courts are not at liberty to break the tie choosing one theory of range management over another."[711]

In summary, only a set of facts which makes a strong showing of agency "irrationality" will overturn a BLM decision made on multiple-use grounds.   As long as this judicial interpretation of BLM discretionary latitude remains good law, all aspects of range improvement, including riparian protection and restoration, will stay firmly within BLM discretion, insulated from meaningful judicial review.[712]   Given the lack of enforceable standards in federal range laws, the Clean Water Act remains practically the only the effective constraint on agency range policies.

Conclusions

Bureau of Land Management Policies are Inadequate to Protect or Restore Riverine Systems and Biodiversity

Grazing Practices Reform is Critically Needed: Because there are no complete inventories of the amount and condition of riparian areas on BLM (or Forest Service) lands, it is not possible to say how many acres on rangelands are seriously degraded and in need of restoration. It is safe to say, however, that there are tens of thousands of miles in a degraded condition and which require affirmative restoration efforts.[713]

FLPMA and PRIA provide strong authority for the BLM to undertake programmatic exclusion of livestock from degraded and vulnerable riparian ecosystems for the purposes of restoring riparian vegetation and aquifer recharge.[714]   However, neither statute mandates any specific range improvements program, leaving the riparian areas of BLM rangelands vulnerable to continued degradation.   Therefore, despite the strong declarations of policy and findings of range degradation in the two statutes, adequate riparian area restoration and protection have not been undertaken by the BLM (or the Forest Service).   Given the lack of enforceable standards in federal range laws, the Clean Water Act is the most effective constraint on agency range policies.

Range Protection and Enhancement Projects are Often Misconceived: The practical problems with many of the range protection-and-enhancement projects undertaken by the agencies is that they are not planned well enough, are not extensive enough, and do not have the proper focus.   For example, fencing is often erected but fails to enclose the entire vulnerable riparian area.   Also, fencing alone does not necessarily ensure the restoration of native vegetation, including large wood.

As a practical matter, it would simply cost too much to fence off every mile of riparian area on BLM lands nationwide. The responsible agencies need to protect the remaining healthy riparian areas and biotic refugia by prohibiting livestock grazing, or restricting it to certain seasons with careful management in those areas.   The BLM must also identify the components of the natural riverine system to determine where native vegetation needs to be replanted and whether large wood was part of the pre-disturbance system in order to restore degraded areas. Furthermore, especially on BLM projects, restoration initiatives should go beyond isolated segments so that the improvements are conducted within the framework of, the entire riverine system. Also, restoration projects often fail because they focus on the construction of in-stream structures which have not proven very effective without first ensuring the protection and recovery of the overall watershed and riparian areas.

There Are No National Bureau of Land Management Riparian Area Protection Policies: The goals and strategies enunciated under the recent BLM document "Riparian-Wetland Initiative for the 1990s" are general and do not set any concrete management guidelines for BLM lands.   Although the agency's goals and strategies are laudable, they are too general to constrain the considerable discretion with which the BLM interprets them and do not constitute legally binding regulations.[715]

As the EPA pointed out, the 1987 BLM policy statement includes a clear policy (that riparian area conditions should not be permitted to decline) but it "doesn't emphasize the value of riparian-dependent   resources   relative   to   other   resource activities."[716] The EPA further observed that, while the BLM has adequate legal authority to execute its policy in FLPMA (via multiple-use mandates including "watershed"), the CWA (requiring that federal agencies comply with state water-quality standards and nonpoint programs), and the Taylor Grazing Act (requiring livestock permits), "the BLM has numerous de facto constraints on its authority." These de facto constraints include:

* Lack of resources to rigorously enforce permit or allotment-plan conditions.

* Dependence on cooperation from permittees to observe permit conditions, such as moving cattle as scheduled, or respecting riparian enclosures. Such cooperation is not always obtained without rigorous enforcement resources.

*The BLM often has no control over degradation in upstream riparian areas which adversely affect its projects.[717]

The   BLM's   policy   statement   indirectly   emphasizes watershed-level planning in that it directs the BLM to cooperate with other public and private landowners. However, although the BLM   has   begun   to   implement   watershed   planning   through participation in land exchanges and coordinated planning agreements, it faces formidable barriers to the implementation of watershed plans. Problems usually stem from the presence of numerous, often uncooperative private landowners within a watershed and from lack of agency resources for plan development.[718]

BLM and the Clean Water Act: Some Potential for Riparian Area Rehabilitation: As discussed previously, the BLM is required to comply with state water-quality standards developed under the CWA, which imposes enforceable constraints on land management decisions by federal agencies.[719] Importantly, citizens may bring suit in federal court to enjoin any BLM (or other agency) plan calling for activities which would not comply with state water quality standards.[720] Therefore, to the extent that an agency action does not demonstrate its compliance with these standards, it is open to attack.[721]

There Are No Policy Statements, Rules, Standards or Guidelines That Even Mention the Need to Identify and Protect the Remaining Healthy Biotic Refuges, Benchmark Watersheds and Biological Hot Spots. To its credit, the BLM has recognized the dire need for restoration on many of the river and streams within its jurisdiction. However, current BLM policy, at all levels, fails to recognize the unique value of the relatively healthy watersheds, biotic refugia and biological hot spots that still remain in riverine systems within BLM lands. These areas must be identified, protected, and secured to provide the natural capital needed to maintain and restore the systems.

Identification and protection of these vital ecological areas is important because most of the remaining relatively undisturbed riverine habitat for many entire riverine systems is on federal lands, especially in the West. Hence, the federal lands will "carry the weight" of long-term maintenance and recovery efforts until habitat restoration on contiguous private land sections downstream takes effect. This was the dramatic conclusion drawn by the Scientific Panel on Late Successional Forest Ecosystems which applies to BLM as well as Forest Service lands. (Please see conclusion #4 following our assessment of the U.S. Forest Service.)

River System-wide Policy Coordination and Alignment Needed: Currently there are no mandates to develop coordinated and aligned river system-wide assessments, management plans or monitoring programs with adjacent federal agencies and private landowners within a watershed. While memorandums of understanding (MOUs) and other informal agreements have been used with some degree of effectiveness, the BLM must promulgate specific rules which require policy coordination, consistency and alignment within a system.

WATERSHED AS A MULTIPLE USE ON FOREST SERVICE AND BUREAU OF LAND MANAGEMENT LANDS

The multiple-use mandates of the FLPMA (applicable to the BLM) and the MUSYA (applicable to the Forest Service), make "watershed" an "equal" multiple-surface use, to be managed for "sustained yield."[722] Although recent agency actions indicate that watershed values are beginning to take their rightful place among the other multiple uses, watershed protection has often lost out to competing economic pressures resulting in commercial activities which destroy watershed integrity. The primary culprits are timber operations, water diversions, roadbuilding, livestock grazing, mineral extraction and intensive recreation.

Pursuant to the MUSYA, "multiple use" for the Forest Service means:

> management of all the various renewable surface resources of the national forests so that they are utilized in the combination that will best meet the needs of the American people; making the most judicious use of the land for some or all of these resources or related services over areas large enough to provide sufficient latitude for periodic adjustments in use to conform to changing needs

and conditions; that some land will be used for less than all of the resources; and harmonious and coordinated management of the various resources, each with the other, and not necessarily the combination of uses that will give the greatest dollar return or the greatest unit output.[723]

The definition for the BLM in FLPMA is nearly identical, except that several phrases were added about the resource needs of future generations and protection of environmental quality.[724]

The MUSYA also refers to the "sustained yield" of products and services, which is defined as the achievement and maintenance in perpetuity of a high-level annual or regular periodic output of the various renewable resources of the national forests without impairment of the productivity of the land.[725] The BLM definition substitutes "consistent with multiple-use" for "without impairment to productivity of the land."[726]

The specific resources subject to the multiple-use/sustained-yield mandate of the MUSYA are listed as: "outdoor recreation, range, timber, **watershed**, and wildlife and fish."[727] Congress expanded this list of principal resources for the BLM in FLPMA to "renewable and nonrenewable resources, including but not limited to recreation, range, timber, minerals, **watershed**, wildlife and fish, and natural, scenic, scientific and historical values."[728] Principal resources for the BLM are:

> domestic livestock grazing, fish and wildlife development and utilization, mineral exploration and production, rights-of-way, outdoor recreation, and timber production.[729]

As one legal scholar concludes, the use of the word "watershed" in both statutes seems to imply that federal agencies' roles are to be "more protective than allocative" under the multiple-use, sustained-yield mandate.[730] On their face, both FLPMA and the MUSYA appear to place "watershed" on a par with other surface uses.[731]

The purported objective of multiple-use/sustained-yield management is to balance commodity production with resource protection. Three clear mandates which emerge from MUSYA and parallel provisions of FLPMA:

> * Congress has rejected economic optimality as the governing management criterion, admonishing the agencies to consider "relative values of the resources and not necessarily" the greatest economic return. This view was confirmed in the case of *Sierra Club v. Lyng*.[732]

> * A substantive prohibition against the permanent impairment of land productivity (or, for the BLM, environmental quality) appears to flow from the statutory language.[733] However, this view has not been universally accepted by courts.[734]

> * A mix of uses is intended, implying that devotion of a large area to a single "use" would violate the mandate.[735]

Judicial review under the multiple-use mandates: Courts have been reluctant to perceive any concrete management directives in the multiple use mandates. For example, in *National Wildlife Federation v. United States Forest Service*, plaintiffs challenged timber-harvesting proposals that allegedly would have caused multiple landslides, concomitant soil erosion, stream siltation and destruction of anadromous fish habitat.[736] Rather than interpreting the MUSYA to require watershed protection, the court found for plaintiffs on procedural grounds under the National Environmental Policy Act, a holding that suggests courts will not grant relief on multiple use grounds in the future.[737]
The court reasoned that:

> the standards in MUSYA are broad, but they do exist. MUSYA is not entirely discretionary. [However] Congress

authorized the Forest Service to decide which areas and resources to emphasize. As long as the Forest Service considers the other competing uses, the courts are reluctant to overrule its decisions.[738]

Thus, multiple use principles require the agency merely to "consider" other uses, and does not mandate any minimum level of protection for any particular use or for the watershed.

Another, even more extreme example of judicial deference to Forest Service implementation of multiple-use, sustained-yield principles is provided by *Sierra Club v. Hardin*[739] The record of that case states that six-tenths of one percent of the Tongass National Forest in Alaska had been reserved from logging, and the management plan for the forest proposed that 95% of the commercial forest land be clearcut. This plan was upheld as within Forest Service discretion, despite the demonstrated "overwhelming commitment of the Tongass National Forest to timber-harvest objectives in preference to other multiple-use values."[740]

Overall, it is safe to say that reviewing courts have not identified any federal law which delineates concrete rules or standards which bind the Forest Service or the BLM in setting multiple-use combinations. Rather, a management decision will stand if it avoids irrationality toward[741] or total ignorance of[742] watershed values. The agency need only "consider" the relative values of all resources, at which point it is at liberty to favor one resource over another.[743]

Implications for riverine management: In practice, despite the guidelines that appear to emerge from the multiple-use, sustained-yield management philosophy, neither courts nor the agencies have interpreted the provisions of MUSYA and FLPMA to impose any strict limitations on agency discretion over riverine management or, for that matter, over management for any other multiple uses. Rather, due to the somewhat nebulous definition of "multiple use," the term's meaning may vary depending on the identity of the user. This is true regardless of Congress' clear assumption that the term implied greater environmental sensitivity and more balanced resource goals than were manifested under prior management frameworks.[744] Over time, it has become clear that the Forest Service, the BLM and the natural resource industries often interpret multiple use to mean that commodity production is the primary management goal, the pursuit of which is constrained only by a degree of administrative discretion.[745] Consistent with this view, the Director of the BLM under the Reagan Administration asserted that multiple-use lands were available only for economic use.[746] Hence, observers are led to believe that federal land managers "typically regard multiple use as merely an affirmation of their administrative right to do whatever they think best under the circumstances."[747] As for "sustained yield," the term has been effectively applied only to the timber resource.[748]

Specific problems for riverine protection include:

* Congress did not indicate the appropriate size of multiple-use management units, stating only that they should be "areas large enough to allow use adjustments.[749] Although the case of *Sierra Club v. Clark* held that the size and configuration of the relevant area must be determined in order to accurately assess the impacts of an agency action,[750] the agency is left to determine what the "relevant area" is when assessing impacts on "watershed" values.

* "Watershed" is not specifically defined in MUSYA, FLPMA, NFMA or any other federal statute or regulation.[751]

Conclusions

Multiple-use, Sustained Yield Principles Do Not Impose Specific, Enforceable Directives on Federal Agencies to Protect or Restore Riverine Systems and Biodiversity

Ideally, multiple-use decisions should consider the impacts of a proposed action on all resources. Biologically speaking, "watershed should be the key element in such consideration, because all other uses ultimately depend on the quality, quantity and stability of the soil and water -- the essence of the watershed resource."[752] Furthermore, watershed protection is consistent with the protection of wildlife habitat and with most forms of recreation.

Unfortunately, the reality is that the watershed values and riverine resources too often lose out to the competing, short-term economic demands of destructive commercial activities. This is true because no specific riverine management directives are derived from the MUSYA mandates. As Professor George Coggins of the University of Kansas observes, multiple-use, sustained-yield principles will never be interpreted to impose specific duties because the agencies are "told to act rationally in choosing among competing land uses" but are "not told what final choices are rational."[753] It appears that without some statutory definition of watershed, and specification standards for its management, "watershed management" by federal agencies "will remain an amorphous concept."[754]

NATIONAL PARK SERVICE RIVERINE MANAGEMENT

The National Park Service is a traditionally decentralized agency governed by relatively few statutory management objectives. Its primary goal is that of park "preservation," and its secondary objective is the enhancement of "public enjoyment" of the parks. There is almost no statutory planning guidance. These goals have become increasingly difficult to reconcile, and the agency's preservation mission is sometimes superceded by recreational priorities when Congress explicitly gives recreation management priority on certain park system lands.

The primary threats to watersheds on National Parks derive from: 1) grazing uses which were grandfathered at the time particular parks were created; 2) mining, especially placer mining in Alaska; 3) recreational uses, and 4) interference with in-stream flows from users outside the parks.[755] Dams built before and during Park designation are also a problem.

The protection of riverine systems and biodiversity within parks would be enhanced by new policies which lessen external threats to park river systems from poor riverine management on adjacent and nearby federal lands and which provide a common scientific basis for assessing activities both inside and outside national parks.

Park purposes under the National Park System Act of 1916 and planning under the National Parks and Recreation Act of 1978: In 1916 Congress enacted the National Park Service Organic Act, which created the National Park Service in the Department of Interior to:

> promote and regulate the use of the Federal areas known as national parks, monuments and reservations . . . by such means and measures as conform to the fundamental purpose of said parks, monuments and reservations, which purpose is to conserve the scenery and natural and historic objects and the wild life [in national parks] and to provide for the enjoyment of the same in such a manner and by such means as will leave them unimpaired for the enjoyment of future generations.[756]

This provision clearly defines the Park Service mission as preservation, and amounts to a virtual prohibition against economic resource development in a national park. However, the Park Service must still use its discretion to regulate the activities of persons with mining claims, reserved grazing rights or other legally authorized land uses within the parks. The Act also empowers the Secretary of Interior to contract for recreational services.[757]

By 1970, the park system had grown to include a wide variety of "superlative natural, historic, and recreation areas in every major region of the United States, its territories and island possession," which led Congress, as part of a single National Park System, to formally recognize these diverse areas which:

> though distinct in character, are united through their interrelated purposes and resources into one national park system as cumulative expressions of a single national heritage; that, individually and collectively, these areas derive increased national dignity and recognition of their superb environmental quality through their inclusion jointly with each other in one national park system preserved and managed for the benefit and inspiration of all the people . . . ; and that it is the purpose of this Act to include all such areas in the System and to clarify the authorities applicable to the system.[758]

The "Redwood Amendments" of 1978 (an Act expanding the Redwood National Park) amended this statement to add:

> The authorization of activities shall be construed and the protection, management, and administration of these areas shall be conducted in light of the high public value and integrity of the National Park System and shall not be exercised in derogation of the values and purposes for which these various areas have been established, except as may have been or shall be directly and specifically provided by Congress.[759]

By statute, the park system includes "any area of land and water now or hereafter administered by the Secretary of the Interior through the National Park Service for park, monument, historic, parkway, recreational, or other purposes."[760] Today, the more than 350 park-system units are variously designated as national parks, monuments, preserves, lakeshores, seashores, historic sites, military parks, battlefields, historical parks, recreation areas, memorials and parkways.

Most of the units of the National Park system are created by specific enabling legislation which details particular purposes and objectives for the subject unit. For example, whereas a national battlefield may have the primary purposes of commemoration and preservation of historical relics, the Gates of the Arctic National Park was created "to maintain the wild and undeveloped character of the area," while maintaining "reasonable" public access and protecting habitat for fish and wildlife.[761] The degree to which individual park units are subject to specific management prohibitions or mandates varies widely; exceptions from general authorities range from provisions permitting the picking of cactus fruit by Papago Indians on a national monument to provisions for sport hunting and other specific exceptions for Alaska Parks made by ANILCA for Alaskan units of the National Park System.[762]

The only system-wide purposes for park units are contained in the Organic Act, which expresses the park's mandate: to *conserve* for *public enjoyment.* The secondary goal of public enjoyment may only be pursued "in such a manner . . . as will leave [the parks] unimpaired for future generations." Thus, conservation of resources is the paramount mandate.

The increasing demand for access to recreation in National Parks has tested park officials' ability to maintain a balance between the Act's conservation and public enjoyment goals. One response to the original Organic Act's lack of direction for park managers in reconciling the public use and conservation goals has been Congressional legislation requiring all park management plans to specify visitor carrying capacities: the National Parks and Recreation Act of 1978 (NPRA).[763]

Park planning: Until the 1960s, Park Service planning efforts focused on facilities development. Today, park planning concentrates on resource protection and the development of "general management plans."[764] Under the NPRA, the Secretary of Interior must submit annually "a detailed program for the development of facilities, structures or buildings for each unit of the National Park System consistent with the general management plans" and a list indicating the plan status for each unit.[765]

Each unit plan must contain four items: 1) Measures for the preservation of the area's resources; 2) Type and intensity of development for public enjoyment; 3) Visitor-carrying capacity and "implementation commitments"; 4) Proposed boundary modifications with explanations as to why they are necessary or desirable.[766]

Unit planning proceeds at three levels. The most general planning document is the Statement for Management (SFM), which compiles relevant information and defines general park objectives. The SFM is then used to prepare the Outline of Planning Requirements, which assigns priorities to further studies and budget requests. The third and final planning document is the General Management Plan (GMP), which is usually issued with an environmental assessment.[767] The Park Service generally encourages public participation in the planning process to the extent required by the National Environmental Policy Act.

The GMP is a general plan which sets forth management philosophies and strategies rather than detailed management prescriptions.[768] According to Park Service regulations, GMPs must address the following subjects: purposes, zoning and land classifications, proposals for resource preservation and public enjoyment of the unit, alternative proposals, schedules and cost estimates, the affected environment, and environmental impacts.[769] More detailed management plans are often included as appendices to GMPs to deal with planning tasks such as: land suitability analyses, land protection plans, legislative proposals, transportation access plans, interpretation strategies, resource management strategies and wilderness reviews.[770]

GMPs are refined by Resource Management Plans, which are prepared to present a comprehensive program for achieving a park's resource-related objectives. Even more detailed "action plans" may then be prepared to address park-specific issues such as backcountry, grazing, pest control, and fisheries management.

As the language of its organic statute makes apparent, the Park Service is not subject to strict land and resource planning requirements. Rather, park managers have wide discretion to determine which subjects shall be included in a specific unit plan as well as the degree of specificity achieved by the plans. In devising plans, the Park Service is obligated only to comply with its general statutory mandate and with such regulations as it has promulgated in interpreting that mandate. Furthermore, unlike land use plans prepared by the BLM or the Forest Service under FLPMA and NFMA, there is no statutory requirement that subsequent parks management actually conform to the plans.[771]

National Park Service discretion over land management decisions: The main constraint on land management decisions is the Organic Act's directive that they must not "impair" the scenic, natural, historic and wildlife values which a particular unit was created to protect. As the Park Service recognizes in its Management Policies, whether an action is an "impairment" is a management determination that rests with the person making the final decision. In reading this determination, managers are directed to "consider such factors as the spatial and temporal extent of the impacts, the resources being impacted and their ability to adjust to those impacts, the relation of the impacted resources to other park resources, and cumulative as well as the individual effects."[772]

The Park Service has made the following statement with regard to the "impairment" standard:

> It is NPS policy to treat potential impairments in
> the same manner as known impairments. When

there is thought to be potential for resource impairment, actions will be based on strategies that retain the resource in an unimpaired condition until such time as doubts are resolved. For example, if a development might impair a park resource, the development will be postponed or reconfigured until it can be established whether 'might' is 'will' or 'will not,' within reasonable limits of certainty. Absent that assurance, action will not be taken.

To fulfill the Park Service's mandate to preserve natural and cultural resources unimpaired for future generations, it is no longer sufficient to consider strategies and actions solely within the boundaries of the parks. While the National Park Service does not support the creation of buffer zones around the parks or seek veto power over activities on adjacent lands, it will work cooperatively with surrounding landowners and managers to help ensure that actions outside the parks do not impair resources and values.[773]

Judicial review of park planning: The judicial deference repeatedly demonstrated in litigation over Park Service planning activities confirms the notion that park planners have wide management discretion. This is not surprising, since traditional principles of administrative law dictate that courts may not substitute their judgment for that of the executive branch in matters entrusted to their discretion. Rather, courts may only invalidate executive branch decisions in specific circumstances where the subject decisions can be shown to be 1) not in accordance with the law, 2) "arbitrary and capricious," or 3) an abuse of discretion. Therefore, the rule is that acts of the Secretary of Interior (i.e. the Park Service) "are presumptively reasonable and in accordance with the law."[774]

It is the rare case in which a court has not upheld Park Service decisions. The most significant such case was *Sierra Club v. Department of the Interior*, 398 F. Supp 284 (N.D. Cal. 1975), commonly known as the "Redwood Park litigation." In that case, the Secretary of Interior was sued for failure to protect the Redwood National Park from damage due to logging operations on surrounding private lands. The statute creating the park invested the Secretary with specific powers to take administrative action designed to protect the park from external threats. These powers included the power to modify park boundaries and the power to acquire other than fee interests in land and to enter into contracts and cooperative agreements with owners of peripheral lands and lands on watersheds tributary to streams within the Park.[775] The Park Service was also obligated by its "public trust duty" under the Organic Act to conserve the parks and provide for public enjoyment of them "in such a manner and by such means as will leave them unimpaired for the enjoyment of future generations."[776]

Based on the Secretary's failure to implement any of the recommendations made by or on behalf of his own agency to protect the parks from external logging impacts -- except to conduct further studies and enter into an ineffectual and unenforceable "cooperative agreement" with timber companies -- the Court found that the Secretary acted unreasonably, arbitrarily, and in abuse of his discretion because he "failed, refused and neglected to take steps to exercise and perform duties imposed" by the Organic Act and the act creating the Redwood National Park.[777] The court then ordered the Secretary to "take reasonable steps within a reasonable time," defined as 60 days, to exercise his powers to protect the park from external logging threats.[778]

In sum, litigation between environmentalists and park managers over planning conflicts between the "conservation" and "public use" mandates of the Park Service organic act has not clearly defined the outer limits of the Interior Secretary's discretion to encourage recreational use at the expense of conservation.[779] To date, no court has enjoined an NPS-approved recreation facility or contract on the grounds that approval exceeded statutory authority or contravened the statutory purposes.[780]

National Park Service resource management guidelines: Park planning is carried out pursuant to a set of mandatory "management policies" last revised in 1988 as well as natural resource "guidelines" first issued in 1991.[781]

The management policies most relevant to rivers management may be summarized as follows:

> Water Quality and Quantity[782]: The NPS will "perpetuate surface and ground waters as integral components of park aquatic and terrestrial ecosystems," and park waters "will be withdrawn for consumptive use only where such withdrawal is absolutely necessary for the use and management of the park and when studies show that it will not significantly alter natural processes and ecosystems." The quality of water originating within the boundaries of parks will be maintained in compliance with all applicable federal, state and local laws through the following management actions:
>
> * Adequate sewage treatment and disposal
>
> * Erosion control
>
> * "Direct pollution by livestock under commercial grazing permits will be prevented by eliminating streamside or lakeside corrals and pastures and associated watering sites wherever possible."
>
> * "Fuel-burning watercraft and marina operations, placer mining and other activities with high potential for water pollution will be regulated and controlled as necessary."

* "Toxic substances, such as pesticides, petroleum products and heavy metals, will be managed to minimize the risk of water contamination."

* "The intensity of use will be regulated in certain areas and at certain times determined to be necessary, based on water-quality monitoring studies."

* The NPS "will enter into agreements or compacts with other agencies and governing bodies to secure their cooperation in avoiding degradation of water resources."

* The NPS will "observe and monitor upstream diversions, adjacent uses, and groundwater withdrawals and their effects on the occurrence, quantity and quality of water necessary for the continued preservation of park biota and ecosystems."

* The NPS "will seek state support in helping to protect and enhance the quality of park waters through special use classifications, such as outstanding resource waters."

Floodplains and Wetlands:[783]   "The occupancy and modification of floodplains and wetlands will be avoided wherever possible. Where no practicable alternatives exist, mitigating measures will be implemented to minimize potential harm to life, property and the natural values of floodplains and wetlands." Management of these areas is subject to EO 11988, 42 U.S.C. § 4321 (floodplain management); EO 11990, 42 U.S.C. 4321 (wetlands protection); the Rivers and Harbors Acts[784] and Section 404 of the CWA. Inventories of wetlands and floodplains potentially subject to public use and existing uses of these areas shall be prepared, and high-hazard areas and appropriate actions will be identified.

Water Rights[785]: The NPS has stated a policy of asserting and adjudicating its federal-reserved water rights "for water quantities determined to be the minimum amounts needed to protect the primary purposes" of a given park.

At best, these policies impose generally soft constraints on the management of riverine and riparian ecosystems. Despite the fact that National Parks may contain some of the few remaining healthy biotic refuges and potential benchmark watersheds, the hardest standards enunciated by these policies leave much to managers' discretion. For example:

* Park waters will be withdrawn only where *"absolutely necessary"* for park purposes **and** it can be demonstrated that the withdrawal "will not *significantly alter* natural processes and ecosystems."

* "Direct pollution by livestock under commercial grazing permits will be prevented by eliminating streamside or lakeside corrals and pastures and associated watering sites *wherever possible . . .* "

* "The occupancy and modification of floodplains and wetlands will be avoided *wherever possible.*"

The Guidelines are intended to help park managers implement the Management Policies, and they generally restate these policies and suggest ways of implementing them. For example, the "Water Quality" section lists ways in which the NPS can participate in state water-quality-standards development and implementation.[786] The Guidelines addressing "Aquatic Habitat Protection and Management"[787] discuss the wide range of aquatic habitats which exist on park lands, including "permanent and intermittent rivers and streams" and "floodplain/riparian habitat," and discuss the physical and ecological factors relevant to this habitat. Potential impacts on aquatic habitats are listed, including: nutrients, pesticides, atmospheric deposition, hydrocarbons and toxics, physical-chemical constituents, hydropattern alteration, physical modifications, biotic factors, and recreational impacts. Although the Guidelines may contribute to park managers' understanding of river-related habitat and threats to it, they do not provide any additional management standards to the general Management Policies.

For riverine-riparian ecosystems, the most significant Guidelines language appears under the heading of "Aquatic Habitat Protection and Management," which states that the NPS seeks to 1) eliminate human-induced impacts on aquatic habitats; 2) limit effects and mitigate damage if impacts are unavoidable; 3) maintain and restore aquatic habitats to protect their ecological and aesthetic character and dependent animal and plant communities; and 4) minimize economic costs to developments from flood hazards.[788]

Need for restoration of riverine ecosystems within parks: As one Park Service official has observed, the primary threats to watersheds in National Parks derive from: 1) grazing uses which were grandfathered at the time particular parks were created; 2) mining, especially placer mining in Alaska; 3) recreational uses; and 4) interference with in-stream water rights from users outside the parks.[789] This is confirmed by a 1987 NPS service-wide natural resources assessment, which identified 480 water-quality issues affecting or potentially affecting 170 parks.[790] The majority of these issues were related to surrounding land-use activities, including oil and gas development, mining, encroaching urbanization, industrial activity, agricultural practices, or land development such as sewage effluent discharge and landfill leaching.[791] On the many millions of acres of Alaskan park lands, years of placer mining in riparian areas have left a lasting impact which demands attention.[792] Not surprisingly, most of these problems relate to non-point sources of pollution.

The degradation of riverine-riparian ecosystems outside of the Parks often leaves those rivers within the Parks as the only remaining healthy areas of biotic refugia. A thorough assessment of the entire riverine system is required to pinpoint the locations of potential refugia, benchmark watersheds and biological hot spots, a process that is rarely undertaken.

Conclusions

Riverine Systems and Biodiversity in National Parks are Threatened by Internal and External Impacts and Lack of Clear Management Directives

National Park Service Lacks Authority to Regulate External Impacts: Riverine systems and biodiversity in National Parks are probably most threatened by numerous activities that take place on federal lands outside park boundaries, but which affect natural patterns of fluctuation (such as soil erosion and deposition), as well as other dynamics of surface and subsurface water. Despite caselaw which indicates that the Park Service must take reasonable steps to protect watershed resources from adverse external impacts,[793] efforts by the Park Service and others to protect parks from external threats have met with limited success.[794] Since external threats represent the greatest danger to the integrity of the parks, they would greatly benefit from expanded authority for park managers to protect riverine systems and biodiversity from external threats.

The National Park Service Lacks Clear Riverine Management Directives: Neither the Park Service authorizing statutes nor their implementing regulations provide: (1) clear riparian protection standards and rules for the National Parks; or (2) policies, rules and standards for identifying and protecting biotic refugia, benchmark watersheds and biological hot spots.

As a result, these statutes have failed to result in the effective, adequate protection for riverine systems and biodiversity on NPS lands. Park managers have wide latitude and are not compelled to pursue any particular course of action to protect park resources, including riparian ecosystems and riverine biodiversity. Neither the NPS Management Policies or the Natural Resource Management Guidelines are specific enough to protect riparian ecosystems from degradation. In any case, the Guidelines do not constitute enforceable regulations.

Also, because current law leaves park management largely to the discretion of park officials, the NPS does not or cannot effectively coordinate with other federal land managers to protect the entire river ecosystem or to identify the role parkland rivers play in maintaining the health of river systems and related biodiversity. The dynamics of interagency relations under the current statutory and regulatory schemes are not conducive to full ecosystem protection because federal land managers need not act in unison, nor manage in cooperation with adjacent private landowners. Rather, they are motivated by diverse, and divergent, statutes and regulations.

River System-wide Policy Coordination and Alignment Needed: At present there are no directives to develop coordinated, consistent and aligned watershed-wide assessments, management plans, or monitoring mechanisms with adjacent federal agencies and private landowners within watersheds.

Additional Funds Needed for Resource Protection: With ever-increasing crowds using Park Service facilities, it seems doubtful that simply reallocating the limited NPS budget to resource management is a sound idea. Instead, Congress needs to appropriate additional funds to the NPS, earmarked specifically for resource management, particularly riverine management and restoration. Only with an infusion of more dollars can the nation's crown jewels be protected and restored.

FISH AND WILDLIFE SERVICE RIVERINE MANAGEMENT

The Fish and Wildlife Service's (FWS) primary land management responsibility is the administration of National Wildlife Refuges. In addition, the FWS is responsible for game regulation[795] and consultation with other agencies.[796] Because all uses may theoretically be permitted on wildlife refuges, the FWS encounters more resource conflicts than the Park Service, whose statutory mandate includes preservation. Like the Park Service, the FWS Organic Act fails to provide clear purposes for the Refuge System, explicit planning authority, or comprehensive management guidance.[797] Because the FWS has not followed a consistent management credo over the years, and because of its decentralized structure, many agency decisions may be characterized as "ad hoc."[798]

The primary statutory management standards which now exist require that public uses permitted on refuge lands be "compatible" with the primary purposes for which the area was established, and not inconsistent with the operations or primary objectives of the area. The absence of legal criteria and public participation requirements for compatibility decisions has contributed to the establishment of uses within refuges which impair riverine systems and biodiversity. However, many instances of riverine degradation on refuge lands are due to off-refuge activities on both public and private lands.

Other problems for riverine systems and biodiversity are created by outstanding third-party agreements providing for mineral rights reservations and the failure of the federal government to acquire subsurface rights at the time a refuge was created. Adverse impacts also derive from the terms of rights-of-way for uses such as powerlines. Incompatible uses also occur where they existed prior to the establishment of the refuge. FWS control is also lacking over areas over which the agency does not have sole management responsibility. For example, in some situations the Army Corps or the BOR have retained jurisdiction over flood control and irrigation activities on refuge lands.

Public uses and refuge planning under the National Wildlife Refuge System Act of 1966: The National Wildlife Refuge System was formally established in 1966 by the National Wildlife Refuge System Administration Act for the "conservation of fish and wildlife, including species that are threatened with extinction."[799] The Refuge System was initially created by consolidating all refuge lands administered by the FWS. Today, the Refuge System is comprised of almost 500 individual units covering 91 million acres of land and water in all 50 states, Puerto Rico, and several United States territories. The Refuge System is comprised of (1) National Wildlife Refuges (89,048,601 acres) established for such management purposes as migratory birds, endangered and other species; and (2) Waterfowl Production Areas and Waterfowl Management Districts managed for the preservation of wetland habitat and the sustenance of indigenous wildlife.[800] These lands are either owned or are managed according to the terms of easements obtained from private landowners.

In a nutshell, lands in the National Wildlife Refuge System (or other federal property under FWS administration) are subject to FWS discretion to allow any use "compatible" with the primary purposes for which the refuge area was designated.[801] Theoretically at least, the FWS may not permit non-recreational uses which impair wildlife habitat, which is closely linked to ecosystem stability. In practice, the "compatibility" standard affords the FWS broad discretion, and the result is that refuges are "dominant use" lands subject to a management standard which, ecologically speaking, falls between the standards governing parks and those governing multiple use lands.[802] For recreational uses, a stricter standard is imposed under the Refuge Recreation Act which permits appropriate incidental or secondary recreational uses "only to the extent practicable and consistent with the primary objectives for which each particular area is established.[803] Under this standard, the Secretary must affirmatively determine that non-wildlife, recreational uses "will not interfere with the [refuge area's] primary purpose."[804]

The compatibility determination for secondary uses: Prior to the Refuge System Act, the Refuge Protection Act of 1962 (RPA) had established a "compatibility" standard pursuant to which the FWS was authorized to permit non-wildlife-related recreational uses on refuge lands, i.e., "appropriate secondary or incidental" recreational uses "not directly related to the primary purposes and functions" of the refuge area.[805] Under the RPA, the Secretary of Interior is required to: (1) "assure that any present or future recreational use will be compatible with and will not prevent accomplishment of the primary purposes" for which an area was established; (2) permit public recreation only to the extent "practicable and not inconsistent with other previously authorized Federal operations" or with an area's "primary objectives"; and (3) permit only those recreational uses which he has determined "will not interfere with the primary purposes for which the areas were established" for which funding is available.[806]

The Refuge System Act expanded the RPA standard to authorize the Secretary, by such regulations as he deems necessary, to "permit the use of any area within the System for any purpose including, but not limited to, hunting, fishing, public recreation and accommodations, and access whenever he determines that such uses are compatible with the major purposes for which such areas were established."[807]

This "compatibility" determination remains the primary statutory standard governing the use of wildlife refuges. In making such a determination, the Secretary bears the burden of establishing a lack of harm and showing that he could not balance the economic or political factors against wildlife welfare.[808] At present, such determinations are informal, are not made based on clear criteria (scientific or otherwise) and are not made with public participation.

According to its Refuge Manual, the FWS has stated that uses may be determined to be compatible if they "will not materially interfere with or detract from the purpose(s) for which the refuge was established. Some compatible uses may be supportive of refuge purposes, while others may be of a nonconflicting nature."[809]

Existing secondary uses on refuges -- the strange case of harmful but compatible: A 1989 study conducted by the General Accounting Office addressed the issues of (1) whether refuges are being managed for the purposes for which they were established, (2) whether these purposes are being effectively met, and (3) the impacts of public uses on refuges. The study concluded many public uses currently permitted on refuge-system lands are not related to fish and wildlife conservation and that such uses are diverting management attention and resources away from fish and wildlife management. The study further found that 59% of refuges had at least one use that could be considered "harmful." The most frequently occurring harmful activities were mining, off-road vehicles, airboat use, waterskiing and military air exercises. The study ultimately recommended that compatibility decisions be based on biological criteria and that permitted uses be subject to periodic evaluation. Where harmful uses occur outside FWS jurisdiction, the study recommended that the authority to control the uses be acquired or that the impacted area be removed from the system altogether.

The FWS took exception to the GAO's characterization of "harmful" uses as "incompatible," and, in response, the agency released its own survey entitled *Secondary Uses Occurring on National Wildlife Refuges* in June of 1990. This review recorded data on 88 different uses on 478 refuge system units. The results were as follows:

* 132 use occurrences were reported as "incompatible." Grazing was the most frequently reported incompatible use.

* 836 use occurrences were reported as "harmful." Grazing and rights-of-way were the most frequently occurring harmful uses.

* 934 use occurrences were reported as "inappropriate" in refuge manager's personal opinions. The most frequent inappropriate uses were military air exercises and oil and gas extraction.

The FWS has taken the rather confusing position that a use may be "harmful," i.e., the "net result of the activity is that it adversely affects the ability of the refuge managers to conserve or manage in accordance with the refuge/wetland management-district goals and objectives,"[810] but may not rise to the level of incompatibility as measured by comparison with a unit's purposes, goals and objectives.[811] Apparently, the FWS seeks to distinguish between harmful uses it has legal authority to control through incompatibility determinations and harmful uses it does not have the authority to regulate.[812] More than half the uses found to be harmful were outside FWS authority, including: military activities, sewage effluent and flowage easements, commercial navigation, private exclusive uses, and other public leases and uses.[813]

Overall, 63% of the refuge units reported one or more harmful activities within their borders, although only 16% were considered "incompatible."[814]

Refuge planning: Each unit of the refuge system has one or more primary purposes for which it was established by executive order or act of Congress. Refuges often have such broad purposes as the conservation of fish and wildlife habitat in their natural diversity, the fulfillment of international treaty obligations, the provision of subsistence use for local residents and the maintenance of water quality and quantity (e.g., Yukon Flats in Alaska). Individual refuges may also have very narrow purposes, such as the preservation and management of single species, e.g., the National Bison Range in western Montana.

Because the National Wildlife Refuge System Act of 1966, the only "organic" Act governing the FWS, is not comprehensive and fails to provide any explicit planning authority, refuge planning is governed entirely by administrative initiatives.[815] The only exception is Alaska, where Congress has separately required the preparation of land use plans with consultation, public hearing and Federal Register publication requirements.[816]

As noted above, the Refuge System Act states a very broad purpose for the Refuge System: "the conservation of fish and wildlife, including species that are threatened with extinction."[817] Regulations promulgated by the FWS state that:

> All national wildlife refuges are maintained for the primary purpose of developing a national program of wildlife and ecological conservation and rehabilitation. These refuges are established for the restoration, preservation, development and management of wildlife and wild habitat; for the protection and preservation of endangered species and their habitat; and for the management of wildlife and wilderness to obtain the maximum benefits from these resources.[818]

The FWS has also informally stated that it believes the goals of the Refuge System are:

> * To preserve, restore, and enhance in their natural ecosystems (where practicable) all species of animals and plants that are endangered or threatened with becoming endangered.

> * To perpetuate the migratory bird resource.

> * To preserve a natural diversity and abundance of fauna and flora on refuge lands.

> * To provide an understanding and appreciation of fish and wildlife ecology and man's role in his environment, and to provide refuge visitors with high-quality, safe, wholesome, and enjoyable recreational experiences oriented toward wildlife, to the extent these activities are

compatible with the purposes for which the refuge was established.[819]

The FWS planning process is entirely discretionary and is not structured by its organic statute. As it deems necessary, the agency develops "field plans," which include plans for individual refuge systems, and may be either general or local.[820] Individual refuges undergo a three-stage-planning process at the field-station level: master plans; refuge management plans; and annual work plans. Field-station plans usually have ten-or twenty-year horizons and set long-term objectives for the management of particular refuges.[821]

The regional director is responsible for deciding whether a master plan should be developed or revised, based on factors which include the role of the refuge in meeting regional and national objectives, the adequacy of existing data and documentation on the subject refuge program and the extent of public interest in and controversy over the existing program.[822]

The absence of specific management directives is a "double-edged sword" for resource protection: Where the agency takes an action, it is likely to be upheld as within agency discretion, particularly since refuge users seldom have any statutory rights to use the refuges.[823] However, where the agency fails to take action or takes inappropriate directions, there is inadequate statutory basis to compel the agency to take any particular action.

Despite its informality, when the FWS undertakes planning actions it can be exceedingly effective in protecting wildlife resources. For example, *New England Naturist Association, Inc. v. Larsen*, 692 F. Supp. 75 (D.R.I. 1988), involved the Trustom Pond Refuge, which provides nesting habitat for the piping plover, a threatened species under the ESA. In that case, the plaintiffs challenged a FWS Master Plan and environmental assessment that proposed fencing off most of the refuge to prevent conflicts between the plover and human recreational uses, which included nude sunbathing. The court rejected the plaintiffs' challenge to closure of the refuge, partly because the Plan itself was considered evidence that the agency's action was not arbitrary or capricious.[824]

Other Management Authorities In addition to its primary responsibility of managing the National Wildlife Refuge System, the FWS has extensive game regulation and inter-agency consultation responsibilities under a variety of statutes.

* The Migratory Bird Treaty Act of 1918 provides for regulations to control the taking of migratory species.[825]

* The Migratory Bird Conservation Act of 1929 provided for the preservation and management of migratory bird habitat in the form of refuges and expressly barred hunting on certain lands.[826]

* The Migratory Bird Hunting and Stamp Act of 1934 provided funding for the acquisition of migratory bird refuges.[827]

* The Endangered Species Act directs the FWS to emphasize management for endangered and threatened species in the acquisition and operation of refuges.

* ANILCA established nine new refuges and expanded seven existing refuges in Alaska, adding more than 54 million acres to the refuge system and requiring "conservation" plans for Alaskan refuges.[828] As a result of this act, the majority of acreage in the Refuge System is in Alaska.

Status of riverine-riparian ecosystems on refuge lands: Although many refuges suffer from severe water quality and water quantity problems, there is limited information available on the status of rivers and riparian areas on refuge lands because no refuge-wide assessment of riverine-riparian ecosystem conditions has been conducted. However, one can safely say that a majority of refuges have flowing water systems associated with them.

We do know that grazing has severely degraded riparian areas on a number of refuges, such as the Sheldon National Wildlife Refuge in Oregon and Nevada where livestock have destroyed native grasses, silted streams, lowered water tables and caused the rapid decline of a now endangered fish species, the tui chub.[829]

We also know that there is a dire problem with toxic pesticides, leached minerals and other contaminants flowing into Refuges from surrounding and urban areas. According to a 1986 study, 85 Refuges have contaminant problems, and these problems are concentrated on refuges which lack adequate supplies of fresh water.[830] A more recent study indicates that refuges suffer from contaminants both from within and from outside refuge boundaries, especially nonpoint-source pollutants. Further, many more cases of contamination are suspected by refuge managers but often remain undocumented.[831]

As with riverine systems and biodiversity on other federal lands nationwide, a thorough biological and ecological assessment is needed.

Conclusions

U.S. Fish and Wildlife Service Riverine System and Biodiversity Management is Inadequate

Despite the fact that the National Wildlife Refuge System was established for the primary purpose of conserving fish and wildlife, activities which degrade riverine systems and biodiversity are nonetheless continuing to occur on these lands. A large part of the problem is that the Refuge System lands are the only federal lands without comprehensive policies to provide clear direction and goals. Legislation which has been proposed in both the House and Senate which will address some of the problems now being experienced on refuge lands but no law has yet been enacted.[832]

Refuge Purposes Should Be Clarified: At present the Refuge System Act states a very broad purpose for the Refuge System: "the conservation of fish and wildlife, including species that are threatened with extinction."[833]   This broad purpose does not provide adequate direction to the FWS for the protection of the habitat upon which fish and wildlife depend, including riparian ecosystems, floodplains, and hyporheic zones so crucial to preserving the integrity of riverine-riparian ecosystems.[834]

The purposes of the Refuge System need to be clearly stated.   Recent legislative proposals have suggested these purposes: "to provide a network of lands and waters to protect fish, wildlife and plants; to provide adequate food, water and shelter and to ensure conservation of natural diversity of native fish, wildlife and plants and their habitats." In addition, language should be added which makes the restoration of riverine and wildlife habitat a specific purpose of the System.

Planning and Management Guidelines Should be Strengthened to Require Planning and Protection for Water Quality and Quantity, Biotic Refuges, Benchmark Watersheds and Biological Hot Spots: The water-quality and water-quantity needs of the Refuge System need to be clearly identified and addressed.   Currently, there is no clear statutory mandate specifically requiring management plans for refuges generally, much less any management plans which specifically address water issues.   A clear strategic-planning mandate which specifically requires that the agency address the water-related issues and the health of riverine-riparian ecosystems and biodiversity is needed. In addition, clear direction must be established for the identification and protection of biotic refugia, benchmark watersheds and biological hot spots.

Compatibility Criteria Needed: Although the individual purposes for refuges generally favor the preservation of riverine-riparian ecosystems in their natural state, the vague statutory standards permitting "compatible" uses in refuges pose a threat to the maintenance of river ecosystems on refuge lands. Currently, the compatibility determination is made as much or more on the basis of local politics than on the basis of biological criteria relating to the impacts of a proposed use on refuge ecosystems. Statutory guidance is required to ensure that compatibility is determined on the basis of scientific criteria and adequate information.

Public Participation Requirements Needed: Currently, there is no formal requirement for public participation in either refuge planning or compatibility decisions. New policies should require public notice and comment on refuge plans and compatibility decisions.

River System-wide Policy Coordination and Alignment Needed: At present there are no mandates to develop coordinated, consistent and aligned watershed-wide assessments, management plans or monitoring programs with adjacent federal agencies and private landowners within a watershed.

Legal Authority Needed to Protect Riverine Systems From External Threats: Currently there is no requirement nor legal authority for refuge managers to protect riverine-riparian ecosystems and biodiversity within a refuge from external threats, despite the fact that these represent the greatest danger to the integrity of the refuges.

THE NATIONAL WILDERNESS-PRESERVATION SYSTEM AND RIVERINE SYSTEM MANAGEMENT

The Wilderness Act targets large roadless and undeveloped portions of the federal lands for special protection as natural areas. Each of the land management agencies is responsible for administering parts of the 91 million acre National Wilderness Preservation System. Because the Act directs that the "wilderness character" of these areas should be preserved, wilderness areas provide greater protections for watersheds and water quality than they would have under the general policies of each of the agencies -- particularly under the multiple use policies of the BLM and the Forest Service. The Wilderness Act also provides a basis for federal riverine restoration efforts. However, the ecological integrity of wilderness areas is still threatened by pre-existing rights and, to some extent, land use restrictions may vary according to specific acts of Congress designating a particular wilderness area.

The wilderness system: The Forest Service has been creating wilderness areas since 1924, when 700,000 acres of the Gila National Forest in New Mexico was set aside as a "natural" area. However, it was not until new wilderness regulations were passed in 1939 that real restrictions on roads, timber harvesting and other non-wilderness uses were imposed in such areas.

The Wilderness Act of 1964 shifted wilderness designation authority and management discretion from the Forest Service to Congress,[835] creating the National Wilderness Preservation System, with an initial endowment of 9.1 million acres of national forest lands. Since 1964, Congress has expanded the System to almost 91 million acres through dozens of separate laws, with more lands recommended for inclusion by interest groups, federal agencies and Members of Congress.[836] The Wilderness System now contains 477 wilderness areas in 44 states. By the end of 1989, the Forest Service administered 32,532,285 acres of wilderness, the BLM administered 465,509 acres, the NPS administered 38,498,124 acres and the FWS administered 19,332,897 acres.[837] More than 60% of this land -- 56.5 million acres -- is in Alaska, which includes most of the wilderness managed by the NPS and the USFWS. One-third of the System is administered by the Forest Service, whose charge comprises 80 percent of wilderness outside Alaska.[838]

As of 1989, the agencies had recommended that 16.9 million additional acres be added to the System, and 118.5 million additional acres (75% of which were in Alaska) were under study.[839] With the recent completion of the BLM's system-wide wilderness review of 27 million acres and recommendations to Congress, BLM wilderness could grow by as much as 10 million acres.[840]

Riverine system and biodiversity protection and restoration in Wilderness Areas: Although Congress recognized that human activities threaten wilderness, the Act does not anticipate total exclusion of humans and their impacts.[841] Under the Act, areas included in the National Wilderness Preservation System are to be managed by the department or agency that had jurisdiction before the land was designated.[842]

Because the Wilderness Act's definition provides only general characteristics for determining wilderness, it leaves considerable room for interpretation.[843] The Wilderness System is subject to the general management directive, requiring the managing federal agencies to "preserve" the "wilderness character" of designated areas.[844] According to the Act's definition of wilderness, preservation of wilderness character generally means maintenance of the natural appearance and ecological health of wilderness areas. Arguably, federal agencies also have an affirmative duty to restore impaired wilderness character in areas suffering from pre-designation activities.

Some commercial activities permitted: Designation as wilderness generally guarantees that many uses which threaten watershed integrity are prohibited, including most commercial activities, roadbuilding, clearcutting, mining, motorized access (except in emergencies), structures and facilities.[845] The Act also provides numerous exceptions to these general prohibitions, including: (a) possible continued use of motorboats and aircraft where such uses were already established; (b) fire, insect and disease control measures; (c) mineral prospecting conducted "in a manner compatible with the preservation of the wilderness environment"; (d) water project developments; (e) continued livestock grazing under permits issued prior to 1964, subject to "reasonable regulation" by the Secretary; and (f) commercial recreation activities.[846]

In addition to these exemptions, the Wilderness Act includes a number of other special provisions applicable to certain commercial and recreational uses. Notably, the Act extended mining and mineral leasing laws for wilderness areas in National Forests for 20 years -- through 1983. New mining claims and leases were permitted in some wilderness areas, "subject, however, to such reasonable regulations governing ingress and egress as may be prescribed by the Secretary of Agriculture."[847]   Although new mineral exploration under these regulations has been limited, some has occurred, and pre-1983 mineral rights remain valid and subject to development at the discretion of the right-holder.[848]

Minimum requirements management: The Wilderness Act contains a general exception provision authorizing wilderness managers to take any action otherwise prohibited where "necessary to meet minimum requirements for the administration of the area for the purpose of [the Wilderness Act]."[849]   This standard requires that two determinations be made. First, is the proposed activity consistent with a purpose of the Wilderness Act, i.e., preservation of wild areas and public uses and enjoyment?[850] Second, is the activity necessary to meet minimum requirements for administration of an area for a legitimate wilderness purpose? Thus, this general exception is constrained by the Act's mandate that wilderness character be preserved and that the least disruptive, or "minimum," methods be used in executing management actions.[851]   However, Congress has sometimes responded to interest group demands by allowing exemptions for certain uses -- usually existing -- in enacting wilderness designations.[852]

Agency regulations for wilderness management: Except for the Park Service, which administers wilderness areas according to the same regulations applicable to all park lands, each of the federal agencies has promulgated regulations specifically applicable to wilderness. Although the FWS regulations do not add significantly to the statutory language contained in Section 4(b) of the Act, the BLM and the Forest Service regulations attempt to interpret those agencies' wilderness management duties in some detail.[853]

Both the BLM and the Forest Service regulations recognize that it is crucial to the preservation of wilderness character that ecological processes not be impaired by human activity, and both permit restrictions on human use where necessary to maintain an area's wilderness character.[854]   Both agencies further interpret the Wilderness Act to authorize management actions which actively restore wilderness character in areas where the natural state has been disturbed.[855]

Wilderness and multiple-use management: It should be noted that one result of the Wilderness Act was that the Forest Service was allowed to retain control of new wilderness areas, rather than being forced to relinquish them to the Park Service. Like National Forests, these areas are managed under the National Forest Management Act (NFMA), which directs that wilderness be considered in forest planning along with other "multiple use" resources. The NFMA regulations further require evaluation of roadless areas in the general forest-planning process.[856] However, the limited uses to which wilderness areas may be put clearly conflict with many conceptions of "multiple-use management."[857]

Wilderness and water rights: Under current law, the question remains unresolved as to whether wilderness designation carries with it implied reserved water rights to enhance watershed protection and maintenance. The Solicitor General has explicitly rejected the idea, stating that "wilderness areas enjoy the benefits of water reserved for underlying parks, forests or refuges but are not entitled to a separate and additional reservation of water."[858] In contrast, a district court in Colorado held that water is reserved for wilderness purposes upon designation.[859] However, this holding was overturned by the Tenth Circuit on the grounds that the issue was not ripe for decision.[860] The circuit court based its finding on the lack of finality in the agency's action: "The Forest Service's principal position is not that federal-reserved water rights do not exist, but rather that their assertion at this time is unnecessary and possibly counterproductive."[861] This issue is bound to be litigated again in the near future, though, as conflicting uses increase the pressures on limited water sources, particularly in the West.

Conclusions

Riverine Systems and Biodiversity in Wilderness Areas Have Limited Protection

The Wilderness Act's Mandate Provides Only General Constraints on Riverine Management: According to the Wilderness Act's definition of wilderness, preservation of wilderness character generally means maintenance of the natural appearance and ecological health of wilderness areas. However, these are only general characteristics which leave ample room for managing agencies to interpret what is required to "preserve" the "wilderness character" of designated areas. Riverine systems would benefit from a more specific description of what constitutes the natural appearance and ecological health of a riverine system.

The Wilderness Act Provides Authority for Restoration of Natural Ecosystems, But The Extent to Which This Mandate Is Acted Upon Depends on Agency Will and Resources: Arguably, federal agencies also have an affirmative duty to restore impaired wilderness character in areas suffering from pre-designation activities. This duty is not, however, an express provision in the Act and is, therefore, not well-defined or consistently exercised. Riverine systems in wilderness areas would benefit from an express mandate for restoration to their natural state to the extent possible, with specific resource appropriations for this purpose.

Exceptions for Pre-existing Uses May Impair Natural Function of Wilderness Riverine Systems: Although designation as wilderness generally guarantees that many uses which threaten watershed integrity are prohibited, including most commercial activities, roadbuilding, clearcutting, mining, motorized access, structures and facilities, the Act also provides numerous exceptions to these general prohibitions, which permit the continuation of pre-existing uses which threaten the ecological integrity of rivers. Such threatening uses include the operation of motorboats, mineral prospecting, water resources projects, livestock grazing and some commercial recreation activities.

The Wilderness Act also contains a general exception for management actions otherwise prohibited where "necessary to meet minimum requirements for the administration of the area for the purpose of [the Wilderness Act]." This general exception is limited to the least disruptive, or "minimum," methods required to meet management goals. However, Congress has sometimes responded to interest group demands by allowing exemptions for certain non-wilderness uses -- usually existing -- in enacting wilderness designations.

FEDERAL REQUIREMENTS FOR CUMULATIVE IMPACT ANALYSIS AND INTER-AGENCY COORDINATION

In addition to the statutes discussed which relate to the duties of specific agencies, there are also a number of statutes and regulations which require individual agencies to cooperate with one another in their land-planning and management decisions, especially where a decision affects adjacent federal lands.[862] Many of these laws encompass coordinated planning regarding water resources. However, the piecemeal effect of these various legislative acts has meant that the comprehensive and effective river system-wide planning needed to protect riverine systems and biodiversity has not occurred.

Cumulative impacts analysis under the National Environmental Policy Act: a basis for watershed-level decision-making: The express language of the National Environmental Policy Act[863] ("NEPA") is consistent with the protection of riverine-riparian ecosystems and biodiversity at the watershed level. In enacting the statute, Congress recognized that human activities tend to upset "the interrelations of all components of the natural environment," and stated several general substantive goals which can be related directly to watershed protection, including: the prevention and elimination of damage to "the environment and biosphere"; the preservation of "an environment which supports diversity"; and the achievement of "a balance between population and resource use."[864]

The basic requirements of NEPA are purely procedural. Under Section 102, NEPA establishes judicially enforceable obligations which require all federal agencies to identify the environmental impacts of their planned activities. This section requires federal agencies to determine whether a proposed action constitutes a "major federal action" which will "significantly [affect] . . . the quality of the human environment." The decision must be placed in a preliminary document called an environmental assessment ("EA"). If the EA determines that the action is major, the agency must then prepare a comprehensive environmental impact statement ("EIS"). These requirements revolutionized federal decision-making by forcing agencies to factor environmental impacts into their normal decision-making processes subject to both public and judicial scrutiny. However, despite Congressional intent that NEPA impose substantive constraints on agency action, the statute's environmental protection provisions are too general to permit judicial reversal of an agency decision based on NEPA alone.[865] In sum, NEPA requires that agencies use their technical expertise to take a "hard look" at environmental consequences in making decisions, but it but does not require that the final decision avoid the identified consequences.[866]

Despite the procedural emphasis of NEPA, however, its requirement that the "cumulative impacts" of federal actions be considered pushes agencies in the direction of watershed-level decision-making.[867] Cumulative impacts are defined as the total impacts, including the incremental impact of the proposed action when added to other "past, present or reasonably foreseeable future actions," regardless of the identity of the proponent.[868] Cumulative action, defined as actions "which when viewed with other proposed actions have cumulatively significant effect," must be considered together.[869]

Judicial interpretation of NEPA's cumulative impacts requirements has determined that agencies must consider the cumulative impacts of all actions, both federal and private, in the area of a proposed action.[870] This requirement has led at least one court to enjoin an agency activity because it did not adequately consider cumulative watershed impacts.[871]

Cumulative impacts analysis must include agency actions not formally proposed if the action is "closely related" or "connected."[872] An action is connected if it will automatically trigger actions requiring environmental impact statements, if it depends on the execution of other previous or simultaneous actions or if it is an interdependent part of a larger action.[873] For example, an agency may be required to assess the cumulative impacts of timber harvesting when it proposes to build a logging road because the timber harvest necessarily flows from the road construction.[874]

The greatest benefit of cumulative impacts analysis is that it requires federal land managers to concern themselves with the activities of public and private entities in the same watershed. While analysis of project impacts of the cumulative level alone may not ensure adequate watershed protection, it most certainly leads to better protection than would entirely uninformed decision-making and certainly provides direction for the agencies to do so.

Interagency coordination requirements in federal land and resource management -- in search of common ground: In addition to the interagency coordination necessitated by NEPA, the federal land management agencies are subject to various general requirements for some degree of interagency coordination which could, theoretically, lead to coordinated watershed management for federal lands. Interagency coordination provisions are contained in various statutes, including the agencies' own organic legislation, NEPA and the WSRA, among others. These provisions generally require that agencies coordinate their land planning and management decisions whenever a decision affects adjacent federal lands. Such coordinated planning requirements may also extend to state and local bodies where federal actions affect private lands. This section briefly outlines some of these provisions and concludes that none provides adequate directives for agencies to develop watershed-wide planning and management mechanisms to protect or restore riverine-riparian ecosystems and biodiversity.

Coordination requirements under the Wild and Scenic Rivers Act:
For federal lands within river corridors in the Wild and Scenic
River System, the WSRA anticipates the need for interagency
planning in order to protect the outstanding natural values of
designated rivers.   Section 3 provides that agencies must
"coordinate" river management plans with the resource plans for
affected adjacent federal lands.[875]   Section 12 broadly requires
federal agencies to take all necessary action to protect the river
corridor from any activities which impair its values[876] and
specifically requires managing agencies to "cooperate" with the
EPA and the states to eliminate or reduce pollution of river
corridors.[877]

To the Act's credit, these requirements apply to all federal
activities whose effects might impair the values of a river corridor,
regardless of whether such activities occur within a corridor
boundary, and the agencies are pointedly reminded to pay
"particular attention" to scheduled timber harvests, roadbuilding
and similar activities.[878]   However, none of these provisions sets
forth any specific interagency planning procedures for watershed
protection, nor is the term "cooperate" defined.[879]   Furthermore,
the impacts of private, extra-boundary activities are not addressed.
The only direction for joint planning between state, local and
federal affected parties is the Act's requirement that the
appropriate federal official enter "written cooperative agreements"
with state or local officials for planning, administration and
management of federal lands included in the System.[880]

It is informative to note that, at least with regard to the
Act's directive that agencies and states "cooperate" to reduce water
pollution in river corridors, political considerations were likely the
reason that more detailed provisions were not enacted.   More
detailed language would probably have created jurisdictional
problems between congressional committees, because the Act
originated in Interior and Insular Affairs, rather than in Public
Works -- the committee with specific jurisdiction over pollution of
navigable waters.[881]

Coordination under FLPMA and NFMA: Interagency coordination is also mentioned in FLPMA provisions which require the BLM to coordinate its planning and management activities with those of other federal land managers.[882] This provision requires that when developing and revising land-use plans, the Secretary of the Interior shall:

> to the extent consistent with the laws governing the administration of the public lands, coordinate the land use inventory, planning and management activities . . . with the land use planning and management activities of other Federal departments and agencies and of the States and local governments within which the lands are located . . . by, among other things, considering the policies of approved State and tribal land resource management programs. In implementing this directive, the Secretary shall, to the extent he finds practical, keep apprised of State, local, and tribal land use plans; assure that consideration is given to [those plans] that are germane in the development of land use plans for public lands; assist in resolving, to the extent practical, inconsistencies between Federal and non-Federal Government plans, and shall provide for meaningful public involvement of State and local government officials, both elected and appointed, in the development of land use programs, land use regulations, and land use decisions for the public lands, including early public notice of proposed decisions which may have a significant impact on non-Federal lands. Such officials in each State are authorized to furnish advice to the Secretary with respect to the development of land use plans [guidelines, rules and regulations] for the public lands within such State and with respect to such other land use

matters as may be referred to them by him. Land use plans of the Secretary under this section shall be consistent with State and local plans to the maximum extent he finds consistent with Federal law and the purposes of this Act.[883]

This language provides ample discretion to ignore conflicts with other agencies, states or localities: the Secretary is vaguely told to "coordinate" planning and "consider" other policies to the extent "practical" and "to the maximum extent he finds consistent" with federal law and the purposes of FLPMA. No specific meaning is given to any of these terms, and no specific coordination procedures are prescribed.

The NFMA contains similar language, requiring the Secretary of Agriculture to "develop, maintain, and, as appropriate, revise land and resource management plans for units of the National Forest System, coordinated with the land and resources management planning processes of State and local governments and other Federal agencies."[884] Again, nowhere is "coordination" defined in any manner which meaningfully constrains the agency's discretion to ignore the opinion of other affected parties.

In forest planning, the NFMA instructs the Secretary of Agriculture to coordinate with all state, local, and other federal agencies and to use a "systematic interdisciplinary approach" which provides for public participation at all stages, including a hearing prior to plan adoption.[885] Plans are also required to comply with the multiple-use and sustained-yield objectives of earlier legislation, the most prominent of which is the MUSYA of 1960.[886]

Conclusions

Agencies Need Common Goals and Uniform Policy Directives to Effectively Plan and Manage at the Watershed and Ecosystem Level

By Itself, Cumulative Impact Analysis Under NEPA is Insufficient to Ensure That Agency Actions Will Protect Riverine Systems and Biodiversity: NEPA revolutionized federal decision-making by exposing it to public scrutiny and imposing judicially enforceable requirements that a wide range of impacts and alternatives to proposed actions be fully examined. The fact remains, however, that NEPA is a primarily procedural statute which forces informed decision-making, but does not compel particular outcomes. Therefore, even though analysis of the cumulative impacts of agency actions will often require an examination of impacts on whole watersheds and riverine-riparian ecosystems, the final decision is not required to meet any particular standards for protection.

Establishing supportable baselines upon which to measure all future cumulative impacts is very difficult. Often, "thresholds" are established that ironically serve to allow agencies to degrade a system down to the barest minimum, rather than restore a system. Further, "thresholds" can serve to place greater stress on healthier systems, as agencies will refocus development actions on those systems still above the "threshold," thus driving them down as well.

However, cumulative impacts analysis does preclude federal agencies from isolating its actions from other federal, state or private actions in the same watershed, encouraging agencies to at least look at the "big picture."

Existing Interagency Coordination Provisions are Discretionary and Do Not Identify Common Goals or Policies for All Federal Agencies: The provisions discussed above are manifestly inadequate to ensure the coordinated management of riverine systems. For numerous reasons, the existence of discretionary authority to reduce conflicts between various federal programs is not enough to compel the successful exercise of that authority. As some analysts have noted, even where agencies have entered into conflict resolution processes, the resulting agreements -- such as the Memorandum of Understanding between the NPS and BLM -- are limited by the agencies tendency to focus on separate agency goals, when a more effective approach would have been to set out common goals from which to proceed.[887]

In order to ensure that federal agencies effectively coordinate their planning efforts to protect riverine-riparian ecosystems, they must start with common goals that supercede all existing legal mandates. New legislation is required which includes specific and uniform interagency policy-alignment provisions for riverine management. For example, uniform goals and policies to protect and restore riparian areas using the same ecological definitions of these areas are needed for all agencies with management responsibilities within a watershed.

It is only fair to note that while existing statutes themselves do not specify common goals or procedures for interagency planning, *de facto* interagency planning procedures have often developed out of necessity. This is especially true for Wild and Scenic rivers, which may be jointly administered by statute, and national parks, which may be surrounded entirely by lands which enjoy less stringent levels of protection. The experience of the federal officials involved in these efforts could provide valuable models for future watershed-level interagency coordination/alignment efforts.

A Scientific, System-wide Framework Should Be Provided As The Basis For Uniform, Aligned Policies: The establishment of common goals and policies is important to enable agencies to protect and restore riverine systems and biodiversity. However, they must also be based on independent scientific assessments of riverine-riparian ecosystem conditions to provide a starting point from which to assess management and restoration alternatives. Because this information is currently lacking and/or has not been effectively integrated or compiled, an assessment of riverine-system health should be prepared which targets both healthier and degraded riparian areas, floodplains, biotic refugia, biological hot spots and riverine-riparian biodiversity, along with water quality and quantity, etc. Coordinated and aligned watershed protection and restoration cannot occur without this.

RIVERINE SYSTEMS AND BIODIVERSITY ON NATIVE AMERICAN LANDS

Because each of the numerous Native American lands enjoy sovereign status, an analysis of Native American law and its potential for the protection and restoration of riverine systems and biodiversity is beyond the scope of this discussion.[888] Suffice it to say that the tribes exercise sovereignty over the rivers on their lands according to tribal laws and treaties unique to the history and location of each tribe. Many Native American tribes have exerted their authority over fishing rights and water flows derived from treaties signed years ago. Some tribes have entered into cooperative agreements with state or federal agencies, while others have assumed independent administration of water-quality control and certification under the Clean Water Act.[889] There are currently several water-rights questions at issue with implications for riverine protection, including whether tribal reserved water rights, usually quantified by courts based on practicably irrigable acreage on a reservation, can be used by tribes to protect minimum in-stream flows.[890]

APPENDIX C

FEDERAL POLICIES AND PROGRAMS AFFECTING RIVERS THAT FLOW THROUGH PRIVATE LANDS

Riverine systems and biodiversity on private (non-federal) lands are being incrementally degraded by numerous activities, and the vast majority of these systems are in significantly worse condition than on federal lands. Unfortunately, most development on private lands is not consistently regulated to protect riverine systems and biodiversity. Private lands and water use are primarily controlled by state and local law nationwide, creating widely divergent levels of protection at the state, county and municipal levels.

Because the causes of degradation to private-land riverine systems are so varied, the protection and restoration of these systems will require strong new federal policies which cut across the many fragmented and often conflicting state and local policies to encourage comprehensive, coordinated and aligned watershed-level conservation. At present, no effective federal policies exist to initiate comprehensive riverine protection or restoration on private lands. The limited policies that do exist often lack solid local support because they are perceived to include the "heavy hand" of the government, or to be inconsistent with local economic development or otherwise be at odds with local public opinion.

This section briefly evaluates the strengths and weaknesses of a number of existing policies and programs affecting the conservation of riverine systems and biodiversity on private lands.

PRIVATE-LAND RIVERINE POLICIES REQUIRING CONGRESSIONAL ACTION

Congress has created several mechanisms to protect private-lands riverine systems, including providing for inclusion of

329

private-land segments in the National Wild and Scenic Rivers System, and geographically specific acts such as the Columbia Gorge National Scenic Area.

THE NATIONAL WILD AND SCENIC RIVERS ACT OF 1968

The effectiveness of the National Wild and Scenic Rivers Act[891] (WSRA) on federal lands has been discussed previously. In general, all of the issues and concerns identified for federal lands are applicable to private-land river segments. For example, a designation generally addresses just a river segment, not an entire riverine system. Protected corridors are limited to an arbitrary 1/4 mile boundary, thus failing to address the vital tributaries and ecological processes within the watershed. Further, there are no clear directives for restoration, despite the fact that private-land river systems nationwide are a great deal more degraded than federal land rivers. In addition to these limits, this section addresses some issues specifically applying to the effectiveness of the Act on private-land rivers nationwide.

The WSRA's application to private-land river segments has improved considerably in recent years, mostly due to the efforts of the National Park Service. Many additional river segments are certain to be included in the system over time. However, to date, the WSRA has not been effective as a tool to comprehensively protect private-land riverine systems or biodiversity. This is demonstrated by the proportionately small number of private-land river segments which have become part of the system.

Purpose: The purpose of the Act is limited to the protection of "certain selected rivers of the Nation which, with their immediate environments, possess outstandingly remarkable" qualities. Standing alone, this language eliminates more than 98% of the nation's rivers and streams from eligibility because most of them have been significantly altered and degraded by human activity.[892] Moreover, as discussed with reference to federal lands, the level of protection afforded designated rivers depends primarily on the values deemed worthy of protection during the designation process. It is, nonetheless, the WSRA's stated intent with regard to all designated rivers to protect the free-flowing condition of the river, to protect its water quality, to ban federally licensed hydroelectric and water-resources projects and to "fulfill other vital national conservation purposes."

The state designation process: The language and legislative history of the WSRA indicate that its framers intended for most private lands rivers to enter the Wild and Scenic River system through the state designation and management provisions.[893] However, few rivers have been designated through the state process. One serious impediment to states' use of this designation process is the Act's failure to provide states with funding for technical assistance to study rivers and create the designation proposals for state governors. Further, state-requested designation requires the state to pay for the management of the designated segment.

Another reason for the underutilization of the state designation process is that the Act outlines even fewer specific land-management requirements for private lands rivers than it does for federal lands. The Act's only direction for the management of private-lands rivers is stated indirectly through a provision limiting property condemnation along designated rivers: Condemnation is prohibited on all lands subject to a "duly adopted, valid zoning ordinance that conforms with the purposes of [the Act]."[894] Further, the federal government may condemn title and easement only where federal ownership of the land is less than 50%. Where federal ownership is greater than 50%, only easements may be condemned. Although the Act further requires that "guidelines specifying standards" for such local ordinances be promulgated by the appropriate Secretary, such standards have never been established.

Limitations: Attempts to designate private-land rivers have resulted in similar reactions by local landowners across the country. The recurring theme is fear of "big government" control and land condemnation. Many concerned citizens mistakenly equate designation with condemnation. While citizens' fears about

Wild and Scenic designation on public lands can be significant, they often pale in comparison with the near-hysterical opposition to private land designation, a sentiment which generally makes most elected officials and public agencies abandon the efforts in haste.

In addition, because the WSRA was created primarily for federal lands, the program does not place emphasis, provide clear direction for, or mandate coordination with local governments. Local governments are considered in the planning process where private properties or inholdings exist within a designated river. Except in the case of rivers designated by means of state designation,[895] the WSRA was designed to be implemented by federal agencies which must assume full responsibility for management after designation. Land acquisition is allowed to mitigate incongruous private-land actions within a river corridor. However, land acquisition is costly and often degrades local support.

Landowner fears also relate to another reason that the Act has been inadequately utilized to protect private lands rivers: The statute calls for the preparation of river management plans after designation, rather than during the study process. This scheme has proven disastrous in numerous cases where concerned citizens find they cannot support designation because they lack clear, specific information on how designation will affect their property. National Park Service officials experienced in dealing with the public's "fear of the unknown" have suggested that designation on private-land rivers stands a much better chance of success where a clear management plan is developed prior to designation.

The WSRA appears to have potential to protect "outstanding" private lands river segments through its call for the creation of local zoning ordinances to protect designated rivers. Politically, this approach seems credible because it does not emphasize federal land acquisition.[896] In practice, however, city and county governments have almost universally failed to implement zoning plans that effectively address the conservation of designated rivers within their jurisdictions. This problem is only exacerbated by federal agencies' failures to develop guidelines for these ordinances. Without local government and landowner cooperation, Wild and Scenic designation cannot provide protection on private lands consistent with the mandate of the Act.

The WSRA (like state river-protection systems modeled after the federal one) requires a study, designation and management-planning process that is slow, costly, and highly politicized. While this process has had some success on federal lands, it has proven almost completely inadequate to protect private-land river segments. Part of the problem is that Congress must generally act both to authorize a river "study" and to approve the final designation. Federal agencies generally will not do a Wild and Scenic "eligibility" or "suitability" study for private-land rivers as part of their federal land-planning process unless their federal lands represent a significant portion of the land ownership in the basin. At best, when the entire study and designation process is finally completed, an extremely small number of river segments are, or probably ever will be, permanently protected. Most often, due to the nature of politics, highly controversial river segments fail to gain congressional designation, even though these can be some of the most important segments.

Conclusions

The Wild and Scenic Rivers Act is Not An Effective Tool for Comprehensive Protection or Restoration for Private-Land Rivers Nationwide:

The Act's "outstandingly remarkable" standard is too limited to encompass the more than 98% of the nation's private-land river miles that need attention.

There are no specific policies that can lead to the restoration of degraded areas within the designated corridors or areas outside the designation that may be influencing the protected section.

Because Congressional designation is a slow, complex and highly controversial process, only a small percentage of private-land river segments have been, or ever may be, protected under the Act.

Individual states generally lack the funding and technical expertise to complete the requirements for state designation.

Because river-management plans are prepared after designation, private landowners often oppose protection because they are unsure of possible effects to their property rights.

The Act is aimed at only discrete segments of rivers and arbitrary 1/4-mile corridors, with no provision for protecting riverine areas on a broader watershed and ecosystem basis.

Though the WSRA's application to private land rivers is improving, and with amendments or administrative changes could be significantly improved, all of these factors lead to the conclusion that the WSRA is not suitable for comprehensive application to private-land river systems or biodiversity nationwide.

COLUMBIA RIVER GORGE NATIONAL SCENIC AREA

Purposes of the Act: Congress passed the Columbia River Gorge National Scenic Area Act in 1986.[897] The goal of the Act was to create a partnership of federal, state and local agencies in order to develop a plan for protection and management of the resources on the one-quarter of a million acres adjacent to the Columbia River in Oregon and Washington. This Act is somewhat unique in that it represents a rare instance of federal intervention in state and local land-use law.

The purposes of the Act are to "protect and provide for the enhancement of the scenic, recreational and natural resources of the Columbia Gorge," as well as to "protect and support the economy of the Columbia River Gorge Area by encouraging growth to occur in existing urban areas and by allowing future economic development" consistent with the protection and enhancement of Gorge resources.[898] Although the Act's purposes are not purely conservationist, the Act does provide a specific mechanism and guidelines for the development of a management plan for the scenic area by the Columbia River Gorge Commission, the regulatory body created by the Act.[899] This management plan is now in the final stages.

Administration: Lands within the scenic area are divided into three categories. Urban areas comprise approximately ten percent of the total scenic area; these lands are essentially exempt from the scope of the Act and the requirements of the management plan.[900] Special management areas are those areas with the most significant scenic, natural, recreational, and cultural values. They comprise approximately forty-five percent of the total scenic area, and are subject to the management authority of the Forest Service.[901] The Commission has direct management authority over the remaining non-federal lands in the scenic area; these lands are known as general management areas.[902]

Congress delegated the requisite authority and $40 million in federal funds to the Secretary of Agriculture, who then delegated it to the Forest Service, in order to acquire additional lands necessary to achieve the purposes of the Act.[903] However, the agency's ability to acquire new lands is quite limited because of the narrow condemnation powers provided in the Act.[904]

The Act does contain certain conservation-oriented land-use provisions. For example, it requires a 40-acre minimum lot size for the scenic area's most significant lands.[905] In addition, new residential development is prohibited from adversely affecting the Gorge's scenic, natural, cultural or recreational values.[906] However, the scope of these provisions is quite limited, since they do not apply to all of the scenic area or to pre-existing development.

Limitations: Many tributary rivers and streams within the scenic area are subject to the same restrictions on the licensing, permitting and exemption from the construction of dams or other water-resource projects as are rivers in the Wild and Scenic Rivers Act.[907]   Not all water resource projects are prohibited in the Columbia River Gorge. However, unless construction of the water resources project can be shown not to have a direct and adverse effect on Gorge resources, any tributary river and stream (with certain exceptions) which flows in whole or in part through a special management area is protected as if it were a Wild and Scenic river.[908]   It is important to note, though, that these restrictions do not apply to those portions of tributary rivers and streams flowing to the Columbia River which flow through or border on Indian reservations.[909]   Moreover, the Act does little to protect or restore the quality of the river or its fishery resource.[910]

In order to appease opponents who thought the Act would harm the economy of the Gorge, Congress included several provisions aimed at economic development and mitigation. These provisions included authorizing more than $32 million in federal funding to the two states and six counties involved for local economic development projects related to the Act.[911]   These grants provide considerable incentive for cooperation and participation by local residents.

Counties are mandated to adopt zoning ordinances consistent with the goals of the Act.[912]   However, forced participation has served to erode much local support of the program and has added to local residents' resentment of the considerable powers of the Commission.   Consequently, the Commission has often been vigorously opposed by local residents and counties.[913]   Yet, many conservationists feel that the Act itself and the management plan do not go nearly far enough in protecting the resource, due to the political trade-offs required to enact the legislation.

Conclusions

While Offering Some Possible Models, The Columbia River Gorge Scenic Area Act Includes Major Drawbacks for Riverine System and Biodiversity Protection:

Urban areas, with their tremendous potential for damage to the Columbia River, are essentially exempt from the Act.

The Act focuses on protecting the lands within the Columbia Gorge or its tributaries. There is no specific focus on riverine-system or biodiversity protection or restoration, except for a few Wild and Scenic River segments that were designated concurrently with the Gorge Act.

Acquisition of private lands along the river which might have significant scenic, natural, recreational or cultural value is extremely limited by the narrow condemnation powers provided in the Act.

Nothing in the Act addresses the dangers to riverine-riparian ecosystems resulting from existing dams and other water- resources projects on the Columbia river or its tributaries.

The goals of the Act and the management plan may ultimately fail due to the recurring political antagonism between local residents and the Commission which the Act failed to eliminate.

The Columbia River Gorge Scenic Area provides an example of how specially tailored federal legislation can be crafted to manage specific riverine resources while providing some level of protection and some degree of local government control. However, its many limitations make it a less-than-ideal model for future riverine protection policies in other regions.

OTHER FEDERAL PROGRAMS AND POLICIES WITH IMPLICATIONS FOR PRIVATE-LAND RIVERS

The Clean Water Act, the National Flood Insurance Act and the Coastal Zone Management Act are several important federal statutes affecting private-land rivers. Although inadequate for the riverine protection or restoration needed on private lands, aspects of these statutes could be adapted in order to induce states and localities to act so as to conserve private lands rivers.

NONPOINT-SOURCE POLLUTION CONTROLS AND WETLANDS PROTECTION UNDER THE CLEAN WATER ACT

An overview of the Clean Water Act was provided in the preceding discussion of riverine system protection on federal lands. This section briefly discusses the Act's effectiveness with respect to riverine systems on private lands.

Nonpoint-source controls under sections 208 and 319: Section 208 of the CWA, entitled "Areawide Waste Treatment Management," provides a mechanism for states or designated regional agencies to develop and implement strategies to control both point and nonpoint-source pollution. The governor of each state is required to designate areas with water-quality problems and to appoint a local government agency in charge of developing areawide management plans for each area. These plans must be submitted for certification by the Governor and approval by the EPA. EPA grants are available for completing the management plans.

Section 208 contains a cost-sharing provision, called the Rural Clean Water Program (RCWP). This program encourages control of agricultural non-point sources of pollution. The Soil Conservation Service (SCS) is authorized to enter into contracts with owners and operators of rural lands to develop and maintain Best Management Practices (BMPs) in areas where water quality management plans are in effect. Control practices specified in the contracts must be certified by the appropriate management agencies and consistent with the water-quality management plan. The SCS is authorized to provide technical assistance and matching grants no greater that 50 percent of the total cost of the BMPs. This percentage can be increased under certain circumstances. If a landowner fails to carry out the provisions outlined in the contract, he or she can be forced to forfeit future payments and refund prior payments with interest. As discussed previously, BMPs have not proven consistently effective in protecting riverine ecosystems and biodiversity and may often lead to violations of water-quality standards.

Section 208 has two main strengths for the protection of private-land rivers. First, it attempts to recognize the relationships between water diversions, water-resources development and water quality. Second, it makes state and local governments responsible for nonpoint-source control, which is a sound strategy if implemented. The main criticism of this program has been that it is unenforceable. Unlike the penalties which threaten point-source violators, the EPA has no authority whatsoever to compel state submission of areawide plans. The only enforcement tool available is withholding of construction grant monies, a disincentive that has proven ineffective.

In response to the deficiencies of Section 208, Congress amended the CWA in 1987 to include Section 319, which required states to prepare nonpoint-source assessment reports, categorize nonpoint pollution, list processes for the identification of necessary BMPs and to discuss available state and local programs on a watershed-by-watershed basis. The new section also requested, but did not require, that states develop nonpoint-source management plans. This time, financial incentives were provided, and most states have now finished their assessments and plans.

Like the 208 program, however, the program lacks real muscle. The state programs are not required to be enforceable by states and do not authorize federal intervention in state and local planning decisions, primarily because Congress was reluctant to intrude into areas of land use which are generally considered non-federal domain.[914] Thus, the main strength of the current nonpoint-source program is its watershed-based focus. Whether this approach will be supported by EPA regulations under Section 319 remains to be seen.

Wetlands policies: Many American cities, such as Washington D.C., Boston, Seattle, Philadelphia and New Orleans, were built on wetlands. Filling wetlands served two human needs: it created additional land for development, and it rid a city of an apparent nuisance. For centuries, wetlands were considered a source of disease, a breeding ground for insects. Congress in the mid-1800s granted millions of acres of swamps to the states with the expectation that the states would convert the vast wastelands into productive areas.[915] Thousands of acres in the Midwest were subsequently drained for agriculture. A few states lost over 90 percent of their wetlands. After centuries of mistreatment, wetlands have shed their image and are finally valued for their enormously important environmental and economic functions, such as flood control, stream-structural health and the provision of wildlife habitat. In the federal land policy-chapters, the strengths and weaknesses of federal wetlands guidelines were examined in depth. In this section we will briefly examine the effectiveness of wetlands policies for rivers flowing through private lands.

In general, states regulate wetlands in two ways: indirectly, as part of broad regulatory programs, such as the coastal-zone management program or the water-quality certification provisions under Section 401 of the Clean Water Act (CWA), and directly, by enacting laws specifically to regulate activities in wetlands. Many states have enacted their own legislation to fill the regulatory gaps in the federal 404 program and protect their remaining wetlands. The resulting programs range from those which regulate activities, such as dredging or draining, to programs that provide tax incentives for permanent wetlands protection.

As discussed previously, in 1977 Congress directed the Environmental Protection Agency (EPA) to turn part of the 404 program over to the states. Under Section 404(g) of the CWA, EPA may delegate administration of the 404 permit program for nonnavigable waters to individual states. The Corps would retain its authority over navigable waters within a state, and EPA would continue to oversee state programs.

For a variety of reasons, states have been disinclined to take over the federal program. The 404 permit program's regulations are cumbersome, its requirements are stringent, and the incentives to assume its administration are few. Oregon seriously considered assuming responsibility of the 404 permit process in 1988, but concluded that since the Corps would retain jurisdiction over much of the state's wetlands, and since the state would have to spend an estimated $410,000 per year to run the program, it simply was not worth it. By the end of 1989, only Michigan had assumed administration of the federal program and only New Jersey was seeking to do so.

State assumption of the federal 404 permit program would substantially reduce duplication and delays caused by overlapping state and federal wetlands regulations. But most states will not seek to assume responsibility for the program until the federal government improves the incentives to do so, such as providing states with financial and technical assistance.

Even if these incentives are provided, though, the wetlands program has significant limitations on protecting riverine ecosystems and biodiversity on private lands. As previously stated, the destruction of wetlands does not include the many riparian areas and floodplains that are not also wetlands under the formal criteria. Further, there is insufficient authority to regulate activities that result in major wetland loss. The policies have so many loopholes and exemptions that almost all wetlands can be legally eradicated.

These provisions of the CWA provide a sound basis for water quality protection but do not consider biological or ecological processes, habitat or the complex interrelationships that exist in these ecosystems. Although section 404 has been somewhat effective in protecting wetlands, the policy has **not** been effective in providing ecosystem-level protection for private-land riparian areas or floodplains, which in many cases overlap with wetlands areas.

Conclusions

The Clean Water Act is Ineffective in Protecting or Restoring Riverine Systems and Biodiversity on Private-Land Rivers

The CWA is Ineffective in Controlling Nonpoint-source Pollution: The CWA is intended to improve water quality in all water bodies of the United States. However, as stated previously, the nonpoint-source pollution measures of CWA have not been effective. There are several sections of the CWA that could be helpful in addressing the nation's private-land riverine systems and biodiversity. First, the basic goals of the CWA are consistent with the establishment of new national goals and policies to protect and restore riverine systems and biodiversity. Second, the planning processes outlined in sections 208 and 319 could serve as models for a federal program to improve riverine-riparian ecosystems and biodiversity at the state and local level. However, for this ever to become really effective, the Act must "climb out of the water and up on the banks." It must effectively address land-management activities. Finally, as discussed below, if expanded to include riparian ecosystems and the structural and functional processes of riverine systems, the section 404 permitting process could limit degradation to riverine systems and biodiversity.

The Section 404 Wetlands Policy is Inadequate But Has Potential: If the definitions could be expanded to include riparian areas and floodplains and the loopholes and exemptions removed and strict monitoring and enforcement provided, the wetlands policy could become more effective in protecting riverine systems and biodiversity. However, the prospects of these actions occurring without the creation of a new national goal and new mandates from Congress seem remote at best.

NATIONAL FLOOD INSURANCE PROGRAM

Established by the National Flood Insurance Act of 1968,[916] the National Flood Insurance Program[917] ("NFIP") is a federal program designed to provide an insurance alternative to disaster assistance to meet the escalating costs of repairing damage caused by floods. Under the program, approximately 2.1 million property owners are provided with federally subsidized flood insurance. Major goals of the program include: protecting property owners against flood losses by assuring the availability of insurance; encouraging construction methods which minimize the risks of flood damage; and establishing alternatives to federal disaster relief for property owners whose businesses or residences suffer flood damage.[918]

The NFIP is based on agreements between local communities and the federal government. If a community agrees to implement measures to reduce flood risks in Special Flood Hazard Areas, the federal government will make flood insurance available to residents of that community. In theory, the program is designed to reward wise flood management practices that are implemented and maintained by communities. The Federal Emergency Management Agency (FEMA) is responsible for administering the program. Local communities must enact flood-plain-management regulations established by FEMA in order to qualify for coverage under the program.

After a community applies for participation in NFIP, a flood risk study is performed by FEMA, which then prepares a flood-hazard-boundary map and a flood insurance rate map to determine insurance premiums.[919] The community then may review the rate map and negotiate alterations to it. Once agreement on the rate map has been reached, though, the community must fully comply with NFIP land-use regulations. Hence, the community must review all proposed building permits to determine whether flood-prone areas are affected, and then whether proposed construction sites in those flood-prone areas will be reasonably protected from flooding. Within special flood hazard areas designated by FEMA, any new construction must employ flood-resistant designs and materials.[920]

Participation in the program is voluntary on the part of communities. However, if the federal government designates an area as a special flood-prone area,[921] communities within that area must participate in the program within one year or risk restrictions in federal financial assistance.[922] For example, owners of floodplain property become disqualified from federally subsidized mortgages and construction loans, loans from the small business administration, and some types of federal disaster relief.[923] Participation means all floodplain landowners must purchase insurance.

Although managed on the federal level, the NFIP mandates considerable input and enforcement on the part of local communities. Communities must incorporate the NFIP into its permitting and planning process. Therefore, new home buyers must purchase flood insurance which, the theory goes, would discourage development on floodplains. In addition, at the request of the Federal Insurance Administrator, each governor designates a state agency to coordinate that state's NFIP program.

Because flood insurance premiums under NFIP are subsidized by the federal government, property owners in flood-prone areas may obtain flood insurance at rates below the market cost. The immediate goal is to encourage those property owners to obtain flood insurance, but the long-term goal of the program is supposed to eventually eliminate subsidies, in order, ultimately, to discourage floodplain development.[924] If the program worked as intended, the NFIP could indirectly provide a few elements of riverine-riparian ecosystem protection by discouraging development in floodplains. However, the record indicates that the program has not been successful overall. In fact, the availability of this insurance appears to have encouraged floodplain development in many areas.

Conclusions

The NFIP Has Not Proven Effective At Preventing Inappropriate Floodplain Development:

Although the goal of the program was to deter floodplain development, the availability of federal flood insurance under the program has acted instead to encourage such development in many areas.

The NFIP is an example of a federal program that provides financial incentives for land-use planning by communities, and can be applied to a wide variety of rivers. However, the program has generally failed to discourage floodplain development, and has been of little benefit to riverine-system and biodiversity protection.

COASTAL ZONE MANAGEMENT ACT

Purposes of the Act: The Coastal Zone Management Act of 1972[925] ("CZMA") was passed by Congress in order to "preserve, protect, develop, and where possible to restore or enhance, the resources of the Nation's coastal zone for this and succeeding generations."[926] Much of the Act is geared toward managing and steering development of coastal energy resources. A small number of riverine systems that are located within the jurisdiction of CZMA programs are affected by the program.

Administration: The CZMA is overseen by the Secretary of Commerce, acting through the National Oceanic and Atmospheric Administration (NOAA). However, the Act focuses on the states as being the key players in the management of coastal-zone areas.[927]

To encourage states to develop coastal management programs, Congress incorporated several major incentives in the CZMA. For example, the Act provides federal grants to states for the development and administration of coastal management programs.[928] The program also provides a mechanism by which a state can allocate some of its funds to a local government or interstate agency, thus encouraging the coordination of coastal management on a regional level.[929]   Finally, the program provides for research and technical assistance from the NOAA.[930]

Management plans must be approved by the Secretary and must include an inventory and designation of areas of particular concern within the coastal zone; a planning process for assessing and controlling shoreline erosion; and a description of the organizational structure proposed to implement the program with specific references to the inter-relationships and responsibilities between various jurisdictions.[931]   If management plans are done properly, the potential for some degree of ecosystem-level protection may exist, although it is not directly mandated by the Act.

Through federal grants and technical assistance, the CZMA provides financial incentives designed to foster local participation. The Act provides resource-management improvement grants that can be used for the preservation or restoration of specific areas of the state that are (a) designated under the management-program procedures because of their conservation, recreational, ecological or aesthetic values or (b) contain one or more coastal resources of national significance.[932]

Federal financial assistance was one of the two major incentives to encourage states to participate and develop coastal management programs under the CZMA. The second incentive was to give states important regulatory authority. Under the Act, federal agencies are not exempted from complying with state programs. Thus, federal projects and activities, as well as federally permitted activities such as off-shore drilling, which affect the coastal zone must be consistent with approved state coastal-zone management programs.[933]   This consistency requirement is not absolute, since the Secretary may allow the activity upon finding that the activity, although inconsistent with the state program, is consistent with the national objectives of the CZMA or necessary to national security.[934]

The Act also sets up the National Estuarine Research Reserve System.[935] Reserves can be designated by the Secretary or by the Governor of the state and must be (1) suitable for long-term research and contribute to the biogeographical and typological balance of the system and (2) must be afforded long-term protection by the law of the state.[936] Through the identification and designation of estuarine reserves, CZMA provides protection of the areas most sensitive and critical to the maintenance of coastal species and ecosystems.

Limitations: Unfortunately, the CZMA affects only a small fraction of American rivers, since it applies only to the extent of their location in coastal areas. Moreover, although some of the land in coastal zones is in private ownership, much of it is actually controlled by the states. However, the CZMA is one of the best examples of an existing program which provides a model for cost-effective protection of large geographic areas. Numerous coastal states have implemented management programs under the CZMA.[937] Other states have failed to implement effective programs, leaving the overall CZMA program with mixed results. Virtually all coastal areas fall under CZMA management authority. A similar structure, improved and specifically applied to rivers nationwide, could provide protection and management guidelines under the Act.

Conclusions

Because of Its Geographical Limitations, the Coastal Zone Management Act Provides Little Protection for Private-Land Rivers But Has Certain Administrative Aspects Which Might Prove Useful in New Riverine Management Policies, Which Include:

Coordination between federal, state, and local agencies is emphasized.

The Act recognizes that energy-resource development must be carefully managed to minimize dangers to the ecosystem.

Specific guidelines required for approval of a management plan are set out in detail.

State cooperation is encouraged through an extensive but flexible structure of grants for the development and administration of management programs.

The estuarine research and reserve section provide long-term protection for critical areas within the ecosystem which are particularly sensitive.

Thus, the framework of the CZMA could be adapted and incorporated into a comprehensive private-lands river policy.

OVERALL SUMMARY

Existing Federal Private-Land Riverine-System Conservation Policies Are Inadequate and Ineffective

Although some encouraging models exist, based on this review we conclude that the federal private-land riverine-system and biodiversity protection and restoration policies are largely inadequate and ineffective in meeting needs nationwide:

All of the federal "protection" options require separate congressional Acts for each river segment or group of rivers protected. Given the limited focus on "high quality" rivers and the controversial nature of designations, all have very limited applicability to comprehensive private land riverine protection.

The Clean Water Act has proven ineffective at preventing non-point pollution on private-land rivers, and does not address the structure, function and biological aspects of riverine systems.

Federal wetlands policies have failed to include riparian areas and floodplains, despite their similarity in many cases with the current federal definition of wetlands. Too many loopholes exist, further weakening the policies.

The National Flood Insurance Program has in many cases stimulated rather than deterred floodplain development.

The Coastal Zone Management Act is too limited to apply to most riverine systems, though it may provide a good structural model for new policies.

Despite the limited effectiveness of the existing federal private-land riverine policies and programs, some positive threads do emerge, and potential models exist within them that could be applicable to new federal policies.

APPENDIX D

STATE AND LOCAL RIVERINE CONSERVATION POLICIES

Different states and municipalities have adopted a variety of programs which are aimed at protecting riverine systems and biodiversity on private lands. In this section we examine some of these approaches.

STATE RIVERINE PROTECTION PROGRAMS ON PRIVATE LANDS

A thorough assessment of all state policies and programs affecting private-land rivers nationwide would require an extremely lengthy and complex analysis, well beyond the scope of this book. One thing is abundantly clear: the degradation of riverine systems on private lands and loss of biodiversity is much greater than on federal lands. For example, in many states, 60%-90% of native riparian vegetation is already lost or seriously degraded.[938] Thus, despite a plethora of programs and policies that may look good on paper, the cold, hard facts are that little is happening on the ground. The problem lies in the almost complete lack of uniformity and enforcement from state to state in governing private-land riverine protection. Some states have practically no statutes or regulations applicable to riverine systems, while others may have a battery of applicable laws. Unfortunately, even among those states which do address riverine-riparian systems, the applicable laws are generally fragmented in a broad spectrum of different state programs, are often conflicting and largely ineffective.

STATE FOREST PRACTICES ACTS

For some states with major timber holdings, state forest-practices legislation includes riparian protection measures. These

351

statutes, and their implementing regulations, affect riparian management on a significant number of bodies of water. For example, the Oregon Department of Forestry has jurisdiction over about 13,000 miles of "class I" streams, more than 13% of the 90,000 stream miles in Oregon.[939]

In general, forest-practices laws and regulations authorize state forestry agencies to enforce state forestry standards on state and private lands and require forest managers to report planned timber harvests to the state. Sensitive harvest areas may be inspected to ensure application of state Best Management Practices (BMPs) requirements. BMPs will vary according to the size of the subject riparian-management area, the category of stream involved and the planned number of trees which must remain.

The applicability of riparian BMPs in state forest-practices acts is sometimes strengthened and broadened by the use of multi-party cooperative agreements. For example, the state of Idaho's Antidegradation Agreement (with its source in the CWA's antidegradation mandate) addresses specific mining, forestry and agricultural (crop and range) land-use practices on both public and private lands. Additionally, through a Memorandum of Understanding, the Forest Service and the BLM are bound to meet or exceed stream protection measures in Oregon's Forest Practices Act.[940]

State forest-practices regulations generally require operators to apply BMPs addressing such concerns as: 1) minimum areas of special consideration at stream sides, with "leave tree" requirements; 2) roadbuilding and equipment-handling constraints in arbitrarily defined riparian-management areas; 3) required removal of slash debris from the riparian management area; and 4) minimization of stream crossings.[941] State agencies' monitoring and evaluation of timber harvest activities varies between states, and so does the available evidence on the effectiveness of these programs. An audit of forestry BMPs by Idaho's Department of Environmental Quality found that while compliance with state forestry requirements generally protected water quality, some of these requirements proved inadequate. Specifically, riparian-area management boundaries did not adequately reflect the natural boundaries of the riparian ecosystem, too little woodsy material was actually left and stream protection classes were not clear.[942]

Likewise, Oregon's Forest Practices Act provides inadequate protection to streams and, partially due to inadequate resources, is not supported by monitoring to demonstrate BMP effectiveness. Even with recent changes in the state rules, Oregon's State Forest Practices Act is considered almost completely inadequate to protect riverine-riparian ecosystems and biodiversity. Washington state is currently conducting a review of its BMPs.[943] The Nevada Forest Practice Act[944] prohibits activities such as tree felling, skidding, road construction or vehicle operation within 200 feet of the high water mark of any stream, lake or other body of water.[945] However, this statute provides an exception, so that such activities can occur within the 200-foot buffer area as long as a special variance is obtained. The variance is available through a committee made up of the state forester firewarden, the director of the department of wildlife and the state engineer. The committee must consider specific statutory factors, including effects on water quality, soil erosion and impact on fish habitat.[946] Nonetheless, the 200-foot buffer is not absolute, but instead is subject to the discretion of state officials.

Most western states' forest-practices acts specifically address water quality and riparian protection.[947] In contrast, among the non-western states with forest-practices acts, those states' acts often lack specific riparian protection provisions.[948] For example, the law governing forest-cutting practices in Massachusetts[949] contains a policy declaration that the goal of the Act is to protect forest lands for various purposes including "conserving water, preventing floods and soil erosion, improving the conditions for wildlife and recreation, [and] protecting and improving air and water quality."[950] However, the statute leaves any specifics regarding riparian protection to the state forestry committee and such rules as it may decide to adopt.[951] Similarly, the policy provision of the Forest Harvesting Law of Mississippi[952] states that the purposes of the act were, among other reasons, "to prevent soil erosion and consequent silting of stream channels and reservoirs; [and] to protect watersheds and reservoirs, and to ensure at all times an adequate supply of water of the highest quality."[953]   However, the statute contains no provisions aimed specifically at stream protection.

In sum, most state forestry programs have limited effect or success due to lack of clear and effective ecosystem, watershed-level, or site-specific standards, inadequate monitoring mechanisms and lax enforcement.   Furthermore, these programs are rarely integrated with adjoining federal-lands riverine management policies.   In any case, these state acts do not generally apply to federal lands directly and are inadequate to protect riparian ecosystems and floodplains where they do.   As the EPA observes, the ideal way to identify "riparian management areas" is by using ecological definitions on a site-specific basis, but most state agencies--if they address this at all-- specify minimum widths of these zones, leave-tree numbers, and percent of required shading on an across-the-board basis which ignores, and is most often at odds with, ecological realities.[954]

WETLANDS LAWS

In other states, riverine protection occurs primarily under the auspices of the state's wetland law,[955] if the law is broad enough to include riparian areas. For example, in Vermont, wetlands protection is linked to growth management.   The Vermont Wetlands Act[956] outlines certain responsibilities for regional and local planning commissions.   In 1988 the state legislature passed a growth management act to foster greater cooperation among state agencies, regional planning commissions and municipal governments in planning for local resources.[957] This growth management act mandates the creation of a planning document will be generated to provide guidance to Vermont towns interested in conducting more detailed wetland inventories and adopting local zoning ordinances.[958]

PUGET SOUND WATER QUALITY AUTHORITY

Wetland law in the state of Washington is also a source of riverine protection. Wetlands and riparian ecosystems are protected by a number of laws administered by several different agencies at federal, state and local government levels. However, of the many existing state regulations, only the wetlands protection element of the Puget Sound Water Quality Management Plan[959] focuses on the protection of wetlands as its primary purpose. The Puget Sound planning effort is a state/federal collaboration which covers the 12 counties in the Puget Sound area and is the most comprehensive local program in existence in Washington State.

The Puget Sound Water Quality Authority (PSWQA) developed regulations concerning the local planning and management of nonpoint-source pollution in Puget Sound. The rules establish a process to identify and rank watersheds in the Puget Sound basin and to develop action plans to prevent nonpoint-source pollution, enhance water quality, and protect beneficial uses. Watersheds are ranked by a committee set up by each county, and action plans are developed by local watershed management committees. Action plans are then submitted by the lead agency and approved by the Department of Ecology. Action plans may be implemented through various voluntary actions including local ordinances or a combination of local, state, and federal laws, regulations, and programs. The action plans describe a coordinated program of effective actions that are designed to prevent and abate nonpoint-source pollution within the watershed. Action plans must contain a source control program if an existing or potential non-point source of pollution is identified as significant or potentially significant.

The action plan program in the Puget Sound region includes several provisions which have a positive impact on riverine protection. For example, the program focuses on nonpoint-source pollution at the basin level, rather than some smaller geographic unit. Moreover, a watershed is prioritized on the basis of scientific and technical data, and then an action plan is based on the watershed's ranking. Watershed rankings must be reviewed every five years, thus minimizing the possibility that new dangers to a watershed will be ignored. The program contains a strong public participation component and provides a strong model of a state program that is implemented at the local level. Finally, the program presents specific guidelines for agricultural practices, on-site sewage disposal, stormwater and erosion, forest practices, marinas and boats and other nonpoint sources.

Nonetheless, the program also has numerous drawbacks. For example, the program has no provisions for property acquisition and does not outline any financial incentives for reducing nonpoint-source pollution on private lands. Although the PSWQA was one of the first agencies in the nation to have enforcement authority over other agencies, including the ability to establish fines, these enforcement powers were so controversial that they have been eliminated. Moreover, funding and state support for implementation have been limited.

Finally, management and abatement of non-point source pollution is important, but is only one factor in riverine-riparian ecosystem and biodiversity protection.

STATE WILD AND SCENIC RIVER PROGRAMS

Through their own river conservation statutes, states have been enacting state law counterparts to the federal Wild and Scenic Rivers Act since the early 1970s. To date, 32 states have river conservation programs in some form.[960] Most state programs are clearly fashioned after the federal act, with similar purposes and a similar focus on maintaining rivers in their free-flowing condition. As a result, many of these statutes, such as Georgia's Scenic Rivers Act,[961] prohibit or restrict dams. Other statutes, such as Maryland's Wild and Scenic Rivers Act,[962] go further and protect designated rivers from channelization or diversion.[963] Most state river laws also require that the legislature must act to include a river corridor in the state system. In Oregon, river segments may also be protected under its State Scenic Waterways Act by a Governor's Declaration or by voter referendum.[964]

Some state programs provide condemnation authority to enable the state to purchase private lands within a targeted river corridor. For example, Georgia's act permits the acquisition of private lands which border a scenic river.[965] Generally, however, state statutes carefully protect private property rights by limiting state acquisition authority. In Michigan, for example, the state's Natural Rivers Act [966] allows the state to purchase private property only with landowner consent.[967] Likewise, the Oregon act does not restrict the use of existing water rights, allow public use of private property or require removal of existing development which is damaging to a designated river segment.[968]

State programs also differ in the legal and policy tools that are used to implement their river protection programs. Most states use a combined approach to authorize various land-use controls and resource management tools and generally proclaim that incompatible uses over the river and its corridor shall be prohibited. The strongest overall protection for rivers is provided in states where river protection is not addressed primarily through the river protection statute itself. Rather, the best protection results from a combined approach where rivers are protected through multiple state and local processes, including land use planning, greenway programs, water quality and waste control, species and natural resource management, energy facility and transportation planning, agricultural land conservation and interagency review or coordination of permit applications affecting rivers.[969]

Maine is one example of a state where rivers receive stronger protection because a combined "all fronts" approach is used. The shoreline zoning program establishes minimum land-use standards applicable to all of the state's river corridors, with more stringent controls applicable to certain designated rivers.[970] Maine also identifies high-priority streams through its statewide rivers inventory. Site-specific, locally developed controls are created for river segments by river corridor commissions.[971]

STATE RIVER PROGRAMS LIMITED BY FEDERAL POLICIES

Like their federal counterparts, most state river protection efforts are limited to the protection of a select group of privately managed river corridors which are deemed to possess outstanding recreational or scenic quality. Therefore, most state programs do not address large numbers of rivers, nor are they ecosystem-based. Rather, like the federal statute, they focus on an arbitrarily defined management corridor. Further, they do not address riverine restoration.

State river programs are limited in a number of ways by current federal policies. A recent study of state programs by the Congressional Research Service identified several policy areas which, states believe, require Federal action to enhance state river conservation efforts. States most commonly identified the following federal policy areas as problems: 1) A lack of coordinated Federal water policy to promote watershed-level planning has placed the burden almost entirely on private organization to foster integrated management within river basins; 2) The narrow focus of the federal Wild and Scenic River System protects few rivers at great cost; 3) Unsatisfactory intergovernmental coordination exists between state and federal programs, and; 4) There is local mistrust of federal intervention due to the federal program's emphasis on exclusive federal ownership and management.[972] States called for more financial and technical assistance to states and for federal policies which provide private landowners with incentives to donate land for inclusion in federal or state river-protection programs. States also recommended that the federal government make a commitment to federal consistency with state standards. Currently, the Environmental Protection Agency may override state river designations or comprehensive water plans, and the Federal Energy Regulatory Commission (FERC) may override state in-stream-flow requirements and authorize condemnation of lands without regard for state river-protection schemes.[973]

In sum, although state river protection programs do provide some degree of protection for a select group of private-land riverine systems, state programs do not generally address large numbers of rivers. Like the federal Wild and Scenic designation process, state designation processes usually require legislative action, making them politically complex and highly controversial. Moreover, no river conservation program we reviewed is ecosystem-based, addresses entire watersheds or includes a meaningful restoration program. Even the best state systems are underfunded, have inadequate statutory authority, lack broad political support and cannot override damaging federal actions such as hydroelectric licensing by FERC. As a result, state programs protect less that one percent of the nation's rivers. Even then, protection is often marginal at best.

STATE EFFORTS AT COOPERATIVE WATERSHED PLANNING

A number of states have attempted to develop cooperative watershed-planning approaches, with the results having varying degrees of success. For example:

> The Michigan Natural Rivers Act[974] requires the state natural resources commission to prepare and adopt a long-range comprehensive plan for the individual, designated natural-river area. The statute requires that state land within the area be managed according to the plan. Moreover, the statute states:
>
> > [S]tate management of fisheries, streams, waters, wildlife and boating shall take cognizance of the plan. The commission shall publicize and inform private and public landowners or agencies as to the plan and its purposes, so as to encourage their cooperation in the management and use of their land. . . . The commission shall cooperate with

federal agencies administering any federal program concerning natural river areas, and with any watershed council... .[975]

The Michigan state river-program manager works with the forest supervisors from the Hiawatha, Huron-Manistee, and Ottawa national forests, in order to develop protection strategies for segments of rivers located on national forest land which are eligible for designation under the federal Wild and Scenic Rivers Act. Segments of the rivers located outside of national forest land are being studied by the state, in coordination with the Forest Service.[976]

Memoranda of understanding, particularly between state and federal agencies, have been used. For example, the BLM, the Forest Service, and the state of Montana have entered into a memorandum of understanding which involves conducting joint studies on more than 60 rivers in Montana. The rivers will be considered for potential protection under the federal Wild and Scenic Rivers Act, or for some type of protection under state law.[977]

State river protection statutes contain explicit provisions which legally require state agencies to plan cooperatively and act only in ways which are consistent with river protection. For example, New Hampshire's Rivers Management and Protection Program Act[978] requires all state agencies to "conform" to the provisions of the act. South Carolina's Scenic Rivers Act,[979] on the other hand, goes even further and requires cooperation between state and local authorities along a river,[980] though the results as of yet are mixed.

According to one legal scholar, the "new federal Coastal Zone Management Act coastal nonpoint-source pollution control requirements provide perhaps the firmest legal foundation for integrated federal, state, and local approaches to coastal water quality problems."[981]

While these attempts at cooperative watershed management are good beginnings, the fact remains that without common goals and uniform policy directives, "cooperative" approaches will find piecemeal success at best.

Conclusions

State Policies and Programs to Protect and Restore Private Land Riverine Systems and Biodiversity are Inadequate:

State forest practices acts are inconsistent, and generally provide inadequate protection for riparian areas and other riverine areas.

Because state forest practices acts focus exclusively on forestry and related issues, the portion of riverine areas which are included within the scope of the acts are protected only from timber harvest and related activities, not from the many other potential impacts on these areas, such as road building.

State wetland programs usually do not include riparian areas in their focus, and so provide only marginal protection for riverine resources.

Even the state wetlands programs which are most protective of riverine systems tend to focus on specific issues such as non-point source pollution, and fail to provide the comprehensive approach needed to protect riverine-riparian ecosystems and biodiversity on private lands.

State river protection programs generally exclude all rivers which do not qualify as "outstanding" recreational or scenic segments, and hence apply to only a minute percentage of rivers.

State river protection programs fail to manage or to address problems on a watershed or ecosystem basis. They also require a "study" and designation process that is resource and time consuming and highly politicized, leaving most programs unable to provide effective or comprehensive protection.

There are no effective state restoration policies that we could identify, even though the degradation to private-land rivers is so extensive nationwide that without restoration programs many systems and biodiversity may collapse.

In sum, state programs play an important role in the overall mosaic of river management tools. With improved enabling policies at the federal and state level, the programs could prove even more effective. However, existing programs are too limited in their scope, application and enforcement to meet the challenge of providing the comprehensive protection and restoration necessary for riverine systems and biodiversity on private lands nationwide.

COOPERATIVE LOCAL APPROACHES TO RIVERINE MANAGEMENT

Some municipal governments have enacted their own laws to help protect riverine systems and other local water resources.[982] However, because such ordinances are so limited geographically, they are of little benefit in protecting extensive riverine systems and biodiversity. In contrast, riverine protection strategies that interface state support with local governments, private organizations and citizens hold the potential to catalyze very effective river protection and restoration programs.

Perhaps the best examples of effective local responses aimed at riverine protection have arisen in the context of attempts to restore individual rivers which have already experienced degradation. Below we describe several such local responses aimed at promoting river conservation and enhancing water quality.

MERRIMACK RIVER

The Merrimack River, which flows through New Hampshire and northern Massachusetts, was one of the most polluted rivers in the country fifty years ago. Under the Clean Water Act of 1977,[983] water quality standards were established, and funds were provided to individual states to meet those standards. Those funds allowed municipalities along the Merrimack to construct wastewater treatment plants which were crucial to a cleanup of the river. Federal funds were also important in implementing several state river protection programs, including the Merrimack River Watershed Initiative and the New Hampshire Rivers Management and Protection Program.[984]

The Merrimack River Watershed Council, a local citizens group, has played an active role in protecting the river, by emphasizing that enlightened, nonpolluting land use is in the public interest. The council has worked to prepare a comprehensive greenway plan, establish river access points, protect trails, and make basin residents aware that the Merrimack is a critical resource in the region.[985]

The river is now a drinking water source for several communities. It is also popular with canoeists and birdwatchers, and efforts are underway by state and federal fish and wildlife agencies to restore populations of anadromous fish.[986] Largely due to the work of citizen groups such as the council, the Merrimack has been designated a local scenic river in Massachusetts[987] and may eventually gain national Wild and Scenic River status.

Thus, the Merrimack has been revitalized by a cooperative effort between citizens and state and local governments. In particular, significant progress has been made in terms of improving the water quality of the Merrimack, especially with regard to sewage-related pollutants. However, as population in the region increases, reduced federal funding for constructing new wastewater treatment plants and upgrading the technology of older plants threatens the future health of the river.

MATTOLE RIVER

Northern California's Mattole River is a prime example of a Pacific Coast river where excessive logging, road building and overgrazing led to the massive erosion which all but destroyed the original salmon habitat. Citizen groups, in conjunction with agencies at all levels of government, continue to work to restore the health of the river.[988]

Efforts began with a small group of residents who called themselves the Mattole Watershed Salmon Support Group. Eventually, the Mattole Restoration Council was incorporated to plan and implement watershed restoration. The council represents the initial residents' group, together with a dozen other member organizations. The council attempts to imitate natural processes as much as possible in its restoration projects, though citizen workers intervene directly in the salmonids' spawning cycle in an attempt to increase reproduction rates.

The council has worked with various government agencies in its efforts to restore the Mattole River through erosion control, reforestation, and salmon habitat repair and enhancement. These cooperative efforts include: coordinating with the State Coastal Conservancy and the Redwood Community Action Agency to conduct surveys of the river channel to monitor sediment movement; engaging in reforestation with the California Conservation Corps and BLM; and conducting a major landslide study involving the California Department of Water Resources and Redwood National Park.

In general, the Mattole River has benefitted greatly from the efforts of area residents. The recovery of native salmon populations is far from assured, but citizen involvement has enhanced the level of public awareness regarding the importance of a healthy watershed and has forced federal and state agencies to focus on the dangers to the river caused by deforestation.

UPPER MISSISSIPPI RIVER

The Upper Mississippi River is a 1300-mile navigation system maintained by the U.S. Army Corps of Engineers. It is also a national fish and wildlife refuge system, encompassing a 280,000-acre corridor.[989] The Izaak Walton League was largely responsible for persuading Congress to create the refuge in 1924[990] and played a major role again in 1974 when it joined with the Sierra Club and 21 western railroad companies to file suit in order to prevent the Corps from constructing a new dam and set of locks near St. Louis. In that suit, the district court ordered the Corps to get congressional consent and gather more information on environmental and economic impacts before proceeding.[991] Congress eventually authorized the construction of a new dam and single lock, imposed a fuel tax on commercial navigation and created a trust fund for the revenues. Congress also ordered that no further expansion of the navigation capacity of the system occur until a Master Management Plan for the river was prepared by the Upper Mississippi River Basin Commission. The plan ultimately became the Environmental Management Program for the Upper Mississippi River System that was authorized as the Upper Mississippi River Management Act of 1986.[992]

The Upper Mississippi River Management Act is designed to ensure the coordinated development and enhancement of the Upper Mississippi River. Congressional consent is given to the states of Illinois, Iowa, Minnesota, Missouri and Wisconsin, or any two or more of those states, to negotiate a cooperative agreement promising mutual assistance when planning the use, protection, growth and development of the Upper Mississippi River system. The Act also gives these states the authority to establish an agency or agencies responsible for carrying-out agreements and mandates necessary to fulfill the goal of the Act.[993]

Most of the funding authorized for the Environmental Management Program is for habitat restoration. The projects are proposed by the FWS and the five states bordering the river; they are then screened by the Corps for program eligibility and engineering feasibility. The program is important because it is among the first in the nation to address conflicting federal mandates for large interstate rivers and to redress habitat degradation caused by alterations within the rivers and their drainage basins.

Minnesota, one of the five states involved in Upper Mississippi management, has a unique program aimed at protecting the river and emphasizing local government involvement. The Mississippi Headwaters Board (MHB)[994] is a joint powers board of eight Minnesota counties organized in 1980 to protect and conserve the natural, cultural, scenic and scientific values of the upper 400 miles of the Mississippi River Corridor. These goals are implemented through administration of local ordinances regulating land use and development in the river corridor and a management plan for public lands. The MHB was organized as an alternative to Wild and Scenic designation.

The authority of the MHB was shaped by a combination of Minnesota's Wild and Scenic Rivers Act of 1973,[995] the state's 1969 law regulating shoreland development,[996] and federal requirements. The MHB is unique in river conservation in that it is concerned both with the corridor of the river and the river itself. The MHB's regulations extend to the corridor only, but the board is broadening its authority to include water quality.

The MHB's provisions for managing land uses in the river corridor and its water-quality program are consistent with an ecosystem protection strategy. Land uses are primarily managed through enactment of the river corridor zoning ordinance by the eight counties. The zoning ordinance contains specific provisions concerning septic systems, building setbacks, and vegetation removal. Unfortunately, development review is performed at the local government level and is subject to different interpretations.

In summary, the programs developed for the Upper Mississippi River have helped protect the river by emphasizing cooperative agreements and maintaining local authority over land uses. Such factors may be useful to consider in formulating a national protection strategy for private-land rivers.

LIMITATIONS OF LOCAL APPROACHES

These local approaches are promising. However, they are currently inadequate in providing comprehensive protection or restoration of riverine systems and biodiversity on private lands nationwide for a number of reasons:

* Local approaches are, by definition, targeted at a small geographical area or a single river (segment), and thus are very limited in scope.

* Local programs often contain no mechanism for protecting or restoring riverine systems on a broad, watershed or ecosystem level.

* Funding for program research, development, administration and implementation is often extremely limited.

Because these approaches depend upon active citizen concern and involvement, they are less likely to be successful in protecting or restoring rivers in remote, less populated regions of the country without some way to involve the larger citizenry.

Without an "umbrella" federal enabling policy that provides legislative direction, financial support and incentives to assist and stimulate local bottom-up programs nationwide, they are most likely to be piecemeal, not commonplace, examples.

Despite these limitations, the successful examples of cooperative local approaches are useful in formulating a model for new national private-land riverine conservation policies.

OVERALL SUMMARY

Existing State and Local Policies and Programs Are Inadequate to Protect and Restore the Nation's Private Land Riverine Systems and Biodiversity

Based on our review of state and local river management policies, we conclude that the existing options are inadequate in meeting riverine system and biodiversity protection and restoration needs nationwide.

In theory, state and local programs could be much more effective. A broad range of land acquisition, county and state land-use regulatory tools, and local partnership strategies are generally available for state and local use. The planning and zoning authority afforded at the county level in many states could be utilized to develop certain types of effective protections for riverine corridors, floodplains, and riparian areas. Successful local efforts are few, however. Generally, imminent threats or a perceived loss of local control is required to mobilize local efforts.

To mobilize effective action, local officials and citizens generally must be encouraged to set river protection as a high priority and must see these efforts as complementary to or not deterring local economic development. Successful programs require that citizens have knowledge of and access to public and private technical assistance, combined with the support of an interconnected and flexible set of regulations, taxes and other incentives. In addition, the programs must generally enhance or sustain the local economy in some way.

The modest number of successful state and local programs indicate the degree of difficulty these approaches face in the absence of complementary federal enabling policies which includes these components. If combined with these types of new policies and incentives, however, state and local protection and restoration efforts could blossom nationwide and possibly provide the key element to restore the nation's private-land riverine systems and biodiversity.

NOTES

1.   Platts, W.S. and D.W. Chapman. 1992. "Status of Chinook Salmon Spawning and Rearing Habitat in the Salmon River Drainage." Don Chapman Consultants, Inc., 3653 Rickenbacker, Suite 200, Boise, ID, 83705.

2.   Master, L. 1990. "The imperiled status of North American aquatic animals." *Biodiversity Network News* (The Nature Conservancy) 3(3): 1-2, 7-8.

3.   Miller et al., 1988. "Regional applications of an index of biotic integrity for use in water resource management." 13(5) *Fisheries* 12-20.

4.   Frissell, C., 1991. "Water Quality, Fisheries and Aquatic Biodiversity Under Two Alternative Management Scenarios for the Westside Federal Lands of Washington, Oregon and Northern California," A Report prepared for The Wilderness Society, at 6.; citing W. Nehlsen., et. al., 1991. "Pacific salmon at the crossroads: stocks at risk from California, Oregon, Idaho, and Washington" 16(2) *Fisheries* 4-21; J.E. Williams, et. al., 1989. "Fishes of North America endangered, threatened or of special concern," 14(6) *Fisheries* 2-21.

5.   Thomas, J.W., E. Forsman, J. Lint, E.C. Meslow, B. Noon, J. Verner, 1990. "A Conservation Strategy for the Northern Spotted Owl," *Interagency Scientific Committee to Address the Conservation of the Northern Spotted Owl*, Portland, OR.

6.   Williams, J.E., J.E. Johnson, D.A. Hendrickson, S. Contreras-Balderas, J.D. Williams, M. Navarro-Mendoza, D.E. McAllister, and J.E. Deacon. 1989. "Fishes of North America endangered, threatened or of special concern," *Fisheries* (Bethesda) 14(6): 2-20.

7.   *See infra* note 14

8.   Jenkinson, J.J., 1981. "Endangered or threatened aquatic mollusks of the Tennessee River System." *Bull. Am. Malac. Union* 1981: 43-45.

9.   *Supra* note 5.

10.   Windell, J.T., 1991. "Streams, Riparian and Wetland Ecology" (University of Colorado, unpublished) cited in U.S. EPA Region 10, *Characteristics of Successful Riparian Restoration Projects in the Pacific Northwest* 9.

11.   Swift, B.L., 1984. "Status of riparian ecosystems in the United States." *Water Resources Bulletin* 2: 223-228.

12.   General Accounting Office, "Water Pollution: More EPA Action Needed to Improve the Quality of Heavily Polluted Waters," (1989)(GAO/RCED-89-38).

13.   Ohio Environmental Protection Agency, *Ohio Water Resource Inventory*, (1990) (evaluating 645 water bodies) cited in Yoder, C., "The Integrated Biosurvey as a Tool for Evaluation of Aquatic Life Use Attainment and Impairment in Ohio Surface Waters," *Biological Criteria: Research and Regulation* (Proceedings of a Symposium), (EPA-440/5-91-005) (July 1991).

14.   Karr, J.R., 1991. "Biological integrity: a long-neglected aspect of water resource management." *Ecological Applications* 1: 66-84. Testimony by James R. Karr before the Subcommittee on Energy and the Environment, House Interior and Insular Affairs Committee, April 29, 1992.

15.   Reinert, R.E., B.A. Knuth, M.A. Kamrin, and Q.J. Stober. 1991. "Risk assessment, risk management and fish consumption advisories in the United States." *Fisheries* (Bethesda) 16(6): 5-12.

16.   Colburn, T.E., A. Davidson, S.N. Green, R.A. Hodge, C.I. Jackson, and R.A. Liroff. 1990. "Great Lakes, Great Legacy?" The Conservation Foundation, Washington, D.C.

17.   Jacobson, J.L., S.W. Jacobson, and H.E.B. Humphrey. 1990. "Effects of in utero exposure to polychlorinated biphenyls and related contaminants on cognitive functioning in young children." *Journal of Pediatrics*, 116:38-45.

18.   *Ibid.*

19.   Karr, J.R., 1993. "Protecting Ecological Integrity." *Yale Journal of International Law*, Vol. 18:297-306.

20.   Water Quality 2000. 1991. "Challenges for the future: interim report phase II." *Water Quality 2000*, Water Pollution Control Federation, Alexandria, VA.

21.   *See generally Restoration of Aquatic Ecosystems, infra* note 22.

22.   This term was originally used by The National Research Council in their 1992 report, *The Restoration of Aquatic Ecosystems*, pp.184-185. Full cite: National Research Council, 1992. *Restoration of Aquatic Ecosystems*, National Academy Press, Washington, D.C.

23.   Skovlin, 1984. "Impacts of Grazing on Wetlands and Riparian Habitat: A Review of Our Knowledge," in National Research

Council/National Academy of Sciences, *Developing Strategies for Rangeland Management* 1001-85.

24. Platts, 1981. "Influence of Forest and Rangeland Management on Anadromous Fish Habitat in Western North America: Effects of Livestock Grazing" 1 (USFS Gen. Tech. Report No. PNW-124). (Riparian ecosystems are the most productive ecosystems in rangelands).

25. Karr, J.R. and I.J. Schlosser. 1978. "Water resources and the land-water interface." *Science* 201: 229-234

26. Restoration of Aquatic Ecosystems, *supra* note 22 at 161.

27. Williams, J.E. and R.J. Neves, 1992. "Introducing the elements of biological diversity in the aquatic environment." Trans. 57th N.A. Wild. & Nat. Res. Conf. 57:345-354.

28. Angermeier, P. and J.R. Karr, "Biological Integrity versus Biological Diversity as Policy Directives in Water Resource Protection"; submitted to *Science*, 1993.

29. Stanford, J.A. and J.V. Ward. 1993. "An ecosystem perspective of alluvial rivers: connectivity and the hyporheic corridor." *J.N. Am. Benthol. Soc.* 1993, 12(1) 48-60.

30. *Infra* note 615

31. *See* note 14 Karr 1991.

32. *Supra* note 22 at 150.

33. See generally *Restoration of Aquatic Ecosystems, supra* note 22.

34. Echevarria, J.D., Pope Barrow, & Richard Roos-Collins, 1989. *Rivers at Risk: A Concerned Citizens' Guide to Hydropower*, Ch.1, Island Press.

35. The National Research Council estimates that the number of stream and river miles affected by channelization and levying is probably much greater than the number of dammed river miles, although it could not find a recent national assessment which contains this specific data. *Restoration of Aquatic Ecosystems supra* note 22 at 150.

36. *see generally* Echevarria, et al. *Rivers at Risk, supra* note 34.

37. *Supra* note 22

38. Benke, A., 1990. "A perspective on America's vanishing streams." *Journal of the North American Benthological Society*, Vol.9, No.1.

39. *See* discussion on "How Dams Harm Rivers" in *Rivers at Risk. supra* note 34 at 1.

40.   Kleinmann, R.L.P., and R. Hedin, "Biological Treatment of Minewater: An Update", in M.E. Chalkey, B.R. Conrad, V.I. Lakshman, and K.G. Wheeland, eds., *Tailings and Effluent Management*, (1989). (Proceedings of the International Symposium on Tailings and Effluent Management, (1989). (Proceedings of the International Symposium on Tailings and Effluent Management, August 20-24, 1989, Halifax. 28th Annual Conference of Metallurgists of CIM. Pergamum Press, NY).

41.   *Supra* note 22 at 203.

42.   Some progress has been made in controlling mining-related pollution. Under the Federal Surface Mining Control and Reclamation Act of 1977 (PL 95-87), mining companies have been required to restore land and water affected by mining and acid mine drainage. In most cases, conditions must be restored to their pre-mining uses. In addition, a federal coal tax funds the restoration of lands abandoned before the Act's effective date, and certain lands are required to be set aside as unsuitable for mining in the future based on their high value for other uses, including habitat for rare or endangered species. There are also a variety of state and local programs designed to deal with the restoration of streams affected by mine drainage and related point sources of pollution.

43.   *See generally Restoration of Aquatic Ecosystems, supra* note 22.

44.   *Infra note 45.*

45.   Association of State and Interstate Water Pollution Control Administrators, in cooperation with the U.S. EPA. "America's Clean Water: The State's Evaluation of Progress 1972-1982" (1984), cited in *Restoration of Aquatic Ecosystems supra* note 22 at 174.

46.   *Ibid.*

47.   Sedell and Everest, "Historic Changes in Pool Habitat for Columbia River Basin Salmon under study for TES Listing" (USDA Forest Service, 1991).

48.   *See generally Restoration of Aquatic Ecosystems, supra* note 22, citing Judy et al., 1984; Guildin, 1989.

49.   Council of Environmental Quality and Interagency Advisory Committee on Environmental Trends, 1989. "Environmental Trends".

50.   *See generally Restoration of Aquatic Ecosystems, supra* note 22.

51.   Allan, J.D. and A.S. Flecker. 1993. "Biodiversity Conservation in Running Waters: Identifying the major factors that threaten destruction of riverine species and ecosystems." *Bioscience*, Vol. 43, No.1

52.   *Ibid.*
53.   *Ibid.*
54.   Achieng, A.P., 1990. "The impact of the introduction of Nile perch, *Lates niloticus* on the fisheries of Lake Victoria." *Journal of Fish Biology* 37 (Supplement A):17-24.
55.   *Supra* note 51.
56.   *Ibid.*
57.   *See* Karr testimony at note 14
58.   Karr, J.R., in press. "Biological Monitoring: challenges for the future." In A. Spacie and S. Loeb (eds.) *Biological Monitoring of Aquatic Ecosystems.*
59.   Karr 1991 at note 14; U.S. Environmental Protection Agency. 1991. "Biological Criteria: state development and implementation efforts." EPA-440/5-91-003. Office of Water. Washington, D.C.
60.   Science Advisory Board (EPA). 1990. "Reducing risk: setting priorities and strategies for environmental protection." SAB-EC-90-021. U.S. EPA, Washington, D.C.
61.   U.S. EPA 1991. "The Watershed Protection Approach: an Overview." EPA 503/9-92-002. Office of Water, Washington, D.C. Ohio Environmental Protection Agency. 1988. "Biological Criteria for the Protection of Aquatic Life." Ohio EPA, Division of Water Quality Monitoring and Assessment, Surface Water Section, Columbus, Ohio. U.S. EPA, 1991. "Biological Criteria: Research and Regulation." Office of Water, US EPA Washington, D.C. EPA 440/5-91-005. J. Lyons. 1992. "Using the index of biotic integrity (IBI) to measure environmental quality in warmwater streams in Wisconsin." North Central Experiment Station, USDA, Forest Service, Minneapolis, MN. General Technical Report NC-149. Taken from Karr, J.R., note 14.
62.   Bella, D.A and W.S. Overton. 1972. "Environmental planning and ecological possibilities." *Journal of the Sanitary Engineering Division, American Society of Civil Engineers* 98 (SAE, June, 1972): 592-599.
63.   Frissell, C., 1993. "A New Strategy For Watershed Restoration and Recovery of Pacific Salmon in the Pacific Northwest." A report prepared for the Pacific Rivers Council, Eugene, OR.
64.   *Ibid.*
65.   Frissell, C.A. and R.K. Nawa. 1992. *Incidence and causes of physical failure of artificial fish habitat structures in streams of western Oregon and Washington.* North American Journal of Fisheries Management 12:182-197.

66.   *Supra* note 63 and references therein.

67.   Yount, J.D. and G.J. Niemi. 1990. *Recovery of lotic communities from disturbance -- a narrative review of case studies.* Environmental Management 14:547-569; Niemi, G.J. and seven coauthors. 1990. *Overview of case studies on recovery of aquatic systems from disturbance.* Environmental Management 14:571-587.

68.   *Supra* note 63 and references therein.

69.   *Supra* note 67

70.   Sedell, J.R., G.H. Reeves, F.R. Hauer, J.A. Stanford, and C.P. Hawkins. 1990. *Role of refugia in recovery from disturbances: modern fragmented and disconnected river systems.* Environmental Management 14-711-724. Moyle, P.B. and G.M. Sato. 1992. *On the design of preserves to protect native fishes.* Pp. 155-169 in W.L. Minckley and J.E. Deacon (eds.) Battle Against Extinction: Native Fish Management in the American West. University of Arizona Press, Tucson. 518 pp.

71.   *Ibid* (Moyle and Sato).

72.   *Supra* note 70 (Moyle and Sato).

73.   *Supra* note 70 (Sedell et al.); *Supra* note 63.

74.   Williams, J.E. 1991. *Preserves and refuges for native western fishes: history and management.* Pp. 171-189 in W.L. Minckley and J.E. Deacon (eds.) Battle Against Extinction: Native Fish Management in the American West. University of Arizona Press, Tucson. 518 pp.

75.   *Supra* note 65.

76.   Beschta, R.L. and W.S. Platts, 1986. *Morphological features of small streams: significance and function.* Water Resources Bulletin 22: 369-379; Elmore, W., and R.L. Beschta, 1987. *Riparian Areas: perceptions in management.* Rangelands 9(6):260-265.

77.   Platts, W.S. and R.L. Nelson, 1985. *Stream habitat and fisheries response to livestock grazing and instream improvement structures, Big Creek, Utah.* Journal of Soil and Water Conservation 40:374-379; *Supra* note 65.

78.   *Supra* note 63; Nickelson, T.E., M.F. Solazzi, S.L. Johnson, and J.D. Rogers. 1992. *Effectiveness of selected stream improvement techniques to create suitable summer and winter rearing habitat for juvenile coho salmon (Oncorhyncus kisutch) in Oregon coastal streams.* Canadian Journal of Fisheries and Aquatic Sciences 49: 790-794.

79.   *Supra* note 63.

80.   *Ibid.*

81.   Weaver, W.E. and seven coauthors, 1987. *An evaluation of experimental rehabilitation work: Redwood National Park.* Redwood National Park Technical report 19, National Park Service, Arcata, CA. 164+pp.

82.   *Supra* note 63.

83.   *Supra* note 63; Frissell, C., W.J. Liss, and D. Bayles. "An integrated biophysical strategy for ecological restoration of large watersheds." Proceedings of a Symposium "Changing Rules in Water Resources Management and Policy." American Water Resources Association, Seattle, WA. 27-30 June, 1993.

84.   *Supra* note 63; Frissell et al., in press.

85.   *Supra* note 81

86.   Bureau of Land Management, U.S. Department of Interior. Bureau of Land Management.   175   Public Land Statistics, 1990   1 (August 1991).

87.   These statistics reflect those published in Congressional Research Service (CRS) Report for Congress, The Major Federal Land Management Agencies: Management of Our Nation's Land and Resources (May 7, 1990) (90-239 ENR). The 1991 edition of the BLM's Public Land Statistics, however, puts the BLM's percentage of total federal lands at 41%, but estimates that only 662 million acres of federal lands exist. The source of the discrepancy is unknown.

88.   CRS, The Major Federal Land Management Agencies, Table 1. The early history of the United States is fraught with controversy over the primary purposes of the federal lands, and policies favoring retention for national purposes often conflicted with those favoring disposition to the states or private parties. By the late 1800s, however, settlement and development had progressed far enough that concerns arose over the preservation of federal lands in an unsettled condition, as well as the reservation of lands for future use. As a result, Yellowstone became the first National Park in 1872, the first "forest reserves" were established in 1891, and the first national wildlife refuge was established in 1905. Since then, federal land laws have continued to shift their emphasis away from disposal towards continued federal ownership, although it was not until the enactment of the Federal Land Policy and Management Act of 1976 (FLPMA)that federal policy was expressly declared to be one of retention of federal lands. *Ibid.*

89.   Wheatley, C., C. Corker, T. Stetson & D. Reed, Study of the Development, Management and Use of Water Resources on the Public Lands 403 (1969) (source cited in *United States v. Mexico*, 438 U.S. 696, 699 n.3 (1978)). The fresh water flowing from federal lands is derived from the hydrologic cycle of precipitation resulting from the evaporation of sea water.

90.   *Ibid.* at 454. Only about 4% of the population in the western states received water from sources "entirely independent" of water yield from the federal lands in 1967.

91.   *Ibid.*

92.   *Ibid.* The federal lands in the western states are also responsible for about 60% of the sediments carried by major streams. *Ibid.* at 416.

93.   16 U.S.C. §§1271-1287.

94.   Personal Communication with John Haubert, Outdoor Recreation Planner, National Park Service, Division of Park Planning and Protection, Washington, D.C. office.

95.   The Act enables the National Park Service to provide river conservation planning assistance to state and local governments, as well as private groups. The availability of this assistance has contributed to the growing national interest in the development of "greenways" and trails along rivers and streams. *See* Little, C., Greenways for America (1990). While popular in urban and suburban areas, and among recreation groups, this assistance has not resulted in biological conservation or the preservation of natural ecological conditions.

96.   16 U.S.C. § 1271.

97.   *Ibid.*

98.   *Ibid.* §§ 1271, 1273(b), 1282(a), 1283(c); Gray, *No Holier Temples: Protecting the National Parks Through Wild and Scenic River Designation*, 58 U.Colo. L.Rev. 551, 560-61 (1988).

99.   16 U.S.C. § 1284(c); Blumm, "Reserved Water Rights" in 4 Water and Water Rights 244 (R. Beck ed. 1991).

100.   *Ibid.*

101.   16 U.S.C. § 1273.

102.   To date, no studies have been conducted by the USFWS or the BLM, although they are authorized to do so.

103.   16 U.S.C. § 1273(a)(ii) (Section 2(a)(ii) of the WSRA).

104.   "Free-flowing" means "existing or flowing in a natural condition without impoundment, diversion, straightening, rip-rapping, or other modification of the waterway," although the existence of low dams, diversion works, and other minor structures at the time a river is proposed for inclusion in the system does not alone bar its consideration for inclusion.

105.   *Ibid.* § 1273(b), 1271.

106.   *Ibid.* § 1273(b)(1).

107.   *Ibid.* § 1273(b)(2).

108.   *Ibid.* § 1273(b)(3).

109.   *Ibid.* § 1286(a).

110.   In September, 1991, the BLM resource management plan for the Stafford District in Arizona found several intermittent streams to be eligible for inclusion, including Turkey Creek and Swamp Springs -- both of which are representative of the Southwest's arid lands ecosystem. American Rivers, *Rivers Receive Interim Protection Through Public Lands Program* in American Rivers page 10 (Newsletter, Winter 1991).

111.   16 U.S.C. § 1274(b).

112.   *Wilderness Society v. Tyrrel,* 701 F. Supp. 1473 (E.D. Cal. 1988) (holding that state-designated rivers are not subject to the same boundary requirements).

113.   *Ibid.* 20 ELR 20661 (E.D. Cal. 1989).

114.   16 U.S.C. § 1274(a).

115.   *Ibid.* § 1281(a).

116.   *Ibid.* § 1274(d)(1) (requiring promulgation of a management plan). This provision was added to the WSRA in 1986 to require that for each river designated after 1985, the managing agency must prepare "a comprehensive management plan" to "achieve the [preservation] purposes of this chapter" within three years of designation. Previously, only rivers designated by Congress, not those designated by the Secretary of the Interior at state request, were required to have management plans.

117.   16 U.S.C. § 1281(b) & (c).

118.   *Ibid.* § 1283.

119.   *Ibid.* § 1283.

120.   *Ibid.* § 1278(a).

121.   *Swanson Mining Co. v. FERC,* 790 F.2d 96, 102-03 (D.C. Cir. 1986) (holding that WSRA prohibits FERC from licensing any project on or directly affecting a river corridor, regardless of whether adverse effect is

shown). We note, however, that Congress has qualified this rule in designating statutes by expressly permitting licensing and development on tributaries of designated rivers outside river corridors. *See Sierra Club v. FERC*, 754 F.2d 1506, 1507 n.1 (9th Cir. 1985).

122.   *Ibid.*

123.   16 U.S.C. § 1280(a)(iii). Otherwise, Congress did not distinguish among the three river classes in defining management standards.

124.   *Chevron, U.S.A. v. Natural Resources Defense Council*, 467 U.S. 837, 843 (1984).

125.   *Ibid.* at 845 (quoting from *United States v. Shimer*, 367 U.S. 374, 383 (1961)).

126.   *See* 16 U.S.C. § 1283 It is also worth noting that Section 7(b) of the Act (16 U.S.C. § 1278(b), "Restrictions on water resources projects"), limits federal agency authority to prohibit water resources projects to developments above or below a potential wild and scenic area which would "invade the area or diminish the scenic or recreational, and fish and wildlife values present" in the area under study. This provision could be interpreted to imply that public **or** private water resources projects could be prohibited where they will cause an "invasion" of a study area and/or the "diminishment" of outstanding resource values.

127.   *Thomas v. Peterson*, 589 F. Supp. 1139, 1151 (D. Idaho 1984), *rev'd on other grounds*, 753 F.2d 754 (9th Cir. 1985).

128.   701 F. Supp. 1473 (E.D. Cal 1988) (enjoining salvage timber sale because it appeared likely to degrade water quality and fish habitat on designated river), *Wilderness Society v. Tyrrel*, 20 ELR 20661 (E.D. Cal. 1989)(granting summary judgment on same, and other, grounds).

129.   16 U.S.C. § 1283(c).

130.   *Supra* note 116 at 1489.

131.   *See Sierra Club v. FERC*, 754 F.2d 1506, 1509 n.1 (9th Cir. 1985) (special provisions in designating legislation take precedence over general provisions of WSRA).

132.   16 U.S.C § 1281(a).

133.   *See, e.g., Chemical Mfrs. Ass'n v. Natural Resources Defense Council*, 470 U.S. 116, 125-26 (1985).

134.   47 Fed. Reg. 39,459 (Sept. 7, 1982).

135.   *Ibid.*

136. USDA, United States Forest Service, Land and Resource Management Planning Handbook (1987); USDI, Manual for Wild and Scenic Rivers (1992).

137. Frost, P.M.K., 1992. *Ensuring that Clean Water Flows in Wild and Scenic Rivers,* Unpublished Manuscript at 9, n. 28 (on file at National Wildlife Federation, Portland, Oregon).

138. *Ibid.* citing Beschta, Robert L., William S. Platts and Boone Kaufmann, Field Review of Fish Habitat Improvement Projects on the Grande Ronde and John Day River Basins of Eastern Oregon 10 (1991) (unpublished report on file with the Northwest Power Planning Council, Portland, OR).

139. 16 U.S.C. Sec. 1284 (c) While this provision claims such water as is necessary to accomplish the statute's purposes, other parts of the Act emphasize that this right need not impair state jurisdiction over water resources. Section 1284(b) states that the statute should not be construed as "an express or implied claim or denial on the part of the Federal Government as to exemption from state water laws," and Section 1284(d) reiterates that the jurisdiction of the states over designated rivers shall remain unaffected by their inclusion in the Wild and Scenic river system, at least "to the extent that such jurisdiction may be exercised without impairing the purposes of this Act or its administration." These provisions are not inconsistent with the reservation of a federal water right, in that they merely express traditional Congressional deference to state water resources law. *See Sierra Club v. Lyng,* 661 F. Supp. 1490 (D. Colo 1987) (interpreting congruent language about state law in the Wilderness Act).

140. *See, e.g., Sierra Club v. Andrus,* 487 F. Supp. 443 (D.D.C. 1980), *aff'd on other grounds sub. nom. Sierra Club v. Watt,* 659 F.2d 203 (D.C.Cir. 1981) (finding no agency duty to assert a federal reserved water right).

141. For details on the status of flow quantification in Oregon and Alaska, see Frost, *supra* note 137 at n. 64.

142. 16 U.S.C. § 1281(a).

143. *See* FLPMA, 43 U.S.C. § 1752(a); 43 CFR 4130.6-3 (1992) (authorizing BLM to modify permit conditions to conform with new law of management needs).

144. Benke, *supra* note 38 at 82.

145. 16 U.S.C. §§ 460zz to 460zz-11 (within the St. Paul/Minneapolis metropolitan area).

146.   *Ibid.* §§ 460xx to 460xx-6.
147.   *Ibid.* § 460ddd.
148.   Benke, *supra* note 38 at 82.
149.   *Supra* note 38 at 77.
150.   *Ibid.*
151.   Source: John Haubert, Outdoor Recreation Planner, National Park Service, Division of Park Planning and Protection, Washington, D.C. office.
152.   16 U.S.C. § 1274(b).
153.   For example, on the Salmon River in Oregon, the BLM and the Forest Service corridor boundaries are different. *See* Environmental Assessment, Salmon National Wild and Scenic River, Mt. Hood National Forest (1992). In some areas, such as on the Grande Ronde and North Umpqua Rivers in Oregon, agencies with joint jurisdiction have voluntarily entered into cooperative planning agreements to avoid this problem.
154.   Frost, *supra* note 137 at 39; *see also* P. Baldwin (Congressional Research Service).
155.   The Act's failure to specifically mandate restoration has been interpreted to conflict with certain types of fish habitat restoration projects. The Office of the General Counsel to the Forest Service recently stated that fish habitat restoration projects cannot be totally accommodated by the policy direction contained in Section 7 of the Act because such projects may fall within the Act's definition of "water resources projects" having "a direct and adverse effect" on the values for which a river was designated. Memorandum from James B. Snow, Deputy Assistant General Counsel, Natural Resources Division Responding to Concerns of Congressman Staggers (December 6, 1991) (citing 16 U.S.C. § 1279(a)). The argument is that since a water resources project is defined as any development affecting the free-flowing characteristics of a river, and "free-flowing" is defined in the Act as " . . . existing or flowing in natural condition without impoundment, diversion, straightening, rip-rapping, or other modification of the waterway . . . . " (16 U.S.C. § 1286(b)), it follows that certain types of fish habitat restoration do not comport with the terms of the Act. Therefore, instream habitat restoration which is dependent on the erection of instream structures is subject to scrutiny, and may be prohibited, unless special language is included in designation legislation or unless the

definition of "free-flowing" is amended in the Act. Fortunately, the most effective, ecology-based types of fish habitat restoration are based on natural stream processes and do not conflict with the terms of the Act.

156.   Gray, *No Holier Temples: Protecting National Parks Through Wild and Scenic River Designation*, 58 U.Colo. L. Rev. 551, ___ (1988).
157.   33 U.S.C. §§ 1251-1387.
158.   *Ibid.* § 1251(a).
159.   *Ibid.*
160.   Ohio Environmental Protection Agency, Ohio Water Resource Inventory, (1990) (evaluating 645 water bodies) cited in Yoder, C., *The Integrated Biosurvey as a Tool for Evaluation of Aquatic Life Use Attainment and Impairment in Ohio Surface Waters*, Biological Criteria: Research and Regulation (Proceedings of a Symposium), (EPA-440/5-91-005)(July 1991).
161.   33 U.S.C. § 1251-1387.
162.   *Ibid.* § 1251(a).
163.   *Ibid.* § 1251(a)(2).
164.   *Ibid.* § 1313 (Section 303).
165.   *Ibid.* § 1323(a) (emphasis added)
166.   40 C.F.R. § 131.10.
167.   *Ibid.* § 131.11. We note that the Clean Water Act's mandate to **fully protect** designated beneficial uses supersedes the Forest Service's NFMA mandate (discussed below) to maintain "minimum viable populations" of native vertebrate species, as restated in 36 C.F.R. § 219.19.
168.   40 C.F.R. § 131.12.
169.   *Ibid.* 140
170.   *Ibid.* §1313(c)(2)(a) (requiring adoption of standards consistent with Act's purposes); §1313(c)(2)(b)(toxics standards based on biological monitoring and assessment should be used where numeric criteria are not available consistent with information published by the EPA on water quality criteria and toxic pollutants under 33 U.S.C. §1314(d)).
171.   EPA, Biological Criteria: National Program Guidance for Surface Waters 9 (April 1990).
172.   33 U.S.C. § 1362(15). Although the EPA must review state water quality standards every three years to check compliance with the Act's mandate, there is no formal mechanism for public participation in the development of state standards to ensure both their enforceability and their biological adequacy.
173.   40 C.F.R. § 130.5

174.   In reality, the technical difficulty of determining quantities of particular pollutants being discharged from certain point sources or land areas have prevented many states from determining these allocations, particularly for non-point sources. Whitman, *Clean Water or Multiple Use? Best Management Practices for Water Quality Control in the National Forests,* 16 Ecol. L. Q. 909, 925 (1991).

175.   40 C.F.R. § 130.6(b).

176.   *See* Or. Admin. R. § 340-41-026; Whitman, *supra* note 174 at 925.

177.   33 U.S.C. § 1362(7).

178.   *See, e.g., Quivera Mining Co. v. EPA* , 765 F.2d 126 (10th Cir. 1985) (including normally dry arroyos with occasional surface flows within the definition of "waters of the United States"); *Utah v. Marsh,* 740 F.2d 799 (10th Cir. 1984) (including isolated lake). For other cases, *see* Blumm & Zahela, *Federal Wetland Protection Under the Clean Water Act: Regulation, Ambivalence, Intergovernmental Tensions, and a Call for Reform,* 60 U.Colo. L. Rev. 695, 716-17 (1989).

179.   33 U.S.C. § 1362(14).

180.   *Ibid.* § 1365 ("Citizen suits").

181.   33 U.S.C. § 1288 (Section 208).

182.   *Ibid.* § 1288(a).

183.   *Ibid.* § 1288(b)(4).

184.   *Ibid.* § 1288(b)(4).

185.   *Ibid.* § 1313(e).

186.   40 C.F.R. § 130.6(c)(4).

187.   *Ibid.* § 130.6(c)(4)(ii).

188.   *Ibid.* § 130.6(c)(4)(iii).

189.   *Ibid.* § 130.6(c)(4)(iv).

190.   The amendments state that "it is the national policy that programs for the control of non-point sources of pollution shall be developed and implemented in an expeditious manner so as to enable the goals of this Act to be met through the control of both point and non-point sources of pollution." 33 U.S.C. § 1251(7) (added as Section 316(b) of the Water Quality Act of 1987). Section 319 sets new deadlines for the adoption of management programs, restates existing requirements more precisely in a single section, and allocates $400 million to state-federal non-point control programs.

191.   Whitman, *Clean Water or Multiple Use? Best Management Practices for Water Quality Control in the National Forests,* 16 Ecology L. Q. 909, 931 (1989).

192.   *Ibid.*

193.   33 U.S.C. § 1329(b)(4). This provision strengthens the Act's existing requirements that Total Maximum Daily Loads be calculated on a water-by-water basis. *See id.* § 303; 40 C.F.R. Part 130 (total maximum daily load calculations).

194.   *See, e.g.,* Office of Water, EPA, Nonpoint Source Controls and Water Quality Standards (Aug. 19, 1987)(guidance document).

195.   33 U.S.C. § 1313(a).

196.   *Northwest Indian Cemetery Protective Ass'n v. Peterson,* 565 F Supp. 586 (N.D. Cal 1983), *modified* 764 F.2d 581 (9th Cir. 1985), *rev'd in part on other grounds sub nom. Lyng v. Northwest Indian Cemetery Protective Ass'n,* 485 U.S. 439 (1988). This case is also significant because it implicitly recognized citizens' groups right to sue federal agencies to enforce state water quality standards against nonpoint source polluters if federal standing requirements under the Administrative Procedures Act are met.

197.   565 F. Supp. at 605.

198.   764 F. 2d at 588.

199.   *Ibid.* at 588-89.

200.   Wetlands are also protected by other statutes and executive orders, the most prominent of which are: The Estuarine Areas Act of 1968, 15 U.S.C. §§ 1221-1226 (1982) (directing all federal agencies to consider the value of estuaries in land and water resource planning); the Coastal Zone Management Act, 16 U.S.C. §§ 1451-1464 (creating a state-run regulatory program which contributes to the ecological preservation of tideland areas); the Coastal Barrier Resources Act of 1982, 16 U.S.C. §§ 3501-3510 (also protecting tideland areas); Exec. Order No. 11,990, 3 C.F.R. § 121 (1977)(requiring federal agencies to restrict uses on federal lands sold or leased, or withhold them from disposal if private use would threaten wetlands values); Exec. Order 11,988, as amended 44 Fed. Reg. 15784 (1979) (stopping a land exchange that did not adequately protect floodplain values). In addition, the FWS is authorized to purchase easements over prairie pothole areas which deny landowners the right to drain this important migratory waterfowl habitat under 1961 legislation codified at 16 U.S.C. §§ 715k-5, 718d(c).

384   *Entering the Watershed*

201.   *Natural Resources Defense Council v. Callaway*, 392 F. Supp. 685 (D.D.C. 1975) (holding that CWA intended to assert full jurisdictional scope permitted by the Commerce Clause of the U.S. Constitution).
202.   *United States v. Riverside Bayview Homes*, 474 U.S. 121 (1985).
203.   33 U.S.C. § 1344 ("Permits for dredged or fill material). For collected discussions of the Section 404 program, *see generally* 50 U.Colo.L. Rev. __ (1989) (focusing on Section 404 issues); Symposium, 7 Va. J. Nat. Res. L. 217 (1988) (collecting current wetlands literature).
204.   33 C.F.R. §320.4(a).
205.   Two critics have commented that the public interest review presumes the district engineers to "possess the wisdom of Solomon." Blumm & Zahela, *supra* note 178 at 695.
206.   33 U.S.C. § 1344(e)(1) (1988).
207.   33 C.F.R. § 330.6(a).
208.   *Ibid.* § 330.5(b)(4).
209.   *Ibid.* §§ 330.5(b)(1)-(5), (7), (10).
210.   758 F.2d 508 (10th Cir. 1985).
211.   *Ibid.* at 512-13.
212.   33 U.S.C. § 1344(r).
213.   Blumm & Zahela, *supra* note 178 at 722-24.
214.   33 C.F.R. § 330.5(a)(26).
215.   *Ibid.* §330.2(b).
216.   *See* Rich & Coltman, Summary and Recommendations: Clean Water Act Section 404 Discharge of Dredged and Fill Materials and Section 401 Water Quality Certification Programs in Arizona 7-5 (Aug. 30, 1991) (prepared for Office of Water Quality, Arizona Department of Environmental Quality by the Herberger Center, College of Architecture and Environmental Design, Arizona State University).
217.   Blumm & Zahela, *supra* note 178 at 726; Addison & Burns, *The Army Corps of Engineers and Nationwide Permit 26: Wetlands Protection or Swamp Reclamation?*, 18 Ecology L.Q. 619, 639 (1991).
218.   Addison & Burns, *supra* note 217 at 643.
219.   *Ibid.* at 637-38.
220.   *Ibid.* at 668.
221.   33 U.S.C. § 1344(b)(1).
222.   *Ibid.* § 1344(c).
223.   *Ibid.* § 1344(f).
224.   48 Stat. 401 (codified as amended at 16 U.S.C. § 662).

225. This "elevation" authority is derived from interagency agreements between the Department of the Army, the EPA and the Departments of Interior, Agriculture, Commerce and Transportation.
226. 16 U.S.C. § 1456(c).
227. 43 U.S.C. § 1340(c)(2).
228. As of 1988, Michigan was the only state with this authority, but in the last three years more states have taken steps to assume administration of their wetlands permitting programs.
229. 40 CFR § 230.10(a).
230. *Ibid.* § 230.10(c).
231. *Ibid.* § 230.3. The Corps uses the same definition. 33 C.F.R. § 328.3. Application of the current "wetlands" definition is accomplished according to the 1989 Federal Manual for Delineating Wetlands, a joint project of the EPA, the Corps, the Soil Conservation Service and the USFWS, but the Bush Administration has indicated its desire to change wetland delineation methodologies -- much to the chagrin of the scientific community. *See* Proposed Revisions to the Federal Manual, 56 Fed. Reg. 40446 (1991). More than one scholar believes that the Manual should be retained because it "yields accurate and repeatable results," based on "scientifically valid and consistent criteria for wetland identification by federal agencies" and should not be replaced by the "severely flawed" proposals to change it.   University of Washington Institute of Environmental Studies Faculty, Review of Proposed Revisions to The Federal Manual for Delineating Wetlands, 1-3 (Nov. 26, 1991).
232. GAO, Wetlands: The Corps of Engineers' Administration of the Section 404 Program 23 (July 1988).
233. *Ibid.*
234. *Ibid.* at 26.
235. *Ibid.* at 27.
236. GAO at 28.
237. *See id.* at 30.
238. *Ibid.* at 23-25 (citing examples of delineation disparities).
239. Blumm & Zahela, *supra* note 178 at 718.
240. *Ibid.*
241. *Ibid.* at 720.
242. *See* Steiner, Pieart & Cook, 1991. *The Interrelationship Between Federal and State Wetlands and Riparian Protection Programs*, 1, Arizona State University.

243.   As several analysts have pointed out, the current CWA shows a "geographic bias" toward eastern and southern states, "where rainfall is abundant, watercourses are perennial and wetlands are areas that are consistently inundated with surface water, allowing hydric soils to develop. The result is that the law is not as easily applied to arid Arizona, with its ephemeral and intermittent streams, dammed rivers, dry washes and riparian areas that are fed as often with ground water as with surface water." Rich & Coltman, *supra* note 216 at 7-10.

244.   *Ibid.* at 7-9.

245.   33 U.S.C. § 1344(f)(2).

246.   EPA Region VII, *Environmental Action Plan for Rainwater Basin Wetlands Project* (September 1986), as cited in GAO, Wetlands: The Corps of Engineers' Administration of the Section 404 Program (July 1988).

247.   *See* Salveson, D., Urban Lands Institute, Wetlands: Mitigating and Regulating Development Impacts (1990).

248.   GAO, Wetlands at 20

249.   33 U.S.C. § 1341; *see also* 33 C.F.R. § 320.4(d).

250.   Rich & Coltman, *supra* note 216

251.   Ransel, K. & E. Meyers, *State Water Quality Certification and Wetland Protection: A Call to Awaken the Sleeping Giant,* 7 Va. J. Nat. Res. L. 339-379 (1988). Part of the reason that the 401 program has not been fully used by states is that the EPA has not given states formal guidance on the full range of federal activities which fall within state jurisdiction under section 401. *Ibid.* Furthermore, states may not seek to bring federal activities within the ambit of certification due to a lack of state resources. *Ibid.*

252.   The 1987 amendments to the CWA explicitly refer to its antidegradation mandate at 33 U.S.C. § 1313(d)(4)(B).

253.   40 C.F.R. § 131.12.

254.   EPA, Questions and Answers on Antidegradation 4 (August 1985).

255.   *Ibid.*

256.   *Ibid.*

257.   The courts have yet to decide how strictly the term "no degradation" may be interpreted by states.

258.   *See e.g.* U.S.E.P.A., Region 9, Guidance on Implementing the Antidegradation Provisions of 40 C.F.R. 131.12 (June 3, 1987); Letter from James A. Rogers, Associate General Counsel, Water and Solid Waste

Division, U.S.E.P.A. to Kenneth Mackenthum, Director, Water Criteria and Standards Division, U.S.E.P.A. (August 15, 1979). For a discussion of antidegradation policy and the protection of river segments included in the Wild and Scenic River System, *see* Frost, P., *Ensuring that Clean Water Flows in Wild and Scenic Rivers* (1992) (unpublished manuscript on file at the National Wildlife Federation, Portland, Oregon).

259.   U.S.E.P.A., National Water Quality Inventory, 1988 Report to Congress.

260.   Livingston, E., et. al., Florida Nonpoint Source Assessment, Volume One, Department of Environmental Regulation (August 1988).

261.   Oregon Department of Environmental Quality, 1988 Statewide Assessment of Nonpoint Source Water Pollution (August 1988).

262.   Thompson, P., 1989. *Poison Runoff: A Guide to State and Local Control of Nonpoint Source Water Pollution.* (Natural Resources Defense Council).

263.   *Ibid.*

264.   Whitman, *supra* note 174 at 928. Although states are not required under the CWA to enforce their plans against nonpoint source polluters, they have the authority to enact nonpoint enforcement mechanisms. *Ibid.,* n. 121.

265.   This is true despite the decision in *Northwest Indian Cemetery Protective Ass'n v. Peterson*, 795 F. 2d 688 (9th Cir. 1986), *rev'd on other grounds sub nom.* Lyng v. Northwest Indian Protective Ass'n, 108 S.Ct. 1319 (1988), holding that under federal law the Forest Service must demonstrate how state water quality standards will be met in its pre-project environmental analyses. *See* Whitman, *supra* 167 at 925.

266.   Anderson, M., *Water Quality Planning in the National Forests* 17 Envt'l L. 591, 610-11 (1987).

267.   Karr and Schlosser. 1978. *Water resources and the land-water interface.* Science. 201: 229-234.

268.   *Ibid.* at 921 (citing a study of mass soil movement caused by logging roads in the Six Rivers National Forest in Northern California).

269.   *Ibid.* On national forest lands, despite the fact that provisions of the National Forest Management Act require that impacts on water quality and fish habitat be considered in determining whether lands are suitable for timber harvest, these considerations are not always factored

into forest planning.   *Ibid.* at 952; *see* discussion of watershed management on forest lands *infra*.

270.   *Ibid.* at 952.   The Forest Service is directed to identify areas unsuitable for timber harvesting under its planning statute, the National Forest Management Act.   *See* discussion *infra*.

271.   Whitman, *supra* note 174 at 955.

272.   *Ibid.* at 956-58.

273.   Whitman, *supra* note 174 at 958 *citing* a survey of BMP implementation in the Shasta-Trinity National Forest.

274.   Wilson, Thomas E., *Watershed Management and Water Quality Protection in* The Public Lands During the Remainder of the 20th Century: Planning, Law and Policy in the Federal Land Agencies, 5 (1987) (proceedings of a symposium)(Wilson is the Chief of the Office of Water Planning, U.S.E.P.A. Region 10).

275.   Karr, J.R., K.D. Fausch, P.L. Angermeier, P.R. Yant, and I.J. Schlosser. 1986. *Assessment of biological integrity in running waters: a method and its rationale.*   Illinois Natural History Survey Special Publication No. 5. Champaign, IL. Karr et. al., 1986. J. Karr, L. Toth, and D.R. Dudley. 1985. Fish communities of midwestern rivers: a history of degradation. BioScience 35: 90-95.

276.   Wilson, *supra* note 274 at 6.

277.   Wilson *supra* note 274 at 7.

278.   Ohio Environmental Protection Agency, Ohio Water Resource Inventory, E. T. Rankin, C. O. Yoder, D. Mishne, eds. in Executive Summary and Vol. I. Div. Water Qual. Planning and Assessment, Ecological Assessment Section (1990) as cited in C. Yoder, *The Integrated Biosurvey as a Tool for Evaluation of Aquatic Life Use Attainment and Impairment in Ohio Surface Waters*, Biological Criteria: Research and Regulation (Proceedings of a Symposium), (EPA-440/5-91-005 July 1991).

279.   U.S.E.P.A., Biological Criteria: Guide to Technical Literature 3 (July 1991).

280.   55 Fed. Reg. 52,097 (19 December 1990).

281.   According to the EPA, habitat assessment for streams and rivers should be based on the evaluation of primary, secondary, and tertiary habitat components.   For more information, see U.S. E.P.A., Biological Criteria: Guide to Technical Literature 3-4 (July 1991).   For a general overview of habitat assessment *see* U.S. E.P.A., Rapid Bioassessment Protocol Guidance Document (1989).

282.   Addison & Burns, *supra* note 217 at 619, 643 (1991).

283.   U.S. Environmental Protection Agency, Region 10: Riparian Area Management Policy. Washington D.C.: March 12, 1991.

284.   Less suspended sediment reduces silt build-up in reservoirs, reduces river clogging and lengthens the life of flood control or water storage basins and dams. Rich & Coltman, *supra* note 216 at 7-8, *citing* Salvesen, 1990.

285.   Anderson *supra* note 266, and sources cited therein.

286.   *See e.g.* Oregon Department of Environmental Quality regulations at OAR 340-41-026 (establishing a nomination process for designation of ONRWs).

287.   *See generally* Anderson, *New Directions for National Forest Water Quality Planning*, Forest Watch, March, 1988, at 22, as cited in Whitman, *supra* note 174 at 925, n.102.

288.   Anderson, *Water Quality Planning for the National Forests* 17 Envt'l L. 591, 608 (1987).

289.   Office of Wetlands, Oceans and Watersheds, Office of Water, USEPA, *The Watershed Protection Approach; An Overview* (November, 1991).

290.   16 U.S.C. §§ 1531-1543 (1982).

291.   *Ibid.* §1532(6).

292.   *Ibid.* §1532(20).

293.   *Ibid.* § 1531(b). Wildlife biologists have described ecosystems as "the populations in a community interacting with their surrounding physical environment by food energy flow and mineral exchange." S. Anderson, Managing Our Wildlife Resources, 27-28 (1985).

294.   *See, e.g.,* H.R. Rep. No. 1625, 95th Cong., 2d Sess. 16, *reprinted in* 1978 U.S. Code Cong. & Admin. News 9453, 9455 (finding that habitat loss is the major cause of extinction); *Defenders of Wildlife v. Andrus,* 428 F. Supp. 167, 169 (D.D.C. 1977) (stating the FWS position that most important factor affecting species survival is quality of habitat); *Tennessee Valley Auth. v. Hill,* 437 U.S. 153, 178-79 (1978)(primacy of ecosystem preservation important in interpreting the ESA).

295.   16 U.S.C. § 1533(a)(3), § 1534 (1988).

296.   *Ibid.* § 1536(a)(2).

297.   *Ibid.* § 1538(a)(1)(B); 50 CFR § 17.3 (1984).

298.   Congress did not provide for the modification of critical habitat once it was designated.

299.   ESA, § 4, 16 U.S.C. § 1533(b)(2) (1988).

300.   By contrast, species are listed as endangered on the basis of biological data only, which gives the broadest possible reach to the status designation process.

301.   16 U.S.C. § 1532(A)(i) (1988).

302.   The ESA defines conservation at "the use of all methods and procedures which are necessary to bring any endangered or threatened species to the point at which measures provided pursuant to this chapter are no longer necessary." 16 U.S.C. § 1523(3); 50 C.F.R. § 424.02(c). According to biologists, this point should be at or above the Minimum Viable Population level. Yagerman, *infra* note 303 at 833, n. 98.

303.   Yagerman. *Protecting Critical Habitat Under the Federal Endangered Species Act*, 20 Envt'l L. at 833, n. 98.

304.   50 C.F.R. § 424.12(b) (1991) (emphasis added).

305.   *Ibid.*   •

306.   *See Cabinet Mountains Wilderness v. Peterson*, 685 F. 2d 678 (D.C. Cir. 1982) (involving controversy over broad use of critical habitat).

307.   16 U.S.C. § 1536(a)(2)(1988).

308.   *Ibid.* § 1536(c).

309.   *Ibid.* § 1536(b)(3)(A).

310.   Yagerman *supra* note 303 at 841.

311.   50 C.F.R. § 402.02 (1989).

312.   Yagerman, *supra* note 303 at 841, n.141.

313.   *See e.g., Chevron U.S.A. v. Natural Resources Defense Council*, 467 U.S. 837 (1984 (parenthetical) Cited in Yagerman *supra* note 300 at 845.

314.   Yagerman *supra* note 303 at 845, n.161.

315.   16 U.S.C. § 1532(19).

316.   50 C.F.R. § 17.3 (1989).

317.   *See Palila v. Hawaii Department of Land and Natural Resources*, 639 F.2d 495 (9th Cir. 1981)("*Palila II*") (holding that destruction of bird's critical habitat through maintenance of non-native species for sport hunting constituted taking under Section 9).

318.   Palila v Hawaii Dep't of Land and Natural Resources, 631 F. Supp. 787, 790 (D. Haw. 1985) *aff'd*, 852 F.2d 1106 (9th Cir. 1988) (*Palila II*).

319.   898 F.2d 1410 (9th Cir. 1990).

320. An affirmative duty to implement "programs for the conservation" of endangered and threatened species was recognized in *Carson-Truckee Water Conservancy Dist. v. Clark,* 714 F.2d 257, 262 n.5 (1984).
321. *Ibid.* at 1412.
322. *Ibid.* at 1418-19.
323. *Ibid.* at 1420.
324. *See e.g., Palila v. Hawaii Dep't of Land and Natural Resources (Palila I),* 639 F.2d 495 (9th Cir. 1981); *Palila v. Hawaii Dep't of Land and Natural Resources (Palila II),* 852 F.2d 1106 (9th Cir. 1988).
325. *Tennessee Valley Authority v. Hill,* 437 U.S. 153 (1978)(holding that the ESA overrides any congressional project authorization and could preclude any project that would violate the ESA).
326. Brooks, C., *Oregon Water Rights and the Endangered Species Act: Conflicting State and Regulatory Mandates* (prepared for CLE International, Oregon Water Law, February 22, 1992).
327. 568 F. Supp. 583 (D. Colo, 1983), *aff'd* 658 F.2d 762 (10th Cir. 1985).
328. 741 F.2d 257 (9th Cir. 1984), *cert denied,* 470 U.S. 1083 (1985).
329. 898 F.2d 1410 (9th Cir. 1990).
330. *United States v. Glenn-Colusa Irrigation Dist.,* 788 F. Supp. 1126 (E.D. Cal. 1992).
331. Previously, the "species" was the predominant management unit. Yagerman *supra* note 303 at 817.
332. The CEQ has said:

> Biological diversity is a broad catchall term including the interconnected and related concepts of genetic diversity, including the genetic variability within individuals, races and populations of a species; species or ecological diversity, including the number or richness of species within a community or habitat; and habitat or natural diversity, including the variety and number of natural habitats and ecosystems.

CEQ 1985 Annual Report 273 (1985) (stating that nations must move beyond legal systems in order to adequately preserve habitat, utilizing economic incentives to permit private property and the market to maintain wildlife and habitat).

333.   Yagerman, *supra* note 303 at 818.

334.   *See e.g.* Mann and Plummer, *The Butterfly Problem,* The Atlantic Monthly (January 1992).

335.   *Supra* note 303 at 811, 829, n.83.

336.   *See Enos v. Marsh,* 616 F. Supp. 32 (D. Haw. 1984), *aff'd,* 769 F.2d 1363 (9th Cir. 1985) (where court failed to understand importance of Minimum Viable Populations and habitat size, finding that the subject site did not appear to be "essential" to the conservation of an endangered plant species). Cited in Yagerman, *supra* note 303 at 829, n.85.

337.   There have been Congressional efforts to create stronger laws to protect ecosystems. e.g. the Natural Resources Subcommittee of the House Science and Technology Committee cleared a bill in 1989 that would establish biological diversity protection as a national goal and require governmental agencies to consider the preservation of natural ecosystems. H.R. 1268, 100th Cong. 2d Sess. (1989).

338.   Remarks by Marvin Plenert, Pacific Regional Director, U.S.F.W.S., at the CLE International Session: The Endangered Species Act (Seattle, Washington, September 24, 1992).

339.   16 U.S.C. §§ 791a-825r.

340.   *Ibid.* § 797 (e).

341.   *Ibid.* § 796(2).

342.   *Ibid.* § 837 et seq.

343.   33 U.S.C. § 1341(a)(1). *See* 18 C.F.R. § 4.38 (1992).

344.   16 U.S.C. § 797(e).

345.   *Udall v. Federal Power Commission,* 387 U.S. 428, 450 (1967).

346.   Echevarria, et al *supra* note 34 at 45.

347.   16 U.S.C. § 797(e) (emphasis added). This provision essentially requires the Commission to give all river uses equal weight in the decisionmaking process.

348.   Amendments are subject to notice and hearing requirements and may not be so major as to constitute a "change" in license conditions without mutual agreement of the parties. Bodi, F.L., *Hydropower, Dams, and the National Parks* in National Parks, and Conservation Association,

Our Common Lands: Defending the National Parks 454 (1988) (D. Simon, ed. 1988).

349.   16 U.S.C. § 803(a). *Udall v. FPC*, 387 U.S. 428, 450 (1967); *Scenic Hudson Preservation Conference v. FPC*, 354 F.2d 608, 620 (2d Cir. 1965), *cert. denied*, 384 U.S. 941 (1966); *Confederated Tribes and Bands of the Yakima Indian Nation v. FERC*, 746 F.2d 466, 471 (9th Cir. 1984), *cert. denied*, 471 U.S. 1116 (1985).

350.   16 U.S.C. §803 (a).

351.   *See, e.g.*, *In re Northern Lights*, 39 FERC P61,352 (June 25, 1987) (proposed project at Kootenai Falls, Montana, rejected by FERC on grounds of protecting aesthetic, fishing and tribal religious interests), cited in Comment, *Fishery Protection and FERC Hydropower Relicensing under ECPA: Maintaining a Deadly Status Quo*, 20 Envtl. L. 929, 967 n.169 (1990).

352.   *See generally* Blumm, M. & B. Kloos, *Small Scale Hydropower and Anadromous Fish: Lessons and Questions from the Winchester Dam Controversy*, 16 Envtl. L. J. 583 (1986).

353.   16 U.S.C. § 803(a).

354.   In fact, FERC has generally refused to prepare such plans. *See* Blumm, M., *Hydroelectric Regulation under the Federal Power Act*, in 4 Water and Water Rights 343 (R. Beck ed. 1991).

355.   *See, e.g.*, *In re City of Fort Smith*, 44 FERC P61,160 (CCH) (July 28, 1988), cited in Rivers at Risk, *supra* note 34 at 49, n.5.

356.   *LaFlamme v. FERC*, 842 F.2d 1063 (9th Cir. 1988).

357.   16 U.S.C. § 803(a)(2)(A).

358.   18 C.F.R. § 2.19.

359.   *Ibid.* § 385.713.

360.   *See, e.g.*, 16 U.S.C. §§ 797(e), 811, 823.

361.   A federal "reservation" is defined as a national forest, tribal lands inside Indian reservations, military reservations, and other federal lands withheld from appropriation under the public land laws, such as some BLM lands. 16 § 796(2). This gives the BLM even more limited authority, since most of its holdings are not considered to be "non-reservation" lands.

362.   16 U.S.C. § 797e.

363.   *Ibid.*

364. *Escondido Mutual Water Co. v. LaJolla Band of Mission Indians*, 466 U.S. 765, 776-79 (1984). *But cf. United States Dep't of Interior v. FERC*, 952 F.2d 538, 544-45 (D.C. Cir. 1992) (employing arbitrary and capricious standard in upholding FERC's licensing of 16 hydro projects in upper Ohio River basin despite protests by Department of Interior and state agencies).

365. *Ibid.* at 780-84.

366. 41 FERC Paragraph 62,442 (CCH) (June 29, 1987) (involving the Lena Lake special management area).

367. 43 U.S.C. § 1761(a)(4).

368. Recently, the BLM threatened to assert its right-of-way authority over the Salt Cave dam near Klamath Falls, Oregon, but no formal exercise was accomplished.

369. 16 U.S.C. § 823(a).

370. *Ibid.* § 2705.

371. *Ibid.* § 2601 et seq. The Public Utility Regulator Policies Act guarantees a market for any facility with a capacity of less than 80 megawatts and which meets statutory tests for "minimal" environmental impacts. Power from qualified projects must be purchased by local utilities at the "avoided cost," i.e. the cost of generating this electricity with alternative fuel.

372. 16 U.S.C. § 823a(c).

373. *Ibid.* § 803(j).

374. *Id* § 803(j)(2). *See United States Dept. of Interior v. FERC*, 952 F.2d at 544.

375. *Ibid.*

376. *See, e.g., Confederated Tribes v. FERC*, 746 F.2d 466 (9th Cir. 1984) *cert. denied*, 471 U.S. 1116 (1985); *Steamboaters v. FERC*, 759 F.2d 1382 (9th Cir. 1985), *reh'g denied*, 777 F.2d 1384 (9th Cir. 1985).

377. 16 U.S.C. § 803(a)(2)(b).

378. *See California v. FERC*, 495 U.S. 490 (1990) (FPA preempted state's requirements for minimum stream flow in river with federally licensed hydroelectric project since California state law did not recognize minimum streamflows as established proprietary rights). *See generally* Blumm, *Federalism, Hydroelectric Licensing, and the Future of Minimum Streamflows after California v. FERC*, 21 Envtl. L. 113 (1991).

379. Bodi, *supra* note 348 at 455.

380.   Cody, CRS Issue Brief, Western Water Supplies: Issues in the 102d Congress (updated Jan. 31, 1992)(Order Code IB91102).

381.   *Ibid.*

382.   *See, e.g.,* Bodi, *supra* note 348 at 456.

383.   16 U.S.C. § 1(a).

384.   *Ibid.* § 791a et seq.

385.   *Ibid.* § 797a.

386.   Bodi, *supra* note 348 at 451.

387.   *Ibid.* at 452.

388.   16 U.S.C. § 799.

389.   16 U.S.C. § 808(a).

390.   FERC, Office of Hydropower Licensing, *Evaluating Relicense Proposals at the Federal Energy Regulatory Commission,* Paper No. DPR-2 (April 1991).

391.   16 U.S.C. §§ 797(e), 803(a), 803(j)(1).

392.   *See* "The Elwha River Ecosystem and Fisheries Restoration Act," H.R. 4844, 102d Cong. 2d Sess (1992)(reported out of committee in late September, 1992).

393.   *See e.g. National Wildlife Federation v. FERC,* 912 F.2d 1471, 1481 (D.C. Cir. 1990) (concluding that decision which rejected fish agency's recommendation was supported by substantial evidence, and that decision need not give "equal weight," only equal "consideration" to environmental values).

394.   *Ibid.*

395.   16 U.S.C. §§ 839-839(h).

396.   *Ibid.* 839b(h)(1)(A).

397.   *Ibid.* § 839(b)(h)(1)(A), (h)(10(A), (H)(6)(E)(i)-(ii).

398.   Blumm & Simrin, *Unraveling of the Parity Promise,* at 667 n. 41 citing H.R. Rep. No. 976, 96th Cong., 2d Sess. 49, reprinted in 1980 Cong. & Admin. News 5989, 6015.

399.   16 U.S.C. § 839b(h)(6)(C).

400.   *Ibid.* § 839b(h)(6)(A).

401.   NWPPC, Protected Areas Amendments and Response to Comments (1988).

402.   Middleton, R., *Fish Habitat Destruction in the Columbia River Basin,* Wana Chinook Tymoo, 5 (Columbia River Inter-Tribal Fish Commission, Issue Two, 1992) (citing the Scientific Panel on Late-Successional Forest

Ecosystems, Alternatives for Management of Late-Successional Forests of the Pacific Northwest).

403.   *Ibid.* (citing Dr. Gordon Reeves, USFS fish biologist).

404.   *Ibid.* (citing Don Chapman, fisheries consultant).

405.   Blumm, *Parity Promise, supra* note 398 at 727.

406.   This summary is based on Blumm & Simrin.

407.   *Supra* note 398

408.   *Ibid.*

409.   *Supra* note 396 at 729.

410.   *Ibid.*

411.   30 U.S.C. §§ 22-54.

412.   *Ibid.*

413.   Mineral Leasing Act of 1920, 30 U.S.C. §§ 181-287.

414.   Coggins, G., and C. Wilkinson, Federal Public Land and Resources Law 503-04 (2d ed. 1987). Uranium is an energy fuel but it remains open for location under the 1872 Hardrock Act. *See* 1 The American Law of Mining, §§ 4.15-.19 (2d ed. 1985); *see also*, Comment, *Ground and Surface Water in New Mexico: Are they Protected Against Uranium Mining and Milling?*, 18 Nat. Res. J. 941 (1978).

415.   Under the Mineral Lands Leasing Act, "Lands . . . may be leased by the Secretary." 30 U.S.C. § 226(a).

416.   *Ibid.* §§ 181, 226(a).

417.   16 U.S.C. § 3148, 30 U.S.C. §§ 187a-b, 188, 195, 199, 226, 226-3.

418.   30 U.S.C. § 226(h).

419.   *Ibid.* § 226(g). *See generally* Sansonetti, T., and W. Murray, *A Primer on the Federal Onshore Oil and Gas Leasing Reform Act of 1987 and Its Regulations*, 25 Land and Water L. Rev. 375 (1990).

420.   30 U.S.C. §§ 601-02.

421.   *Ibid.* § 611. Such common varieties of minerals can be sold unless the deposit "has some property giving it distinct and special value." *Ibid.* § 601.

422.   *Ibid.* §§ 351-59. Federally acquired lands make up about 8 % of all federal lands. Coggins and Wilkinson, *supra* note 412 at 421.

423.   *Ibid.* §§ 1001-25. Developing geothermal resources is actually more akin to building hydroelectric generators than it is to mineral or fuel extraction. However, the requirements and procedures contained in the Geothermal Steam Act are similar to those contained in the 1920

Leasing Act. *See generally*, Olpin and Tarlock, *Water That Is Not Water*, 13 Land & Water L.Rev. 391 (1978).

424. *Ibid.* Wilkinson and Anderson, *Land and Resource Planning in the National Forests*, 64 Or. L. Rev. 1, 259 (1985), U.S. Dep't of Agriculture, Forest Service, Minerals Program Handbook § 1.33 (1981).

425. 30 U.S.C. §§ 201 *et seq.*

426. *Ibid.* §§ 1201-1328.

427. *Ibid.* § 1202(a).

428. *See* 30 CFR §§ 700-707, 730-845 (1985). *See also* Kite, *The Surface Mining Control and Reclamation Act of 1977: An Overview of Reclamation Requirements and Implementation*, 13 Land & Water L.Rev. 703 (1978).

429. 30 U.S.C. § 1272.

430. *Ibid.* § 1272(e)(1).

431. *Ibid.* § 1272(e)(2).

432. *Ibid.* § 1281.

433. *Ibid.* § 1272(a)(3).

434. *Utah Int'l v. Department of the Interior*, 553 F. Supp. 872, 882 (D. Utah 1982).

435. 42 U.S.C. §§ 4321-4370.

436. FLPMA also introduced the requirements that all old claims as well as new locations must be recorded with BLM, or they will "conclusively" be deemed abandoned. 43 U.S.C. § 1744(c).

437. Act of June 4, 1897, ch. 2, 30 Stat. 35 (codified at 16 U.S.C. §§ 477, 478 (1978)).

438. 30 U.S.C. § 352.

439. *Ibid.* § 601.

440. *Supra* note 424, 64 Or. L.Rev. at 251-53.

441. 16 U.S.C. §§ 528-531.

442. *Ibid.* § 531(a).

443. 36 C.F.R. Part 228. These regulations were ultimately upheld: "While prospecting, locating, and developing of mineral resources in the national forests may not be prohibited nor so unreasonably circumscribed as to amount to a prohibition, the Secretary may adopt reasonable rules and regulations which do not impermissibly encroach upon the right to the use and enjoyment of placer claims for mining purposes." *United States v. Weiss*, 642 F.2d 296, (9th Cir. 1981).

444.   *See, e.g.*, 43 C.F.R. § 3111 (oil and gas). The BLM promulgated its mining regulations in November 1980; These generally coincide with the Forest Service regulations. *See* 43 CFR Part 3800 (1985). The Fish and Wildlife Service proposed regulations in December of 1980 governing the impacts of mining within wildlife refuges, but final rules were never promulgated. *See* 45 Fed. Reg. 86,512 (1980).

445.   Wilkinson and Anderson, *supra* note 422, 64 Or. L. Rev. at 269, citing Forest Service Manual § 2860.2 (1984).

446.   *Ibid.*, citing Forest Service Manual §§ 2822.21, 2860.3 (1984).

447.   30 U.S.C. § 1272(e). *See also* 43 Fed. Reg 57,662 (1978) (unsuitability criteria adopted under FLPMA.)

448.   *See Udall v. Tallman*, 380 U.S. 1 (1965) (lands within National Wildlife Refuge System); *see also Duesing v. Udall*, 350 F.2d 748 (D.C.Cir. 1965); *Rosita Trujillo*, 21 IBLA 289 (1975) (land under study for possible inclusion in the Wild and Scenic Rivers System).

449.   16 U.S.C. § 1604(f)(1), (2).

450.   *Ibid.* § 1604(g)(2)(a), (c).

451.   *Ibid.* § 1607(b).

452.   30 C.F.R. §§ 219.1(b)(2), 219.22.

453.   *Supra* note 424, at 267.

454.   *Ibid.* at 272.

455.   Hocker, *D.C. Dallies*, Clementine, Winter 1992, at 404-11.

456.   *See* Barnhill, *Role of Local Government in Mineral Development*, 28 Rocky Mtn. Min. L. Inst. 2121 (1983); Note, *State and Local Control of Energy Development on Federal Lands*, 32 Stan. L.Rev. 373 (1980).

457.   These eight states are: California, Colorado, Idaho, Montana, Oregon, Utah, Washington, and Wyoming.

458.   General Accounting Office (GAO), Report on Federal Land Management: An Assessment of Hardrock Mining Damage 16 (April 1988). (hereinafter "GAO" Report)

459.   Arizona, Nevada, and New Mexico.

460.   GAO Report, *Supra* note 458 at 16.

461.   *See, e.g.*, Schwartz, *Community Action on Mining: East-to-West*, Clementine (Winter 1991), 15, citing examples from the following communities: Haines, Alaska (area residents and city and borough governments fighting waste water discharge permit for underground gold mine); Warren, Maine (citizens' organization working to establish local

land ordinances to prevent degradation of ground and surface water quality from metals mining); Santa Fe, New Mexico (citizen groups working to stop the development of a cyanide heap-leach gold mine); and Ladysmith, Wisconsin (construction on open-pit metals mine halted after law suit filed by Lac Court Oreilles Chippewa tribe and the Sierra Club).

462.   Arizona, California, Colorado, Idaho, Montana, Nevada, New Mexico, Oregon, Utah, Washington, and Wyoming.

463.   GAO Report, *Supra* note 458 at 2.

464.   *Ibid.* at 12.

465.   *Ibid.*

466.   42 U.S.C. §§ 9601-9675, as amended by Superfund Amendments and Reauthorization Act of 1986 (SARA), Pub. L. No. 99-499, 100 Stat. 1613 (1986).

467.   *Mines of Poison*, Clementine, Autumn 1988, at 11.

468.   *Ibid.*

469.   *See* Durbin, K., *Closed Smelter Complex Poses Cleanup Challenge*, The (Portland) Oregonian, April 6, 1992, at A1, A10; K. Durbin, *Tribe Sues Mining Companies over Cleanup of Wastes*, The (Portland) Oregonian, April 7, 1992, at B1, B4.

470.   Leshy, J., 1987. The Mining Law of 1872: A Study in Perpetual Motion 188.

471.   In contrast, all US non-mining industries combined generate less than 300 million tons of hazardous waste annually. *Mines of Poison*, Clementine, Autumn 1988, at 11.

472.   *Ibid.*

473.   *Ibid.*

474.   *See* Leshy, J., The Mining Law of 1872: A Study in Perpetual Motion (1987); Anderson, *Federal Mineral Policy: The General Mining Law of 1872*, 16 Nat.Res.J. 601 (1976); Hagenstein, *Changing An Anachronism: Congress and the General Mining Law of 1872*, 13 Nat.Res.J. 480 (1973); Senzel, Revision of the Mining Act of 1872, (Study for the Senate Comm. on Energy and Nat. Res., 95th Cong., 1st Sess.) (1977).

475.   *Mines of Poison*, Clementine, Autumn 1988, at 11.

476.   For example, the Superfund site on the Clark Fork River in western Montana stems from copper mining and smelting which the Anaconda Company began in the 1880s. *See* Toole, K.R., Montana, An Uncommon Land 169 (1959).

477.   Hocker, *supra* note 455 at 12.

478.   *See, e.g.*, Entickap and Kirch, *Report from Windy Cragg*, Clementine, Winter 1991, at 4 (dangers to the Tatshenshini and Alsek rivers from a huge proposed copper mine in northwestern Canada).

479.   *See* Kriz, M., *Hard Rock Realities*, 23 National Journal 1744-47 (July 13, 1991).

480.   In 1977, Morris K. Udall, D-Ariz., was forced to abandon his attempts to reform the 1872 Act when miners in his state initiated a campaign to recall him from office. In 1988, Sen. John Melcher, D-Mont., lost his bid for reelection due to bitter opposition by miners and other supporters of resource development. *Ibid.* at 1746. The power of the mining lobby in the West is not limited to national campaigns, however. It has been a major force influencing governments in certain western states for a long time. *See, e.g.*, K. R. Toole, *supra* note 468, at 244-45, 249 (regarding the control exercised by the Anaconda Company in Montana). *See also* Mullon, *State of Utah vs. Kennecott Corporation: Snuggling with the Enemy*, Clementine, Winter 1991, at 7-11 (regarding unfair settlement in CERCLA suit).

481.   *See* Wilkinson and Anderson, *supra* note 424, at 267.

482.   *Ibid.* at 272.

483.   Hocker, *supra* note 455 at 404-11 (discussing the need for better mineral planning and new leasing structure).

484.   Salvesen, 1990, *supra* note 247 at p. 43. Cited in Steiner, Pieart & Cook, *supra* note 242 at 18.

485.   Griffin, C., *Protection of Wildlife Habitat by State Wetland Regulations: The Massachusetts Initiative*, Transactions of the 54th North American Wildlife and Natural Resources Conference 22-31 (1989), cited in Steiner, Pieart & Cook, *supra* note 242 at 25.

486.   Kusler, J., *A Call for Action: Protection of Riparian Habitat in the Arid and Semi Arid West* in Johnson, R.R., C.D. Ziebell, D.R. Patton, P.F. Fjollion, and R.N. Hamre, eds. Riparian Ecosystems and their Management: Reconciling Their Uses 6 (1985) (published by the U.S. Forest Service, Tuscon, Arizona), cited in Steiner, Pieart & Cook, *supra* note 238 at 18.

487.   Or. Rev. Stat. § 308.792-803 (property tax exemption for designated riparian lands); *see also* Or. Rev. Stat. Sec. 316.084 (25% income tax credit for fish habitat improvement).

488. Washington State Laws Ch. 90.58.030(1)(d)(definition of shorelines of the state).

489. Steiner, Pieart & Cook, *supra* note 242 at 18. According to Griffin, *supra* note 485, as of 1989 only 13 states nationwide had comprehensive inland wetland protection laws.

490. Wyo. Stat. §§ 35-11-308 to -311.

491. Steiner, Pieart & Cook, *supra* note 242 at 22.

492. *Ibid.*

493. 43 U.S.C. § 383 (1988).

494. *See e.g. California v. United States*, 438 U.S. 645 (1978).

495. 33 U.S.C. § 1251(g).

496. Opinion of the Solicitor, Department of Interior, M-38914 (Supp. 1), "Non-Reserved Water Rights - United States Compliance with State Law," (September 11, 1981)(Codiron Opinion).

497. 43 U.S.C. § 666.

498. For a discussion of the problems inherent to the riparian system, *see* Sherk, 1990. *Eastern Water Law: Trends in State Legislation*, 9 Virginia Env. L. J. 287. (reviewing existing water allocation law and proposed legislation in the eastern states).

499. 207 U.S. 564 (1908).

500. *United States v. New Mexico*, 438 U.S. 696 (1978).

501. *Cappaert v. United States*, 426 U.S. 128 (1976) (finding implied reservation to protect desert pupfish which justified denial of water right application to drain aquifer).

502. Federal Water Rights of the National Park Service, Fish and Wildlife Service, Reserve, Bureau of Reclamation and Bureau of Land Management, 86 ID 553 (1979).

503. Opinion of the Attorney General (July, 1988).

504. *Sierra Club v. Block*, 622 F. Supp. 842 (D. Colo. 1985), *rev'd on other grounds sub. nom, Sierra Club v. Yeutter*, 911 F. 2d 1405 (10th Cir. 1990) (dismissed for lack of ripeness).

505. *Sierra Club v. Watt*, 659 F.2d 203 (D.C.Cir. 1982)(finding no federal water rights reserved under FLPMA).

506. 426 U.S. 128 (1976)

507. *United States v. New Mexico*, 438 U.S. 696 (1978) (holding that the general preservation purpose of the USFS Organic Act is merely a restatement of the timber and watershed purposes).

508.   *See e.g. Sierra Club v. Andrus*, 487 F. Supp. 443 (D.D.C. 1980), *aff'd on other grounds, sub. nom.* Sierra Club v. Watt, 659 F.2d 203 (D.C.Cir. 1981)(finding no agency duty to assert a federal reserved right).

509.   Blumm, *Reserved Water Rights* in 4 Water and Water Rights 256 (R.Beck ed., 1991). Though federal agencies are apparently becoming more assertive of implied rights, the governments duty to do so is still unclear. *Ibid.*

510.   16 U.S.C. § 528.

511.   *Ibid.* § 1604(g)(E)(iii).

512.   *Ibid.* §§ 473-482 (partially repealed 1976).

513.   *Ibid.* § 475 (emphasis added).

514.   16 U.S.C. § 472.

515.   Coggins, 1991. *Watershed as a Public Natural Resource*, 11 Va. Env. L.J. 1, 5.

516.   744 P.2d 491 (Colorado 1987).

517.   The Supreme Court affirmed the Forest Service's authority to manage for nonstatutory uses early in the century. *Light v. United States*, 220 U.S. 523 (1911).

518.   16 U.S.C. §§ 528-531 (1982).

519.   *Ibid.* § 528. The definition did not include minerals because, at the time, the BLM was the sole manager of this resource.

520.   H.R. Rep. No. 1551, 86th Cong., 2d Sess. 4 *reprinted in* 1960 U.S. Code Cong. & Admin. News 2377, 2379 *cited* in Coggins, G., Public Natural Resources Law, at 16-4, n. 38 (1992); *see* discussion and critique of multiple use/sustained yield policy as applied, in Part II.C, *infra* notes 720-752).

521.   16 U.S.C. § 528.

522.   One Third of the Nation's Land: A Report to the President and to the Congress by the Public Land Law Review Commission 45 (Washington D.C.: Government Printing Office, 1970).

523.   42 U.S.C. §§ 4321-4370 (1982 & Supp. III 1985).

524.   *Ibid.* § 4321.

525.   To date, EISs are rarely prepared for specific projects. The following cases discuss the level of planning at which NEPA compliance must be demonstrated: *Thomas v. Peterson*, 753 F.2d 754 (9th Cir. 1985); *National Wildlife Fed'n v. United States Forest Service*, 592 F. Supp. 931 (D. Or. 1984); *appeal dismissed as moot*, 801 F.2d 360 (9th Cir. 1986). *Cf.*

California v. Block, 690 F.2d 753 (9th Cir. 1982); *National Wildlife Federation v. Coston*, 773 F.2d 1513 (9th Cir. 1985).
526.   *Thomas v. Peterson*, 753 F.2d. 754 (9th Cir. 1985); *Northwest Indian Cemetery Association v. Peterson*, 795 F.2d 699 (9th Cir. 1986); *rev'd on other grounds*, 485 U.S. 439 (1988); *Sierra Club v. United States Forest Serv.*, 843 F.2d 1190 (9th Cir. 1988); *Save the Yaak Comm. v. Block*, 840 F.2d 714 (9th Cir. 1988).
527.   16 U.S.C. §§ 1600-1614.
528.   16 U.S.C. §§ 1600-1616 (1982).
529.   Coggins, G., 1990. *The Developing Law of Land Use Planning on the Federal Lands*, 61 U. Colo. L. Rev. 307, 335.
530.   16 U.S.C. § 1604(g)(E) (emphasis added).
531.   Coggins, *Developing Law, Supra* note 529 at 335.
532.   *See id.* at 340-44 for summary of specific NFMA harvest provisions.
533.   16 U.S.C. § 1601(a)(1988).
534.   *Ibid.* § 1602.
535.   *Ibid.* § 1606(c).
536.   *Ibid.* § 1606(a) & (c).
537.   Coggins, *Developing Law, supra* note 529 at 337.
538.   36 C.F.R. § 219.4(a) (1989).
539.   16 U.S.C. § 1603.
540.   *Ibid.*   The NFMA mandate for replanning in the event that conditions change may be compared to a similar situation under NEPA. Although the statutory language of NEPA does not specifically require a supplemental EIS whenever conditions change, such a requirement is implied. Thus, the regulations of most agencies specifically provide for such an occurrence. *See, e.g., Marsh v. Oregon Natural Resources Council*, 490 U.S. 360, 370-71 (1989) (requiring the Army Corps of Engineers to follow its regulations requiring that a supplemental EIS be completed upon the introduction of significant new information). *See also Seattle Audubon Society v. Evans*, 952 F.2d 297, 303 (9th Cir. 1991) (allowing Portland Audubon Society to amend complaint to challenge BLM's decision to proceed with logging without first preparing a supplemental EIS addressing new information on the spotted owl).
541.   *Ibid.* § 1604.
542.   *Ibid.*

543.   *Ibid.* § 1604(g)(E) (emphasis added).

544.   *Ibid.* § 1604(g)(3)(B).

545.   *Ibid.* § 1604(k).

546.   Arjo, 1990. *Watershed and Water Quality Protection in National Forest Management*, 41 Hastings L.J. 1111, 1121 citing 122 Cong. Rec. S33,838 (Sept. 30, 1976) (statement of Senator Randolph).

547.   *Ibid.* at 1321, citing Behan, *Political Popularity and Conceptual Nonsense: The Strange Case of Sustained-Yield Forestry*, 8 Envt'l L. J. 309, 338 (1978) (ultimately concluding that "enforceable standards" are not desirable from Behan's point of view).

548.   *Ibid.* § 1604(g).

549.   *Ibid.*

550.   36 C.F.R. §§ 219.18., 219.19, 219.21, 219.22, 219.24, 219.25, 219.26.

551.   *Ibid.* § 219.1. We note that the Forest Service will be accorded wide discretion in determining "net public benefits" under MUSYA principles. *See, e.g.,* Burgess, *Standards for Judicial Review of Forest Plans: Will the Courts not See the Forest for the Trees?* in The Public Lands During the Remainder of the 20th Century (U.Colo. School of Law, 1987).

552.   522 F.2d 945 (4th Cir. 1975) (the *"Monongahela"* case) (finding that language in the Organic Act which limits harvesting to mature trees and requires marking before cutting also precludes clearcutting); *see also Zieske v. Butz*, 406 F. Supp. 258, 259 (D. Alaska, 1975)(following *Monongahela* holding).

553.   *See, e.g.,* 16 U.S.C. § 1600(3) & (5), 1601(d)(1), 1602, 1604(e)(1), 1604(g), 1604(g)(3)(A), 1607, 1611(a) (1988).

554.   36 C.F.R. § 219.27(e).

555.   *Ibid.* § 219.27(f).

556.   16 U.S.C. § 1604(g)(3)(E)(iii)

557.   36 C.F.R. § 219.27(e).

558.   16 U.S.C. § 1604(3)(E)(iii); 36 C.F.R. § 219.19, requires that management plans provide adequate fish and wildlife habitat to maintain viable populations of existing vertebrate species..." *See* (Seattle Audubon Society v. Evans, 9th Cir. 1991, discussing requirements of minimum viable population regulation.)

559.   *See* Anderson, 1987. *Water Quality Planning in the National Forests,* 17 Envt'l Law 591, 632-639 (discussing debates over the draft forest plans in Idaho).

560.   Wilderness Society, 19xx. National Forests: Policies for the Future, Volume I/"Water Quality and Timber Management" 9.
561.   *Ibid*; FSM 2526.03; 2630.2, 2634.02.
562.   *Ibid*. at 638 & n. 203 (1987).
563.   *Ibid*.
564.   "Demand Letter" from the Sierra Club Legal Defense Fund representing the Oregon Rivers Council, the Wilderness Society, et al, to Ron Stewart, USFS Regional Forester, Region 5, John Butruille, USFS Regional Forester, Region 6, and Regional Foresters for Regions 1 and 4, April 2, 1992. (Challenge also based on agency's failure to manage fish and wildlife habitat for maintenance of minimum viable populations throughout the national forests.)
565.   36 C.F.R. § 219.14((a)(2).
566.   *Citizens for Environmental Quality v. United States,* 731 F. Supp. 970 (D. Colo. 1989) (upholding regulations but remanding for identification of available technology)(GET CASE).
567.   Wilderness Society, 1988. National Forests Policies for the Future, Volume I/"Water Quality and Timber Management" 7.
568.   FSM 2412.14.
569.   *Supra* note 567
570.   36 C.F.R. § 219.13
571.   *Ibid*. at 646.
572.   *Ibid*. §§ 219.14-26.
573.   Because these standards were not developed pursuant to a formal rulemaking procedures, their legal effect has been questioned. *See* O'Riordan & Horngren, 1987. *The Minimum Management Requirements of Forest Planning,* 17 Envt'l L. 643 (arguing that, as implemented through MMRs the forest planning process violates the rulemaking requirements of the NFMA).
574.   36 C.F.R. § 219.27(e).
575.   O'Riordan & Horngren, *supra* note 573 at 647.
576.   FSM, 2526.05, Definitions, Riparian Areas.
577.   FSM 2526.02.
578.   FSM 2526.03.
579.   EPA, Riparian Policy, at 9 (1991).
580.   *United States v. Fifty-Three Eclectus Parrots,* 685 F.2d 1131, 1136 (9th Cir 1982) (holding that "general statements of policy" contained in agency

manuals are not enforceable against the agency); *Lumber Prod. & Indus. Workers Log Scalers v. United States*, 580 F. Supp. 279 (D. Or. 1984).

581.   592 F. Supp. 931 (D. Or 1984), *appeal dismissed as moot*, 801 F.2d 360 (9th Cir. 1987)

582.   764 F. 2d 581 (9th Cir. 1985), *rev'd in part sub. nom. Lyng v. Northwest Indian Cemetery Protective Ass'n*, 485 U.S. 439 (1988) (dealing only with Indian religious freedom, EIS and water pollution holding below intact).

583.   592 F. Supp. 931 (D. Or 1984) (the *"Mapleton Case"*), *appeal dismissed as moot*, 801 F.2d 360 (9th Cir. 1987).

584.   *National Wildlife*, 592 F. Supp at 936.

585.   Arjo, *Watershed and Water Quality Protection in National Forest Management*, 41 Hastings L. J. 1111, 1123, n. 102 (1990).

586.   *National Wildlife*, 592 F. Supp. at 940.

587.   565 F. Supp. 586 (N.D. Cal. 1983), *affirmed in part, vacated in part*, 764 F. 2d 581 (9th Cir. 1985), *revised in part sub. nom. Lyng v. Northwest Indian Cemetery Protective Ass'n*, 485 U.S. 439 (1988).

588.   *Ibid.* at 606.

589.   764 F.2d at 585-88.

590.   *See also* discussion of the Clean Water Act's requirements, *infra* notes 152-285 and accompanying text.

591.   764 F.2d at 588-89.

592.   *Ibid.* at 589; *see also Oregon Natural Resources Defense Council v. U.S. Forest Service*, 834 F.2d 842 (9th Cir. 1987) (recognizing citizens' action under Administrative Procedures Act for non-point violation of state water quality standards).

593.   731 F. Supp. 970 (D. Colo. 1989).

594.   For a more complete discussion of the case's other aspects, *see* Coggins, Public Natural Resources Law, 13-47 to 13-50.

595.   36 C.F.R. § 219.14(a)(2) (1987). This regulation modifies the NFMA requirement that timber be harvested only where "soil, slope, or watershed conditions will not be irreversibly damaged." 16 U.S.C. § 1604(g)(3)(E)(i) (1988).

596.   *Rio Grande, supra* note 593 at 984-85.

597.   *Ibid.* at 985-86.

598.   *Ibid.* at 992. The court held that because the agency's good faith is assumed, plaintiffs must exhaust administrative remedies on any claims arising after a plan is completed. *Ibid.*

599.   USEPA Region 10, Nonpoint Sources Section, Riparian Policy: Summary and Analysis 8 (February 1991).

600.   EPA, Riparian Policy, at 11.

601.   *Ibid.* at 8.

602.   Tongass Timber Reform Act of 1990 (PL 101-626).

603.   Pub. L. No. 96-487, 94 Stat. 2371 (codified in 16 U.S.C. §§ 3101 et seq., and in scattered sections of 10 U.S.C., 16 U.S.C., and 43 U.S.C.).

604.   EPA, Riparian Policy at 9.

605.   National Marine Fisheries Service revised Policy for Riparian Habitat Protection in Alaska (May 3, 1988) (cited in Southeast Alaska Conservation Council, Defending the Promise Of Tongass Reform, 14 March 1992).

606.   *Ibid.* at 15.

607.   *Ibid.* at 8; Or. Rev. Stat. §§ 527.610-.770, .990(1), .992 (1991).

608.   *See, e.g.*, 33 U.S.C. § 1288(b)(2)(F) (1986) (requiring the agency to identify agriculturally and silviculturally related nonpoint sources of pollution and set forth procedures "to control to the extent feasible such sources"). *See also* Whitman, 1989. *Clean Water or Multiple Use? Best Management Practices for Water Quality Control in the National Forests*, 16 Ecology L. Q. 909, 910.

609.   *See* discussion of mining law *infra*, notes 411-483 and accompanying text.

610.   Organic Act, 16 U.S.C. § 475, MUSYA, 16 U.S.C. §§ 528-531.

611.   16 U.S.C. §1604(g)(3)(E)(iii).

612.   *See* discussion of riparian-related regulations *infra* notes 542-563 and accompanying text.

613.   36 C.F.R. 219.27(e).   The Forest Service manual's broader definition of riparian areas does not constitute a binding regulation, nor is it universally applied in forest planning.

614.   36 C.F.R. § 219.27(e).

615.   Franklin, J., J. Gordon, K. Norman Johnson, J.W. Thomas, Alternatives for Management of Late-Successional Forests of the Pacific Northwest: A Report to the Agriculture Committee and the Merchant Marine and Fisheries Committee of the U.S. House of Representatives; October 8, 1991.

616.   36 C.F.R. §§ 219.19, 219.27(a)(6).

617.   *See* Anderson, *Water Quality Planning in the National Forests*, 17 Envt'l Law 591, 632-639 (1987) (discussing debates over the draft forest plans in Idaho).

618.   16 U.S.C. § 1604(k).

619.   36 C.F.R. 219.14(a)(2).

620.   FSM 2412.14.

621.   Wilderness Society, 1988. National Forests: Policies for the Future, Volume I/"Water Quality and Timber Management" 7.

622.   *Ibid.* at 9 citing USFS 1987 Policy Statement

623.   *Ibid* at 591

624.   U.S. Department of the Interior, BLM, "Riparian-Wetland Initiative for the 1990's," 1 (September 1990).

625.   *Ibid.* at 23.

626.   Coggins, *Watershed, supra* note 515 at 21.

627.   43 U.S.C. §§ 1701-1784 (1982).

628.   *Ibid.* § 1732 (a).   Despite the open-endedness of the FLPMA planning mandate, the enactment of FLPMA, combined with legal developments immediately preceding it, dramatically altered the prior legal and political context for BLM decisionmaking. *See Natural Resources Defense Council v. Morton*, 388 F.Supp. 829 (D.D.C. 1974) (requiring the BLM to produce EISs under NEPA with which to document the effects of present and proposed grazing on specific areas of the BLM public lands, causing subsequent BLM decisions to undergo an unprecedented degree of public scrutiny).

629.   Coggins, *The Developing Law of Land Use Planning on the Federal Lands*, 61 U. Colo. L. Rev. 307, 317 (1990) (hereinafter cited as *Developing Law.*)

630.   43 U.S.C. § 1712(c).

631.   *Ibid.* § 1711(1).

632.   *Ibid.* § 1712(c)(3).

633.   *Ibid.* § 1712(c)(8).

634.   *Ibid.* § 1732(b).

635.   Coggins, *Developing Law, supra* note 629 at 323.   For a summary of substantive judicial review of BLM plans *see id.* at 326-333 and cases cited therein. *See also, California Wilderness Coalition*, 101 IBLA 18 (1988) (deferring to agency judgment);*Sierra Club v. Clark*, 756 F.2d 686 (9th Cir.

1985) (BLM area plan provision allowing off-road vehicle (ORV) use did not violate BLM regulations, FLPMA, MUSYA principles or CEQ guidelines because BLM decision was "not unreasonable" and within BLM discretion to decide when ORV use is "appropriate"); *Sierra Club v. Clark*, 774 F.2d 1406 (9th Cir. 1985) (BLM amendment to area plan allowing ORV race held not to contravene BLM policy or FLPMA, effectively giving BLM sole discretion in determining where ORV use is appropriate); *Natural Resources Defense Council, Inc. v. Hodel*, 624 F. Supp. 1045 (D. Nev. 1986), *aff'd*, 819 F.2d 927 (9th Cir. 1987) (pre-FLPMA grazing plan upheld); *cf. Headwaters, Inc. v. BLM*, 684 F. Supp. 1053 (D. Or. 1988) (upholding a BLM decision to engage in extensive timber activity, but only after finding that the decision was derived from a plan which fully considered all potential uses for and values of the area).

636.   43 U.S.C. § 1732(a); Coggins, *Developing Law, supra* note 629 at 323.   Tracts which are dedicated to specific uses under other laws are excepted as being governed by such other applicable law.

637.   *Ibid.* § 1712(e)(1).

638.   *Ibid.* § 1712(e)(2).

639.   *Ibid.* § 1712(e)(3).

640.   *See, e.g. California Wilderness Coalition*, 101 IBLA 18, 29 (1988); *Wilderness Society*, 90 IBLA 221 (1986).

641.   *See, e.g., National Wildlife Federation v. Burford*, 835 F.2d 305, 322-23 (D.C.Cir. 1987).

642.   43 U.S.C. §§ 1712 (a) & (f).

643.   *Ibid.* § 1712 (c)(2).

644.   Coggins, *Developing Law, supra* note 629 at 320; The BLM employs fewer resource specialists and experts than do the other federal agencies. *Ibid.* at 320, n. 120.

645.   *Ibid.* at 320; 43 C.F.R. §§ 1601.0-1601.8 (BLM planning regulations).

646.   *Ibid.* at 321.

647.   43 C.F.R. §1601.0-6 (1986).

648.   Williams, Public Land Management: Planning, Problems and Opportunities, in Public Lands During the Remainder of the 20th Century (Univ. Colo. L. School Natural Resources Law Center, 1987); Williams, 1987. *Planning Approaches in the Bureau of Land Management*, Trends No. 2, 17.

649.   Coggins, *Developing Law, supra* note 629 at 320.

650.   On sample planning procedures see: *National Resources Defence Council v. Hodel*, 624 F. Supp. 1045 (D. Nev. 1986), *aff'd*, 819 F.2d 927 (9th Cir 1987) (BLM grazing planning in some districts); *National Wildlife Fed'n v. Burford*, 677 F. Supp. 1445 (D. Mont. 1985) (BLM coal lease planning).

651.   43 U.S.C. § 1702 (a). The statutory definition of ACE is repeated in the BLM planning regulations at 43 C.F.R. § 1601.0-5(a). Congressional intent to cease and reverse damage to ACECs is also manifested in several other provisions of the FLPMA. *See, e.g.,* 43 U.S.C. S§ 1711(a) (mandatory inventories of lands and resources to give priority to ACECs); 1712(c)(3) (land use plans to prioritize ACECs); 1701(a)(11) (declaration that regulations and plans for ACECs be promptly developed).

652.   Braun, 1986. *Emerging Limits on Federal Land Management Discretion: Livestock, Riparian Ecosystems and Clean Water Law*, 17 Envtl L. 43, 60, n. 54.

653.   *See Sierra Club v. Hardin*, 325 F. Supp. 99, 123, 123 n. 48 (D. Alaska 1971), *rev'd unreported sub. nom. Sierra Club v. Butz*, 3 Envt'l L. Rep. (Envt'l L. Inst.) 20292 (9th Cir 1973); BLM, Areas of Critical Environmental Concern -- Policy and Procedures (1980).

654.   43 U.S.C. § 1751(b)(1).

655.   *Ibid.* FLPMA's intent that the BLM act to restore degraded riparian ecosystems was reinforced two years later with enactment of the Public Rangeland Improvement Act of 1978 (PRIA), discussed below.

656.   43 C.F.R. § 4130.6-3(a)(1984). Because these regulations contradict prior policy and were arguably promulgated outside agency authority, they were attacked in *National Resources Defense Council, Inc. v. Hodel*, 618 F. Supp. 848, 875 (E.D. Cal. 1985) (striking down numerous cooperative management agreement program regulations because the agency violated its duties under the Taylor Grazing Act, FLPMA, PRIA, and NEPA).

657.   43 U.S.C. § 1712(c)(8).

658.   Pursuant to the Supreme Court's decision in *California Coastal Commission v. Granite Rock Co.*, 480 U.S. 572 (1987), states may impose all types of "environmental" regulations (not "land use" regulations) on any federal land activity.

659.   *Northwest Indian Cemetery Protection Ass'n v. Peterson*, 764 F.2d 581 (9th Cir. 1985).

660.   43 C.F.R. §1725.3.

661.   *Ibid.* § 1725.3-3(a).

662.   *Ibid.* § 1725.3-3(g).

663.   *Ibid.* 43 C.F.R. § 1725.3-3(b).

664.   *Ibid.* § 1725.3-3(h).

665.   *Ibid.* BLM, Public Land Statistics (1990).

666.   43 U.S.C. §§ 1181a-1181j.

667.   *Ibid.* § 1181a.

668.   *Ibid.*

669.   *See e.g.* Durbin, K., *BLM will try turning over a new leaf to save old growth*, The Oregonian C1 (Sept. 27, 1992).

670.   These are the Salem, Eugene, Coos Bay, Roseburg and Medford BLM Districts and the Klamath Falls Resource area of the Lakeview District.

671.   Durbin, *supra* note 669 at C1.

672.   U.S. Department of the Interior, Bureau of Land Management, August 1992. Executive Summary: Wester Oregon Draft Resource Management Plans/Environmental Impact Statements.

673.   BLM, "Riparian-Wetland Initiative," at 3.

674.   *See generally* BLM, "Riparian-Wetland Initiative for the 1990s," (September 1990).

675.   Burford, Robert J., BLM Director, "Riparian Management Policy," (January 22, 1987). This policy was adopted in response to a suggestion by the Public Lands Advisory Council after discussions about riparian management arose from the Omnibus Range Bill of 1984. The policy statement was developed with input from BLM field offices, other federal agencies and interested groups. EPA Region 10, Riparian Policy 12 (February 1991).

676.   "Riparian Initiative," *supra* note 673 at 1.

677.   *Ibid.* at 11.

678.   EPA Region 10, Riparian Policy at 14.

679.   *Ibid.* at 14.

680.   *Light v. United States*, 200 U.S. 523 (1911); *United States v. Grimaud*, 220 U.S. 506 (1911).

681.   General Accounting Office (GAO), June 1988. Public Rangelands: Some Riparian Areas Restored, but Widespread Improvement Will be Slow.

682.   BLM, Public Land Statistics, 1990.

683.   GAO, Public Rangelands, *supra* note 681 at 13.

684.   *Ibid.* at 13.

685.   43 U.S.C. §§ 1901-1908 (1982).

412   *Entering the Watershed*

686.   *Ibid.* §§ 1701-1784 (1982).
687.   16 U.S.C. §§ 1600-1614.
688.   Department of the Interior, Bureau of Land Management, 1990. Public Land Statistics 22-23. An AUM is usually defined as the amount of forage needed to support a 1,000 pound cow or five sheep for one month, which is generally considered to range between 800 and 1000 pounds of forage. GAO, Public Rangelands at 12; *cf.* 43 C.F.R. § 4100.5 (AUM is "the amount of forage consumption necessary for the sustenance of one cow or its equivalent for one month").
689.   *Ibid.*
690.   The current Forest Service grazing regulations are contained in 36 C.F.R. 222 -- Range Management, Subpart A, Grazing and Livestock Use. These regulations provide for the issuance of grazing permits pursuant to "allotment management plans." Allotment management plans set forth the conditions pursuant to which livestock operations will be conducted to meet multiple use, sustained yield principles. BLM grazing regulations appear at 43 C.F.R. § 4100.0-1.
691.   43 U.S.C. §§ 315-315r (1982). The BLM is authorized to grant "grazing permits" under Section 315b of the Taylor Act, and to grant "grazing leases" under Section 315m, both of which will be referred to as permits during this discussion.
692.   *Ibid.* § 1715(b)(1).
693.   *Ibid.*
694.   *Ibid.* § 1753(b) (limiting role of grazing boards to offering advice on allotment plans and use of range improvement funds).
695.   43 U.S.C. §§ 1901-1908 (1982).
696.   Braun, *supra* note 652 at 54.
697.   16 U.S.C. §§ 580k-580l (1982).
698.   43 U.S.C. § 1903(b).
699.   *Ibid.* § 1901(a)(3).
700.   *Ibid.* § 1903(b) (directing the BLM only).
701.   Braun *supra* note 652 at 62, n.64 (citing legislative history).
702.   43 U.S.C. § 1901(a)(1).
703.   *Ibid.* § 1901(a)(3).
704.   Braun, *supra* note 652 at 62 and n. 61.
705.   Braun *supra* note 652 at 62 (citing legislative history).
706.   43 U.S.C. § 1902(f).
707.   *Ibid.* § 1752(d).

708.   Coggins, *Watershed, supra* note 515 at 22, citing Braun, *supra* note 652 at 44; *NRDC v. Morton,* 388 F. Supp. 829, 840 (D.D.C. 1974); BLM, Range Condition Report (USGPO, Doc. No. 207, 1975).

709.   Coggins, *Watershed* at 22.   There is some hope that a plaintiff could succeed if it were argued "that watershed is the key resource upon which all others depend and that watershed integrity is a precondition to improving range condition, which is PRIA's fundamental management command." *Ibid.* A few courts have required further agency action where poor rangeland conditions are made an issue or when watershed damage caused by other activities was clear. *NRDC v. Hodel,* 618 F. Supp. 848, 879-80 (E.D. Cal. 1985); *NRDC v. Morton,* 388 F. Supp 829, 839-41 (D.C.C. 1974); *Sierra Club v. Penfold,* 857 F.2d 1307, 1319-22 (9th Cir. 1988), *aff'd* 664 F. Supp. 1299 (1987); *Nat'l Wildlife Fed'n v. United States Forest Service,* 592 F. Supp. 931, 940-43 (D. Or. 1984), *appeal dismissed,* 801 F.2d 360 (9th Cir 1986); *Sierra Club v. Dept. of Interior,* 398 F. Supp. 284, 293-94 (N.D. Cal. 1975).

710.   624 F. Supp. 1045 (D. Nev. 1985).

711.   *Ibid.,* quoting *Perkins v. Bergland,* 608 F.2d 803, 807 (1979).

712.   It is likely that courts will be more willing to review BLM decisions for conformity with forthcoming land use plans. *NRDC v. Hodel,* 624 F. Supp. at 1060 (indicating court's willingness to scrutinize BLM decisions for conformity with plan provisions).

713.   GAO, Public Rangelands at 37 (1988).

714.   Braun, 17 Envtl L. at 63.

715.   *See United States v. Fifty-Three Eclectus Parrots,* 685 F.2d 1131, 1136 (9th Cir 1982) (holding that "general statements of policy" contained in agency manuals are not enforceable against the agency); *Lumber Prod. & Indus. Workers Log Scalers v. United States,* 580 F. Supp. 279 (D. Or. 1984).

716.   EPA Region 10, Riparian Policy at 12.

717.   *Ibid.* at 12.

718.   *Ibid.* at 13.

719.   *See also,* Braun, *supra* note 652 at 67-78.

720.   *Oregon Natural Resources Defense Council v. U.S. Forest Service,* 834 F.2d 842 (9th Cir. 1987) (recognizing citizen plaintiffs' right to enforce state water quality standards against federal nonpoint violators under the Administrative Procedures Act).

721.   It is worth noting, however, that an agency's plan can be upheld as meeting water quality standards before it is implemented, only to result in a violation of those standards. Generally, a plan will call for "Best Management Practices," and, absent evidence that such practices will not meet water quality standards, it will be upheld. After a plan has been implemented, citizens do not have the same legal handle available to them as they do for point sources, and must rely on the state agencies to prosecute violators.

722.   43 U.S.C. § 1732(a); Coggins, *Watershed, supra* note 515 at 21.

723.   16 U.S.C. § 531(a).

724.   43 U.S.C. § 1702(c) (1982).

725.   16 U.S.C. § 531 (b).

726.   Coggins, *supra* note 515 at 16-9.

727.   16 U.S.C. § 528 (emphasis added).

728.   43 U.S.C. § 1702(c) (emphasis added). Although Congress apparently intended the last four, less quantifiable resources to be given "equal weight" with the other, more conventional resources, Congress failed to list those values as "principal" resources. *See* Coggins, Public Natural Resources Law *supra* note 520 16-5, n.41.

729.   43 U.S.C. § 1702(l)

730.   Coggins, *supra* note 520 at 16-6. *See California v. United States*, 438 U.S. 645 (1978); Tarlock, Law of Water Rights and Resources.

731.   However, FLPMA does not duplicate MUSYA's command to the Forest Service that the agency give "due consideration" to all of these resources.

732.   *694 F. Supp. 1260, 1269 (E.D. Tex. 1988)* citing *Texas Comm'n on Nat. Res. v. Bergland*, 573 F.2d 201, 212 (5th Cir), *cert. denied*, 439 U.S. 966 (1978).

733.   Coggins, 1983. *The Law of Public Rangeland Management IV: FLPMA. PRIO, and the Multiple Use Mandate*, 14 Envt'l L 1, 58-61 (hereinafter cited as *Public Rangeland Management IV*).

734.   *Sierra Club v. Clark*, 756 F.2d 686, 691 (9th Cir. 1985); *NRDC v. Hodel*, 624 F. Supp. 1045, 1061-62 (D. New 1985) *aff'd* 819 F.2d 927 (9th Cir. 1987).

735.   *Cf. Sierra Club v. Hardin*, 325 F. Supp. 99, 122-24 (D. Alaska 1971), *rev'd unreported*, 3 ELR 20292 (9th Cir 1973).

736.   592 F. Supp. 931, 934-35 (D.Or. 1984), appeal dismissed, 801 F.2d 360 (9th Cir. 1987).

737.　*Ibid.* at 942-45; Coggins, *Watershed, supra* note 515 at 19.

738.　592 F. Supp. 931, 938 (D. Or. 1984).

739.　325 F. Supp. 99 (D. Alaska 1971).

740.　325 F. Supp. at 123.

741.　*Perkins v. Bergland,* 608 F.2d 803, 807 (9th Cir. 1979).

742.　*Sierra Club v. Hardin,* 325 F. Supp. 99, 123 & n. 48 (D. Alaska 1971), *rev'd sub. nom. Sierra Club v. Butz,* 3 Envt'l L. Rep. (Envtl. L. Inst.) 20292 (9th Cir. 1973).

743.　*Headwaters, Inc. v. Bureau of Land Management,* 684 F. Supp. 1053, 1056 (D. Or. 1988), *vacated as moot,* 893 F.2d 1012 (9th Cir 1989).

744.　Coggins, *The Law of Public Rangeland Management IV: FLPMA, PRIA, and the Multiple Use Mandate,* 14 Envt'l L. 1, 16 (1983).

745.　*See California v. Block,* 690 F.2d 753 (9th Cir. 1982); Comment, *Managing Federal Lands: Replacing the Multiple Use System,* 82 Yale L.J. 787 (1973).

746.　Burford, Address, New Mexico State Bar Ass'n, Santa Fe, New Mexico, Sept. 25, 1987, as cited in Coggins at 16-3, note 27.

747.　*Supra* note 520.

748.　*See generally* Behan, 1978. *Political Popularity and Conceptual Nonsense: The Strange Case of Sustained Yield Forestry,* 8 Envtl. L. 309.

749.　14 Envt'l L. 1, 53-54 (1983).

750.　Coggins, *supra* note 520, at 16-8.

751.　*See generally* cases cited *supra* note 515.

752.　*Ibid.* at 18.

753.　Tarlock, *The Law of Public Rangeland Management or How Professor Coggins Proposes to Transform the Bureau of Land Management's FLPMA Discretion into Duties,* in NC/NAS Report at 1977-78, cited in Braun, *supra* note 644 at 65, n.68.

754.　Coggins, *supra* note 515 at 10.

755.　Personal Communication with Bill Jackson, Chief of Water Operations Branch, National Park Service, Fort Collins, Colorado (Dec.17, 1991).

756.　16 U.S.C. § 1.

757.　*Ibid.* §3, 20-20g.

758.　*Ibid.* § 1a-1.

759.　*Ibid.*

760.　The General Authorities Act of 1970, 16 U.S.C. § 1c(a).

761.   U.S.D.I., 1988. Introduction to National Park Service Management Policies 1:2 citing the Alaska National Interest Lands Conservation Act of December 2, 1980.

762.   NPS Management Policies, 1:13 (1988).

763.   16 U.S.C. §1a-7(b)(3) (1986).

764.   Coggins, *The Developing Law of Land Use Planning on the Federal Lands*, 61 U. Colo. L. Rev. 307, 311 (1990).

765.   16 U.S.C. §§ 1a-7(b).

766.   *Ibid.*

767.   *Supra* note 764 at 312.

768.   *Ibid.* at 312.

769.   See 36 C.F.R. Part 219 (1991).

770.   *Supra* note 767

771.   *Ibid.* at 313. We note, however, that the Park Service incurred judicial reproach for failing to implement its planning efforts in the Redwood National Park litigation, *Sierra Club v. Department of the Interior*, 398 F. Supp. 284 (N.D. Cal. 1975).

772.   Department of Interior, National Park Service, 1988. NPS Management Policies, 1:3.

773.   *Ibid.* at 1:4.

774.   *Sierra Club v. Department of the Interior*, 398 F. Supp 284, 286 (N.D. Cal. 1975).

775.   *Ibid.* at 286-87.

776.   *Ibid.* at 287.

777.   *Ibid.* at 293.

778.   Among the numerous cases in which Park Service decisions are upheld as within agency discretion are: *NRA v. Potter*, 628 F. Supp. 903 (D.D.C. 1986) (upholding prohibition on hunting); *Organized Fishermen of Florida v. Hodel*, 775 F.2d 1544 (11th Cir 1985), *cart. denied*, 476 U.S. 1169 (1986) (upholding rules' limitations on fishing, including establishment of no-fishing sanctuaries and prohibition of commercial fishing); *Wilderness Public Rights Fund v. Kleppe*, 608 F.2d 1250 (9th Cir. 1979), *cert. denied*, 446 U.S. 982 (1980) (deferring to Park Service on permitting methodology for raft access to Grand Canyon as well within discretion granted under the NPSA, its implementing regulations, and the CPA); *Biderman v. Morton*, 507 F.2d 396 (2d Cir. 1974)(road access to Fire Island);

Sierra Club v. Hickel, 433 F.2d 24 (9th Cir. 1970), *aff'd on other grounds*, 405 U.S. 727 (1972)(road-building in Sequoia National Park).

779.   *See, e.g., National Wildlife Federation v. National Park Service*, 669 F. Supp. 384 (D. Wyo. 1987).

780.   Coggins, Public Natural Resources Law at 17-17. *But cf. Sierra Club v. Lujan*, 716 F. Supp. 1289 (D. Ariz. 1989) (NPS enjoined from major hotel development on North Rim of Grand Canyon because of noncompliance with NEPA).

781.   The guidelines were written under an Editorial Board of senior natural resource employees. Personal Communication with K. Jope (7/24/92).

782.   These policies are found at page 4:15-16 of the National Park Service Management Policies (December, 1988).

783.   NPS Management Policies at 4:16-17.

784.   Codified at scattered sections of 33 U.S.C.

785.   NPS Management Policies at 4:17.

786.   NPS Resource Management Guidelines, Chapter 2, page 52.

787.   *Ibid.* at 65-86.

788.   *Ibid.* at 65-66.

789.   Personal Communication with Bill Jackson, Chief of Water Operations Branch, National Park Service, Fort Collins, Colorado (Dec.17, 1991).

790.   NPS Natural Resources Guidelines (NPS-77), Chapter 2, page 49 (1991).

791.   *Ibid.*

792.   Prior to the passage of the ANILCA, about 50 active placer mines were operating in park lands. At present, one Park Service official has estimated there are about half a dozen active mining operations.

793.   *Sierra Club v. Department of the Interior*, 398 F. Supp. 284 (N.D. Cal. 1975).

794.   Coggins, Public Natural Resources Law *supra* note 520 at 14-10(1992).

795.   *See, e.g.* 16. U.S.C. §§ 703-711 (1982).

796.   *Ibid.* § 1536.

797.   *Supra* note 764 at 314.

798.   *Ibid.*

799.   16 U.S.C. §§ 668dd-668ee, § 668dd(a) (1982).

800.   U.S. Department of the Interior, Fish and Wildlife Service, Compatibility Task Group, June 1990. Secondary Uses Occurring on National Wildlife Refuges 9.

801.   16 U.S.C. § 668dd(d); *see infra* notes 793-812 and accompanying text.

802.   *Supra* note 520 at 14-13.

803.   16 U.S.C. § 460k.

804.   *Ibid.*

805.   *Ibid.* §460k to 460k-4 (1982).

806.   *Ibid.* § 460k.

807.   *Ibid.* § 668dd(d)(1)(A) (emphasis added).

808.   *See Defenders of Wildlife v. Andrus*, 720 F.2d 571 (D.D.C. 1978) (finding regulations permitting powerboats in refuge violated Refuge Recreation Act because use was not incidental or secondary and would interfere with refuge's primary purpose).

809.   5 Refuge Manual 20.6.A (May 8, 1986 release).

810.   *Supra* note 800 at 17.

811.   *Ibid.* at 18, 23.

812.   *Ibid.* at 23. ("the FWS must have the authority to unilaterally regulate a use on a particular refuge in order for that use to have the potential to be "incompatible").

813.   *Supra* note 800 at 24.

814.   *Ibid.* at 25.

815.   16 U.S.C. §§668dd-668ee.

816.   Alaska National Interest Lands Conservation Act of 1980, (ANILCA), § 304, 94 Stat. 2371 (1980).

817.   16 U.S.C. § 668dd(a).

818.   50 C.F.R. § 25.11(b).

819.   *Supra* note 798 at 11.

820.   *Supra* note 520 at 13-10.

821.   *Ibid.*

822.   *Supra* note 520 at 13-10 *citing* Verburg & Coon, 1987. *Planning in the U.S. Fish and Wildlife Service*, 24 Trends No. 2. As of 1990, about 100 master plans were in effect, with 15 in preparation. Coggins, *supra* note 527 at 315.

823. *Compare Schwenke v. Secretary of the Interior*, 720 F.2d 751 (9th Cir.
1983) (upholding order by Secretary of Interior transferring exclusive
control of livestock grazing on wildlife range to Fish and Wildlife Service
to administer according to Wildlife Refuge Act rather than Taylor
Grazing Act, despite objection by ranchers), *with Coupland v. Morton*, 5
Envtl. L. Rep. (Envtl. L. Inst.) 20504 (E.D. Va. 1975), *aff'd* 526 F.2d 588
(4th Cir. 1975) (upholding validity of Department of Interior regulations
severely restricting motorized traffic by recent and seasonal residents in
national wildlife refuge).
824. 692 F. Supp at 80. *See also, Schwenke v. Secretary of the Interior*, 720
F.2d 571 (9th Cir. 1983) (users exert pressure to allow use of refuges for
recreation and commodity production); *Defenders of Wildlife v. Andrus*, 11
Env't Rep. Cas. (BNA) 2098, 455 F. Supp 446 (D.D.C. 1978) (striking down
regulations allowing power boat use in refuge).
825. 16 U.S.C. §§ 703-712.
826. *Ibid.* §§ 715-715s.
827. *Ibid.* §§ 718-718j.
828. ANILCA, § 304(g).
829. Eaton & Waltman, April 1992. *Bold Actions in Refuge System Law
to Maintain Compatibility* (paper presented at the North American Wildlife
and Natural Resources Conference).
830. U.S. Fish and Wildlife Service, 1986. Survey of Contaminant
Issues of Concern on National Wildlife Refuges.
831. Source: Fish and Wildlife Service Refuge Manager Questionnaire,
Part IV. Environmental Contaminants, Dec. 1991 using Calendar Year
1989 Information. U.S. Fish and Wildlife Service, Rm.130, 4401 N. Fairfax
Drive, Arlington, VA 22203.
832. *See S.1862* "National Wildlife Refuge System Management and
Policy Act" (sponsored by Sen. Bob Graham); and its companion house
bill, HR 3688 (sponsored by Rep. Sam Gibbons), H.R. 2881, "National
Wildlife Refuge System Act" (sponsored by Rep. Gerry Studds).
833. 16 U.S.C. § 668dd(a).
834. *Ibid.*
835. Pub. L. No. 88-577, 78 Stat. 890, codified as amended at 16 U.S.C.
§§ 1311-36.
836. Gorte, R., Aug. 4 1989. CRS Report for Congress, Wilderness:
Overview and Statistics (89-460 ENR).
837. *Ibid.* at 19.

838.   *Ibid.*

839.   *Ibid.*

840.   McClaran, 1990. *Livestock in Wilderness: A Review and Forecast*, 20 Envtl. L. 857, 859 n.19.

841.   *See generally* Rohlf & Hannold, 1988. *Managing the Balances of Nature: The Legal Framework of Wilderness Management*, 15 Ecol. L. Q. 249, 255-58 (discussing the purposes of the Wilderness Act). Wilderness is described in Section 2(c) of the Wilderness Act as

> an area where the earth and its community of life are untrammeled by man, where man himself is a visitor who does not remain. . . . an area of undeveloped Federal land retaining its primeval character and influence, without permanent improvements or human habitation, which is protected and managed so as to preserve its natural conditions and which (1) generally appears to have been affected primarily by the forces of nature, with the imprint of man's work substantially unnoticeable; (2) has outstanding opportunities for solitude or a primitive and unconfined type of recreation; (3) has at least five thousand acres of land or is of sufficient size as to make practicable its preservation and use in an unimpaired condition; and (4) may also contain ecological, geological, or other features of scientific, educational, scenic, or historical value.

842.   *Ibid.* § 1133(b).

843.   However, as one commentator noted, even these imprecise guidelines are more specific than those provided for determining new units of the National Park System or the National Wildlife Refuge System. Wilderness: Overview and Statistics, *supra* note 836 at 5, n.8.

844.   16 U.S.C. § 1133(b).

845.   *Ibid.* 16 U.S.C. § 1133(c).

846.   *Ibid.* § 1133(d)(1)-(5).

847.   This authority to permit on-site exploration was not exercised until James Watt ascended to the post of Secretary of Interior in 1981. Congress responded by placing a moratorium on leasing and exploration in wilderness areas for 1983 and 1984.

848.   Wilderness: Overview and Statistics, *supra* note 836, at 6; *see* Mathews, Haak, and Toffenette, 1985 *Mining and Wilderness: Incompatible Uses or Justifiable Compromise?* 27 Environment 12-17, 30-36.

849.   16 U.S.C § 1133(d).

850.   Clearly this is not one, but two, purposes, and there are at least two other purposes implied in the Act as well: accommodation of local and commercial interests and the protection of the health and safety of persons within the area. *See* discussion in Rohlf & Hannold, *supra* note 839 at 260-61.

851.   *Ibid.*

852.   Wilderness: Overview and Statistics, *supra* note 836 at 5.

853.   50 C.F.R. § 35.2; Rohlf & Hannold, *supra* note 841 at 262.

854.   43 C.F.R. § 8560.0-.6 (BLM regulations); 36 C.F.R. § 293.2(Forest Service regulations containing substantially similar language).

855.   *See* Rohlf & Hannold, *supra* note 841 at 272-73 (discussing uncertain scope of Act's mandate to restore wilderness character).

856.   36 C.F.R. § 219.17.

857.   Not surprisingly, the Wilderness Act was the source of a long-term controversy over its implementation, particularly with regard to Forest Service review of roadless areas within the national forests. Eventually, wilderness review standards were worked out which allowed the inclusion of areas exhibiting evidence of previous development, and the consideration of other factors, such as whether a particular ecosystem or land form was already represented in the system and whether system components were adequately distributed from the perspective of public access.   However, because there were significant differences in the commercial potential of some potential wilderness areas -- some overlay valuable reserves of oil and gas, while others had negligible commercial significance -- the Forest Service's decision not to emphasize economic questions of resource allocation in wilderness designations caused considerable debate and political opposition from wilderness opponents. *See, e.g.*, Ferguson, 1978. *Forest Service and BLM Wilderness Review Programs and their Effect on Mining Law Activities*, 24 Rocky Mtn. Min. L. Inst. 717, 723-33.

858.   Solicitor's Opinion on Federal Water Rights in Wilderness Areas, 96 I.D. 211 (1988) (reversing 86 I.D. 553 (1979)).

859.   *Sierra Club v. Block*, 622 F. Supp. 842 (D. Colo. 1985).

860.   *Sierra Club v. Yeutter*, 911 F. 2d 1405 (10th Cir. 1990).

861.   *Ibid.*
862.   *See, e.g.,* 42 U.S.C. §§ 4321, 4331(b) (NEPA); 40 C.F.R. § 1501.1(b) (NEPA implementing regulations); 43 U.S.C. § 1712(c)(9) (FLPMA); 16 U.S.C. § 1604(a) (NFMA); 16 U.S.C. §§ 661-666c (Fish and Wildlife Coordination Act of 1958).
863.   42 U.S.C. §§ 4321-4370(c)).
864.   *Ibid.* §§ 4431(b)(1)-4431(b)(6).
865.   *See e.g. Calvert Cliff' Coordinating Committee, Inc. v. Atomic Energy Commission,* 449 F.2d. 1109 (D.C. Cir. 1971) (implicitly finding that NEPA's enforceable requirements are procedural and that agency decisions will not be reversed on their merits unless they are arbitrary or clearly erroneous); Hildreth, note 865 at 3.
866.   *Robertson v. Methow Valley Citizens Council,* 490 U.S. 332 (1989).
867.   *See* Hildreth, R. *et. al.,* 1992. Integrated Watershed Management, Cumulative Impacts and Implementation of Nonpoint Source Controls: Legal and Policy Analysis.
868.   *See* 40 CFR § 1508.7).
869.   40 CFR 1500.25.
870.   *See e.g. Natural Resources Defense Council v. Callaway,* 524 F.2d 79 (2d Cir. 1975) (finding that the Army Corps failed to consider other parties' dumping in the same geographical area as its proposed dumping).
871.   *Sierra Club v. Penfold,* 857 F2d 1307 (9th Cir. 1988) (upholding lower court injunction on placer mining pending BLM completion of cumulative impacts assessments), cited in Hildreth at 2.
872.   40 C.F.R. § 1500.25.
873.   Hildreth, *supra* note 867 at 2.
874.   *See e.g. Thomas v. Peterson,* 753 F.2d 754 (9th Cir. 1985), *cited* in Hildreth, *supra* note 865 at 2.
875.   16 U.S.C. § 1274(d)(1).
876.   *Ibid.* § 1283(a).
877.   *Ibid.* § 1283(c).
878.   As already discussed, the Act was interpreted to constrain federal actions outside a river corridor in *Wilderness Society v. Tyrell,* where the Forest Service was informed that it must evaluate proposed logging outside the boundary of a river corridor on the South Fork of the Trinity River to determine whether such logging would jeopardize the values

which caused the river to be protected under the Act. 918 F.2d 813, 820 (9th Cir. 1990).

879.   Whether a managing agency has "cooperated" with the EPA and state agencies is a question of fact. Wilderness Society v. Tyrrel, 918 F. 2d 813, 820 (9th Cir. 1990) (holding that the district court could not determine as a matter of law that the Forest Service had not cooperated with the EPA and state agencies, even though the EPA and the state agencies opposed proposed logging).

880.   16 U.S.C. §1281(e). *See also* § 1283(a) (coordination required for state-initiated river segments).

881.   Tarlock, A.D. & R. Tippy, 1970. *The Wild and Scenic Rivers Act of 1968,* 55 Cornell L. Rev. 707, 739 (as cited in P. Frost, *Ensuring that Clean Water Flows in Wild and Scenic Rivers,* unpublished manuscript on file at the National Wildlife Federation, Portland, Oregon).

882.   43 U.S.C. § 1712(c)(9). The implementing regulations appear at 43 C.F.R. §§ 1610.3-1 & 1610.302.

883.   *Ibid.*

884.   42 U.S.C. § 1604(a).

885.   16 U.S.C. § 1604.

886.   *Ibid.*

887.   *See e.g.* Our Common Lands at 28 and passim.

888.   For more information on Indian water rights, see Getches, D. and C.Wilkinson, 1986. Federal Indian Law 651-715 (2d. ed.).

889.   For example, in Michigan and Oklahoma, cooperative agreements have been reached between state and certain tribal governments regarding the issuance of permits under the Clean Water Act. Likewise, the Confederated Salish and Kootenai Tribes is considering assuming such duties on their reservation in Montana. Steiner, Pieart, and Cook, *supra* note 238, at 39-40.

890.   *See* Williams, S., 1990. *Indian Winters Water Rights Administration: Averting New War,* 11 Public Land Law Review 53 (focusing on Wind River reservation in Wyoming); *see also United States V. Adair,*723 F.2d 1394, 1412-14, (9th Cir, 1983), *cert. denied,* 467 U.S> 1252.

891.   16 U.S.C. §§ 1271-1287.

892.   It is estimated that even if fully-implemented, as currently written the Act would only protect about 100,000 river miles.

893.   These provisions permit rivers to enter the system upon the application of a state governor to the Secretary of the Interior. 16 U.S.C. § 1273(a)(ii).
894.   16 U.S.C. § 1277(c).
895.   *Ibid.* § 1273(a)(ii).
896.   *Ibid.* § 1277.
897.   *Ibid.* §§ 544-544p.
898.   *Ibid.* § 544a(1), (2).
899.   *Ibid.* § 544c(a)(1).
900.   *Ibid.* §§ 544b(e), 544d(c)(5)(B).
901.   *Ibid.* § 544f.
902.   *Ibid.* § 544e(a).
903.   *Ibid.* §§ 544g(a), 544n(a)(1).
904.   *Ibid.* § 544g(b).
905.   *Ibid.* § 544d(d)(4), (5).
906.   *Ibid.* § 544d(d)(8).
907.   *Ibid.* § 1278(a).
908.   *Ibid.* § 544k(a)(1).
909.   *Ibid.* § 544k(b).
910.   *See generally* Blumm, M. and A. Simrin, 1991. *The Unraveling of the Parity Promise: Hydropower, Salmon, and Endangered Species in the Columbia Basin,* 21 Environmental Law 657.
911.   16 U.S.C. §§ 544i, 544n.
912.   *Ibid.* § 544f(h).
913.   *See, e.g., Columbia River Gorge United v. Yeutter,* 960 F.2d 110 (9th Cir. 1992) (upholding constitutionality of Act and of Commission's powers).
914.   *Supra* note 867, at 10
915.   43 U.S.C. §§ 981 et seq.
916.   42 U.S.C. §§ 4001 et. seq.
917.   *Ibid.* §§ 4011 et. seq.
918.   DeMeo, R. and D. Merriam, 1988. *Flood Damage Protection: Impact of the National Flood Insurance Program,* 11 Zoning and Planning Law Report 65.
919.   *Ibid.* at 66, citing 44 C.F.R. sec. 59.3.
920.   *Ibid.* at 67.
921.   *Ibid.* § 4101.

922.   *Ibid.* § 4105.
923.   *Ibid.* secs. 4012, 4106.
924.   *See* 1968 U.S. Code Cong. & Admin. News 2969.
925.   16 U.S.C. §§ 1451-1464.
926.   *Ibid.* § 1452(1).
927.   *Ibid.* § 1451(i).
928.   *Ibid.* § 1455(a).
929.   *Ibid.* §§ 1454(g), 1455a(e), 1455(f).
930.   *Ibid.* § 1456c.
931.   *Ibid.* § 1454(b).
932.   *Ibid.* § 1455a(b).
933.   *Ibid.* § 1456(c).
934.   *Ibid.* § 1456(c)(3)(A). See also Whitney, S., R. Johnson, and S. Perles, *State Implementation of the Coastal Zone Management Consistency Provisions--Ultra Vires or Unconstitutional?*, 12 Harvard Environmental Law Review 67 (1988); Archer, J., and J. Bondareff, 1988. *Implementation of the Federal Consistency Doctrine--Lawful and Constitutional: A Response to Whitney, Johnson & Perles*, 12 Harvard Environmental Law Review 115.
935.   16 U.S.C. § 1461.
936.   *Ibid.* § 1461(b).
937.   *See, e.g.,* Cal. Pub. Res. Code §§ 30000 et seq.; S.C. Code Ann. §§ 48-39-10 et seq.
938.   *Supra* note 11.
939.   EPA Region 10, Riparian Policy: Summary and Analysis iii (1991).
940.   *Ibid.* at 15.
941.   *Ibid.*
942.   *Ibid.* at 16.
943.   *Ibid.*
944.   Nev. Rev. Stat. secs. 528.010 to 528.090.
945.   *Ibid.* sec. 528.053(1).
946.   *Ibid.*
947.   *See, e.g.,* Cal. Pub. Res. Code secs. 4511-4628; Idaho Code secs. 38-1301 to -1314; Wash. Rev. Code Ann. secs. 76.09.010 - 76.09.935.
948.   *See, e.g.,* Ann. Mo. Stat. secs. 254.010-254.300; N.H. Rev. Stat. Ann. secs. 79:1-79:30; N.M. Stat. Ann. secs. 68-2-1 to -28; N.Y. Conserv. Law

secs. 3-1101 to -1151; Va. Code Ann. secs. 10.1-1100 to -1181; Vt. Stat. Ann. tit. 10, secs. 2621-2624.
949.   Mass. Ann. Laws ch. 132, secs. 40-46.
950.   *Ibid.* sec. 40.
951.   *Ibid.* sec. 41.
952.   Miss. Code Ann. secs. 49-19-51 to -77.
953.   *Ibid.* 49-19-53.
954.   *Ibid.* at 15. The EPA notes research which supports a 66 to 100 foot riparian management area within which logging would be limited or prohibited. *Ibid.* at 15-16.
955.   *See generally* discussion of wetlands *infra* notes 195-243 and accompanying text.
956.   Vt. Stat. Ann. tit. 10, § 905.
957.   *Ibid.* tit. 24, § 4302.
958.   Steiner, Pieart & Cook, *supra* note 242 at 32.
959.   Wash Code Ann. 400-12-100 through -720.
960.   Cody, B., J. Zinn, G. Siehl. July 17, 1992. River and River Corridor Protection: Status of State and Federal Programs and Options for Congress, Congressional Research Service Report for Congress; *See, e.g.,* Alaska Stat. secs. 42.23.400-.510 (Recreation Rivers Act); Ark. Code Ann. secs. 15-23-301 to -315 (Natural and Scenic Rivers System Act); Cal.. Pub. Res. Code secs. 5093.50-.69 (Wild and Scenic Rivers Act); Conn. Gen. Stat. secs. 22a-1 to -27 (River Protection Commission's Act); Fla. Stat. Ann. sec. 258.501 (Scenic and Wild Rivers Program); Idaho Code sec. 42-1734a-I (Comprehensive State Water Plan and Protected Rivers Act); Ind. Code sec. 13-2-26-1-11 (Rivers Preservation Act); Iowa Code secs. 108A.1-A.7 (Protected Water Areas Program); Ky. Rev. Stat. Ann. secs. 146.200-.290 (Wild Rivers Program); La. Rev. Stat. tit. 56, secs. 1841-1856 (Natural and Scenic Rivers Act); Me. Rev. Stat. Ann. tit. 12, secs. 401-407 (Maine Rivers Policy); Mass. Gen. L. ch. 21, sec. 17B (Scenic Rivers Program); Minn. Stat. secs. 104.31-.40 (Wild, Scenic and Recreational Rivers Program); N.H. Rev. Stat. Ann. secs. 483:1-483:15 (Rivers Management and Protection Program Act); N.J. Rev. Stat. secs. 13:8-45 to -63 (Wild and Scenic Rivers Act); N.Y. Envtl. Conserv. Law secs. 15-2701 to -2723 (Wild Scenic and Recreational Rivers System); N.C. Gen. stat. sec. 113A-30 to -44 (Natural and Scenic Rivers System); Ohio Rev. Code Ann. secs. 1501.16 to -.19.1 (Wild, Scenic and Recreational River Act); Okla. Stat. tit. 82, secs. 1452-1471 (Scenic Rivers Act); Pa. Stat. Ann. tit. 32, secs. 820.21-.24 (Scenic Rivers Act); R.I.

Gen. Laws secs. 46-28-1-13 (Rivers Council Act); S.C. Code Ann. sec. 49-29-10-230 (Scenic Rivers Act); S.D. Codified Laws Ann. secs. 46A-1 to -9 (Water Resources Management Act); Tenn. Code Ann. secs. 11-13-101 to -117 (Scenic Rivers Act); Vt. Stat. Ann. tit. 10, secs. 1422(9) et seq. (Comprehensive State River Policy Act); Va. Code Ann. secs. 10.1-400 to -418 (Scenic Rivers Program); Wash. Rev. Code secs. 79.72.010-.900 (Scenic Rivers System); W.Va. Code secs. 20-5B-1 to -17 (Natural Streams Preservation Act); Wisc. Stat. sec. 30.36 (Wild Rivers Program).

961.   GA. Code Ann. secs. 12-5-351 to -354.

962.   Md. Nat. Res. Code Ann. secs. 8-401 to -411.

963.   *Ibid.* sec. 8-406.

964.   Or. Rev. Stat. §§ 390.805 - 390.925.

965.   GA. Code. Ann. Sec. 12-5-354(2).

966.   Mich. Comp. Laws secs. 281.761 to -776.

967.   *Ibid.* sec. 281.765.

968.   Or. Rev. Stat. §§ 390.805 - 390.925.

969.   Cody, et al., at 7.

970.   *Ibid.*

971.   *Ibid.*

972.   Cody et. al., at 14-16

973.   Cody et. al., at 19.

974.   Mich. Comp. Laws secs. 281.761-.776.

975.   *Ibid.* sec. 281.763.

976.   Coyle, K. and C. Brown, Conserving Rivers: A Handbook for State Action (July 1992 draft).

977.   *Ibid.* at 235.

978.   N.H. Rev. Stat. Ann. secs. 483:1-483:15.

979.   S.C. Code Ann. sec. 49-29-10-230.

980.   K. Coyle and C. Brown, at 235-36.

981.   *Supra* note 867 at 66; see also *id.* at 18-19, 42.

982.   For example, in Connecticut, municipalities are required by the state wetland law to regulate wetlands within their boundaries. Steiner, Pieart & Cook, *supra* note 242 at 22.

983.   33 U.S.C. §§ 1251 et seq.

984.   N.H. Rev. Stat. Ann. §§ 483:1 - 483:15.

985.   For detailed information on the Merrimack, contact: the Merrimack River Watershed Council, 604 Main Street, West Newbury, MA 01985.

986.   See David, S., 1992. "The Merrimack River," in National Research Council, *Restoration of Aquatic Ecosystems* 463-69.
987.   See Mass. Ann. Laws ch. 17, § 17B.
988.   Berger, J., 1992. "Citizen Restoration Efforts in the Mattole River Watershed," in National Research Council, Restoration of Aquatic Ecosystems 457-63.
989.   See Sparks, R., 1992. "The Upper Mississippi River," in National Research Council, Restoration of Aquatic Ecosystems 406-12.
990.   16 U.S.C. §§ 721-731.
991.   *Atchison, Topeka & Santa Fe Ry. v. Callaway*, 431 F. Supp. 722 (1977).
992.   33 U.S.C. § 652.
993.   *Ibid.* § 652(e).
994.   See Minn. Stat. Ann. § 103F.367. *See generally id.* §§ 103F.361 - 103F.377 (governing Mississippi headwaters planning and management in the state of Minnesota).
995.   *Ibid.* §§ 103F.301 - 103F.345 (formerly *id.* §§ 104.31 - 104.40).
996.   *Ibid.* § 105.485.

BIBLIOGRAPHY

Achieng, A.P., 1990. "The impact of the introduction of Nile perch, Lates niloticus on the fisheries of Lake Victoria." *Journal of Fish Biology* 37 (Supplement A).

Addison and Burns, 1991. "The Army Corps of Engineers and Nationwide Permit 26: Wetlands Protection or Swamp Reclamation?," 18 *Ecology L.Q.*

Allan, J.D. and A.S. Flecker. 1993. "Biodiversity Conservation in Running Waters: Identifying the major factors that threaten destruction of riverine species and ecosystems." *Bioscience*, Vol. 43, No.1

Anderson, H. M., 1976. "Federal Mineral Policy: The General Mining Law of 1872," 16 *Nat.Res.J.*

Anderson, H. M., 1987. "Water Quality Planning in the National Forests" 17 *Envt'l L. J.*

Anderson, H.M., 1988. "New Directions for National Forest Water Quality Planning," *Forest Watch*, Cascade Holistic Economic Consultants, Portland, OR.

Angermeier, P. and J.R. Karr, 1993. "Biological Integrity versus Biological Diversity as Policy Directives in Water Resource Protection"; submitted to *Science.*

Archer, J., and J. Bondareff, 1988. "Implementation of the Federal Consistency Doctrine--Lawful and Constitutional: A Response to Whitney," Johnson and Perles, 12 *Harvard Environmental Law Review.*

Arjo, 1990. "Watershed and Water Quality Protection in National Forest Management," 41 *Hastings L.J.*

Association of State and Interstate Water Pollution Control Administrators, in cooperation with the U.S. EPA, 1984. "America's Clean Water: The State's Evaluation of Progress 1972-1982."

Barnhill, 1983. "Role of Local Government in Mineral Development," 28 *Rocky Mtn. Min. L. Inst.;* (Note: "State and Local Control of Energy Development on Federal Lands", 32 *Stan. L.Rev.* 1980).

Behan, 1978. "Political Popularity and Conceptual Nonsense: The Strange Case of Sustained Yield Forestry," 8 *Envtl. L.*

Bella, D.A and W.S. Overton. 1972. "Environmental planning and ecological possibilities." *Journal of the Sanitary Engineering Division, American Society of Civil Engineers* 98 (SAE, June, 1972).

Berger, J., 1992. "Citizen Restoration Efforts in the Mattole River Watershed," in National Research Council, *Restoration of Aquatic Ecosystems.*

Beschta, R.L. and W.S. Platts, 1986. "Morphological features of small streams: significance and function." *Water Resources Bulletin.*

Beschta, Robert L., William S. Platts and Boone Kaufmann, 1991. "Field Review of Fish Habitat Improvement Projects on the Grande Ronde and John Day River Basins of Eastern Oregon" 10 (unpublished report on file with the Northwest Power Planning Council, Portland, OR).

Blumm, M. and B. Kloos, 1986. "Small Scale Hydropower and Anadromous Fish: Lessons and Questions from the Winchester Dam Controversy," 16 *Envtl. L. J.*

Blumm, 1991. "Reserved Water Rights" in 4 *Water and Water Rights* (R. Beck ed.).

Blumm, M., 1991. "Hydroelectric Regulation under the Federal Power Act," in 4 *Water and Water Rights* (R. Beck ed.).

Blumm, M. and A. Simrin, 1991. "The Unraveling of the Parity Promise: Hydropower, Salmon, and Endangered Species in the Columbia Basin," 21 *Environmental Law*.

Blumm, M. and Zahela, 1989. "Federal Wetland Protection Under the Clean Water Act: Regulation, Ambivalence, Intergovernmental Tensions, and a Call for Reform," 60 *U.Colo. L. Rev.*

Bodi, F.L., 1988. "Hydropower, Dams, and the National Parks" in *National Parks, and Conservation Association, Our Common Lands: Defending the National Parks* (D. Simon, ed.).

Braun, R., 1986. "Emerging Limits on Federal Land Management Discretion: Livestock, Riparian Ecosystems and Clean Water Law," 17 *Envtl L. J.*

Brooks, C., 1992. "Oregon Water Rights and the Endangered Species Act: Conflicting State and Regulatory Mandates" (prepared for CLE International, Oregon Water Law.

Burford, Robert J., 1987. Director, Bureau of Land Management, "Riparian Management Policy".

Burgess, W.D., 1987. "Standards for Judicial Review of Forest Plans: Will the Courts not See the Forest for the Trees?" in *The Public Lands During the Remainder of the 20th Century* (U.Colo. School of Law).

Cody, B., CRS Issue Brief, "Western Water Supplies: Issues in the 102d Congress" (updated Jan. 31, 1992)(Order Code IB91102).

Cody, B., J. Zinn, G. Siehl, July 17, 1992. "River and River Corridor Protection: Status of State and Federal Programs and Options for Congress," *Congressional Research Service Report*, No. 95-575 ENR.

Coggins, G., 1983. "The Law of Public Rangeland Management IV: FLPMA. PRIO, and the Multiple Use Mandate," 14 *Envt'l L. J.*

Coggins, G., and C. Wilkinson, 1987. *Federal Public Land and Resources Law*, Foundation Press, University Casebook Series, (2d ed).

Coggins, G., 1990. "The Developing Law of Land Use Planning on the Federal Lands," 61 *U. Colo. L. Rev.*

Coggins, G., 1991. "Watershed as a Public Natural Resource," 11 *Va. Env. L. J.*

Coggins, G., 1992. *Public Natural Resources Law*, Clark-Boardman publishers.

Colburn, T.E., A. Davidson, S.N. Green, R.A. Hodge, C.I. Jackson, and R.A. Liroff, 1990. "Great Lakes, Great Legacy?" The Conservation Foundation, Washington, D.C.

Backiel, A., M.L. Corn, R. Gorte, et al., Congressional Research Service (CRS), May 7, 1990. Report for Congress, "The Major Federal Land Management Agencies: Management of Our Nation's Land and Resources" (90-239 ENR).

Council of Environmental Quality and Interagency Advisory Committee on Environmental Trends, 1989. *Environmental Trends.*

Coyle, K. and C. Brown, 1992 (draft). "Conserving Rivers: A Handbook for State Action."

David, S., 1992. "The Merrimack River," in National Research Council, *Restoration of Aquatic Ecosystems.*

DeMeo, R. and D. Merriam, 1988. "Flood Damage Protection: Impact of the National Flood Insurance Program," 11 *Zoning and Planning Law Report*

Durbin, K., "Closed Smelter Complex Poses Cleanup Challenge," The (Portland) *Oregonian,* April 6, 1992.

Durbin, K., "Tribe Sues Mining Companies over Cleanup of Wastes," The (Portland) *Oregonian,* April 7, 1992.

Durbin, K., "BLM will try turning over a new leaf to save old growth," The (Portland) *Oregonian,* Sept. 27, 1992.

Eaton, P. and J. Waltman, 1992. "Bold Actions in Refuge System Law to Maintain Compatibility,". (paper presented at the North American Wildlife and Natural Resources Conference, April 1992). Available from Jim Waltman, Audubon Society in D.C.

Echevarria, J.D., Pope Barrow, and Richard Roos-Collins, 1989. *Rivers at Risk: A Concerned Citizens' Guide to Hydropower,* Ch.1, Island Press.

Elmore, W., and R.L. Beschta, 1987. "Riparian areas: perceptions in management." *Rangelands* 9(6)

Entickap, P. and K. Kirch, 1991. "Report from Windy Cragg", *Clementine,* Winter, Mineral Policy Center, Washington, D.C.

FERC, Office of Hydropower Licensing, 1991. "Evaluating Relicense Proposals at the Federal Energy Regulatory Commission", Paper No. DPR-2.

Ferguson, 1978. "Forest Service and BLM Wilderness Review Programs and their Effect on Mining Law Activities," 24 *Rocky Mtn. Min. L. Inst.*

Franklin, J., J. Gordon, K. Norman Johnson, J.W. Thomas, "Alternatives for Management of Late-Successional Forests of the Pacific Northwest: A Report to the Agriculture Committee and the Merchant Marine and Fisheries Committee of the U.S. House of Representatives"; October 8, 1991.

Frissell, C.A., 1991. "Water Quality, Fisheries and Aquatic Biodiversity Under Two Alternative Management Scenarios for the West-side Federal Lands of Washington, Oregon and Northern California," A report prepared for The Wilderness Society.

Frissell, C.A., 1993. "A New Strategy For Watershed Restoration and Recovery of Pacific Salmon in the Pacific Northwest." A report prepared for the Pacific Rivers Council, Eugene, OR.

Frissell, C.A. and R.K. Nawa. 1992. "Incidence and causes of physical failure of artificial fish habitat structures in streams of western Oregon and Washington." *North American Journal of Fisheries Management* 12.

Frissell, C.A., W.J. Liss, and D. Bayles, 1993. "An integrated biophysical strategy for ecological restoration of large watersheds." Proceedings of a Symposium "Changing Rules in Water Resources Management and Policy." American Water Resources Association, Seattle, WA. 27-30 June, 1993.

Frost, P.M.K., 1992. "Ensuring that Clean Water Flows in Wild and Scenic Rivers," Unpublished Manuscript (on file at National Wildlife Federation, Portland, Oregon).

General Accounting Office (GAO), 1988. *Report on Federal Land Management: An Assessment of Hardrock Mining Damage.*

General Accounting Office (GAO), 1988. *Public Rangelands: Some Riparian Areas Restored, but Widespread Improvement Will be Slow.*

General Accounting Office (GAO), 1988. *Wetlands: The Corps of Engineers' Administration of the Section 404 Program.*

General Accounting Office, (GAO), 1989. *Water Pollution: More EPA Action Needed to Improve the Quality of Heavily Polluted Waters,* (GAO/RCED-89-38).

Getches, D. and C. Wilkinson, 1986. *Federal Indian Law* (2d. ed.).

Gorte, R. 1989. "Wilderness: Overview and Statistics." CRS Report for Congress, 89-460 ENR.

Gray, B.E., 1988. "No Holier Temples: Protecting the National Parks Through Wild and Scenic River Designation," 58 *U.Colo. L.Rev.*

Griffin, C., 1989. "Protection of Wildlife Habitat by State Wetland Regulations: The Massachusetts Initiative," Transactions of the 54th North American Wildlife and Natural Resources Conference.

Hagenstein, 1973. "Changing An Anachronism: Congress and the General Mining Law of 1872," 13 *Nat.Res.J.*

Hildreth, R. *et. al.,* 1993. "Integrated Watershed Management, Cumulative Impacts and Implementation of Nonpoint Source Controls: Legal and Policy Analysis." Found in Appendix D of Integrated Watershed Analysis and Implementation of Nonpoint Source Controls, Oregon Water Resources Research Institute, Oregon State University, Corvallis. Report submitted to EPA, Region X.

Hocker, P., 1992. "D.C. Dallies", *Clementine*, Mineral Policy Center, Washington, D.C.

Jacobson, J.L., S.W. Jacobson, and H.E.B. Humphrey. 1990. "Effects of in utero exposure to polychlorinated biphenyls and related contaminants on cognitive functioning in young children." *Journal of Pediatrics*.

Jenkinson, J.J., 1981. "Endangered or threatened aquatic mollusks of the Tennessee River System." *Bull. Am. Malac. Union*.

Karr, J.R., 1991. "Biological integrity: a long-neglected aspect of water resource management." *Ecological Applications* 1. Testimony by James R. Karr before the Subcommittee on Energy and the Environment, House Interior and Insular Affairs Committee, April 29, 1992.

Karr, J.R., 1993. "Protecting Ecological Integrity." *Yale Journal of International Law*, Vol. 18.

Karr, J.R., in press. "Biological Monitoring: challenges for the future." In A. Spacie and S. Loeb (eds.) *Biological Monitoring of Aquatic Ecosystems*.

Karr, J.R. and I.J. Schlosser. 1978. "Water resources and the land-water interface." *Science* 201.

Karr, J., L. Toth, and D.R. Dudley. 1985. "Fish communities of midwestern rivers: a history of degradation." *BioScience* 35.

Karr, J.R., K.D. Fausch, P.L. Angermeier, P.R. Yant, and I.J. Schlosser. 1986. "Assessment of biological integrity in running waters: a method and its rationale." *Illinois Natural History Survey Special Publication No. 5*. Champaign, IL.

Kite, 1978. "The Surface Mining Control and Reclamation Act of 1977: An Overview of Reclamation Requirements and Implementation", 13 *Land and Water L.Rev.*

Kleinmann, R.L.P., and R. Hedin, "Biological Treatment of Minewater: An Update," in M.E. Chalkey, B.R. Conrad, V.I. Lakshman, and K.G. Wheeland, eds., *Tailings and Effluent Management*, (1989). (Proceedings of the International Symposium on Tailings and Effluent Management, (1989). (Proceedings of the International Symposium on Tailings and Effluent Management, August 20-24, 1989, Halifax. 28th Annual Conference of Metallurgists of CIM. Pergamum Press, NY).

Kriz, M., 1991. "Hard Rock Realities" 23 *National Journal.*

Kusler, J., "A Call for Action: Protection of Riparian Habitat in the Arid and Semi Arid West" in Johnson, R.R., C.D. Ziebell, D.R. Patton, P.F. Fjollion, and R.N. Hamre, eds. *Riparian Ecosystems and their Management: Reconciling Their Uses* 6 (1985) (published by the U.S. Forest Service, Tuscon, Arizona).

Leshy, J., 1987. "The Mining Law of 1872: A Study in Perpetual Motion".

Livingston, E., et. al., 1988. "Florida Nonpoint Source Assessment, Volume One," Department of Environmental Regulation.

Lyons, J., 1992. "Using the index of biotic integrity (IBI) to measure environmental quality in warmwater streams in Wisconsin." North Central Experiment Station, USDA, Forest Service, Minneapolis, MN. *General Technical Report* NC-149.

Mann and Plummer, 1992. "The Butterfly Problem," *The Atlantic Monthly*

Mathews, Haak, and Toffenette, 1985. "Mining and Wilderness: Incompatible Uses or Justifiable Compromise?" 27 *Environment*.

McClaran, 1990. "Livestock in Wilderness: A Review and Forecast," 20 *Envtl. L. J.*

Middleton, R., *"Fish Habitat Destruction in the Columbia River Basin,"* *Wana Chinook Tymoo*, 5 (Columbia River Inter-Tribal Fish Commission, Issue Two, 1992) (citing the Scientific Panel on Late-Successional Forest Ecosystems, *Alternatives for Management of Late-Successional Forests of the Pacific Northwest*).

Miller et al., 1988. "Regional applications of an index of biotic integrity for use in water resource management." 13(5) *Fisheries*.

Moyle, P.B. and G.M. Sato. 1992. "On the design of preserves to protect native fishes," in W.L. Minckley and J.E. Deacon (eds.) *Battle Against Extinction: Native Fish Management in the American West*. University of Arizona Press, Tucson.

Master, L. 1990. "The imperiled status of North American aquatic animals." *Biodiversity Network News* (The Nature Conservancy) 3(3).

Mullon, D.A., 1991. "State of Utah vs. Kennecott Corporation: Snuggling with the Enemy," *Clementine*, Mineral Policy Center, Washington, D.C.

National Marine Fisheries Service revised Policy for Riparian Habitat Protection in Alaska, May 3, 1988. (cited in Southeast Alaska Conservation Council, *Defending the Promise Of Tongass Reform*, 14 March 1992).

National Research Council, 1992. *Restoration of Aquatic Ecosystems*, National Academy Press, Washington, D.C.

Nehlsen., W., J.E. Williams and J.A. Lichatowich, 1991. "Pacific salmon at the crossroads: stocks at risk from California, Oregon, Idaho, and Washington" 16(2) *Fisheries*.

Nickelson, T.E., M.F. Solazzi, S.L. Johnson, and J.D. Rogers. 1992. "Effectiveness of selected stream improvement techniques to create suitable summer and winter rearing habitat for juvenile coho salmon (Oncorhyncus kisutch) in Oregon coastal streams." *Canadian Journal of Fisheries and Aquatic Sciences* 49.

Niemi, G.J. and seven coauthors. 1990. "Overview of case studies on recovery of aquatic systems from disturbance." *Environmental Management* 14.

Ohio Environmental Protection Agency, 1990. "Ohio Water Resource Inventory," E. T. Rankin, C. O. Yoder, D. Mishne, eds. in Executive Summary and Vol. I. Div. Water Qual. Planning and Assessment, Ecological Assessment Section, Columbus, cited in Yoder, C., 1991. "The Integrated Biosurvey as a Tool for Evaluation of Aquatic Life Use Attainment and Impairment in Ohio Surface Waters," *Biological Criteria: Research and Regulation* (Proceedings of a Symposium), (EPA-440/5-91-005).

Olpin and Tarlock, 1978. "Water That Is Not Water," 13 *Land and Water L.Rev.*

Oregon Department of Environmental Quality, 1988. "1988 Statewide Assessment of Nonpoint Source Water Pollution," Portland, OR.

O'Riordan, W.H., and S.W. Horngren, 1987. "The Minimum Management Requirements of Forest Planning," 17 *Envt'l L. J.*

Platts, W.S., 1981. "Influence of Forest and Rangeland Management on Anadromous Fish Habitat in Western North America: Effects of Livestock Grazing" 1 *(USFS Gen. Tech. Report No. PNW-124)*. (Riparian ecosystems are the most productive ecosystems in rangelands).

Platts, W.S. and R.L. Nelson, 1985. "Stream habitat and fisheries response to livestock grazing and instream improvement structures, Big Creek, Utah." *Journal of Soil and Water Conservation* 40.

Platts, W.S. and D.W. Chapman. 1992. "Status of Chinook Salmon Spawning and Rearing Habitat in the Salmon River Drainage." Don Chapman Consultants, Inc., 3653 Rickenbacker, Suite 200, Boise, ID, 83705.

Ransel, K. and E. Meyers, 1988. "State Water Quality Certification and Wetland Protection: A Call to Awaken the Sleeping Giant," 7 *Va. J. Nat. Res. L.*

Reinert, R.E., B.A. Knuth, M.A. Kamrin, and Q.J. Stober. 1991. "Risk assessment, risk management and fish consumption advisories in the United States." *Fisheries* (Bethesda) 16(6).

Rich and Coltman, "Summary and Recommendations: Clean Water Act Section 404 Discharge of Dredged and Fill Materials and Section 401 Water Quality Certification Programs in Arizona" 7-5 (Aug. 30, 1991) (prepared for Office of Water Quality, Arizona Department of Environmental Quality by the Herberger Center, College of Architecture and Environmental Design, Arizona State University).

Rohlf, D. and D. L. Hannold, 1988. "Managing the Balances of Nature: The Legal Framework of Wilderness Management", 15 *Ecol. L.Q.*

Salveson, D., 1990. Urban Lands Institute. *Wetlands: Mitigating and Regulating Development Impacts.*

Sansonetti, T., and W. Murray, 1990. "A Primer on the Federal Onshore Oil and Gas Leasing Reform Act of 1987 and Its Regulations," 25 *Land and Water L. Rev.*

Schwartz, T. J., 1991. "Community Action on Mining: East-to-West," *Clementine*, Mineral Policy Center.

Science Advisory Board (EPA), 1990. "Reducing risk: setting priorities and strategies for environmental protection." SAB-EC-90-021. U.S. EPA, Washington, D.C.

Sedell, J.R., G.H. Reeves, F.R. Hauer, J.A. Stanford, and C.P. Hawkins. 1990. "Role of refugia in recovery from disturbances: modern fragmented and disconnected river systems." *Environmental Management* 14.

Sedell, J.R., and F. Everest, 1991. "Historic Changes in Pool Habitat for Columbia River Basin Salmon under study for TES Listing" (USDA Forest Service, Corvallis, OR).

Senzel, 1977. "Revision of the Mining Act of 1872," (Study for the Senate Comm. on Energy and Nat. Res., 95th Cong., 1st Sess.)

Sherk, G.W., 1990. "Eastern Water Law: Trends in State Legislation," 9 *Virginia Env. L. J.*

Skovlin, P., 1984. "Impacts of Grazing on Wetlands and Riparian Habitat: A Review of Our Knowledge" in National Research Council/National Academy of Sciences, *Developing Strategies for Rangeland Management.*

Sparks, R., 1992. "The Upper Mississippi River," in National Research Council, *Restoration of Aquatic Ecosystems.*

Stanford, J.A. and J.V. Ward. 1993. "An ecosystem perspective of alluvial rivers: connectivity and the hyporheic corridor." *J.N. Am. Benthol. Soc.* 12.

Steiner, Pieart and Cook, 1991. "The Interrelationship Between Federal and State Wetlands and Riparian Protection Programs," 1, Arizona State University.

Swift, B.L., 1984. "Status of riparian ecosystems in the United States." *Water Resources Bulletin* 2.

Tarlock, A.D., "The Law of Public Rangeland Management or How Professor Coggins Proposes to Transform the Bureau of Land Management's FLPMA Discretion into Duties," in NC/NAS *Developing Strategies for Rangeland Management.*

Tarlock, A.D. and R. Tippy, 1970. "The Wild and Scenic Rivers Act of 1968," 55 *Cornell L. Rev.* (as cited in P. Frost, "Ensuring that Clean Water Flows in Wild and Scenic Rivers," unpublished manuscript on file at the National Wildlife Federation, Portland, Oregon).

Thomas, J.W., E. Forsman, J. Lint, E.C. Meslow, B. Noon, J. Verner, 1990. *A Conservation Strategy for the Northern Spotted Owl,* Interagency Scientific Committee to Address the Conservation of the Northern Spotted Owl, Portland, OR.

Thompson, P., 1989. "Poison Runoff: A Guide to State and Local Control of Nonpoint Source Water Pollution." (Natural Resources Defense Council).

USDA, Forest Service, 1985. *Minerals Program Handbook.*

USDA, Forest Service, 1987. *Land and Resource Management Planning Handbook.*

USDI, 1992, *Manual for Wild and Scenic Rivers.*

USDI, Bureau of Land Management, 1991. 175 *Public Land Statistics 1990.*

USDI, Bureau of Land Management, August 1992. *Executive Summary: Western Oregon Draft Resource Management Plans/Environmental Impact Statements.*

USDI, Fish and Wildlife Service, 1986. *Survey of Contaminant Issues of Concern on National Wildlife Refuges.*

USDI, Fish and Wildlife Service, Compatibility Task Group, 1990. *Secondary Uses Occurring on National Wildlife Refuges.*

USDI, Fish and Wildlife Service, 1991. *Fish and Wildlife Service Refuge Manager Questionnaire, Part IV. Environmental Contaminants,* using calendar year 1989 Information. U.S. Fish and Wildlife Service, Rm.130, 4401 N. Fairfax Drive, Arlington, VA 22203.

USDI, National Park Service, 1988. Introduction to *National Park Service Management Policies.*

USEPA, Region 7, 1986. *Environmental Action Plan for Rainwater Basin Wetlands Project.*

USEPA, Region 10, 1991. *Riparian Policy.*

USEPA, Office of Water, 1991. *Biological Criteria: state development and implementation efforts.* EPA-440/5-91-003. Washington, D.C.

USEPA, Office of Water, 1991. *The Watershed Protection Approach: an Overview.* EPA 503/9-92-002, Washington, D.C.

USEPA, Office of Water, 1991. *Biological Criteria: Research and Regulation.* Washington, D.C. EPA 440/5-91-005.

USEPA, Region 9, 1987. *Guidance on Implementing the Antidegradation Provisions of 40 C.F.R. 131.12* .

USEPA, 1988. *National Water Quality Inventory*, 1988 Report to Congress.

USEPA, 1987. Office of Water, *Nonpoint Source Controls and Water Quality Standards* (guidance document).

USEPA, 1989. *Rapid Bioassessment Protocol Guidance Document.*

USEPA, 1991. *Biological Criteria: Guide to Technical Literature.*

USEPA, 1991. *Region 10: Riparian Area Management Policy.* Washington D.C.

USEPA, Region 10, Nonpoint Sources Section, 1991. *Riparian Policy: Summary and Analysis.*

Verburg and Coon, 1987. "Planning in the U.S. Fish and Wildlife Service," 24 *Trends* No. 2.

Water Quality 2000. 1991. "Challenges for the future: interim report phase II." *Water Quality 2000*, Water Pollution Control Federation, Alexandria, VA.

Weaver, W.E., et al, 1987. "An evaluation of experimental rehabilitation work: Redwood National Park." *Redwood National Park Technical Report 19*, National Park Service, Arcata, CA.

Wheatley, C., C. Corker, T. Stetson and D. Reed, 1969. "Study of the Development, Management and Use of Water Resources on the Public Lands." (as cited in *United States v. Mexico*, 438 U.S. 696, 699 n.3 (1978)).

Whitney, S., R. Johnson, and S. Perles, 1988. "State Implementation of the Coastal Zone Management Consistency Provisions--Ultra Vires or Unconstitutional?," 12 *Harvard Environmental Law* Review.

Whitman, 1989. "Clean Water or Multiple Use? Best Management Practices for Water Quality Control in the National Forests," 16 *Ecology L.Q.*

Wilderness Society, 1988. *National Forests: Policies for the Future, Volume I/*"Water Quality and Timber Management".

Wilkinson, C. and H. M. Anderson, *1981. "Land and Resource Planning in the National Forests,"* 64 *Or. L. Rev.*

Williams, D.C., 1986. "Planning Approaches in the Bureau of Land Management," *Trends* No. 2.

Williams, D.C., 1987. "Public Land Management: Planning, Problems and Opportunities," in *Public Lands During the Remainder of the 20th Century* (Univ. Colo. L. School Natural Resources Law Center, proceedings of 8th Annual Summer Program).

Williams, S., 1990. "Indian Winters Water Rights Administration: Averting New War," 11 *Public Land Law Review.*

Williams, J.E. 1991. "Preserves and refuges for native western fishes: history and management." Pp. 171-189 in W.L. Minckley and J.E. Deacon (eds.) *Battle Against Extinction: Native Fish Management in the American West.* University of Arizona Press, Tucson.

Williams, J.E., J.E. Johnson, D.A. Hendrickson, S. Contreras-Balderas, J.D. Williams, M. Navarro-Mendoza, D.E. McAllister, and J.E. Deacon. 1989. "Fishes of North America endangered, threatened or of special concern," *Fisheries* (Bethesda) 14(6).

Williams, J.E. and R.J. Neves, 1992. "*Introducing the elements of biological diversity in the aquatic environment.*" Trans. 57th N.A. Wild. and Nat. Res. Conf. 57.

Wilson, Thomas E., 1987. "Watershed Management and Water Quality Protection in the Public Lands During the Remainder of the 20th Century: Planning, Law and Policy in the Federal Land Agencies." US EPA.

Windell, J.T., 19xx. "Streams, Riparian and Wetland Ecology," (University of Colorado, unpublished) cited in USEPA, Region 10, *Characteristics of Successful Riparian Restoration Projects in the Pacific Northwest.*

Yagerman, 1990. "Protecting Critical Habitat Under the Federal Endangered Species Act," 20 *Envt'l L.*

Yoder, C., 1991. "The Integrated Biosurvey as a Tool for Evaluation of Aquatic Life Use Attainment and Impairment in Ohio Surface Waters," *Biological Criteria: Research and Regulation* (Proceedings of a Symposium), (EPA-440/5-91-005).

Yount, J.D. and G.J. Niemi. 1990. "Recovery of lotic communities from disturbance -- a narrative review of case studies." 14 *Environmental Management.*

ABOUT THE AUTHORS

Bob Doppelt, M.A., is Executive Director and co-founder of the Pacific Rivers Council, Inc. He is recognized as a national leader in river protection and conservation efforts, and sustainable development. He was the key strategist for the Oregon Omnibus National Wild and Scenic Rivers Act (1988), the largest river protection act in the nation's history for the lower 48 states.

Chris Frissell, Ph.D., is an aquatic ecologist and a consultant with the Pacific Rivers Council, Inc. Dr. Frissell's research interest is the study of fish meta-populations and their habitats. He has also led scientific workshops on new strategies for watershed restoration.

James Karr, Ph.D., is Director of the Institute for Environmental Studies at the University of Washington. Dr. Karr has developed the Index of Biotic Integrity (IBI), a biologically based method to evaluate the quality of water resources, which is now widely used throughout North America. Current research interests concentrate on water resources, landscape ecology, avian demography and conservation biology.

Mary Scurlock, J.D., is staff policy analyst for the Pacific Rivers Council, Inc., providing legal and policy analysis and research for PRC's National Rivers Policy Project. She is currently working on issues related to funding for watershed and fish habitat restoration.

INDEX